June 18

2

W9-BCW-033

Praise for *Lives in Limbo*

"*Lives in Limbo* is one of the most important books in immigration studies of the past decade. The moving and heartbreaking narratives of struggle, support, and heroism in this book should be read by every American."
—Hirokazu Yoshikawa, author of *Immigrants Raising Citizens: Undocumented Parents and Their Young Children*

"*Lives in Limbo* vividly documents the experiences of belonging and exclusion that mark the everyday lives of undocumented youth as they transition to adulthood. Through his careful attention to the ways in which these young people navigate these contradictory processes, Roberto G. Gonzales puts a human face on the many victims of America's broken immigration system. Theoretically rich, beautifully written, and cogently argued, this brilliant book is a landmark study of the human costs of American policy failures."
—Mary C. Waters, coauthor of *Inheriting the City: The Children of Immigrants Come of Age*

"This necessary book documents in tragic detail how American public policies prevent hardworking children from pursuing their lives as full members of the society in which they were raised. The scholarly and personal commitment required to produce a work of this caliber is evident in the intimacy of the ethnographic work. This theoretically skillful book is one of the best examples of high-quality academic scholarship that also fully engages the policy debates of our times. An impressive achievement that will set the standard for others."
—Robert C. Smith, author of *Mexican New York: Transnational Worlds of New Immigrants*

"Written after years of fieldwork, this book brings into sharp focus the plight of undocumented children transitioning to adulthood in America. Lack of a path to citizenship condemns hundreds of thousands of these youths to a life of permanent marginality. This is must reading for anyone wishing to understand the realities of contemporary immigration."
—Alejandro Portes, coauthor of *Immigrant America*

"This extraordinary study provides important details about a generation of immigrants that, through the courageous organizing and leadership of its members, has already permanently altered the national debate on immigration reform, politically united the Mexican American community across all generations of presence in the United States, and launched the most vibrant youth movement this country has seen in four decades. The book powerfully demonstrates the national shame in failing to enact, nearly a decade and a half after its first introduction, the congressional legislation that would permit the United States to benefit fully from the intellect, ingenuity, and perseverance of this generation of young immigrants."

—Thomas A. Saenz, President and General Counsel, MALDEF (Mexican American Legal Defense and Educational Fund)

"This book accomplishes something truly remarkable. Its ethnographic commitment makes a solid contribution to scholarship without compromising on allowing the reader to experience the poignancy, sadness, distress, and emotional trauma society has inflicted on these unfortunate young people. A must-read for anyone interested in the victims of the current stalemate over immigration reform."

—Leo R. Chavez, author of *Covering Immigration: Popular Images and the Politics of the Nation*

"*Lives in Limbo* is a book of tragic beauty. It recounts with moral clarity, conceptual precision, and empirical rigor what Hannah Arendt, writing in another terrible time, called 'the calamity of the right-less.' It is about what happens in a society, our society, when children and youth who are de facto but not de jure members of the family of the nation lose the right to have rights. It fearlessly narrates the quotidian empire of suffering and shattered dreams our barbaric immigration system has begotten. Reading it will bring tears and joy. It will make you mad and it will make you sad. It will stand as the definitive study of the undocumented coming of age in our midst. It is a book every teacher, every policy maker, indeed every concerned citizen should read and ponder."

—Marcelo M. Suárez-Orozco, author of *Latinos: Remaking America*

THE ATKINSON FAMILY
IMPRINT IN HIGHER EDUCATION

The Atkinson Family Foundation has endowed this imprint to

illuminate the role of higher education in contemporary society.

The publisher gratefully acknowledges the generous support of the Atkinson Family Imprint in Higher Education of the University of California Press Foundation, which was established by a major gift from the Atkinson Family Foundation.

Lives in Limbo

Lives in Limbo

Undocumented and
Coming of Age in America

Roberto G. Gonzales

With a foreword by Jose Antonio Vargas

UNIVERSITY OF CALIFORNIA PRESS

University of California Press, one of the most
distinguished university presses in the United States,
enriches lives around the world by advancing scholarship
in the humanities, social sciences, and natural sciences. Its
activities are supported by the UC Press Foundation and
by philanthropic contributions from individuals and
institutions. For more information, visit www.ucpress.edu.

University of California Press
Oakland, California

Library of Congress Cataloging-in-Publication Data

Gonzales, Roberto G., 1969– author.
  Lives in limbo : undocumented and coming of age in
America / Roberto G. Gonzales ; with a foreword by Jose
Antonio Vargas.
    pages cm
  Includes bibliographical references and index.
  ISBN 978-0-520-28725-9 (cloth : alk. paper) —
  ISBN 978-0-520-28726-6 (pbk. : alk. paper) —
  ISBN 978-0-520-96241-5 (ebook)
    1. Children of illegal aliens—United States—Social
conditions. 2. Children of illegal aliens—United States—
Education. I. Title.
  JV6600.G66   2016
  305.23086′9120973—dc23
                                        2015022454

Manufactured in the United States of America

24 23 22 21 20 19 18 17
10 9 8 7 6 5

In keeping with a commitment to support
environmentally responsible and sustainable printing
practices, UC Press has printed this book on Natures
Natural, a fiber that contains 30% post-consumer waste
and meets the minimum requirements of ANSI/NISO
Z39.48–1992 (R 1997) (*Permanence of Paper*).

For Sara and Joaquin

Every year my students read *Night* by Elie Wiesel.
Following completion of the book, I assign them
the tasks of writing their own memoir. Maria came

to America when she was five years old, wrote that
she had to cross a river before she ever knew what
it meant to swim, ran through knee-high grass as if

the field were made of landmines, hid under the belly
of trucks amid concrete and fertilizer so as not to
leave a scent for the dogs. She did not know why

she was running, but she knew that her mother cried
every night for her father, she knew she was beginning
to forget her daddy's face, she knew that he worked

eighteen hours a day just to provide them with food
they could barely find at home, she knew
that he loved them & wanted to remember what

it felt like to hold his daughter in his arms. But Maria
was five. She doesn't remember life in Mexico. She
remembers Kindergarten & sleepovers & middle

school graduations. She is more American than any
slice of apple pie but that is not what we tell her. We
punish Maria for following directions, for being a child

simply listening to her parents. We tell her parents that
they are wrong for wanting a better life for their family.
We tell her that a 4.0 isn't good enough.

We tell Maria that college wasn't meant for girls like her.

Too much brown skin.
Too much accent.
Where'd you come from?
You don't have a number
    you don't exist.

There is apathy under the eyelids of this country
& we cannot see what's right in front of us. It's hard
to convince someone to do well in school when the law tells

them that it won't matter—when you're a number before you're a face. How convenient that we forget our own history. A country of immigrants who were once told we didn't belong.

An assemblage of faces simply waiting for our country to see us.

—Clinton Smith, "Memoir"

Contents

Foreword by Jose Antonio Vargas   *xi*

Preface   *xv*

Acknowledgments   *xxiii*

1. Contested Membership over Time   *1*
2. Undocumented Young Adults in Los Angeles: College-Goers and Early Exiters   *35*
3. Childhood: Inclusion and Belonging   *58*
4. School as a Site of Belonging and Conflict   *73*
5. Adolescence: Beginning the Transition to Illegality   *92*
6. Early Exiters: Learning to Live on the Margins   *120*
7. College-Goers: Managing the Distance between Aspirations and Reality   *149*
8. Adulthood: How Immigration Status Becomes a Master Status   *176*
9. Conclusion: Managing Lives in Limbo   *208*

Notes   *237*

References   *257*

Index   *279*

Foreword

Roberto G. Gonzales, the preeminent academic expert on the struggles of undocumented immigrant youth, has written more than a book. *Lives in Limbo* is a unique, essential wake-up call. Using qualitative research methods to elicit the stories of young Latinos who grew up in Los Angeles, Gonzales does something no journalist has done: he follows them over twelve years. *Lives in Limbo* breaks new ground in placing their stories in context by examining the sociological, historical, political, and cultural forces that shape the outcomes for these young undocumented Americans. In doing so, Gonzales brings value to the research itself, by saying these lives are worth examining, these outcomes are worth understanding, and these stories are worth telling.

Gonzales is among countless people—many of them educators and teachers who are allies and mentors to undocumented students—I met while traveling the country through my work with Define American, the media and culture organization I founded in 2011. Define American was born when the *New York Times Magazine* published my essay in which I revealed my status as one of more than eleven million undocumented Americans. Like the young undocumented people whose stories are shared in *Lives in Limbo,* I struggled with conflicting realities of belonging and exclusion and still do. My mother and I have not seen each other in person for over twenty years, not from deportation, but from an equally unyielding US immigration policy that prevented her, a single parent with limited means, from legally joining me in California when my grandfather smuggled me over from the Philippines at age twelve.

I weathered that transition as best I could, buoyed by the blissful ignorance Gonzales writes about, an ignorance that envelops undocumented children at younger ages when neither they nor their teachers understand their status. Four years later, I felt like the all-American kid, riding my bike to high school, joining the newspaper, drama club, and choir, feeling proud of my English and my grades, and excited about the future.

Then, at age sixteen, a storm hit. But I was so fortunate, because as I reached that terrible moment in every undocumented child's life, the moment of realizing the import and impact of one's immigration status—when panic leads to anger, confusion, and alienation—I had wonderful, caring mentors to calm me and catch me: my teachers, friends, high school principal and superintendent, internship supervisors, even a parent from my high school who offered to pay my college tuition. These good, kind, law-abiding citizens readily stepped up to help me navigate a future path that would require me to join the millions of people like me who would have to "transition to illegality," as Gonzales puts it.

Gonzales's dedication to developing the long-term qualitative research presented in this book will help us to more fully understand the lives of young undocumented Americans and the impossible circumstances in which they find themselves.

At its heart, this research is about stories of belonging and wanting to belong. Alexia, Chuy, Pedro, Gloria, and the others in this book are real people whose lives have been profoundly shaped by our complex and unpredictable immigration system. Gonzales's research shows that the trajectories of their individual lives vary profoundly, depending on the political climate of the communities in which they live and where they fall in the de facto educational tracking to which they are subjected. Whether you can get a driver's license, pay in-state tuition and apply for financial aid for college, earn a green card, purchase health care, and travel without being subjected to checkpoints depends on where you live in this country. But equally consequential are the impacts of being singled out as one of the "good immigrants" with "college potential" or being routed to the separate and unequal lower tracks of America's public schools.

America needs this book. We've always needed it, but we need it now more than ever. By contextualizing the individual lives of his subjects, Gonzales helps us see not only the humanity of all the people who allowed him into their lives but the larger forces shaping their outcomes.

Community and civic leaders would do well to read this book, because it will help them understand how neighborhoods, cities, and states can promote integration over illegality by making it simpler for immigrants to navigate their daily lives within the law. California provides a clear example of a state whose government moved from criminalizing to legalizing many of the necessary activities of its residents. For example, after generations of having a "Don't ask, don't tell" philosophy regarding immigrants, the state went through a series of approaches to regulating immigration issues.

In 1994, California's voters passed Prop. 187, effectively prohibiting noncitizens from accessing health care, education, and other public services. My dear friend Karen Willemsen, a teacher and Define American's education director, remembers the chilling effect of the law. The day after the election, thousands of immigrant children failed to show up for school, and teachers spent much of their time calling parents to reassure them that their children were still welcome. The law never took effect, having been found unconstitutional in federal court, in violation of *Plyler v. Doe,* the landmark case that ruled that the state has a vested interest in the education of undocumented minors.

For educators, these stories show the limits of *Plyler v. Doe.* The reasoning in *Plyler,* Gonzales explains, was that the social cost of denying education to so many children would be likely to have a significant negative impact on the state. But, as Gonzales also notes, the current debate over which immigrants might be worthy of a path to full citizenship betrays that state interest in educating all students. The majority of educators and education organizations advocate for educating undocumented students to their fullest potential. In practice, however, Gonzales shows that they are tracked, as the majority of public school students are, so that a small percentage considered to have college potential are culled into advanced placement and honors classes and the majority are shunted to lower tracks, where they receive little to no individualized attention or mentoring.

I was lucky. I was deemed one of the "good kids," the kind of immigrant you want to have around. Significant adults took an interest in me. Don't get me wrong—I am grateful they did. Because of them, I have had many more opportunities than some. For example, I was able to start Define American and produce and direct *Documented,* a documentary film, which, like Gonzales's research, contextualizes my own story of growing up undocumented. Moreover, inspired by the work of Gonzales and other educational scholars, I was able to launch a curriculum to accompany *Documented.*

In lectures, in interviews, and in my own writing, I often ask the question: "What have you done to earn your citizenship?" It is a complicated question that gets at the root of what Gonzales's study shows us—that America is dividing its immigrants into categories: legal versus undocumented, college-worthy versus "street kids," good immigrants versus "criminals." The truth of the matter is that children don't aspire to live lives circumscribed by illegality. But failure to fully understand how America is shaping the lives of immigrant children means we risk losing more generations of young people to the shadows of illegality. These young people are American—they are just waiting for their own country to recognize them.

Jose Antonio Vargas

Preface

In 1951, Langston Hughes posed a question fundamental to the predicament of African Americans living amid racial segregation and social marginalization: "What happens to a dream deferred?"[1] Put in sociological terms, what are the long-term impacts of being only partially recognized members of a social group? And what effects do these forms of denial have on the individual psyche? For twelve years, I explored these very questions as they played out in the lives of undocumented immigrant young adults at the intersection of belonging and illegality. The answers this book provides show that many of these young people's dreams of inclusion were encouraged when they were children before being deferred by the realities of adulthood.

Beginning in the late 1980s, the young people in my study left their communities in Mexico along with their parents, siblings, and sometimes extended family members to make a new life in Los Angeles. They joined the hundreds of thousands of other Mexican families who would settle in the five-county metropolitan area for the next decade and a half.

The growth in settlement among undocumented children throughout the 1990s and early 2000s coincides with my own sustained engagement with their families over the last two decades as a youth worker, researcher, and university professor. Several years before undertaking this study, while I was still in my twenties, I met dozens of other undocumented children and teenagers in my role as a youth worker in Chicago. From 1992 to 2002 I lived and worked on the near northwest side of the city, in a port-of-entry community for Mexican and Polish immigrant families that had started to gentrify.[2] During this time I was employed by two social service agencies in former settlement houses. While in college I had read about Jane Addams and others who had established these houses to provide education and recreational facilities to European immigrants and their children at the turn of the twentieth century. I was also inspired by Chicago community leaders like Rudy Lozano, Esther Nieves, and Inhe Choi, and I was honored to be part of a long tradition. But I also knew that this particular moment was different.

Living and working in the same community, I was privy to many of the details of family life. Undocumented immigration status curbed daily activity for many families, and our programs did what they could to address their needs. As the children in our programs began to enter their teenage years, it became increasingly clear that many were left without answers to a growing number of questions that their own immigration status and encroaching adulthood presented. These young people felt at home in the United States but faced a mounting number of exclusions that forced them to confront their outsider status. Many left school because of a growing frustration, while a smaller number attempted to make difficult transitions to college. The changes they experienced were confusing.

I spent countless hours talking with teenagers and trying to counsel parents. But few resources were available. While there were growing community efforts to gain rights for undocumented immigrant workers, little attention was being paid to the unique circumstances of their children. There was no in-state tuition at the local public universities for aspiring teens, so financing college was an impossibility for most families. And, beyond that, there was nearly no research evidence to guide best practices for serving these youth.

During this time, while I was working with a broad range of neighborhood youth, I noticed that in school they were receiving varying levels of assistance. A small group of youth I worked with had access to good classes and the resources of high-quality instruction and individualized assistance. When they needed letters of recommendation or adult guidance, their teachers and counselors were quick to help. Other youth were stuck in large classes and were invisible to most of their schools' staff. They had difficulty finding help from their schools. Many of them became so discouraged they simply gave up. As I witnessed natural relationships—neighbors, relatives, kin, and childhood friends—transform into deepening divisions within the school system and the community, I began to question the motives for such divisions. I enrolled in a master's program at the University of Chicago School of Social Service Administration, where the likes of Jane Addams, Graham Taylor, John Dewey, Julia Lathrop, and Edith Abbott had taught, just across the Midway from a prominent group of sociologists studying urban life. For three years I balanced school and full-time work.

Back in my neighborhood, as undocumented families were being illegally forced out of their rental homes to accommodate newer, more expensive developments, many of the neighborhood's youth were being rounded up in neighborhood gang sweeps. When we attempted to integrate neighborhood youth into our programs, our decisions were scrutinized by teachers and community leaders who questioned our inclusion of "bad kids," warning us that these young people could not be "saved."

The circumstances of one child, in particular, directed my attention to what I came to believe was a growing social problem. I met Alex when he was six years old.[3] The son of a Mexican mom and a Guatemalan dad who had met in Mexico City, Alex made the journey to the United States with his parents and older brother when he was four years old. I was the director of a youth program at the time, and his mom enrolled him in one of my after-school programs. Alex was shy but inquisitive for his age. Over the years, through his participation in the program, I got to know him better.

Eventually, Alex started channeling his intellectual curiosity and growing talents into the arts. It was not long before it became obvious that he had a unique talent for drawing and painting. Along with two other members of my staff, I encouraged him to sharpen these talents and to pursue art. We enrolled him in art classes. We also purchased paints, sketch pads, and other supplies. By the time Alex was in eighth grade he had already participated in three community murals and was receiving accolades from the broader community.

We wanted to capitalize on his burgeoning talents, so we persuaded his parents to let him apply to a private art school. However, we faced the startling realization that not everyone shared our enthusiasm. Alex, who had lived in his community for ten years, was told by an admissions officer at one of the schools that he did not belong, that because he was an "illegal immigrant," he would not be considered for admission to the school. Disappointment turned into frustration and despair as he enrolled in his neighborhood high school, a place where about one of every two entering freshmen graduated.

During his first semester, Alex became noticeably withdrawn and disconnected from teachers and other school officials. He learned that because of his immigration status he would not be able to receive a driver's license or take an after-school job. A multitude of barriers blocked Alex's path. For the first time in his young life, he felt as though he was an outsider. His anger masked his pain, and instead of identifying him as needing help, his teachers saw him as a troublemaker. Internalizing that label, Alex left school and started hanging out with some of the guys in the neighborhood gang. A few short months later, he was shot and killed in broad daylight by three men wearing masks, alleged to be from a gang that was antagonistic to his neighborhood gang.

What had happened in Alex's young life to send him spiraling downward so fast? And how did his community fail him? His death deeply affected me, and I was consumed by these questions for a long time. I took the questions very personally and ended up leaving community work in the months after. The year following his death, I started graduate school in Southern California and began exploratory research in nearby Santa Ana. I immediately began meeting young people like Alex. The themes so prevalent in my work in Chicago—difficult transitions, conflicted feelings of belonging and outsiderness, and the dichotomous labels that had framed youth's lives—were abundant in these young Angelenos' narratives.

They had moved to the United States with their parents at very young ages (e.g., at six months, two years, five years) and had grown up alongside American-born peers; they thought of themselves as Americans. Compared to their parents, they had come a great distance. They had received many more years of formal education, and they spoke English with much greater fluency. They had years of Americanizing experiences, having grown up with Barney and the Power Rangers, the Los Angeles Dodgers, and trips to Disneyland. Socially and culturally, they were largely indistinguishable from their American-born friends. During their late high school years, however, they started to experience the limits of their immigration status. There were the lucky few who made it—who did not get picked up in raids, who managed to have good mentors in school, who rose to the top of their class. But many others did not have even the possibility of reaching that level. Could they have if their schools and community organizations had done more to help them, particularly early on? Quite possibly.

I soon began a research project that would permeate my life for the next twelve years as I finished graduate school, began an academic career, married, and became a father. While I have worked hard to achieve methodological rigor and the advancement of scholarly theory, this book is also intensely personal.

Between 2003 and 2014, I traversed dozens of communities across greater Los Angeles, volunteering in schools and after-school programs, attending community meetings, and listening to the stories of the many young adults I met. I have published many of my findings in journal articles and policy reports. I have sat on panels with many of our nation's leaders, and I have been asked to consult with city councils, school boards, and community associations across the country. I have also corresponded with hundreds of undocumented young people.

We typically view illegality as a *process* that begins when migrants cross a political border and that continues as they navigate life in the shadows.[4] Some scholars and policy makers see this process as culminating in immigrants' attempts to become legal.[5] This understanding of illegality matches a common assumption about assimilation and intergenerational mobility—that these processes are unidirectional and positive. This book shows the opposite to be true. For the young people I came to know, time and the transition to adulthood multiplied their exclusions and forced them to live shadowed lives.

While undocumented immigrants typically work for long periods in undesirable, poorly paid jobs, their children soon surpass them in human capital accumulation and English language proficiency. We may be tempted to see this outcome as a sign of intergenerational progress. However, most of these young people end up either in the same position or only a small step ahead of their parents because of their undocumented status: they, too, face strained financial circumstances, family need, and a lack of employment options. The young people in my study transitioned to illegality over time, with illegality becoming a master status by the time they reached adulthood. Illegality in its contemporary manifestations mattered more than other statuses and achievements in a greater number of situations and interactions.

Lives at the intersection of illegality and belonging are complex. Early experiences of inclusion provided my respondents opportunities to become intimately acquainted with their communities; adult lives of illegality pushed them to the margins and placed them in closer contact with law enforcement and immigration officials. Through childhood and early adolescent interactions with peers and teachers, my respondents joined an inclusive circle. But as they grew older, their connections became strained and sometimes broke. They were left behind as friends started driving, taking new jobs, applying to college, and starting careers. They began to withdraw from social activities and networks. As each year passed, they were defined more centrally by their undocumented status.

In adulthood, constant worries about apprehension altered daily routines and dramatically circumscribed their worlds. As their options dwindled, their responsibilities increased. They learned to embrace spaces and times that provided opportunities, as one young man described to me, to "be themselves." They formed relationships, joined dance groups and sports teams, and started families. Over time, however, all of these young people watched opportunities slip through their fingers. Most were unable to accumulate job experience outside low-wage sectors. Accumulated stress and the grind of poorly paid work increased their susceptibility to injury and took a serious toll on their health, well-being, and future outlooks.

Over the last few decades, California's population has become increasingly immigrant and noticeably Mexican. Newcomers to the area inhabit both ends of the economic spectrum. But Southern California communities expose the growing reality that in urban areas race, immigration status, and questions of who belongs mark the major fault lines of inequality. Densely populated Mexican neighborhoods and de facto segregated Mexican schools stand in close proximity to affluent neighborhoods.

My deep engagement in this project has taught me a great deal about Southern California and about our country as whole. I have learned much about Mexican immigrant families and especially the young people in the communities in and around Los Angeles. My fieldwork has also helped me understand the ways in which a *condition of illegality* marks, directs, and frames the lives of undocumented young people. While I was not new to this population when I began this study, my research afforded me the opportunity to critically and deeply engage what C. Wright Mills called the "sociological imagination"—that is, the relationship between broad structural and historical contexts and individuals' own biographies.[6] Thinking about these young people also helped me to disentangle ideas about membership, including how it is structured and how it is experienced by people who live on its margins.

Indeed, while the lives of young people like Alex and those I have met in Los Angeles are importantly framed by their undocumented immigration status, their everyday worlds are quite different from those of their parents, whose lives take place in the shadows. Their relationship with their community and their sense of place and belonging grow out of deeper, more intimate and local, experiences. Thus these young people are perhaps more vulnerable to the effects of a dysfunctional immigration system that marks them as insiders *and* outsiders. And they are hostages to time. While their dreams are on hold, they must manage the pressures of finding employment, paying the bills, and supporting family members. "Meantime," as Bob Dylan wrote years ago, "life outside goes on / all around you." [7]

Acknowledgments

I thank all of those who made this book possible.

This project simply would not exist without the mentorship and support of two people, Rubén G. Rumbaut and Leo R. Chávez. Each contributed invaluable insights and ideas over the years. Their ongoing encouragement, respect, and humor helped make the journey enjoyable, and their confidence in my project and my value as a scholar provided the affirmation needed to carry on. I can only hope to be such an example to my current and future students.

Over the last twelve years I have benefited greatly from the support of many individuals and institutions. I am indebted to Eddie Uehara of the University of Washington, Neil Guterman of the University of Chicago, and Jim Ryan of Harvard University for providing me teaching relief so I could write and continue fieldwork, and to the National Poverty Center at the University of Michigan and the West Coast Poverty Center at the University of Washington, which provided summer grants that allowed me to travel and continue the research. I benefited greatly from the generous assistance from the University of California Institute for Mexico and the United States (UC MEXUS), the National Sciences Ford Fellowship Diversity Program, the Center for Research on Latinos in a Global Society, and the Public Policy Institute of California for dissertation support that began this project. I have presented earlier drafts of this research, and I am grateful to the following institutions for their invitations: the University of Wisconsin Institute for Research on

Poverty; the Radcliffe Institute for Advanced Study at Harvard University; the Center for Latin American and Caribbean Studies at Indiana University's Centre College; the Arizona State University School of Social and Family Dynamics; the Stanford University Department of Sociology; the Illinois State University Department of Sociology; the University of Chicago Katz Center for Mexican Studies; the Cornell University Institute for the Social Sciences; UC Davis Law School; the University of Pennsylvania Department of Sociology; the University of Texas at San Antonio Mexico Center; the UCLA School of Public Affairs, the UC Berkeley Center for Latino Policy Research; the University of Kansas Hall Center for the Humanities; Connecticut College, Brown University; the University of Washington Center for Studies in Demography and Ecology; the Berlin Center for Metropolitan Studies; Universitat Autònoma de Barcelona, Centre d'Estudis i Recerca en Migracions; and the Centre on Migration, Policy and Society of Oxford University.

I owe a great deal of gratitude to a large community of colleagues who helped me in ways big and small. They include Leisy J. Abrego, Robert C. Smith, Nando Sigona, Veronica Terriquez, David Takeuchi, Mark Courtney, Luis Fraga, Douglas S. Massey, Grace Kao, Steven Raphael, Patricia Gandara, Hiro Yoshikawa, Michael Olivas, Hiroshi Motomura, Audrey Singer, Charlie Hirschman, Cynthia Garcia Coll, Marcelo Suárez-Orozco, Carola Suárez-Orozco, Sheldon Danziger, Evelyn Nakano Glen, Philip Kazinitz, Mary Waters, Hector Codero-Guzman, Susan Coutin, Helen B. Marrow, Becky Pettit, Harriett Romo, Annette Lareau, Shannon Gleeson, Van Tran, Irene Bloemraad, Luisa Heredia, Genevieve Negrón-Gonzales, Katharine Donato, Tanya Golash-Boza, Jody Agius-Vallejo, Ernesto Castañeda, Michael Jones-Correa, Maria Cook, Els de Graauw, Kara Cebulko, Caitlin Patler, Alexis Silver, Rubén Hernández-León, Lisa Garcia-Bedolla, Kristel Acacio, Louis Desipio, Diego Vigil, Rudy Torres, Gil Conchas, Raul Fernandez, Gilbert Gonzalez, Michael Montoya, Charlie Morgan, Golnaz Komaei, Monica Trieu, Mark Leach, Armando Ibarra, Rosaura Tafoya-Estrada, Matthew Mahutga, Wai Kit Choi, Sylvia Martin, Jim Bachmeier, Magnus Lofstrum, Helen Lee, Debbie Reed, Caroline Danielson, Hans Johnson, Laura Hill, Sarah Bohn, Amelia Gavin, Marsha K. Meyers, Gunnar Almgren, Scott Allard, Waldo Johnson, Natasha Kumar, Ming Hsu Chen, Elaine Chase, Cathy Cohen, and Karen and Nate Robinson. I give special thanks to David Snow and Cal Morrill, whose ethnography class planted the initial seeds that grew this project, and to Frank D. Bean, whose ongoing enthusiasm provided validation, often at the perfect moments.

Joanna Dreby and Cecilia Menjívar read large portions of the manuscript and offered valuable comments. I am indebted to Tomas Jimenez, David S. Fitzgerald, Phil Wolgin, Eve Ewing, Deepa Vasudevan, Barbara Davenport, and the two anonymous reviewers for providing critical and useful feedback and to M. Katherine Mooney and Jessica Cobb for all of their substantive feedback. I am grateful to Naomi Schneider for her belief in this project and unwavering support, and I am appreciative of the work of the production team at the University of California Press, especially Ally Power, Dore Brown, and Elisabeth Magnus.

Across the state of California, I would like to acknowledge other individuals who have contributed to this project: Art Guerrero, Serafin Serano, Sister Eileen McNerney, Marisela Sandoval, and Patricia Rodriguez. For all of their hard work on behalf of undocumented students, I give special thanks to Gil Cedillo, Kathy Gin, Ed Kissam, Jo Ann Intili, Rafael Magellan, James Montoya, Adriana Flores-Ragade, Elena Macias, Irma Archuleta, Jamie Johnson, Sy Abrego, Sara Lundquist, Lilia Tanakeyowma, Alfred Herrera, Angela Chen, Santiago Bernal, Kent Wong, Janna Shadduck-Hernandez, Meng So, Ruben Elias Canedo Sanchez, Janette Hyder, and Alejandra Rincón. Nationally, I am appreciative of the efforts Angela Kelley, Eun Sook Lee, Dae Joong Yoon, Inhe Choi, Margie McHugh, Jeanne Batalova, Wendy Cervantes, Felipe Vargas, the National Immigrant Youth Alliance, United We Dream, and the dozens of undocumented student groups around the country.

I would be remiss if I did not thank my current and former students, in particular Benjamin Roth, Kevin Escudero, Thomas Swerts, Michele Statz, Marcelle Medford Lee, Ariel Ruiz, Joanna Perez, Maria Luna Duarte, Rachel Freeman, Matthew Shaw, and Stephany Cuevas.

To all of those who gave their time for this study, who invited me in to your worlds, and who shared your time so generously, I am indebted to you especially. You are my heroes. I am sorry that confidentiality precludes me from mentioning your names. But you know who you are.

I would like to express my gratitude for the continued support and sacrifices my family has made as I worked on this book. To my mother, Martha Patricia Gonzales, and my sister, Aimee Gonzales, and her wonderful children, I am thankful beyond words. Last, I want to recognize and appreciate my late godson, "Alex," whose short life inspired this research.

This book is for my wife, Sara, and our son Joaquin. Sara's love has been the single greatest source of motivation and encouragement in all aspects of my life. She is a constant reminder of why I do what I do. Joaquin has deepened our lives in ways I could never have imagined. Their gifts of unconditional love, companionship, nurturance, and laughter are more than I could ever ask for.

CHAPTER 1

Contested Membership over Time

It was what many had been hoping for: some sort of relief. But did it come too late? And was it enough? On the evening of Thursday, November 20, 2014, US president Barack Obama went on live television to announce a new administrative action to reform the US immigration system. Obama began, "Today, our immigration system is broken, and everybody knows it. . . . It's been this way for decades. And for decades, we haven't done much about it." Responding to growing discontent among immigrant rights groups, the president and the Department of Homeland Security (DHS) together issued a memorandum expanding the Deferred Action for Childhood Arrivals (DACA) program of 2012. DACA—instituted by a DHS directive rather than congressional action—provided temporary work permits and deportation relief to more than 664,000 young undocumented immigrants who had lived in the United States since childhood.[1] The 2014 expansion announced by President Obama eliminated DACA's upper age ceiling of thirty-one years and introduced a new program, Deferred Action for Parents of Americans and Permanent Residents (DAPA), to provide deportation relief and work permits to an estimated 3.5 million undocumented immigrants with US-born children.

The president's actions followed a series of aborted legislative attempts to provide the nation's eleven million undocumented immigrants with a pathway to legalization. Legislation targeting undocumented immigrant youth, formally known as the Development, Relief, and Education for Alien Minors (DREAM) Act, had gained some political traction since first being introduced in 2001 but had not been able to pass Congress.[2] As time passed without congressional action, immigrant communities grew increasingly desperate for reform. Their world was shrinking. Ramped-up deportations sowed fear across the country. Every passing day presented another blocked opportunity to get an education or to work, to connect with family members in one's country of origin, and to make a true home in the United States.

These actions also came more than thirteen years after the initial introduction of the DREAM Act and many years of disappointment that young people and their families had experienced watching time go by without legislation being passed. Policy makers like to say that change takes time and occurs incrementally. But legislative decisions take place at a great distance from people's lived reality. For those waiting for immigration reform, time has been cruel and unyielding.

I was wrapping up this book and trying to figure out what these administrative changes would mean for a group of undocumented young adults in Los Angeles whom I had been following for nearly twelve years. I was especially curious about what this new program would mean for them, how they would respond, and who would be left out.

Back in Los Angeles, Maria Betancourt, one of the young people whose lives I had followed between 2003 and 2014, reacted to the president's announcement with mixed emotions.[3] In 2012, she had been an undocumented resident eligible for the DACA program, and she had been excited to apply, saving for over six months to come up with the $465 application fee. But now, as a thirty-one-year-old with only a high school diploma, her DACA status was not sufficient to raise her standard of living. With her work permit, Maria was able to apply legitimately for a cashier job at a local drug store, but her hourly wage was not enough to lift her family out of poverty.

When she was younger, Maria had aspired to become a dental assistant. She had enrolled in community college but had quit by the end of the semester because her studies would be useless without "those nine digits." Now, even with the nine-digit social security number granted by DACA, Maria did not expect to be able to return to school. She had two children and was expecting a third. Her husband Ramon, also undocumented, was unable to apply for immigration relief or a work permit because of the long shadow cast by previous gang ties and crimes he had committed as a teenager.

In the November 2014 announcement, Obama forcefully argued, "We're going to keep focusing enforcement resources on actual threats to our security. Felons, not families. Criminals, not children. Gang members, not a mom who's working hard to provide for her kids." But the distinction between "criminals" and caring, productive family members was not so clear for the Betancourts. Ramon had worked hard over the years to establish a life removed from gang ties and to be a good husband and father. He had severed ties with many of the guys from his old neighborhood, he had begun volunteering at his church, and he had worked very hard so he could help to financially support his family. But the president's words provided no offer of relief for people like Ramon, no notion of rehabilitation. Though his crimes had been committed long ago, these new programs provided Ramon with little hope for the future. Despite his connection to his church, his many years of hard work, and the steps he had taken to get his life on track, Ramon was structurally locked out.

Across the country in Milwaukee, Wisconsin, Esperanza Rivas was firmly situated among the politically "deserving"—with the exception of her undocumented status. In contrast to Ramon's criminal past, Esperanza's teen years made her a poster child for the proposed DREAM Act legislation. She had been adored by teachers and classmates alike when she was in high school in Long Beach, California, where she was at the top of her class, ran cross-country, and was a member of the marching band.

But time was not on Esperanza's side. When she graduated from the University of California in 2006, no federal programs existed to provide her with a legal work permit. She was forced to take a job from a narrow range of bad choices. She kept her hopes up by advocating for the passage of the DREAM Act with a group of friends, but her advocacy could not provide an escape from the strains of low-wage work and life "under the radar."

In 2012 Esperanza moved to Milwaukee to be close to her mom and sister. Even after receiving DACA status later that year, Esperanza struggled to support her one-year-old son as a single mom. She used her work permit to secure one job at a bank and another at a hotel—jobs similar to those she had held as an undocumented worker. At age thirty-two, her work history did not allow her to compete for jobs commensurate with a University of California education. "What sucks about this," she told me, "is yeah, I have a work permit. So what? I've missed out on so much time. While my friends have been busy building their careers with internships and entry-level jobs that have given them real experience, on the job, I've got to start from scratch. Nobody is going to hire a thirty-two-year-old for those jobs. Besides, it's hard to make any long-term plans. [DACA] isn't legal status. It's not citizenship. I don't know when it might end. I might get my hopes up and then I'm back where I was before. This is so tiring."

A change in immigration status years ago might have made a huge impact on Esperanza's life, but after years of lost opportunities its arrival is less consequential, as it is for many others like her. And for those like Maria, and especially Ramon, it just may have come too late. Now that they are in their early thirties, DACA fails to meet their fuller needs. What they require is an entire set of policies that would support and integrate them. Policies based on the deserving/undeserving distinction disadvantage far more of the population than they benefit, and do not even adequately address the life complexities of those singled out as "deserving."

Why do high-achieving undocumented young adults like Esperanza ultimately share similar work and life outcomes with their less educated peers, even as higher education is treated as the path to integration and success in America by politicians advocating for immigration reform? And what is the function of school if all of these young people are destined to be laborers? Drawing on interviews and fieldwork over nearly twelve years with 150 undocumented young adults in Los Angeles, this book provides some interesting answers.

EXCLUSION AND BELONGING FOR THE 1.5 GENERATION

Maria, Ramon, and Esperanza have much in common. All three were born in Mexico but migrated to the United States before the age of twelve and have spent most of their lives in Los Angeles. Their time lived in the United States provides them important experiences from which to make claims about their social membership, but their immigration status dramatically shrinks their everyday lives. Scholars refer to these young people as "Americans in waiting" and as "impossible subjects,"[4] but their experiences of belonging are far more complex than indicated by political or academic discourse. Indeed, a complex web of polarizing rhetoric regarding the place of immigrants in American society entangles the lives of these young undocumented Mexican immigrants. Descriptions such as "innocent" and "deserving" vie with ones such as "illegal" that conflate nationality, immigration status, and outsiderness.

Current academic debates on immigration focus on questions of membership and rights, joining a long tradition in social science that examines borders and exclusion from formal citizenship within the boundaries of liberal democratic states.[5] The general public is also keenly interested in immigration issues and questions of inclusion and exclusion.[6] Formal and informal, public and private conceptions of citizenship are tied to questions of belonging.

Historically, national membership has been defined in relation to a bounded community where the rules of legal citizenship set the parameters of belonging and exclusion. But recent work in the field of immigration studies takes a different view of membership, treating citizenship as "the rules and meanings of political *and* cultural membership."[7] More and more scholars have been challenging the long-standing belief that the nation-state is the sole actor to determine membership and endow rights. Recent trends in globalization, human rights, and multiculturalism have made national boundaries less consequential for determining membership, and as persons with a long-term presence in receiving states undocumented immigrants like Maria, Ramon, and Esperanza enjoy spaces of belonging that supersede legal citizenship.[8] Differing old and new views of membership raise critical questions about the relevance of territorial presence for belonging—they beg the question: is residing within a community sufficient grounds for asserting membership, or does one first need to be recognized as a member?

Scholarly debates around the definition of "citizenship" are not just abstractions; these debates have real consequences for the lives of noncitizens. Migrants today cross national borders in almost every Western nation, not only to work but also to make their homes. Increased global interdependence of capital and markets for goods, services, and workers has led to unprecedented levels of settlement of undocumented migrant populations in traditional immigrant-receiving countries as well as countries that have not historically seen significant levels of immigration. Undocumented migrants create families and establish homes in territories where they have come to work yet do not have full legal rights. Regulating undocumented (also known as unauthorized, irregular, or illegal) populations is a high-priority objective of national policy in host countries,[9] with each nation finding its own answers to the questions of political inclusion and social welfare provision for undocumented residents.

Throughout my many years of community and academic work I have met hundreds of undocumented young people struggling to reconcile these conflicting meanings of membership. Despite wide acceptance of children as a protected class, countries like the United States face the growing challenge of how to best provide for children's well-being given the political popularity of strong enforcement stances and stringent policies against undocumented immigration.[10] This tension has produced a broad range of responses, with implications for local communities, services, and protections. In many countries, the scales tip more toward enforcement than protection.[11] Since the mid-1990s in the United States, immigration laws and enforcement practices have diminished noncitizens' rights and have made neighborhoods and public spaces insecure.[12] Even mundane acts such as driving, waiting for the bus, or socializing in a public park can lead to police questioning, detention, and deportation. These trends instill fear and anxiety within large, settled immigrant populations that include citizens, legal immigrants, and undocumented residents. At the same time, however, policies aimed at integrating immigrants have increased their access to higher education, given them means to participate in local elections, and allowed them access to a baseline of services such as health care. These inclusionary acts provide important opportunities for undocumented residents to establish connections, form relationships, and participate in the day-to-day life of their communities.

Many immigrants living in the United States today belong to mixed-status families, where some members have some form of immigration status while others do not, and some members are adults and others are children. In this book I focus on undocumented members of what sociologist Rubén G. Rumbaut termed the 1.5 generation, young people who were born in Mexico and who began their American lives as children.[13] Together, undocumented immigrants like these number 2.1 million people;[14] almost half of them are now adults.[15]

Young people in the 1.5 generation were raised with the expectation that as adults they would find better opportunities than those afforded to their parents.[16] Their schooling prepared them for better jobs. Instead, as undocumented Americans, they must reconsider their basic assumptions about the link between their efforts to acculturate and the rights they have as adults and must revise their long-standing expectations about their futures while watching their documented and American-born friends advance, weighing options and beginning careers. They must negotiate membership in the national community as part of a group that is culturally integrated but legally excluded. As sociologists Richard Alba and Victor Nee point out, "Assimilation . . . happens to people while they are making other plans."[17] The limitations faced by undocumented young people make clear that successful assimilation and full membership depend on the host country's willingness to include them.[18] As the saying goes, "It takes two to tango."

This book wrestles with conflicting understandings of undocumented immigrants to reveal the gap between individual feelings of belonging and the exclusion enforced by the society in which they live. It focuses on undocumented Mexican young adults living in Los Angeles, California. Mexicans constitute the largest immigrant group in the United States. They also make up the largest share among undocumented immigrants. And more undocumented immigrants—the majority of whom are of Mexican descent—live in Los Angeles than any other place in the country. Given the racialized history of Mexicans in the United States, this book's framing questions of belonging and exclusion play out in complex ways. However, while the circumstances of undocumented Mexican youth merit special attention, it is important to point out that many of the issues raised in this book relate to the broader population of undocumented immigrant youth and young adults living in the United States.

For twelve years, I listened to the stories and observed the daily activities of young men and women with "roots on the wrong side of their lives."[19] Their stories of being *ni de aquí ni de allá* (from neither here nor there) describe personal experiences of belonging and exclusion under the contemporary US immigration system. Sitting on factory benches, living room couches, and folding chairs in community centers across the five-county Los Angeles metropolitan area, I listened to personal narratives of belonging and exclusion and how these conflicting experiences often changed over time. Despite painful experiences of exclusion in their own lives, many of my respondents maintained faith in the American dream. And despite vitriolic public discourse and government practices designed to keep them at the margins, these young people found or fashioned ways to engage in the social and political life of their communities.

During my visits with these young people over the years, I have observed changes in their lives—different partners, new jobs, accumulated debt, and flattened aspirations. I have often been surprised by the ways in which they have responded to change. Despite the differences in their educational trajectories, they now view illegality as the most salient feature of their lives, trumping all of their achievements and overwhelming almost all of their other roles and identities.

The narratives of 1.5 generation undocumented Mexican young adults teach us about the double-edged nature of citizenship. Their life histories show how young people sustain a sense of belonging in community even as they are excluded from opportunities to step into adult roles, and denied many privileges and rights. To account for the contradictions between official policy and actual lived experience, we need theories that, as sociologists Irene Bloemraad, Kim Voss, and Taeku Lee put it, "disentangle the meaning and implications of new narratives outside formal, legal citizenship."[20]

INVESTIGATING THE TRANSITION TO ILLEGALITY

How do young people who migrate to the United States as children experience undocumented status as they transition into adulthood? This book moves away from a political debate on the terms for the legal inclusion of undocumented young people like Maria, Ramon, and Esperanza to focus instead on how these young people perceive and experience membership over time. The young people I profile straddle the worlds of their immigrant parents and their native-born peers. As they move toward adulthood, they struggle with the widening gap between their identity as "Americans" and their legal designation as undocumented immigrants. Their immigration status prevents them from fully participating in adult pursuits, yet they cannot afford to linger in a prolonged childhood. They try to reconcile competing messages about (social and cultural) belonging and (political and legal) exclusion. And as they strain to cope with contradictory messages, anti-immigrant animosity, and the stigma of exclusion, they seek ways to balance their identities as Mexican immigrants and de facto Americans.

Liminal Lives

The concept of liminality draws attention to the various transitions that occur as people move from one life stage to another. Immigration scholars have found liminality useful for understanding the experience of immigration in general and the lives of migrants with uncertain or undocumented status in particular. Arnold van Gennep, an ethnographer and folklorist, originated the concept. In his classic work *Rites of Passage*, van Gennep emphasized the importance of transitions along the life course—birth, coming of age, marriage, beginning an occupation, and death—whereby individuals move from group to group and from one social status to another.[21] Three important stages are involved in each transition. There is a period of segregation from the individual's previous way of life (the preliminary stage); a state of transition from one status to another (the liminal stage); and a process of introduction to the new social status and new way of life (the postliminal stage). Anthropologist Victor Turner elaborated on van Gennep's concept of transition, stating that individuals or entities in the liminal stage are "neither here nor there; they are betwixt and between the positions assigned and arrayed by law, custom, convention, and ceremony."[22] The liminal stage is characterized by ambiguity, which ends when the individual reaches the new social status.

In her study of Central American immigrants living in uncertain legal status and caught in the legal limbo of Temporary Protected Status (TPS), sociologist Cecilia Menjívar introduced the concept of liminal legality to highlight the gray areas of immigrant lives.[23] Menjívar observed that many immigrants live in a state of legal limbo that can persist indefinitely, in some cases without ever leading to citizenship or permanent legal status. This long-term uncertainty, or "permanent temporariness," is characterized by ambiguity, endowing immigrants with characteristics of both legal *and* "illegal" statuses. This real-life condition underscores the inadequacy of binary approaches to membership.

The state of living across national borders without legal recognition as an undocumented adult can be considered a form of *legal liminality*—a concept that inverts Menjívar's term to draw attention to the socio-legal construction of immigration status. When immigrants leave their country of origin, they also leave behind the roles that define their membership in that national community—citizen, community member, neighbor. Migrants possessing visas can move into van Gennep's third stage and develop new membership. But migrants without any form of legal immigration status remain stuck in the second liminal stage. Their new lives are characterized by uncertainty and instability in many realms, including employment, housing, and physical, and emotional well-being. Even the length of their stay in the host country is uncertain. For many, this liminality—this tenuous life in the shadows—is long term and indefinite.

Children who cross into the United States without legal residency status have a different experience of liminality. Their legal integration in K-12 schools allows them a more stable point of entry into American society. Open access to public school affords them the important opportunity to integrate into the country's legal and cultural framework, albeit temporarily. As members of a community of students, many young immigrants achieve a social status that has profound implications for their transition into new identities as American children. Their (temporary) integration provides positive messages about belonging, and their cultural, social, and political lives are rooted *inside the circle.* During the life stage of preadolescence, their exclusion from the American way of life is temporarily suspended. In effect, young undocumented immigrants are able to leave the liminal phase, crossing over socially and culturally although still not legally.

Coming of Age Undocumented

Research on immigrant children's transition to adulthood is important and timely. At no other point in the last century have immigrants represented such a significant percentage of the nation's population. What's more, their children are the fastest-growing segment of children under the age of eighteen. They are diverse in their backgrounds and the places where they grow up. As they come of age, academics and policy makers are concerned with measures of their productivity, including their educational attainment and employment.

We typically think about becoming an adult as the process by which young people assume the tasks and responsibilities of adulthood. Traditionally, this process entails the transition from full-time schooling to full-time work and from living with one's parents to establishing a separate home and starting a family of one's own. Moreover, we have come to associate the transition to adulthood with a normative time line— certain milestones should be achieved by a certain age—despite considerable evidence that this time line is slowing for the current generation of young adults.

In the twenty-first-century United States, a college degree is a major determinant of future success. Young Americans, especially those from middle- and upper-middle-class families, spend more time in postsecondary schooling and delay major transitions, including exiting the parental household, beginning full-time work, and starting families of their own.[24] By extending time in the parental home to acquire additional education and training, young people build human capital to compete in the high-skilled labor market. Some parents provide financial support to their young adult children to aid this process, paying college tuition, providing down payments for their children's first homes, and defraying some of the costs associated with having children.[25]

These parental strategies allow postadolescent children to delay assuming adult responsibilities. But young people from less-advantaged households do not have these same opportunities. Instead, some defer college because their families' financial needs and expectations of their contributions make it impossible for them to afford tuition and the time required to be a student.[26] For undocumented youth, the transition to adulthood is accompanied by a *transition to illegality.*

Difficult transitions stem from conflicting and contradictory laws that provide undocumented children access to K-12 schools but deny them the means to participate in the polity once they become adults. In 1982 in *Plyler v. Doe,* the Supreme Court struck down a Texas statute that denied funding for the public education of children who had not been "legally admitted" into the United States, and the Court voided a municipal school district's attempt to charge these students tuition to compensate for lost state funding. The justices ruled that the Texas law violated the equal protection provisions of the Fourteenth Amendment and that states could not discriminate against children on the basis of immigration status in the provision of public elementary and secondary education. Citing the "pivotal role of education" in the life of a child and the nation, Justice William Brennan noted that, while education is not a fundamental right, denying K-12 education to undocumented children amounted to inflicting a "lifetime of hardship on a discrete class of children not accountable for their disabling status." Brennan also stated that "by denying these children a basic education, we deny them the ability to live within the structure of our civic institutions, and foreclose any realistic possibility that they will contribute in even the smallest way to the progress of our Nation. In determining the rationality of [the Texas statute], we may appropriately take into account its costs to the Nation and to the innocent children who are its victims."

The Court's decision in *Plyler v. Doe* was a watershed moment in immigration policy. By establishing the legal inclusion of "innocent" undocumented immigrant children in the American public school system, the ruling laid the groundwork for them to benefit from the same opportunities for inclusion that had existed for generations of immigrant schoolchildren before them.

Though the *Plyler* decision mandated the inclusion of hundreds of thousands of undocumented children "within the structure of our civic institutions," its reach was limited. It guaranteed access only to K-12 education. Beyond that, support in schools, counseling, and other critical services are not guaranteed and are very hit-or-miss. Moreover, the ruling did not address education beyond K-12, nor did it provide any means for individuals to change their immigration status. Given that undocumented children have no practical way to adjust their immigration status, as they near the end of high school and begin adult lives their lack of legal citizenship closes off access to good jobs, creates barriers to enrolling in college, and heightens the chances for detainment and deportation.

In Western societies, adolescence marks a liminal phase both culturally *and* legally. Adolescence is arguably the most "betwixt and between" stage of life. In most US states, turning eighteen represents a crucial legal threshold of adulthood. All young people in the United States must reposition themselves when they reach the age of majority, adjusting to the responsibilities and consequences that accompany legally defined adulthood. It is the age at which a child ceases to be considered a minor and assumes responsibility for his or her actions and decisions. Eighteen-year-olds with legal immigration status generally have the right to vote, to make a will and exercise power of attorney, to become an organ donor, to obtain medical treatment without a parent's permission, to enlist in the armed forces, and to apply for credit. When individuals cross this legal threshold, they can be tried as adults, they are eligible for jury duty, and, if they are male, they must register with the Selective Service. In most states, even before adolescents reach eighteen, they are eligible to undertake certain adult activities, such as working and driving.

But for undocumented youth turning eighteen is a profoundly different experience. Most aspects of childhood do not require legal residency status as a basis of participation; most adult pursuits do. For documented and native-born adolescents, the age of majority marks a time of opportunity. Driving, voting, going to college, and working are markers of their increasing maturity, autonomy, and adult standing. For an undocumented eighteen-year-old, they are at least problematic, at worst prohibited, blunt reminders of their tenuous status. The interaction among age, cultural milestones, and state and federal law means that as undocumented youth come of age they transition to illegality, a process that not only shapes their lives socially and emotionally but also redefines their rights, access, and ability to stay in the country.

As children, undocumented youth learn the rules of society, discover the world around them, and form attachments to people and institutions and places. But time brings changes that are unexpected, unwanted, and often cruel. As they come of age, they experience dramatic ruptures in their expectations and their possibilities. Adolescence initiates a period of intense turmoil, uprooting their identity, their future goals and plans, and their sense of belonging. Youthful feelings of belonging give way to new understandings of the ways that they are excluded from possibilities they believed were theirs. As they watch their peers' lives expanding, in work and education, in autonomy and relationships, undocumented young adults must learn to navigate a severely reduced arena of safety. Conflicting terms of inclusion leave them feeling out of place, longing for the protected status that they enjoyed in school.

The Role of Schooling in Shaping the Transition to Illegality

These processes do not unfold evenly. The range of experiences among my respondents shows that belonging and barriers to belonging are shaped by local laws and practices. Adult immigrants typically become incorporated into their new homeland through the world of work. For children, however, school is usually the primary institutional introduction to their new lives as Americans.[27] Indeed, the connection between schooling and the training of a standard citizenry is well established.[28] But, as Justice Brennan's opinion in the *Plyler v. Doe* case reinforces, schools also importantly shape the parameters of *social membership*. They determine how pupils are incorporated into the larger community, they control access to scarce resources, and they make their own decisions about deservingness, setting terms of their own for inclusion and exclusion.

Historically, public schools have wielded the power to either replicate societal inequalities or equalize the playing field. However, many large urban school districts across the country lack the human resources—the number of teachers and counselors and their workload—to meet the needs of the entire student body. In these schools, adults' decisions are often influenced by differential access to information, their own personal prejudices and beliefs, and scarcities of time, materials, staff, and space. Teachers and counselors often expend their limited resources on students they have designated as "worthy." School stratification is especially disadvantageous for students in the lower tracks, who constitute the vast majority in most schools.[29] Highly differentiated curricula and de facto tracking are particularly harmful for disadvantaged students.[30] A general perception that tracking is based on meritocracy, rather than racial or class-based discrimination, normalizes the achievement gap.

Children from poor and minority families have consistently lagged behind their white, middle- to upper-class peers in schooling outcomes.[31] Sociologist Karolyn Tyson argues that despite desegregation efforts in the post–*Brown v. Board of Education* era, contemporary American public high schools use racialized tracking practices to segregate students.[32] However, scholars have also found that student outcomes remain diverse, even within schools with high concentrations of poor and minority students.[33] Relationships with school officials and high-achieving peers, some researchers argue, can provide low-income students of color with access to important sources of social capital and resources necessary for school success.[34] By fostering young people's integration into school-based networks, nurturing positive school relationships, and providing access to institutional resources (e.g., academic counseling and honors and advanced placement classes), school personnel play a vital role in facilitating students' sense of belonging.[35]

Students who are "chosen" early on for better classes and smaller learning communities have access to a wider range of resources, including teacher time and visits to college counselors. Their positive positioning allows them greater opportunities to form trusting relationships with adults in their schools. Those on the wrong side of tracking decisions must contend with larger classes, outdated materials, more competition for attention, and fewer adult advocates. Some students receive adult support and resources; others are ignored, negatively labeled, and pushed out of the educational system.

School decisions—though structured by school inequality, tracking processes, and resource constraints—have the effect of presenting school failure as the result of individual actions.[36] Moreover, what is and is not provided to these students has a strong bearing on future educational and occupational paths.

Though school curriculum tracking decisions affect all students, poor positioning within the school curriculum hierarchy can be a double disadvantage for undocumented students. Placement in the lower or middle curriculum tracks of their schools undercuts their ability to form trusting relationships with high-achieving peers, teachers, and other school personnel. As a result, many students never receive the support and guidance they need to seek out information critical to school success. Whether these students exit the school system before high school graduation or fail to make the transition to college, their entry into the world of low-wage work and their early struggles with their legal limitations have consequences for their adult options and their ability to define themselves as included members deserving of rights.

Once undocumented youth leave school, their experiences set them on different pathways. High achievers who make successful transitions to college find a productive pursuit in higher education that allows them to expand their learning and develop skills that would enable them to do the kind of work they hoped to do. It provides them positive and affirming experiences that buoy their hopes for the future.

Those who either drop out of school or do not continue schooling after graduation face a dramatic shrinking of their worlds. Without the protection or pretext of being in school, they face frequent exclusions and a growing number of encounters that drive home their status as outsiders.

Ultimately, for these undocumented young adults, at some point in adulthood their illegality dominates their feelings of belonging in most situations and interactions. Illegality becomes a *master status*.

Undocumented Status as a Master Status

The concept of master status was introduced nearly seventy years ago by sociologist Everett Hughes, who noted the tendency of particular human traits, labels, or demographic categories to dominate all other statuses and to prevail in determining a person's general social position.[37] Hughes argued that while some statuses carry prestige and honor, others mark individuals more negatively. He also observed that particular statuses or traits carry a degree of stigma that can dominate and subsume all other traits. In the United States, race and gender are statuses that play key roles in ranking social position and shaping access.[38] These are also statuses that physically mark individuals. Despite attempts to legislate an end to social inequalities based on race and gender, certain practices remain. Race, for instance, can affect whether and to what degree an individual is suspected of taking part in illegal activity and labeled as a criminal, is passed over for promotions, and is denied loans.[39]

For undocumented 1.5 generation young adults, undocumented status, while less consequential in childhood, becomes a master status in adulthood. It frames their lives in such a way that years lived in the United States, acculturation to American norms and behavior, and educational attainment are all inconsequential to their everyday routines as undocumented immigrants. This is the case because much of what they need to carry out adult lives—driver's licenses, jobs, valid forms of identification—require legal immigration status. Moreover, the stigmatizing mark of illegality means that they find themselves increasingly associated with the common perceptions of criminality and outsiderness, pushing them further out onto the margins.

RESEARCHING UNDOCUMENTED MEXICAN YOUTH

Drawing on participants' narratives of their lives and my own observations of their everyday routines, this book provides an intimate account of the conflicting processes involved in living both inside and outside the circle of belonging. This perspective reveals the cruel and damaging flaws of our contemporary immigration system. I show that while undocumented young people are substantively integrated into American society and can make certain claims to belonging, full membership is denied them by capricious immigration policies. Ultimately, the experiences of my study participants challenge long-standing assumptions among academics and policy makers about the link between acculturation and political and economic incorporation.

This book draws from a longitudinal research study of undocumented young adults in the five-county Los Angeles metropolitan area conducted between 2003 and 2014, involving participant observation, 150 in-depth interviews, and detailed field notes of my engagement with respondents, particularly those with whom I met on more than one occasion. All 150 young people I interviewed were undocumented for most of their childhood, adolescence, and adulthood. They grew up in one or more of the five counties—Los Angeles, Riverside, San Bernardino, Ventura, and Orange—that make up the Los Angeles metropolitan area, and they went to large high schools. With the exception of eight Central Americans (from Guatemala and El Salvador), all were born in Mexico. Most respondents had parents who were undocumented (92 percent) and who had fewer than six years of schooling (86 percent). Most respondents were raised by two parents; thirty-eight were raised by single parents; and six were raised by other family members.

This study is the most comprehensive effort to date to understand the experiences of young undocumented immigrants of the 1.5 generation, and it is the first to follow them as they transition into their adult lives.[40] My sampling strategy involved theoretical and snowball sampling.[41] Because of the delicate nature of my study and the precarious immigration status of respondents, the work of building long-term, trusting relationships was central to my research process. As anthropologist Philippe Bourgois points out, such relationships are necessary "to ask provocative personal questions, and expect thoughtful, serious answers."[42] To build trust, I made multiple contacts with each person before I raised the possibility of audio-recording our conversations, and I was careful to avoid asking potentially intrusive questions early on.

My broad plan included recruiting Mexican immigrants who came to the United States at twelve years or younger and who were undocumented as a result of clandestine crossing or visa overstay. Their ages at the time of the first interview ranged from twenty to thirty-one. I understood from my previous work with youth that many potential participants in my study had experienced severe setbacks in their lives at the hands of adults and institutions and were generally distrustful of them. I knew it would be crucial to gain their trust and support for my project. I also knew that it would not be accomplished in a short time. To the community stakeholders and the young adults alike, I presented myself as an outsider with a sincere interest in the lives of immigrant families, but also as an insider who had the community experience and sensibility adequate to initiate and navigate relationships of trust. My ten years working with youth in Chicago during the 1990s gave me some currency with community members. Staff of organizations often treated me as a colleague, introducing me to program participants, taking me on neighborhood tours, and sharing their own insights.

My initial fieldwork strategies led me to contact with undocumented young adults at community meeting places—job training programs and support groups for troubled young people, soccer fields and basketball courts, continuation schools and GED classes, after-school enrichment programs and DREAMer clubs. To generate a sample that included a broader range of coming-of-age experiences, I sought out ways to find young adults who were not connected to mainstream community organizations. Generating snowball samples outside community institutions also allowed me to find young people who were not at the educational extremes.

Interviews focused on respondents' experiences growing up undocumented in Los Angeles. They included questions about family, community, education, work, and civic participation as well as broad themes of belonging and illegality. I also asked about respondents' hopes and expectations for the future. The interviews form the basis of the project.

THE LAW AND THE CLOCK: CHANGES IN THE POLITICAL CONTEXT OVER TIME

What I learned from undocumented Mexican young adults made clear that the illegality-belonging dynamic is profoundly shaped by time. Historically, studies of immigrant incorporation have viewed time as a given. After all, it takes time to learn the language, customs, and culture of the host society. There has been much debate about whether time lived in the United States (even if it takes several generations), as opposed to structural conditions, is the recipe for incorporation. Nevertheless, time has been undertheorized, particularly as it relates to the here-and-now experiences of immigrants and their children.[43]

Time allows young people to accumulate experiences that shape their identities and to define the world around them. Time turns innocent playful children into adults with greater responsibilities. It alters the institutional landscape that young people rely on, and it changes the requirements for participation. Time moves immigrant children in and out of legal categories and legalization channels.[44] It distorts youths' visibility within in their local community and the perception that they are innocents who deserve protection. But time also plays out on a grander scale.

Contemporary Mexican Migration

The plight of America's estimated 2.1 million undocumented young people can best be understood in the broader historical context of migration from Mexico.[45] Their presence and their vulnerability are the result of a long history of labor migration dating back to the end of the Mexican-American War in 1848 and legislative attempts to crack down on undocumented migration. Mexicans have long been viewed as a source of cheap, flexible labor, meeting labor demands in America's railroads, factories, mines, and fields. While this dependence on Mexican labor reached an apex during World War II, the legal character of Mexican migration began to change dramatically in the mid-1960s.

In 1964, the burgeoning civil rights movement put an end to the Bracero Program, a twenty-two-year-old guest-worker initiative that supplied cheap and flexible Mexican labor to America's farms. Southwestern growers who had become accustomed to a cheap Mexican labor force nevertheless continued to rely on Mexican migrants to harvest their crops.[46] A year later, in 1965, Congress passed the Hart-Celler Act, eliminating restrictive immigration policies and creating new family and skilled-worker preference categories for entry. These changes opened up immigration from Asian and African countries and refueled debates about immigration, membership, and belonging.[47] New ethnic enclaves emerged in several US cities, and existing ones expanded. Meanwhile, migration from Mexico also surged. However, as sociologists Douglas S. Massey and Karen Pren argue, this increase in migration occurred *in spite of* rather than because of the new system.[48]

Before 1965, there were no numerical limits on immigration from the Western Hemisphere. But the 1965 amendments to existing immigration law, including changes in the Hart-Celler Act, marked an end to open borders and made the likelihood of illegality even greater for newly excluded Mexicans. When the law went into effect in 1968, it limited annual immigration from the Western Hemisphere to 120,000 and established country quotas of 20,000.[49] These changes, which came shortly after the Bracero Program ended, led many employers to view undocumented migration as their only source of cheap labor.[50]

The restrictions under Hart-Celler also altered the legal auspices under which Mexican immigrants arrived to the United States. Between 1965 and 1986, twenty-eight million Mexicans entered the United States as undocumented migrants.[51] These legally vulnerable migrants met a growing demand for unskilled labor in the service, retail, and construction industries fueled by the growth of cities and suburbs.[52] These jobs required little English-language proficiency and were well suited for immigrants willing to work for low pay, often in poor working conditions. As the Mexican population grew in US cities, undocumented Mexicans became more visible and the public reaction became more hostile. Mexican migrants were characterized as criminals who were inherently outsiders and as a threat to public safety, health, and the American way of life.[53]

By the early 1980s, unauthorized immigration from Mexico was a hot political issue in the United States. In 1986, Congress passed the Immigration Reform and Control Act (IRCA) in an effort to curb unauthorized migration in the face of growing public hostility. IRCA legalized 2.7 million migrants. This was a major success as a vehicle for bringing migrants out of the shadows and for promoting economic mobility opportunities. However, IRCA did nothing to grant legal visas to subsequent cohorts of workers, thus perpetuating the problem. Moreover, IRCA was the first in a series of laws to impose an increasing number of immigration restrictions that dramatically changed migration patterns. In response to calls for tighter security, efforts to fortify the nearly two-thousand-mile US-Mexico border produced a longer and taller fence, a greater number of agents along the border, and an increased use of technology to detect migrant crossings.[54] But IRCA failed to address the underlying causes of unauthorized immigration, and the undocumented population continued to grow over the next three decades.

Effects of the Legal Context on Immigration Flow

With immigrants' shift to permanent settlement, the number of undocumented children living in the United States grew rapidly. Prior to the 1980s, undocumented Mexicans were mostly seasonal labor migrants whose families remained back home. However, greater militarization of the border made the act of crossing much more difficult, costly, and dangerous. Instead of returning home to their families in Mexico, migrants started bringing their spouses and children to the United States to live with them.[55] Throughout the 1990s and into the twenty-first century, the number of undocumented immigrants residing in the United States grew substantially, as did the number of children who would grow up in the United States without legal immigration status.[56]

The passage of IRCA and associated militarization of the border is the most frequently cited explanation for this change in migration patterns. But at least two additional processes contributed to the growth of the undocumented Mexican child population in the United States. In 1996, the Illegal Immigration Reform and Immigrant Responsibility Act (IIRAIRA) established new and far-reaching grounds of inadmissibility. These include three-year, ten-year, and permanent bars to reentry for persons unlawfully present in the country.[57] Under IIRAIRA, if a migrant spends more than 180 days in the United States and lacks an appropriate visa extension, he or she is automatically prohibited from legally immigrating for at least three years. The bars are activated upon *departure* from the United States—a provision that is especially draconian given the expiration of another legal provision, known as 245(i), just before IIRAIRA went into effect. Under 245(i), individuals were allowed to adjust their status while they were still within the United States.[58] With that provision no longer in effect, undocumented residents are required to return to their countries of origin to apply for legal status. But leaving the United States triggers bars to reentry, making it impossible for undocumented immigrants to maintain their lives in the United States while regularizing their status.

This Catch-22 produced a population of settled and now highly vulnerable migrant families—one consisting mainly of Mexicans—with few rights and no practical way to legalize their immigration status. It also stunted the long-term prospects of undocumented children as they come of age. Twenty years ago, many undocumented young people who grew up in the United States eventually legalized their status through employment sponsorship or marriage. Now, because of the immigration bars, pathways to legal status are far more limited, and the population of undocumented young adults has grown to unprecedented levels.

In less than two decades, the number of undocumented immigrants living in the United States increased ninefold, from 1.3 million in 1990 to a peak of 12.1 million in 2007.[59] The population of Mexicans in the United States also increased during this time, by roughly half a million people per year. Undocumented immigrants accounted for 80 to 85 percent of the increase.[60] At an estimated 2.1 million, the children of undocumented immigrants constituted close to one-fifth of the overall 11.2 million undocumented immigrants living in the United States in 2012.[61]

As political discourse around illegality has grown increasingly vitriolic, legislative efforts have focused disproportionate attention on enforcement as the chief means of addressing unauthorized migration.[62] These measures have had particularly disastrous effects on children of deported parents and on undocumented children as they transition to adulthood with greater fears of their own safety.

Blurred Boundaries between Immigration and Crime

In 1996 Congress amended the Immigration and Nationality Act of 1952 by passing the Antiterrorism and Effective Death Penalty Act (AEDPA) and the Illegal Immigration Reform and Immigrant Responsibility Act (IIRAIRA).[63] Taken together, AEDPA and IIRAIRA greatly expanded the number of crimes to be considered deportable offenses and made deportation mandatory for all immigrants sentenced to a year or more. In addition, the 1996 laws eliminated a "suspension of deportation" practice, which had previously allowed immigrants without a criminal history protection from deportation.[64] As a result, the 1996 laws increased the number of noncitizens who could be removed and sharply reduced the number of noncitizens eligible for any form of relief from removal proceedings, thus subjecting both noncitizens convicted of crimes and those with past criminal convictions to mandatory detention and deportation without the avenues of relief previously available. Equally consequential, the deportation provisions of these laws are applied retroactively to immigrants who would not have been deported under the laws in place at the time of their original convictions. Under these laws, immigrants are left with no recourse to judicial review or appeal. And since immigration courts are civil rather than criminal, the right to counsel does not apply.

Today, not only are noncitizens vulnerable to retroactive convictions of deportable offenses—including minor crimes like shoplifting committed years earlier—but these convictions trigger an irreversible chain of events that ends in permanent banishment from the United States. Hence, a one-time offense and youthful indiscretion committed years ago automatically results in detention without bond, restriction from access to counsel, no appeals process, deportation, and a lifetime separation from one's family—no matter how long ago their crime was committed and regardless of time served. Factors such as an immigrant's ties to the community, lawful good behavior, and tax-paying work history are no longer considered grounds for relief.

Growing Up in a Hostile Environment

Today, undocumented Mexican children are coming of age amid a storm of anti-immigrant discourse and activity.[65] As hate crimes directed largely against Latino immigrants have gained increasing visibility, federal immigration enforcement activity has also intensified. Since 1997, formal agreements between federal Immigration and Customs Enforcement (ICE) and local law enforcement created a climate of racial profiling and community insecurity.[66] In the first five and a half years, the Obama administration deported over two million people, with deportations reaching a peak of over four hundred thousand in 2012.[67] Over 90 percent of those deported have been of Latino descent.[68] And nearly all of these recent deportees have been Latino men.[69]

In April of 2014, the *New York Times* reported that nearly two-thirds of the two million deportations during the Obama presidency involved either people with no criminal records or those convicted of minor crimes.[70] That same month, researchers at Syracuse University cautioned that ICE's broad definition of criminal behavior included very minor infractions such as exceeding the speed limit.[71] Given the scope and intensity of enforcement efforts, Latino families and communities have experienced disproportional anxiety and disruptions.

While the federal government sets a general framework based on immigration categories that bestow rights to some while denying access to others, it also grants limited local authority to states. This provides possibilities for pockets of inclusion or exclusion, depending on how such authority is exercised. In other words, success or failure is a matter of chance. Where a person lives matters a great deal. Whether a child grows up in a place with harsh or lenient enforcement is highly consequential to his or her outlook and life outcome. Between 2005 and 2011, state legislative activity focused on immigration increased more than fivefold, from (in 2005) legislators in twenty-five states considering approximately 300 immigration-related bills and enacting 39 of them, to (in 2011) legislators across forty-two states and Puerto Rico introducing 1,607 immigration-related bills and resolutions and passing 306 of them.[72] The stances of states, counties, and cities have ranged from unsympathetic, unwelcoming, and even inhospitable to very supportive and favorable. However, the more hostile measures have received the most attention.

In 2010, Arizona passed Senate Bill 1070, an unusually broad and harsh immigration law. Its controversial enforcement provision—commonly known as "Show me your papers"—conflated Mexican, immigrant, and "illegal," resulting in a legal justification for racial profiling.[73] Following the lead of Arizona, several other states levied sanctions against employers and empowered local police to check for citizenship status.[74] Lawmakers in Alabama went considerably further in 2011.[75] They sought to deny immigrants access to virtually every facet of regulated life, from water utilities to rental agreements to dog tags.[76] Across the country, an even larger number of municipal and county ordinances attempted to cut off access to a wide array of common services.[77]

Meanwhile, several states have attempted to restrict the participation of undocumented immigrant students in public two- and four-year postsecondary educational institutions.[78] In 2008, South Carolina became the first state to ban undocumented immigrants from enrolling in any college or university that receives state dollars. That same year, the Alabama State Board of Education passed a policy barring undocumented students from the state's two-year public colleges. In Georgia, in 2010, educational officials similarly voted to bar undocumented students from attending the state's five most selective public universities.[79]

Taken together, these trends have produced a hostile climate, ratcheting up levels of alarm and fear in immigrant communities.[80] According to the Pew Hispanic Center, more than one in two Latinos worries about discrimination and deportation.[81] Law professor Michael Olivas, noting increased levels of hostility and prejudice at the community level, warns of "an ethnic and national origin 'tax' that will only be levied upon certain groups, certain to be Mexicans in particular."[82]

California's Varied Immigration Stances

The young people in my study came of age during a time of intense turmoil and anti-immigrant sentiment in California. In the early 1990s Republican governor Pete Wilson fanned nativist flames by evoking images of "floods of Mexicans," "hostile takeovers," and "uncontrollable" and "unchecked" "illegal" migration.[83] This rhetoric portrayed Mexican migrants as unwanted criminals who were outsiders and a threat to public safety, health, and the American way of life. In 1993 Wilson signed into law a measure that required driver's license applicants to provide a Social Security number, effectively excluding undocumented immigrants. In 1994 California residents voted in favor of the controversial Proposition 187 ballot initiative, which aimed to prohibit undocumented immigrants in the state from using health care, public education, and other social services. In 1996 Californians voted in favor of Proposition 209 to abolish the state's public affirmative action program in employment, contracting, and public education. And in 1998 they effectively eliminated bilingual education in California with Proposition 227.

After growing support to allow undocumented immigrants in the state to drive, Governor Gray Davis signed a bill giving undocumented immigrants access to driver's licenses in 2003. However, his actions caused a public outcry that helped spur his recall from office. Arnold Schwarzenegger, who was elected in the recall, persuaded the state legislature to repeal the never-enacted driver's license bill. He later vetoed subsequent attempts at legislation in 2004 and 2006.

By the time my research was nearing its end, changed demographics and public opinion favored increased access for undocumented immigrants, and the state began to take great strides toward integrating them.[84] These efforts, signed into law by Governor Jerry Brown in 2013, included the TRUST Act, which sets minimum standards to limit immigration hold requests in local jails; A. B. 60, legislation that allows undocumented immigrants to receive California driver's licenses;[85] two measures (A. B. 263 and S. B. 666) that target employers who retaliate against workers by threatening to report their immigration status; A. B. 1159, a measure that imposes regulations to protect consumers from being defrauded by unqualified individuals who charge a fee to help immigrants gain legal status; and A. B. 1024, a bill that allows undocumented immigrants who pass the state bar exam to be licensed as attorneys. Also, local ordinances have created "sanctuary cities" and have targeted unfair towing practices.

While most of my respondents did not receive any institutional financial assistance while in college, eligible students in the system in 2012 began to receive state-level financial aid. The California Dream Act—divided into two bills, A. B. 130 and A. B. 131—made undocumented students who qualify for in-state tuition under A. B. 540 eligible for institutional scholarships and state-based financial aid such as Cal Grants, State University Grants, and Board of Governor Fee Waivers. The bills went into effect in 2012 and 2013 respectively.

California has taken giant steps to integrate undocumented immigrants. Nevertheless, federal immigration enforcement continues to exacerbate levels of fear and vulnerability. And old convictions, like those of Ramon, render many immigrants ineligible for many of these programs. Furthermore, while immigrants in California may enjoy certain benefits, the circumstances of those in states like Alabama and Arizona have arguably worsened.

Deferred Action for Childhood Arrivals

On August 15, 2012, DACA went into effect, providing undocumented young people a temporary reprieve from deportation and giving them legal access to work permits. For those who had come to the United States before the age of sixteen, had been in the country continuously for the previous five years, and had not turned thirty-one prior to the president's announcement, this policy change represented an important step forward and a chance to begin to realize deferred dreams. As of March 31, 2015, more than 664,000 applications had been approved.[86]

For many college graduates, the program's work permit allows beneficiaries to make the most of their advanced degrees in jobs that match their educational preparation and credentials. For college-bound and students currently enrolled in postsecondary institutions, DACA provides an additional incentive to invest in education and skills.

In California, DACA has had tremendous reach. With over seventy-one thousand approvals, California is home to the greatest number of DACA beneficiaries.[87] In 2012, DACAmented Californians became eligible for driver's licenses when A. B. 2189 was signed into law. In addition, they are eligible for Medi-Cal, a health program serving low-income families.[88] Beginning in 2012, many Californians were poised to take advantage of increased access to driver's licenses, health care, jobs, and opportunities to travel.

By mid-2015, a significant segment of those estimated to be eligible for the program nationwide had not applied. Explanations vary. Many older individuals may not have been aware that community organizations were able to assist them with the application process; older individuals also may have had more difficulty proving their continuous residence, given that they arrived in the United States earlier and have been out of school for many years.[89] The low uptake rates by DACA-eligible youth may also be attributable to educational barriers. An earlier analysis of what might happen if legislation aimed at legalizing undocumented immigrant young people was enacted suggested that barriers to postsecondary education, especially its high cost and family poverty, would lead as many as 62 percent of those eligible under a DREAM Act bill not to pursue it.[90]

Many of my respondents have not welcomed DACA with the kind of enthusiasm it has received among a younger demographic. Time away from school, dreams deferred many years ago, and strained personal budgets have deterred many from applying. In addition, a lack of experience in relevant job sectors has weakened the impact of the status among my respondents who received DACA.

Deepening Divisions between Deserving and Undeserving Immigrants

DACA has highlighted the growing distance between the college educated and the rest of the undocumented youth population. But it should not be surprising that such a divide exists. Increasingly, immigrant integration proposals and legislation have exacerbated divisions between high achievers and other undocumented youth, rewarding the meritorious with an easier pathway to access while leaving others further behind.

By 2015, eighteen states had in-state residency tuition policies for undocumented immigrant college students.[91] In 2011, California joined Texas and New Mexico in allowing undocumented immigrant students to receive state financial aid.[92] These measures provided undocumented students increased access to institutions of higher education and boosted their enrollments. However, they also signaled a troubling trend: policy proposals during this time have been driven by a singular focus on undocumented youth qua students, with little consideration of their experiences outside school. DACA is an excellent example. The main criterion for eligibility is graduation from high school or attendance in an educational program.

Conversely, the federal government has shown zero tolerance for immigrants who commit even the slightest offense or infraction. Since 1996 the government has increasingly expanded the definition of immigrant criminality, using standards that do not apply to US citizens. An immigrant pulled over today for an improper lane change or a broken tail light—crimes that might result in a fine or suspended sentence for nonimmigrants—could face arrest, detention, deportation, and a bar from returning to the United States if he or she pled guilty to a misdemeanor that has since been defined a deportable offense.[93]

In the early stages of advocacy for undocumented students, educators, legislators, and lobbyists tried to paint a portrait of undocumented students that would appeal to all who love the American dream. The prevailing image of undocumented immigrants had been that of lawbreaking, inassimilable, and uneducated masses using public benefits, lowering wages, and having babies in the United States.[94] This uncontrollable tide, led largely by Mexicans, was said to be a threat to US culture, politics, the economy, and national security. To gain public sympathy for DREAM-eligible youth, advocates began to distance them from the familiar characterizations of undocumented immigrants. They depicted undocumented youth as innocent of the "criminal" decision to break US laws by crossing the border. They were framed as clean-cut, college-bound youngsters who spoke fluent and largely unaccented English. Images of valedictorians, class presidents, and model citizens wearing business suits or caps and gowns, the trappings of academic and professional success, multiplied in the media. Stories of educational achievement and American dreaming humanized the plight of undocumented immigrants.

However, these depictions also deepened divisions not only between "innocent" youth and their "lawbreaking" parents but also between high-achieving students and the more general population of undocumented youth unable to go to college. By framing the issue around school, they moved the discussion away from immigrant rights to one that distinguishes "worthy" immigrants from "unworthy ones," "innocent" and "deserving" immigrants from felons and gang members. While a fraction of the population was successfully navigating the education system, those out of school faced greater odds of being ensnared by immigration enforcement, contributing to what legal scholar Jennifer Chacon has called a "school-to deportation" pipeline.

But college-going immigrants too enter the low-wage workforce and find that the target is also on their backs. One then must ask: What, ultimately, is the value of characterizations emphasizing undocumented youths' high achievement and youthful innocence? Do they benefit only a dwindling number of high-achieving adolescents, while leaving the majority behind?

STUDYING UNDOCUMENTED ADULTS OVER TIME

Undocumented immigrants who begin their lives in the United States as children represent a significant share of the nation's undocumented immigrant population. It is imperative that researchers develop a better understanding of how this group negotiates liminal lives between belonging and exclusion. Both early exiters and college-goers bear powerful witness to the human costs of a broken and inhumane immigration system. Long-cherished national ideals underlying belief in meritocracy and the American dream rest on the assumption that US institutions—including the immigration system—operate fairly and predictably. But the system is rarely consistent or just. The politically and culturally marked lives of undocumented young people starkly reveal its cracks and contradictions.

When I began my study, many of my respondents were in their late teens. Most are now in their late twenties and early thirties. Robert Courtney Smith calls this kind of endeavor "life-course ethnography," an oxymoronic categorization that defies the logic embedded in these different approaches to research because it requires focused, in-depth immersion in the culture and everyday life of research subjects but also entails a longer, sustained view of their lives across time. Like Smith, I argue that this kind of deep and long engagement not only is possible but is an effective way to understand how vulnerable populations make sense of, contend with, and respond to the material conditions of their lives. By deeply immersing myself in the worlds of these young people I was able to gain an on-the-ground view of the big questions of migration and membership as they unfolded in the more personal themes of home, time, and place.

My twelve-year engagement with undocumented young adults in the Los Angeles metropolitan area began as an ethnography in 2003 of young adults in Santa Ana, California, the county seat and second most populous city in Orange County. After spending several months in community organizations and observing 1.5 and second-generation Mexican young adult participants, I conducted the first set of interviews with thirty adult children of undocumented immigrants, twenty-two of whom were undocumented. Then, from 2003 to 2006, I expanded my ethnographic fieldwork to the five-county Los Angeles metropolitan area to learn more about how young adults who came to the United States as children were affected by their undocumented status. In 2007 I interviewed seventy-eight undocumented young adults,[95] and then in 2009 I interviewed an additional fifty. This third wave of interviews gave me the chance to refine questions about adult transitions and to further diversify the sample. Social media and relationships with community members have allowed me to follow up with most of my respondents through the years.

In the first few years of my study I spent countless hours in community spaces. I tutored, volunteered, attended group meetings and town hall forums, and presented workshops. I also advertised my project to clubs and at community meetings, and I explained my project to potential research subjects. This field experience served as the basis for my ethnography and the foundation of my study. I located participants through participant observation and through referrals from community and family members I had met. My early research entailed following young people throughout their daily lives. I observed them in home, at school, in their local communities, and at work. I was present for many of their accomplishments, and I listened to their stories of frustration and sometimes desperation. I watched them earn GEDs and graduate from college, struggle to find and keep jobs, enter graduate schools, have children, and face deportation. I explored how respondents internalized, critiqued, and responded to contradictory messages about belonging and membership.

By the end of my study, there were dozens of undocumented immigrant student groups in almost every state in the country as well as national organizations composed of undocumented young adults. But during the early stages of my research, little public attention was paid to the plight of undocumented young people. Locating undocumented student groups and gaining their trust took time. And enlisting the participation of out-of-school undocumented young adults required a great deal of community immersion and ongoing contact with potential study participants.

Given the respondents' immigration status, I have gone to great lengths to establish and maintain confidentiality. Respondents provided verbal consent rather than leaving a paper trail with a written consent form. Having gone through a thorough human subjects process, I took several measures to avoid any identifiers that would directly link data to specific respondents. I gave pseudonyms to all respondents at the time of the initial meeting, and I never collected home addresses. I have replaced the names of respondents and their family members, schools, workplaces, and residences. I have also altered other types of identifying information, including gender, year of arrival, and birthplace, during multiple phases of deidentification to protect confidentiality. I also destroyed all audiotapes immediately after transcription.

Methodological Considerations

One long-standing difficulty in developing a better understanding of undocumented children is the lack of reliable demographic and empirical data. Large-scale surveys do not ask about immigration status, so we know very little about this population's earnings, expenses, mental and emotional health, and other important characteristics.[96] High-achieving undocumented college students are an attractive convenience sample for university researchers, politicians, and journalists, but this group is not representative of the undocumented population as a whole. Efforts to evaluate the potential impact of proposed DREAM Act legislation have generated more reliable data on the numbers of undocumented young people and where they live. But researchers are still unable to generate a detailed picture of trends in undocumented youths' academic trajectories.

Immigration scholar Nancy Foner makes a persuasive case for ethnography as a method to engage and understand hard-to-access populations. While acknowledging the important role large-scale survey research has played in the field of migration studies, she draws attention to the uniquely valuable, and often complementary, insights that ethnographies can provide. The in-depth study of a smaller number of people, carried out over a longer period of time, produces denser, deeper knowledge of individuals and reveals subtleties in meaning and behavior that large-scale surveys often miss or, in some cases, get wrong.[97] To move beyond conjecture, this study takes an ethnographic research approach that yields deep familiarity with the lives of the undocumented 1.5 generation. As Agnieszka Kubal notes, inquiry into the power of the state is most fertile at "the level of lived experience, where power is exercised, understood, and sometimes resisted."[98] Understanding how young adults experience power required a methodology deeply rooted in their lives.

My research on the 1.5 generation involved multiple ethnographic methods, including participant observation, in-depth life-history interviews, and unstructured interviews. This triangulation generated a "thick description" that situated the study participants' lived experiences, everyday processes, and subjective realities within their broader socioeconomic and historical contexts.[99] The research approach was grounded in daily and weekly contact, which enabled me to observe young men and women as they engaged in practices and interactions rather than to rely solely on verbal reports.

Unlike the few existing studies of this population, my own study deliberately sought undocumented young adults who were not high academic achievers.[100] There are dangers inherent in telling only one story about the lives of many people.[101] Limiting the study of any group to an investigation of its most successful members runs the risk of obscuring the bigger picture. To be sure, the dominant media narrative—of undocumented students' school achievement and exemplary civic participation—is an important one. It underscores their perseverance and remarkable ability to overcome obstacles. Ultimately, however, such depictions reify the Horatio Alger story, highlighting triumphs and ignoring the contextual forces that shape, constrain, and promote inclusion and mobility.[102]

The inclusion of young people who left school at or before their high school graduation in my study makes clear the effects of undocumented status on individuals who do not have the protections afforded by school involvement and by accumulated social and cultural capital. Well-intentioned descriptions of undocumented youth as "American at heart" ignore the multiple ways they are prevented from feeling American. The young people I met all contended with significant troubles: family poverty, exclusion, constant fear of apprehension, stigma, daily stress, and worry. To frame their experiences solely in terms of college access and career advancement neglects the serious cumulative effects of these broader issues. Through deeply involved ethnography with undocumented youth with a wide range of educational experiences, this research questions the structures that position this group outside the American community. In doing so, it reveals these actors' capacity to resist their circumstances and presents a fuller view of their agency.

Representing Liminal Experiences

President Obama's rhetorical use of "felons, not families" in his November 20 speech reflects and expands on efforts to present undocumented immigrants in a binary fashion: as innocents and high achievers or as undeserving threats to an American way of life. Indeed, the former depiction has emerged only recently as a political counternarrative to portray undocumented youth as worthy of membership. However, this dichotomization is equally problematic. It excludes and marginalizes many undocumented youth and adults not captured by this narrow vision of innocence, and it obscures their nuanced and similar experiences.

The young people I came to know came of age in complex social worlds, and their personal stories are highly nuanced. I share the concern Philippe Bourgois expressed regarding the possible misinterpretation of his ethnographic account of young men enmeshed in a drug culture.[103] Like him, I worry that the life stories and events presented in this book may be misread as negative stereotypes of young adults at the margins.[104] But I believe that the depth of my research process provided me with the ability to humanize my subjects, departing from the one-dimensional caricatures of undocumented youth as either superstar students or dangerous criminals. Any up-close exploration of a socially marginal population risks problems of representation. However, resisting binary depictions of these young men and women requires moving beyond sanitized and decontextualized sound bites that obscure the everyday realities of being undocumented, poor, and a racially marked other.

Avoiding a one-dimensional depiction of educational success can lead to a different problem—that of perpetuating the narratives of inferiority commonly used to characterize those on the margins. To avoid this trap, I constructed an alternative narrative that draws from a rich set of comparisons to present a critical interrogation of the US immigration system, the public school system, and poor, segregated, urban communities of concentrated poverty. This approach allows me to (re)tell stories of struggle and agency alongside a wider narrative of structural inequality and exclusion. Accompanying the many accounts of struggle in this book are diverse examples of individual triumph, resistance, and difficult choices made in the face of mounting obstacles.

The book addresses the varied levels of inclusion experienced by undocumented young adults who have been blocked from full legal access to membership in American society. Subsequent chapters draw on data from my larger sample of interviews as well as field notes from the time I spent interacting with and observing a smaller group of respondents. My analysis primarily focuses on young people's interpersonal experiences of their undocumented status, with attention to the influence of social structures at the local level, including schools, families, communities, and labor markets. I explore critical transition points that move college-goers and early exiters in and out of spaces of inclusion and exclusion. I pay close attention to the choices they make under sometimes conflicting circumstances. The participants' experiences of commonality and of difference have much to do with individual characteristics, but examined together they also demonstrate the force of the law in constricting immigrants' day-to-day worlds and limiting adult lives.

PLAN OF THIS BOOK

Chapter 2 presents the college-goers and early exiters in their social world of Los Angeles. It examines their social, political, and legal circumstances and how they understood those circumstances. This chapter provides a glimpse into the legal and economic challenges that the two groups faced in early adulthood, as well as the mechanisms that shaped their daily lives and future aspirations. While the college-goers enjoyed institutional protections that buffered experiences of illegality, early exiters bore the brunt of legal limitation and poverty. College-goers' ongoing presence in the academic world allowed and encouraged them to continue to dream and to plan bright futures. In contrast, early exiters had trouble looking past immediate needs of survival and making ends meet.

In Chapters 3, 4, and 5 I examine young adults' transitions from spaces of belonging to spaces of exclusion, from acceptance to rejection, from protected lives to illegal ones. In tracing the transition to illegality, I outline three stages: (1) integration; (2) discovery; and (3) learning to be illegal. I also show how factors outside the formal immigration system shape experiences of belonging.

Chapter 3 explores the issue of belonging through the early life experiences of undocumented youth. My respondents' narratives support claims of belonging based on presence, place, relationships, and accumulated experiences in communities. But undocumented young people did not experience belonging uniformly. Chapter 4 focuses on the primary and secondary school experiences of college-goers and early exiters. I explore how teachers and counselors included some young people while casting out others.

Chapter 5 examines the tumultuous discovery stage in the transition to illegality. I incorporate a life-course perspective to understand the role of adolescent and adult transitions in defining liminality, belonging, and exclusion. As respondents reached their late teenage years, the contradictions between laws that provided educational access and laws that denied their participation came into sharp relief. Almost overnight, feelings of inclusion and belonging were replaced by experiences of rejection and a heightened awareness of their unauthorized status. For many respondents, legal barriers brought a profound experience of stigma. The chapter highlights the divergent responses of college-goers and early exiters to experiences of exclusion.

For generations, scholars have touted education as the primary means of upward mobility. But my respondents experienced the rewards of educational attainment differently. By their mid- to late twenties, college-goers had finished higher education pursuits and early exiters had settled into work and family routines. In Chapters 6 and 7, I show how the two groups responded to exclusions, narrowed access, and everyday lives of illegality.

Chapter 6 draws on observations and interviews to describe the post–high school experiences of the early exiters. As they entered the world of low-wage clandestine work, they "learned to be illegal," a transformation that involved the almost complete retooling of daily routines, survival skills, aspirations, and social patterns. As they underwent this transformation, early exiters endured hardships, but they also demonstrated agency and resilience—forming relationships, taking part in social activities, and interacting with community institutions.

Chapter 7 turns to the college-goers, who, in contrast to the early exiters, enjoyed a seamless transition from high school to the legal pursuit of postsecondary education. On their college and university campuses, many found support from caring staff and undocumented peers. These relationships helped them secure the resources needed to move out from behind their stigmatized identities. Some asserted claims of membership through local and national activist efforts. However, the condition of illegality overwhelmed many college-goers as they struggled to finance college and reconcile their dual identities as students and undocumented immigrants. Even after completing college and attaining degrees, many college-goers experienced a regressive slide into a life of limited choices and the fear of deportation.

While the trajectories of college-goers and early exiters diverged during their late teens and early twenties, they ultimately and dramatically converged as these undocumented young adults approached their thirties. Chapter 8 builds on the evidence provided in the preceding chapters to describe illegality as a master status. In a legal environment that promoted enforcement and punishment at the expense of integration, all respondents' adult lives were framed by illegality.

Chapter 9 revisits the key issues raised in chapter 1 and uses the study's findings as a basis for recommendations for national and local policies to address the untenable position of undocumented youth. This chapter also discusses the potential reach and limitations of the DACA program, assesses the possibilities for federal legalization, and examines local-level integration efforts and their limitations.

CHAPTER 2

Undocumented Young Adults in Los Angeles

College-Goers and Early Exiters

Driving through the sprawling metropolis of Los Angeles, I am often struck by the dramatically different worlds its residents inhabit. Known for its ethnic diversity, the "City of Angels" has become increasingly immigrant over the last few decades.[1] The largest populations of Cambodians, Filipinos, Guatemalans, Iranians, Koreans, Salvadorans, and Vietnamese outside their respective countries live in this five-county area. There are also many Armenians, Chinese, Indians, Laotians, Russian and Israeli Jews, and Arabs from several countries.[2] There is no denying it— Los Angeles is the contemporary capital of Immigrant America.

At the same time, Los Angeles is a city of haves and have-nots, splintered by fault lines of inequality that closely track those of race and immigration status. To understand its divisions, for several years I traveled across Los Angeles's five counties to meet with, observe, and interview the subjects of this book. Over the course of this study I spent countless hours in a car and logged thousands of miles. Because of the sprawling nature of the municipality, most people in Los Angeles drive. It is widely known that public transportation, with its inconvenient schedules and multiple transfers, is a last option in Los Angeles, reserved for those with the fewest resources. Over the course of my study, I witnessed many of the city's disparities through the windshield of my 1988 Volvo station wagon.

As I exit the 405 freeway on my way to a community meeting, I drive past the Paseo luxury apartment complex—a half mile of identical

Spanish colonial–style units in uniform clay tones. An imposing fifteen-foot-high olive-colored stucco wall separates its upwardly mobile tenants from the dozen or so Mexican and Central American immigrants waiting for the city bus outside. After passing luxury complexes and several blocks of corporate high-rises made of glass and steel, the streets and sidewalks become more congested, with car and foot traffic in every direction. The mostly Mexican, working-class neighborhood is teeming with life. Women push strollers. Older men push carts filled with *raspadas, chicharrones,* and *frutas.* Groups of fast-food workers in matching hats and T-shirts stand near bus stops. *Ranchera* music can be heard from passing cars. I pass a donut store where more than fifty young men congregate in the parking lot. They squeeze together along picnic-style benches and tables, talking and drinking coffee. They wait, hoping today they will be picked up for work.

Indeed, "There are many LAs."[3] But Los Angeles is also distinctly Mexican. Not only does Los Angeles have the largest concentration of Mexicans outside Mexico City and Guadalajara, but Angelenos of Mexican descent make up the municipality's single largest ethnic group. In this respect, Los Angeles reflects broader demographic trends in the United States.

Mexican immigrants are the single largest country-of-origin group in the United States. Nearly 34 million people of Mexican origin now live in the United States, including 11.4 million foreign-born immigrants (accounting for nearly 30 percent of the country's 40 million immigrants) and 22.3 million native-born citizens.[4] The size of the country's Mexican-origin population has grown dramatically over the past four decades as a result of one of the largest and longest migrations in modern history, from less than a million in 1970 to a peak of 12.5 million by 2007.[5]

Contemporary Mexican migration is principally an undocumented story. More than half (51 percent) of Mexican immigrants in the United States are undocumented. Conversely, contemporary undocumented migration is largely a Mexican story. While the numbers of undocumented immigrants from countries outside Latin America have risen slightly since 2000, the vast majority of undocumented immigrants come from Mexico. In fact, no other sending country accounts for even a double-digit share of the total.[6]

In both of these stories, the state of California, for its part, has emerged as a uniquely significant hub. Home to 2.6 million of the nation's estimated 11.2 million undocumented immigrants, California has a larger undocumented population than any other state; this group constitutes

7 percent of the state's total population and 9 percent of its labor force.[7] California's undocumented immigrants are overwhelmingly Mexican (65 percent) and have lived in the country longer on average than those in other states.[8] With its diverse labor markets, the five-county Los Angeles metropolitan area is home to more than 60 percent of the state's undocumented population, making it the largest destination in the country for undocumented immigrants as well as home to the highest shares of undocumented children.[9]

These numbers swarm in my head as I continue to my meeting. A few blocks down the street, I hear the laughter and squeals of more than two hundred brown-skinned children dressed in white shirts, dark pants, and colorful backpacks as they congregate on the Jefferson elementary school playground. In contrast, Cesar Chavez Continuation High School, a second-chance credit recovery program a mere two blocks away, is quiet and relatively empty. Despite the brightly colored mural on the side of the building depicting a pair of hands, palms up, offering hope to neighborhood youth, "*Sí, Se Puede!* You Can Do It," only a few students are visibly walking its campus.

Many immigrant communities in Los Angeles are characterized by de facto segregation, dense poverty, low-performing schools, high rates of crime, and few opportunities for their residents. Empirical studies support the argument that overall, US Latinos are experiencing some degree of *spatial* assimilation, particularly along class lines. Residential integration is occurring much less frequently among Latino immigrants, however. For them, there is a trend toward growing spatial isolation rather than integration.[10] Growing up under these circumstances has direct consequences for children's academic attainment because neighborhood characteristics such as density, ethnic and racial character, and poverty shape school quality. According to data from the Civil Rights Project, Latino students in California attend schools that are 84 percent nonwhite and where three-fourths of students are poor.[11]

California's immigrant communities face clear educational challenges. The state ranks last in the nation in its ratio of students per counselor, at 945 to 1—double the national average of 477 to 1.[12] Low-income schools are marked by high teacher turnover and a relatively high proportion of teachers lacking proper qualifications.[13] As of 2013–14, eight of California's ten largest school districts are majority-minority, and six of these are in the Los Angeles Metropolitan Area.[14] Each of these school districts has a Latino student majority; statewide, native- and foreign-born Latinos graduate at rates significantly below whites.[15] The Los Angeles and Santa Ana Unified School Districts have 89.6 percent and 96.6 percent minority student populations, respectively, with more than 75 percent of their students receiving free or reduced lunches. California ranks thirty-second in the nation in high school completion, and graduation rates are especially low in the Los Angeles area; thirty-five Los Angeles County high schools are counted among the lowest-performing 5 percent of California schools receiving Title I funding, and only two-thirds of Los Angeles Unified School District students graduate from high school. These conditions are particularly disadvantageous to low-income, immigrant, and Latino students.

As California's public schools face increased segregation and overcrowding, its colleges and universities face problems of the opposite nature. While California K-12 education enrollments rose dramatically since the mid-1980s and into the 1990s, college and university enrollment, after steadily increasing from the mid-1990s, dropped during the early 2000s because of fee hikes and funding constraints.

The California Master Plan was established in 1960 to provide coherence to public postsecondary education statewide and to ensure educational access, quality, and affordability to any student who could benefit from postsecondary education.[16] Under the plan, the top 12.5 percent of California high school graduates would be accepted into one of the University of California campuses, the state's premier research system; the top third of high school graduates would be able to enter the California State University system; and any student who would "benefit from instruction" was accepted into the California Community Colleges system.[17] From the community colleges, all who qualified were to be offered transfers into a public university.

Soon after their implementation, these policy efforts made some difference in the lives of black and Latino students. During the 1970s, because of affirmative action policies and civil rights legislation, college completion in California improved more among blacks and Hispanics than among whites. However, by the 1990s, bachelor's degree completion surged among whites and Asians, and the gap with whites grew larger for Latinos and African Americans. In 1996, race-based admission policies at public universities in California ended with the passage of Proposition 209. Today, Latino students in California fare worse than their white and Asian counterparts in the University of California system at every step of the university process, and they are also underrepresented in the California State University system. While first-time freshmen in the community college system are representative of the racial and ethnic composition of the California high school seniors, Latino students are underrepresented among students transferring to four-year programs.

As I drive past the elementary school and the high school, the Los Angeles landscape visibly changes again. I cross an industrial area where steel and glass distributors and assembly plants line railroad tracks. Many undocumented immigrants—including my research participants—find work in areas like this, but their jobs offer little in the way of job mobility, decent wages, or protections. Undocumented immigrants account for one in twenty people in the US workforce; in California this ratio is nearly one in ten.[18] Los Angeles has incorporated large numbers of unauthorized migrant workers in its low-wage workforce over the last several decades.[19] However, Los Angeles–based families of undocumented workers earn less than half the average California income, and they are 43 percent larger than the average American family.[20] Overall, the Los Angeles area workforce is less well paid, less educated, and more impoverished than anywhere else in the state. Families absorb the consequences of these employment conditions. The gross mismatch between undocumented workers' low wages and Los Angeles's high cost of living pushes families into marginal neighborhoods. Scholars suggest that most undocumented immigrants live in areas with large concentrations of other undocumented individuals.[21] In Los Angeles, where the gap between the rich and the poor has steadily widened since the 1970s, and where the working poor cannot keep up with the rising cost of living, these conditions drive undocumented immigrants increasingly out to the margins.

The lives of undocumented young adults and their families described in this book cannot be understood without an examination of the broader contexts of their communities, schools, and workplaces. This chapter introduces the two key groups studied in this research—early exiters and college-goers—in their daily worlds. Drawing on the voices of college-goers and early exiters, this chapter provides a glimpse into how diverse family, school, and work experiences shape pathways of belonging and illegality that are different and unequal. We get to know many of the characters in this book, what distinguishes them as college-goers and early exiters, and how they view their futures.

SETTING THEIR SIGHTS: COLLEGE-GOERS AND EARLY EXITERS

Early exiters and college-goers in Los Angeles share common struggles. Their everyday worlds are framed by the same broad conditions—

undocumented immigration status, family poverty, and the limitations of both. Their lives are characterized more by similarity than by difference.

But their narratives, coupled with my own observations, suggest a more nuanced underlying story. Diverse family, school, and work experiences shaped pathways of belonging and illegality that were different and unequal.

Throughout my fieldwork of observing, interviewing, and interacting informally with the young adults whom I eventually categorized as either college-goers or early exiters, I was also struck by their dissimilar worldviews. These young men and women had very different thoughts about their futures—thoughts that had begun to develop much earlier on, when they were in school. Does one's situation cause one's outlook or vice versa? Or are they intertwined?

Anthropologist Nicolas de Genova draws attention to an important characteristic of illegality that he calls "an enforced orientation to the present."[22] He argues that the uncertainties that arise from the possibility of apprehension and deportation yield a heightened awareness within individuals of their revocable futures. In other words, many people have taught themselves to live with the knowledge that all they have can be taken away in an instant.[23] This enforced orientation to the present inhibits many undocumented immigrants from committing to long-term plans because they experience their assets—including jobs, friends, and material possessions—as temporary. Each event that forces them to confront their legal limitations and each threat of apprehension and deportation reminds them of the stark reality that at any moment their lives could change.

When I asked questions about their expectations for the future, the differences in the perspectives of the two groups were remarkable.

After a tutoring session one day in 2004, I sat across the table from Dora, a twenty-two-year-old young woman who was studying to take the GED exam. Over a half-dozen meetings, Dora and I had begun to build rapport. That day, instead of asking Dora about her past, I found myself fielding questions about my own education. My age (thirty-five at the time) came up during our conversation, and Dora was surprised that I was still in school. Dora had a daughter of her own—she had left high school when she became pregnant—and was pursuing her equivalency degree to fulfill a promise to her mother.

Dora: Shouldn't you be married by now?

Roberto: Well, my mom would probably agree.

Dora: I don't mean to laugh, but you're kinda old to still be in school. Don't you work?

Roberto: Yeah, it is a little funny. It's hard to explain. I'll finally be out of school in a few years, and then with my degree I hope to get a job as a professor.

I laughed off Dora's questions, which I heard frequently from my own family members and from old friends. "When are you going to get a real job?" they asked, struggling to make the connection between my many years in school and a future payoff. It was hard for them to see the point in delaying work for so long. As I fielded Dora's questions I wondered if she might be thinking of her own future, perhaps even of returning to school too. But once I raised that topic, the mood of the conversation quickly changed.

Roberto: What about you? What do you think you'll be doing in five years?

Dora: I don't know, probably the same thing. It's really frustrating. I don't feel like I can do anything on my own right now. I'm like a little kid. I don't know how I can get out of this.

Roberto: Are there goals you want to accomplish between now and then?

Dora: That's the thing. I really don't know. I don't know how. I mean, I don't see any way I could. It's gonna come crashing down anyway. I just try not to think about it.

Dora's frustration arose from her inability to find work as an undocumented immigrant. Her undocumented status combined with her inexperience with full-time work and fear of rejection left her in a state of limbo. She had been job-hunting for weeks to no avail. Most employers preferred to hire workers with more experience. Dora eventually gave up on her job search to give birth to her second child.

Like Dora, Pedro was undocumented and without a high school diploma or GED. At twenty-six, Pedro was older than Dora and had been regularly working without papers for nearly ten years. I met Pedro at a nonprofit community center where he was using employment services to supplement his patchwork of temporary jobs and entrepreneurial activities. During a chat that Pedro and I had on the front steps of the community center, I asked him a few questions about his present life and his hopes for the future.

Roberto: When you were younger did you imagine your life the way it is now?

Pedro: It's like, sometimes I wanna do this, but sometimes I can't. Sometimes I have to do that. But, I, I just try to maintain one single path because, you know, we change our clothes day by day, you know.

Roberto: That's an interesting way to look at it. What do you want for yourself in the future?

Pedro: Right now, I want to take care of my legal status, clean up my record, and get an education and a decent job. I'm thinking about five years from now. I don't want to extend it any longer. I wish it could be less, you know. But I don't want to rush it either, because when you rush things they don't go as they have to be. Maybe ten years from now . . . I wouldn't mind living in a mobile home.

As for Dora, Pedro's struggles prevented him from planning very far into the future. These young adults faced a gauntlet of obstacles as they looked for work. They competed with more recently arrived immigrants for scarce jobs, and the available work was often unfamiliar or difficult. Even after the hiring process began, a Social Security Administration no-match letter might arrive, forcing them to abandon the job and again hunt for work.[24] These common challenges eroded the young people's future aspirations and pushed them further to the margins of society. When I first met Pedro in 2003, he had not seen the inside of a school in nearly a decade. When I spoke to him again in 2014, he still had not earned his GED. In the years since Pedro first left school, he has gained useful experience in the low-wage labor market and he has assumed responsibility for providing for himself. But as his answers to my questions make clear, he was careful not to plan very far in advance. For Dora, a lack of work experience made it difficult to compete successfully for the only types of jobs within her reach.

Not all my respondents voiced such tamped-down expectations. Unlike the early exiters, when I asked college-goers questions about their expectations for the future, they were much more ready and able to articulate their educational and career goals.

In 2005, at a regular meeting of a community-based student group, I spoke to two of the group's members, Rosalba and Nimo, about their plans for the future. Their answers could not have been more different from Dora's and Pedro's.

Rosalba: If it takes me another five years, I'm going to become a teacher. I have faith that everything will work out. Right now I'm doing all of the things I need to do to prepare myself for that day.

Roberto (turning to Nimo): And what about you?

Nimo: Nothing stands in my way. I don't think giving up is an issue. . . . I kind of want to start doing internships before [I leave school] because then you have practice in the field, and then when you go on the real job you are familiar with it. You need to learn how to plan for things.

Rosalba's and Nimo's responses conceal the important detail that legally neither could "go on to the real job." Moreover, like most undocumented youth, both grew up contending with the limitations of poverty. Given their legal and economic profiles, it would not be surprising to find these young adults embittered and worn down, with little thought about the future. Instead, they were optimistic. Legal exclusions did not stop them from building their résumés and preparing for their futures in a manner similar to that of many other young people their age.

School experiences shape our lives. Empirical studies repeatedly confirm the importance of educational attainment for securing good jobs and higher income, for pursuing healthy lifestyles, and for enjoying better overall quality of life.[25] But elementary and secondary schooling affect more than students' opportunities for college and/or work. As I explain in this chapter, school life informs students' expectations for the future and their sense of belonging. College-goers have different orientations to time than early exiters. The pursuit of education helps them look beyond the present. And their teachers have conditioned them to be future thinkers and planners at every step of the school process, working to stand out in middle school to get into competitive high school programs, maintaining a high grade point average in high school to gain admission to college, and taking advantage of internships and summer opportunities during college to make themselves competitive for good jobs in the high-skilled workforce if that opportunity arises.

The school experiences of college-goers and early exiters provide useful evidence to suggest that schools structure optimistic attitudes as well as pessimistic outlooks. A growing body of research on school culture reports that academic success and failure are largely contingent upon whether school officials actively create a culture that facilitates positive interactions among students, teachers, and staff.[26] When schools take the time and effort to assist students, they can be an important source of social capital.[27] But when students feel disconnected from the schooling process, they have few opportunities to form relationships with individuals who can guide their academic progress.[28]

Unlike other researchers who have compared bounded friendship groups, I have chosen to group my respondents into relatively broad categories.[29] There is much heterogeneity within these groups, and many respondents moved across categories during their lifetimes. However, what separates the young people in the study are the experiences that led some to leave school system and those that enabled others to persist in educational settings.

It is estimated that only 5 to 10 percent of undocumented immigrant students successfully matriculate to postsecondary institutions and that even fewer graduate. While the two groups in my study are based on broad categorizations, those in the college-goer group represent a much more unique and homogeneous experience. Among the college-goers, many have earned bachelor's degrees and some have even earned post-baccalaureate degrees. All of them have at least two years of higher education. Early exiters, on the other hand, represent a much more common and varied experience. Some dropped out of high school, others graduated but did not go on to college, and some started college but were unable to persist. Their decisions regarding school were structured by a range of factors: trouble with teachers or the law, early parenting, frustration with their immigration status, economic needs that forced them to take on full-time work, or the inability to finance college.

In total, I followed seventy-seven college-goers and seventy-three early exiters. As of 2012, twelve college-goers had earned advanced degrees, twenty-nine had bachelor's degrees, sixteen had started but had not completed degrees at four-year universities, and twenty had accumulated at least two years' worth of credits at community colleges. The majority of the college-goers attended a California public college or university. Of the seventy-three early exiters, twenty-five had not earned a high school degree or equivalent and forty-eight had earned a high school diploma or GED (table 1).

The differences in the two groups' attitudes were shaped by some of the same forces driving divisions among young Americans more generally. These include educational inequalities, differential levels of opportunity, and varying messages about belonging. In adulthood, early exiters' daily routines reflect a concern with immediate needs, such as keeping jobs, paying mounting expenses, and taking care of their families. In contrast, college-goers occupy the highest strata of their schools and communities. They are future oriented, and their daily lives are shaped by a commitment to the pursuit of more ambitious goals. When Pedro and Dora try to think about the future, they have difficulty seeing

TABLE I. HIGHEST LEVEL OF EDUCATIONAL ATTAINMENT OF STUDY
PARTICIPANTS BY GENDER ($N = 150$)

Educational Attainment	Male	Female	Total
Less than high school	14	11	25
High school graduate/GED	23	25	48
2 + years community college	9	11	20
University enrollment	9	7	16
Bachelor's degree	11	18	29
Advanced degree	5	7	12
Total	71	79	150

NOTE: Educational attainment data are as of 2012.

beyond their current circumstances of limitation and struggle. Nimo and Rosalba not only believe in their futures; they plan for them.

The expectations and aspirations Nimo and Rosalba expressed were forged much earlier in their lives through the contributions of teachers and parents and through accumulated positive and affirming experiences. I arranged to meet with Rosalba in January 2007 at a public library in Riverside where she tutored neighborhood children. "I never had any doubts," she told me. ". . . It was ingrained that my only obligation was to go to school [college]. . . . Teachers have expectations that you're going to go [to college]; they help prepare you. . . . So for me, I didn't even think about not going."

Perhaps the most important factor contributing to the college-goers' optimism was their impressive social networks. Most reported that, beginning when they were young, a long line of teachers, counselors, coaches, and community and church leaders shepherded them around obstacles to achieve school success. In Rosalba's case, supportive community members and school officials provided a wide net of comfort and safety that taught her not to take "no" for an answer. Her many mentors also opened numerous doors. She elaborated:

I've made it because I've had a support system. At every step of my education, I have had a mentor. A mentor holding my hand. In high school, it was a counselor that enrolled me in honors courses. And he talked to a teacher already, so that she would take me into her class and give me that chance. And that teacher became my mentor for all four years at my high school. When I transferred to [community college], I had big, big mentors [people in high positions] there who then found me mentors at Cal State. And the mentor I had at Cal State found me a mentor to help me out at a private university for my master's. There's a chain. And being involved in student government is where I found my support system. That's where I increased my support system. . . . So it is being involved that leads you to the right people. They are always looking out for you, looking [for] scholarships for you.

It's a thousand times much harder without a mentor. Being undocumented, it's not about what you know, it's who you know. Who do you know? You might have all of the will in the world, but if you don't know the right people, then no, as much as you want to, you're gonna have to take a quarter off to raise more money, when a mentor would have said, here's that one-thousand-dollar scholarship from this organization, apply to it. And little things. For example, most majors require you to do fieldwork, and fieldwork requires you to get fingerprinted. How do you go get fingerprinted when you're undocumented? But if you know someone else who has done it already, and has found a way to go around it, or you have a mentor to speak upon your behalf to the organization that you want to do your internship, and they can help you out or put you in another internship. But yeah, every kid should have a mentor. . . . You need someone to lead the way.

When I first met Rosalba in 2005, she was twenty-six and had more education than most of her similarly aged US-born peers. She had earned a BS in mathematics, had fulfilled all the requirements for a California teaching credential, and was only one semester away from an MS in mathematics. Between 2005 and 2007, I visited her several times at the same public library. Over those two years, Rosalba had started to see cracks in her future plans. Tutoring was not enough for her. But she had successfully overcome struggles enough times that she maintained an optimistic attitude. While she was not yet in command of her own classroom, she continued to believe that she would reach her goal.

Though nearly four years younger than Rosalba, Dora was already worn down by experiences of exclusion and rejection. Despite her promise to her mom, Dora seemed unlikely to finish school. She had not connected with anyone at her high school after leaving and had no models in her life to demonstrate the tangible benefits of an education. Dismissing the possibility of getting "a fancy office job," she began applying—with no success—for much less appealing positions. As she hunted for work, she was saddened and frustrated by the way potential employers looked past her, never giving her serious consideration. Dora and I lost contact between 2004 and 2005. When I saw her again in 2006, she told me that she felt trapped. She had very little evidence to convince her that life would get better. "It's frustrating. Sometimes you have everything to get the job, but you don't have the papers. You can do it, but you don't have papers. It's very, very frustrating because you don't know what to do. Sometimes you find a job that you think you can do it, and you like it, but if you don't have the papers, you're not gonna get the job. They don't care if you have experience."

At twenty-four, Dora found that she was defined not by what she had to offer an employer but rather by what she lacked—"papers." For Dora, the future was as illusory as her papers. Whereas Rosalba's vision of the future was consistent with an ideal of meritocracy (i.e., her hard work earned her a high place in her school and community, and she expected to continue to reap the rewards she had earned), Dora could not get past potential employers' demeaning attitudes and closed doors.

As they moved into adulthood, college-goers and early exiters both faced an uphill climb. Legal constraints and financial responsibilities circumscribed their opportunities. Early exiters tend to see their glass as half empty and marred by a small hole that, despite their best efforts, defied plugging, allowing the contents to slowly drain. The college-goers viewed their glass as half full and then went looking for a faucet to fill the glass to its brim. While college-goers and early exiters do not represent homogeneous categories or bounded friendship groups, in early adulthood the divergence in orientation and access between college-goers and early exiters is unmistakable and consequential.

LIVING IN THE PRESENT: THE EARLY EXITERS

As a group, the early exiters are much more diverse than the college-goers. Because the bar for college admittance is so high for undocumented youngsters, very few make it. Those who do tend to have much in common. Statistically, most undocumented immigrant youth leave the schooling pipeline before college. Whereas the path to higher education is relatively narrow and predictable, undocumented youth who exit early do so following many different pathways. Some find it difficult to move from high school to college because of family need or a lack of money for tuition and related expenses. Others simply fall through the cracks at their large high schools, failing to stand out in overcrowded classrooms. Still others are actively pushed out of the school system because of excessive truancies, gang affiliations, fighting, or teen pregnancy.

Pushing against Structural Forces and Limited Options

The young men and women in my study who did not complete high school or who did not pursue postsecondary options after graduating bore the brunt of powerful structural forces, including an outdated immigration system, failing neighborhood schools, and struggling communities. Early exiters' lives were marked by the pressures of survival. They had to find and keep jobs to earn enough money to meet their basic needs. They had to figure out how get to work on time in a context of poor public transportation and without access to a driver's license. They had to avoid encounters with law enforcement and in their neighborhoods. And they had to uphold their responsibilities as family members caring for parents, siblings, and children of their own.

Options for work are limited for young adults without legal work permits or higher education. Early exiters thus reluctantly settled into poorly paid, often physically exhausting jobs. Felipe had been fortunate to find steady work. When his uncle, who owned a landscaping business, secured a contract for ongoing work on a University of California campus, he needed extra workers and asked Felipe to join his crew. During his lunch break one day in 2009, Felipe and I talked about his job:

Roberto: How do you like working here?

Felipe: Well, I can say that this is the longest I've been at one job for a long time. Do I like it? I don't know how to answer that question. I think really different now than I used to.

Roberto: Do you mean that you feel like you've lowered your expectations? Your standards?

Felipe: Yeah. Look, I'm twenty-seven. I'm obviously not where I'd like to be. This work is rough. I've gotten used to it. I'm much faster now than I used to be. But I'm not gonna lie. It's rough. My body has been beaten up so much, it's just hard.

Roberto: What do you think is the hardest part about it?

Felipe: I think I've accepted things, but I know I could do a lot better if I just had a chance. I think it's too late for that now. Probably the hardest part is, well, it's the physical. I look at my dad and he has back problems. My mom has arthritis. I'm strong now, but what's going to happen to me when I'm older?

Roberto: That's a good question. Where do you see yourself? [Pause] Let's say in five years?

Felipe: I don't know. Maybe I'll move back to Mexico, buy a farm or something. Right now, I can't really see it. I mean, what I'm going to do. It's just hard.

As for other early exiters, time slowed down for Felipe after he left high school. In his adult life, he could not see beyond his current circumstances. A life of limitations and long hours spent toiling in dead-end jobs conditioned his thoughts and behaviors. Felipe also told me that his work allowed him little social time. He moved closer to his work site to be able to get rides from his immigrant coworkers, but he did not know anyone living in the area, limiting his social contacts. Every aspect of his daily world felt temporary; jobs, friends, and possessions could all be lost when a new obstacle presented itself.

The Multiple Pathways of Early Exiters

As a group, early exiters did not share any natural or intrinsic set of personal characteristics. Rather, their undocumented status and poverty conspired to dramatically limit their adult options. Their life experiences were very different from those of their peers who went on to complete at least two years of college. Full-time work in low-wage jobs presented a qualitatively different experience from attending college full time.

When young adult undocumented immigrants leave the confines of their schools and the routines that have structured their days since childhood, they leave the last line of defense against the consequences of illegality. Of course, school is not a panacea. It does not assure all students of upward mobility; nor does it promote a sense of connectedness or an optimistic outlook for every child. But for young people who continue to pursue education into the early years of adulthood, school affirms their identities and supports the development of goals. For those who leave school early, work is unable to fulfill this affirming role. Instead, early exiters' experiences with low-wage, dead-end jobs curtail their aspirations. Without the buffer of schooling, legal exclusions mark even the most mundane aspects of adult life, driving undocumented youth toward precarious work patterns and complicated strategies for daily survival. Few practices last long enough to become routine, however. Immigration and Customs Enforcement raids of factories, bus stations, and apartments, random DUI checkpoints, and Social Security no-match letters force modifications and weaken attachments to habits and routines.

The condition of illegality penetrates the being of early exiters. They think constantly about ways to avoid immigration officials, police, and other authorities. They are always looking over their shoulders, avoiding potentially dangerous situations, and spending their time worrying. The stress of illegality is palpable and overwhelming.

The following profiles illustrate several of the reasons respondents in the early exiter group did not go to college.

Family Need

Nationwide, adolescent and young adult children from working-class, minority, and immigrant households carry heavy responsibilities for contributing to family bills, groceries, and rent.[30] As I described earlier, most undocumented immigrants in Los Angeles have trouble making ends meet on their meager wages. The high cost of living in the region forces families to make difficult decisions. Undocumented parents often must rely on their adult or even adolescent children for financial support. Many early exiters began working and contributing to family earnings as teenagers. Their *internal remittances* were much more substantial than those of college-goers, averaging a little more than $400 a month (as opposed to $250 for college-goers; among early exiters, men contributed $100 more than women).

The long hours respondents spent in grueling, low-wage jobs took time away from other pursuits. This commitment had negative consequences for their schoolwork. In 2005, Flor was twenty-seven years old and had been living in the United States for eighteen years. When she was a child, her family moved frequently. By the time Flor started high school, she had lived in nine apartments spread across three counties and had attended eight schools. She never felt connected at school. Flor's family included ten undocumented members, so every one of the eight able-bodied family members was required to pitch in. At the age of fourteen, she joined her mother and older sisters cleaning houses. Flor's family obligations were decidedly gendered, but in contrast to many of the female college-goers Flor was expected to work outside the home. She often had to miss school when her family had big jobs. After two years, she was suspended from school for excessive truancies and never returned.

At twenty-seven, Flor was married with two children. She had earned a GED after seven years of juggling the demands of work, family life, and school. When I asked if she wanted to continue her education, she responded this way: "If I go to college, I'm not gonna have much time to spend with my kids, you know. Well, it's kinda like in the middle, since my son is already attending kindergarten and he's there for four hours. I would just have to leave my daughter alone for those four hours, let's say. But it's kinda like in between, you know. I'm kinda attached to her [laughs]. These are tough decisions that I have to make."

Flor had worked for almost half of her life. She found it difficult to see beyond the immediate needs of caring for her family. Life was a struggle, but she had few other choices. Flor's ambivalence regarding her future was also related to her lack of experience with school as something that could change her circumstances. She had never really been able to give schooling much of a chance. As with many other early exiters, including men who began working in construction or landscaping as teenagers, immediate family need eclipsed the future-oriented pursuit of education, disrupting the normal pattern of schooling and with it their view of the future.

Pushed Out

Among the early exiters is a group of young people who were pushed out of the school system. Many of these young people were engaged in illicit activity, such as gang involvement or selling drugs. Trouble with the law not only marked them as teenagers; it also followed them as adults.

Josue spent much of his life on the streets. His ability to hustle and navigate the informal economy to his own advantage cushioned some of the effects of illegality. When I first met him in 2003, he was working for a large pizza chain. Prior to this, however, he had spent many years supporting himself by selling drugs. The lifestyle appealed to him. Josue felt powerful on the streets of Inglewood. He had autonomy and was not subjected to the ill treatment received by most undocumented immigrants with little protection or recourse. Still, over time, he began to worry that without legal immigration status and with little formal job training he would not be able to craft a secure future.

> In a way, it's hard to get a job, you know. Get paid the way we want to be paid. Back then I used to skip that. "You know what? I'm not gonna work for a job. I'm not gonna bust my ass for someone who can be yelling at me for like $5.75, five bucks an hour. Nah, nah. Hell no. If I get a job, I wanna get paid twenty bucks an hour." Because I thought that, "Man, I speak English. I do good. I do that." But actually, I didn't have any real experience for my age, and I decided to start selling drugs, you know. Because I thought, "This is easy. I got my own schedule. I can do whatever the hell I want to the whole day. I can scream at them; nobody is gonna scream at me. Nobody is gonna do nothing to me because I am the one in control."

In Josue's adult life, his work choices were limited. Selling drugs provided him with a sense of control and some cash, but this illicit work increased his chances of coming to the attention of the authorities. Working for a restaurant chain provided a secure paycheck in the short term, but Josue's lack of papers almost guaranteed that a Social Security no-match letter would eventually surface and he would have to look for another job.

Another group of early exiters that was pushed out of the school system was teen parents. Like many American youngsters, several respondents initiated sexual activity during high school. While not all young men who became teenage fathers accepted their new roles or responsibilities, several took on extra work to provide financial support. Options were fewer for young women who became pregnant, as they confronted multiple burdens associated with early child rearing. For some, their pregnancy created strain in their families. Others were left by their partners to raise children on their own. Nearly all of these young women were steered into alternative educational options, including night school, by school administrators.

Out of Options

The majority of early exiters found themselves with dwindling options after high school. Many of these young people finished high school, but steep barriers to college, a lack of guidance about postsecondary options, and the need for financial independence limited their ability to make college transitions. Many of these young people attempted to start college through community colleges. But as they balanced school with part-time or full-time work and other family responsibilities, they came to experience college as a revolving door.

After Eric finished high school, his father asked him what he was going to do for full-time work. With a sick mother who had been out of work for more than a year, his family desperately needed him to contribute to household expenses. His two older brothers had already been working for several years, but money was still tight. He told his dad that he wanted to go to college. "My dad only went to school up to the sixth grade, so he doesn't really, he doesn't know the system, like, and doesn't really know what college is for. So, when I graduated he thought, 'Okay, now you are done with school it's time to work.' I wanted to continue in school and I thought I could maybe take some classes at [the community college]."

After several "heated arguments," Eric's father agreed to let him go to college, on the condition that Eric would pay for his tuition, fees, and books. "So, I worked all summer and saved money for my first semester so I could take full-time classes. I wasn't sure how I was going to be able to afford the next semester, but I was like, 'Hey, I'll figure something out.' I started working nights and had to drop one of my classes. [Work] really affected my time I had to study and my grades went down."

Eric did not enroll in college the next semester, but he was determined to get back to school. The next fall, he signed up for two classes. The balancing act Eric was trying to manage became too much for him and he left school for good. Like so many other early exiters, full-time work at unfulfilling and undesirable jobs became his central pursuit.

Flor, Josue, and Eric never formed a deep connection to school. Eric kept to himself but did well enough in his high school classes to get by. He did not stand out and, as a result, did not form tight bonds with teachers or high-achieving peers. Flor and Josue did not spend much time in school. Flor's time was diverted to housecleaning work, while Josue's daily pursuits were mostly illegal. For all three, their lives were structured by similar factors: a lack of resources to meet mounting expenses; the watchful eye of immigration officials, police, and supervisors; and restricted work options that were a constant reminder of their legal limitations.

LEARNING TO DREAM: THE COLLEGE-GOERS

Despite the pressures to bypass college to work and the barriers associated with earning a postsecondary degree, in many low-income communities going to college is a sign of success, a guarantor of upward mobility. College-going youth are cited as an affirmation that hard work pays off and that no barrier is too high for those who truly want to succeed. It is not surprising then, that college-goers are the public face of undocumented youth. Over the last few years, their stories of resilience and academic success have earned them the label DREAMers.[31] They dream of futures free of the constraints of their immigration status and envision a time when they can put their degrees to use. Their internalization of the seductive notion that their hard work will pay off in the form of future success buoys their optimism. Among the undocumented young people in my study, the college-goers had the most to lose in adulthood. Many of those I interviewed were at the top of their graduating classes, prominently represented on school councils, and leaders in clubs and on athletic teams. They were college undergraduates, bachelor's degree holders, and graduate students in pursuit of terminal degrees in law, business, social work, health, and education; some were even PhD hopefuls.

The Chosen Ones

College-goers were fully aware that going to college shielded them from some of the stress and worry of living as an undocumented adult. They were also well aware that their families provided them with certain privileges and support. In many cases, other family members took on added responsibilities and carried additional burdens to provide college-goers with the time and space to pursue their education. College-goers believed that their parents made selective investments in their children's education, weighing several factors, including immediate needs, family composition, gender, and future contributions. Most felt that their parents had identified them as the family member with the best chances of college success.

> *Julio:* I was very good at math. My brothers didn't make it past eighth grade. So my dad told me I would be the one to make a lot of money.
>
> *Gina:* It's not as though my parents sat us down and said, "Okay, you're going to work with us and you're going to get to go to school." No, we didn't have to draw straws or anything like that. It was just that ever since I was a kid, I would bring home good grades. You know, like that. I was studious and I think they saw that.
>
> *Rafael:* My parents always supported me in school. I remember when I was on the academic decathlon team in high school, my mom would brag to her friends that I was the brains in the family.

In some cases, teachers intervened when financial needs compelled parents to make decisions to send their children to the labor force instead of pursuing postsecondary education. Take Marisol, for example. When her parents made the difficult but economically motivated decision that Marisol would not go to college, her teacher gently intervened. Each of Marisol's three brothers had started working by age fifteen, but her parents allowed her to finish high school on the understanding that she would start helping out once she graduated. After her teacher arranged a meeting with them to explain that Marisol "was special and would be much more of a help to the family by going to college," they finally decided to let her "give it a try." Marisol went on to earn a bachelor's degree in communications at California State University and a master's in social work at a private university in Los Angeles.

In many families, beliefs about gender influenced decisions regarding the distribution of household labor. This was true of Lupita's family. "I always thought my mom kinda favored me," Lupita told me. "She would say I was going to be the one in the family to have a successful career. But it was also like, my dad, you know, my parents were very traditional. They would rather have me in school than working. And my brothers, they came from Mexico when they were teenagers. I think my dad, you know, he had two strong healthy boys he could bring to work with him."

Regardless of a family's ethnicity or immigration status, in many working-class homes parents assign roles to their children based on normative conceptions of gender.[32] Many of the young women I met felt that their parents' restrictions had prevented them from going out with friends, participating in activities like sports after school, and taking jobs. Their brothers were often given greater freedom outside the home, while girls were left to take care of younger siblings and help out with cooking, ironing, cleaning, and other household chores. These arrangements funneled males into the workforce while the enforced time at home led females to devote more attention to their studies.[33]

> *Scarlet:* I started cooking when I was eight. Ironing when I was ten. From there, I took care of most of the chores. I also had to get my brother ready for school. My mom worked two shifts, so she was barely home during the day.
>
> *Lupita:* My parents didn't like me to go out. I couldn't sleep over at friends' house[s], and even for school things I had to be home early. I know they were trying to protect me, but I didn't feel like I had any freedom.
>
> *Iris:* It's like, I think I was so good in school because I had nothing else to do [laughs]. My parents kept me at home, so I said, "You know what? I don't have anything better to do. I might as well use this time for my homework." I really became a bookworm.

This gender pattern was not universal. Many male respondents found time to devote to school pursuits. But in some cases this was because their families saw them as unsuitable for hard labor.

> *Alan:* My dad took me out with my uncles in their landscaping business. It was hard and I couldn't really keep up with them. They told me it was because my hands were too soft. It was kind of embarrassing.
>
> *Ricardo:* I was always the smallest. My dad would ask my brothers first. I used to resent that a lot. It made me sad when my dad and brothers would go out to work but I had to stay behind.

The Power of Positive Expectations

In addition to family and teacher support, most of the college-goers benefited from the general belief that they possessed special qualities.

Their school success was seen as a product of their hard work and talent. They were good students, model citizens, and among a select few who were widely expected to succeed. These beliefs were shaped in childhood and reinforced over time as these young women and men achieved more success, earned more praise, and occupied more select environments.

> *Rafael:* I think my parents realized that this is what I was supposed to be doing. They said, "Yeah, you've got talent and drive. We want to support that."

> *Nimo:* Ever since I was young, my mom has been behind me 100 percent. I think I'm really lucky. I've always had the support of teachers and my mentors. It really fills me up and encourages me to keep going. They believe in me, so I want to show them I can do it.

For Rafael, Nimo, and many others, early experiences of affirmation by parents and teachers fostered positive attitudes that allowed them to visualize a successful future within a community of high-achieving peers and caring and supportive teachers.

School culture places value on setting and meeting goals—passing exams, writing papers, earning good grades, graduating from high school, successfully competing for college admission, entering specialized fields of study, obtaining good jobs, and advancing in one's career. Each step of this process sets the stage for another goal. This value system generated an orientation toward the future, providing college-goers with the means not only to suspend the consequences of undocumented status but also to redirect their fears and anxiety into the pursuit of future goals. College-goers defined themselves through their strong alignment with school values of upward mobility.

ASSESSING FUTURE POSSIBILITIES

Growing up undocumented in Los Angeles is a challenge. But for early exiters and college-goers different sets of contexts shape expectations and aspirations. The early exiters lead lives pushed to the margins. Compared to the college-goers, they have a heightened awareness of limitations and an inability (or perhaps an unwillingness) to envision the future. This is not surprising. The possibility of apprehension and deportation creates uncertainty that leads many undocumented individuals to understand their own futures as revocable.[34] They learn to live with the knowledge that all they have can be taken away in an instant. College-goers also inhabit a world narrowly circumscribed by their legal limitations. But for them these limitations are temporarily eclipsed by a pervasive sense of promise and optimism. Freed from burdensome family responsibilities and the need to take on full-time jobs, college-goers are less threatened than early exiters by the worries of daily survival and possible apprehension. Their world extends farther, reaching outward to their college campuses and into the lives of teachers, mentors, professors, and a diverse group of peers. In early adulthood, college-goers' lives reflect a sense of belonging, cultivated much earlier in childhood, which provides them with a longer view into the future and a stronger belief in possibility.

CHAPTER 3

Childhood

Inclusion and Belonging

I first met Elizabeth at a continuation school where she was earning missing high school credits toward graduation. Tall with a caramel-colored complexion and dark curly hair that fell around her shoulders, Elizabeth was a connector. Popular among her peers at the school, she was often at the center of conversations during breaks and was often sought out for advice. Elizabeth was one of the first people I met in my early stages of fieldwork. She was very generous with her time and introduced me to several of her friends who were not part of the continuation school. We talked several times over a period of roughly three months as I sat in on her classes and observed the informal weekly group meetings where she received educational support from the school's career development staff. When I finally asked Elizabeth if she was interested in being interviewed, she invited me to her home "so," as she said, "you can get a better picture of how I live."

After rescheduling our first visit (Elizabeth's mom, a seamstress, was sick, so Elizabeth had to help her finish a job), we decided it would be best to meet on a weekend. I arrived at her apartment on a Saturday morning, shortly before 9:00 a.m., and the first thing I noticed was that there seemed to be a grassy area nearby where children might play. I wondered what it was like for Elizabeth arriving here when she was seven—did she go outside, or did she stay in with her mother? Elizabeth's community had the distinction of being one of the poorest neighborhoods in her city and a hub for gang activity; a teacher at Elizabeth's continuation school warned me not to go there at night. According to estimates from the city, more than twelve thousand people squeezed into the apartment complex's five square blocks of stucco, concrete, and blacktop. However, beyond the headline-grabbing statistics, most of the residents of the complex were hard-working immigrants, and many did not have papers. They cleaned houses and office buildings, hung dry-wall and toiled in factories, cooked in restaurants, and took care of other people's kids. Elizabeth had lived in this apartment since her mother had sent for her in Mexico. Now, at twenty-two, Elizabeth told me that her mom would leave the neighborhood if she could afford to go elsewhere, but Elizabeth felt at home there.

I pulled into the complex and found Elizabeth's apartment. I was about to knock on the door when I heard an uncertain voice from behind me: "You must be the young man doing the school report."

"Si, Señora. Soy Roberto," I replied in Spanish.

"I'm Guadalupe, Elizabeth's mother," she responded in English.

Guadalupe's face was freshly made up with rouge and a cranberry-colored lipstick. Her wide smile defied the wrinkles carved into her face and the knots that had formed on her fingers from arthritis.

She smiled as we made small talk and led me inside where Elizabeth stood in the living room. Elizabeth's hair was tightly pulled back into a high ponytail. Her more formal dress—a white-collared shirt, pressed black slacks, and black pumps—was a departure from the more casual sweatshirts and sneakers I was accustomed to seeing her wear to school. Initially, I thought she might be going to a job interview after our meeting, but I soon realized from her formality during our conversation that she had dressed up for my visit.

The one-bedroom apartment where Elizabeth and her mom lived could not have been more than 450 square feet. But it was well taken care of—tidy and brightly decorated with candles, pictures, and framed inspirational posters on the walls that Elizabeth later told me covered up water stains from a leaking pipe. There was also a colorful altar dedicated to Elizabeth's father, adorned with a portrait of him in his twenties, a burning candle, a pint bottle of tequila and a shot glass, faded *papel picado* (delicately decorated tissue paper) in purple and pink, and a large crucifix wrapped in a rosary.

Guadalupe asked me to take a seat on the plastic-covered couch and offered me *pan dulce* (Mexican pastries) and *champurrado*, a warm and thick Mexican drink typically prepared with chocolate and corn flour. Elizabeth sat down in a chair next to the couch. The rising sun, in hues of orange and pink, splashed through the living room curtains, and the warm drink felt good in my stomach. After nearly twenty minutes of small talk, Guadalupe pulled out an old family album, handed it to Elizabeth, and excused herself.

Opening the album, Elizabeth directed my attention to a faded and coffee-stained photo on the first page. "This is me, my brother, sister, my mom, and my dad on *mi abuelito's rancho* [my grandfather's ranch]. I was just a baby, like eight months old there." There were a few more photos on the page—a portrait of her parents, a photo of Elizabeth and her sister playing on a dirt road, and a black-and-white class photo of her father—and the yellowing obituary of her father, who had been killed in a traffic accident in Mexico. "This is all we have from Mexico," Elizabeth told me as she turned the page. "There was a fire and we lost a lot of our stuff. I only have a few things to connect me back there." These were the remnants of Elizabeth's life in Mexico—a patchwork of photos and scenes loosely stitched together from secondhand stories. She had been young when she left, and most of her own memories of her birthplace were foggy.

> *Roberto:* And how do you feel about that?
>
> *Elizabeth:* It makes me sad, you know. Like that's where my roots are, but I barely remember anything about Mexico. My brother is four years older than me, and my sister is six years older. I mean, they have more memories of being there, in Mexico, you know. We haven't been able to go back since we left, so all I have are these pictures and my mom's stories.
>
> *Roberto:* Do you remember much about your life there?
>
> *Elizabeth:* I mean, I do and I don't. Like, I remember the little things. My *abuelo's ranchito*, all of the animals. I remember sitting on my dad's lap. He had a really nice voice and he would sing to me. I really miss him. But it's mostly like just scenes. A little here and there. I was very little when we left and I haven't been able to go back.

As Elizabeth proceeded to turn the pages of the album, her childhood in California came to life in multiple colors and dimensions. The album was stuffed with photos and mementos spanning several years. She showed me photos of a class trip to Disneyland, birthday parties at McDonalds, her first communion, holiday celebrations, and graduations. There were report cards and notes from teachers, drawings and letters, a prom program, and a few red rose petals from a former boyfriend pressed into the album. Elizabeth had stories to tell for each photo and item. Before we had gone through even half of the album, it was clear to me that Elizabeth's narrative was an American one. The pages in that album provided ample proof of her claims to belonging.

CULTURAL AND SOCIAL BELONGING

According to sociologist Nira Yuval-Davis, belonging is about emotional attachment, about feeling "at home."[1] Given what is generally known about undocumented immigrants and their experiences of settlement, we might expect young immigrants to feel isolated, anxious, and impermanent—the opposite of feeling "at home." Indeed, Elizabeth, like most of the other study participants, had grown up in a tough neighborhood and in difficult financial circumstances. She had contended with negative comments about Mexicans from her classmates and strangers. But also like most other study participants, Elizabeth remembered spending her childhood and early adolescence thinking of herself as American. She lived in the sunshine, not in the shadows. And like her native-born peers, she had no reason to even notice that fact.

Legal and community contexts shape immigrants' experiences of inclusion and exclusion and their feelings of belonging.[2] Existing research on adult immigrants and their children shows that these two groups' lives are patterned by different sets of contexts, some of which confer advantage and some, disadvantage.[3] This difference is especially evident in the experiences of undocumented immigrants. They are an increasingly visible part of America's communities and of its labor force, yet their daily lives are constrained by laws that prohibit their full participation. The threat of deportation shapes their awareness of the future as revocable and confines undocumented adults to a narrowly circumscribed present.[4]

The worlds of undocumented immigrant children are much wider. Compared to their parents, undocumented youth are much more connected to the people and places that surround them. Though they still feel the constraints of family poverty and their parents' unauthorized status, their everyday lives are also woven into the fabric of their schools, their neighborhoods, and the broader tapestry of American society and culture. Not yet burdened by the need to work, they have time to explore their surroundings and to develop attachments to the blocks, parks, schoolyards, and neighborhoods. With the passage of time they grow increasingly familiar with their surroundings, and an accumulation of experiences locates them within their communities and renders them indistinguishable from their peers. Relationships with native-born peers and teachers instruct them to believe that if they work hard and play by the rules they will have opportunities to become whatever they choose. Over time, this vision of control over their own destiny is naturalized, conditioning undocumented young people to expect that their efforts will produce a bright future and the right to call themselves Americans.

For most undocumented adult immigrants, the act of leaving their country of origin involves intense feelings of separation and profoundly conflicting emotions.[5] These immigrants must let go of family members, friends, and the places and objects of their sentimental attachment, taking with them only their memories. But the young sons and daughters of these newcomers experience less of a personal loss. They are removed from many of the events that prompted their parents' decision to leave and to form a deep attachment to their homeland, so they lack what labor economist Michael Piore calls a "dual frame of reference."[6] For young people like Elizabeth, most reference points originate in the United States, not in the country where they were born.

Nevertheless, undocumented children face two critical challenges: negotiating family circumstances and acculturating to the norms and values of American life.[7] These two important processes uniquely position them in-between their immigrant parents, who are similarly struggling to find their place in their new country, and their American-born peers, who are also experiencing the growing pains of adolescence and coming of age. While children's adjustments are much deeper and take place over extended periods of time, parental adjustments to their new settings and life in the shadows have more immediate effects.

FREQUENT MOVES AND TIGHT QUARTERS

Elizabeth left her family ranch in Guanajuato when she was seven years old. Two years prior, Guadalupe made the decision to look for work in the United States. Leaving Elizabeth, along with her older brother and sister, behind in the care of her grandparents, Guadalupe joined a small group from a neighboring village on a trek covering more than one thousand miles over the course of several days. The journey was not easy, according to Guadalupe. But once in the United States, she made her way to Carson, California, where she located an uncle who had been living there for several years. She stayed with his family until she could establish herself.

Shortly after her arrival, a cousin introduced her to a friend who worked as a seamstress in Los Angeles' garment district. Guadalupe worked long hours in order to save money to send for her children. She complained of backaches, and her fingers were in chronic pain. By the time Guadalupe returned to Guanajuato, Elizabeth had begun to forget her.

Elizabeth's migration story was not uncommon among respondents. Of the 150 young people I interviewed, sixty-two were left behind in Mexico while parents made initial migrations to find work and housing and to get settled.[8] Most of them were left to be cared for by grandparents.

Most of my respondents' memories of their journeys were less detailed. They held only fragments of memories of their crossing. While most crossed the border without proper papers, thirty-one respondents arrived in the United States on a tourist visa.

For Elizabeth, the most vivid memory was the motel room that she, her siblings, and her mom piled into, along with what she remembers to have been about a dozen others. "It was hot and sweaty," she told me. "We just had to stay there. I felt like I couldn't breathe. I wanted to be back in Mexico."

Eventually, Elizabeth and her siblings, like other respondents, were introduced to their new home. Times were tough for the family, especially in the early years. Their apartment was cramped, and their mom's work schedule left Elizabeth and her siblings little time with her.

Undocumented parents, like those of my respondents, face numerous barriers. They have trouble accessing health insurance or opening a bank account.[9] Because of a fear of deportation, undocumented parents of eligible children are less likely to apply for food stamp benefits and children's health care benefits. Undocumented status keeps families in the shadows, avoiding the very institutions intended to benefit immigrant families, and their children are less likely to receive urgently needed services.[10] Such indicators of disadvantage have particularly strong effects in early childhood.[11] These facts drive home an important truth: because of their parents' undocumented status, large proportions of our nation's student population grow up significantly behind the starting line.

Meeting high costs of living on meager wages is an ongoing struggle for families whose solutions must always be considered temporary. Problems that cannot be resolved pile up, compounding families' daily struggles and increasing their instability. The constraints of undocumented life narrow parents' range of choices. For adults without papers and without job security, the chances of finding decent housing, neighborhoods, and good schools for their children are very low.

Respondents described a range of challenges that stemmed from parental undocumented status, poverty, and housing insecurity. Ana summed up the experience of undocumented immigrant families this way: "Being an immigrant is difficult. If you don't have the papers, you don't have the credit to get anything. And you don't get a stable job, a job that pays you well, that will allow you to provide for your family."

Respondents' narratives make clear that poverty was a major source of stress in their early lives. Lacking legal status, accumulated capital, and credit, nearly all respondents' families initially settled in communities of dense poverty to find affordable housing, thus sacrificing safety for affordability. Housing instability, another direct consequence of parental constraints, was a common experience in respondents' childhoods.[12]

Because of parental immigration status and poverty, undocumented immigrant youth face considerable barriers. Many undocumented immigrants settle in areas characterized by de facto segregation and high levels of poverty.[13] These immigrants' children are much more likely to be poor, to live in crowded housing, to lack health care, and to reside in households where families have difficulty paying for food and rent.[14] According to the Pew Hispanic Center, the average income of families with at least one undocumented parent is 40 percent lower than that of either native-born families or legal immigrant families.[15] Parents who lack lawful immigration status often work in low-paying, unsafe jobs for long periods of time. As anthropologist and migration scholar Leo Chavez finds, they forgo job mobility in lieu of stability.[16]

For families with limited resources, relocation decisions are often unpredictable. Moves occur for various reasons, including family stress and disruption, the inability to pay rent and bills, poor or unsafe housing conditions, and fears of detection and apprehension. Family relocation is most consequential for children, influencing social adjustment, behavioral patterns, and academic performance.[17]

Alonso recalled that as a child he had not lived in any one place for more than a year: "I couldn't ever remember my address," he told me. "We moved so many times." Similarly, Luisa described her parents' troubles coming up with enough money for rent each month.

I moved like ten times from the age of four to fourteen. I can count the times by all the schools I went to [counts on her fingers]. Yeah, I went to ten different schools. We lived in Los Angeles when I was younger, in another family's garage, and then a couple other places. From there we moved to Pasadena. We lived in one house with like three or four families. Packed. From there we moved to another house in Pasadena, divided into three small sections, all five of us in one bedroom. I think we also had an uncle living with us for a while. After that we moved into another house in Pasadena, and then from there we moved to South Pasadena and then we moved to San Bernardino.

Luisa's narrative provides insight into another major challenge that emerged in many of my respondents' stories: life at home was uncomfortably cramped. For undocumented parents in Southern California, making ends meet on low and unstable wages required a patchwork of strategies. One common strategy among Mexican immigrants is to share costs among a network of extended family members, kin, and strangers.[18]

Many of my subjects' childhoods were spent crowded into dining rooms, kitchens, and even closets where mattresses were laid down at night.[19] For several years, Ana, who moved to the United States at the age of six, lived in a three-bedroom house in Montebello with fifteen others. Until the age of fourteen, she shared a bed with her two sisters. Neither she nor her siblings had adequate privacy or space and lighting to study. "It was horrible," she recalled, "because even when we got two beds, our situation was too much. You know, five of us [Ana, her two parents, and two sisters], with three girls in one bed."

Not all of my respondents' families remained in conditions of extreme poverty. Living arrangements improved at least modestly for many respondents' families over time as parents and other adult family members gained experience in the workforce. This was especially true for the fifteen respondents who had at least one parent with a college degree. These gains were often small; most families spent their initial years in the United States renting rooms in shared apartments or houses, and many were eventually able to move into apartments of their own. At least eight respondents' families purchased homes (although three of these families eventually lost their homes because of foreclosure). Additionally, roughly one-fifth of my respondents had family members who were able to adjust their immigration status. For some families, a combination of time of arrival, a better-than-average investment in human capital, and a change in immigration status provided a little breathing room from their previous lives of poverty. Nevertheless, most respondents' parents were not in occupations with retirement plans, and most are likely to retire without any retirement income.

OVERWORKED AND SOMETIMES ABSENT PARENTS

In addition to her overcrowded living environment, Ana contended with feelings of loneliness and loss because her mother was rarely home from work. When I met Ana, her stepfather was working more than sixty hours a week cleaning ovens at a fast-food restaurant for seven dollars an hour. His earnings were not enough to pay the bills, but he stayed because his boss treated him well. To make ends meet, Ana's mother also worked, making and delivering meals for migrant workers and waiting tables at a nearby restaurant. Throughout her school years, Ana was not able to spend much time with her mother. "Things were not really stable because my mom had to work all the time," she told me. "Well, she wasn't really a mom. So, like I stayed with my grandmother, with my godfather, with my uncles, anyone who was home."

As Ana's comments underscore, undocumented life constrained respondents' parents to low wages and long hours at work, taking valuable time from their children.[20] Even when they were at home, parents were often exhausted or busy tending to household business, further limiting time spent bonding with their children. In families like Ana's, children paid a price no less steep than the one paid by their parents.

Pedro spent his early childhood away from his mother. When he was a year old, she left him in the care of his grandparents in Mexico while she traveled to the United States to find work. Pedro was six years old by the time his mother had finally saved enough money to bring him to the United States.[21] Even after his arrival, Pedro did not feel closely bonded to her. His mother worked long hours cleaning houses and was rarely home before he went to bed.

> My mom always had a schedule. Early, like eight, we would go to school, and when we came back, my grandma would babysit us, or we had to have a babysitter. But, every time we saw her, she would come home tired from work and mad because we wouldn't be in bed. And then when, like, we would see her, I tried to get closer [and] she would be like, "Ahhh, nooo, get away." And I felt bad. She put me in the Boy Scouts and she wouldn't go to my meetings because she had to work.

As a single parent, Pedro's mom did what she had to do to meet her family's basic needs. But this meant that she did not have the time or energy to care for the emotional needs of the family she was working so hard to support.

THE RELATIONSHIP BETWEEN BELONGING AND PLACE

While respondents' parents toiled in low-wage jobs, their childhoods were freed up from responsibilities and the accompanying stress of undocumented adult life. Compared to their parents, undocumented children have many more opportunities to develop connections to people and places. Like most other children, they have regular opportunities to develop bonds with friends, school, neighborhood, and country. They develop deep attachments to *place* because they are able to accumulate experiences through repeated exposure and interaction over a number of years. Through relationships forged with friends and peers, they become insiders included in the social and physical worlds of others. Alongside their American-born friends and peers, they develop common pursuits rooted in their shared experiences. In childhood, unlike adulthood, legality is not a prerequisite for participation. Children's central pursuits—school and playtime activities with friends—are not governed by officially recognized citizenship status. With the question of legal citizenship temporarily suspended, children have more opportunities for membership.

Despite perceptions of community violence, respondents felt connected to the world outside their homes. After our interview, Elizabeth took me on a walk through her neighborhood. She showed me her school and the places where she used to play as a child. She pointed out gang graffiti and explained their meanings. Neighborhood tours like this one served as a stroll back through time, where my respondents could reconnect with the past and feel nostalgia for a time when life was much simpler.

My respondents' connections to various places are part of their biographies and key elements of their selves. For adults, immediate surroundings shape access to services, information, and opportunities. For children, surroundings also influence values, worldview, and behavior.[22]

Indeed, political and legal claims to membership require formal citizenship. But my respondents' narratives make it clear that there are other ways of belonging and forms of inclusion that are not political or legal. Familiarity with physical space and territorial markers such as parks, street names, schools, churches, and businesses provides evidence of people's presence in a place and helps them stake claims to social and cultural membership.

One of my respondents, Dani, described her neighborhood with the clarity and fondness of someone who knew it intimately:

> Our neighborhood was kind of weird. We had a huge alley in the back that was only for the people who lived there. It was fenced off so people from the outside couldn't come in and cars didn't drive through. There was a gate with a lock so people couldn't get in. The fence had an opening, though, like a hole we could squeeze through. My mom liked it because she didn't have

to worry so much. It felt safe for her. Growing up, all the kids would go back there and play, you know, tag, hopscotch, whatever. Even though we were in downtown L.A., we could leave our stuff out there without it getting stolen. We all knew each other because everyone went to the same elementary [school] and the same junior high. Sometimes there would be drama, like disagreements or whatever, but we all got along for the most part. I still see some of them I've been knowing since we were kids.

For some respondents, including college-goer Lilia, memories evoked the smells, sounds, and flavors of their childhoods. At one point during our interview, Lilia closed her eyes, her thoughts drifting back to her old East Los Angeles neighborhood:

> I loved summertime on my block. I remember all of the street vendors, like the lady who sold lemonade and the men who pushed the *paleta* [ice cream] carts up and down the street. Oh, and the *eloteros* [corn vendors] that would pass by my building. I would call out to them from my window and run outside after them. My brother always teased me because I'd get the butter and cheese all over my mouth. The *chile* would burn my tongue, so I'd have it sticking out. He would say I looked funny. Then upstairs we had this rocker guy and he'd always be playing his music all loud. My mom hated it. His girlfriend once gave me a bracelet. And then there would be yard sales, like the first Sunday of every month. We'd go after church. You would see a lot of people out there. You know—different kinds of people. I loved my neighborhood.

Knowing and Being Known

Detailed descriptions and sensory memories such as Lilia's suggest deep attachments to place. Elizabeth's neighborhood and Dani's back alley were the kinds of places where, as geographer Yi-Fu Tuan put it, "a deep though subconscious" attachment came with "familiarity and ease, with the assurance of nurture and security, and with the memory of sounds and smells of communal activities and homely pleasures accumulated over time."[23] Tuan suggests that children come to know their surroundings more intimately than do adults because they interact with their local world on a deeper level.

> Abstract knowledge *about* a place can be acquired in short order if one is diligent . . . but the "feel" of the place takes longer to acquire. It is made up of experiences, mostly fleeting and undramatic, repeated day after day and over the span of years. It is a unique blend of sights, sounds and smells, a unique harmony of natural and artificial rhythms such as times of sunrise and sunset, of work and play. The feel of a place is registered in one's muscles and bones. . . . Knowing a place in the above senses clearly takes time. It is a subconscious kind of knowing.[24]

Tuan's analysis of belonging as familiar spaces and repeated experiences is consistent with many respondents' descriptions of their neighborhoods. I visited many of them at their homes, and some took me to the places where they had grown up. During a visit with Pedro on his old block, he pointed out places where he used to hang out or play. He remembered with strong familiarity the sidewalks, lots, and hiding places of his youth, and he was quick to notice what had changed. Despite ambivalent feelings and a troubled past, Pedro had returned to live in his childhood neighborhood. In connecting his past and present lives, he recognized that he had left an imprint of his own on the neighborhood:

> It has its problems, but it's where I am from. I left when I was fourteen and came back at twenty-six. My face hasn't changed much. I mean, I've grown and everything, but people recognize me. They come up to me and say, "Hey, are you Pedro? I used to live around you." Or, "I remember when you were just a kid. You've really filled out [noting his very large frame]." I love my old neighborhood. I know my way around here. I know the people. And I know the streets like the back of my hand. It's where I'm from, you know.

Respondents' attachments to their neighborhoods were acquired over time. They readily recalled rich details that directly connected places to the events of their childhoods. These types of associations helped them cultivate feelings of affiliation and membership. Alexia, who had moved to Northern California to attend college, poignantly articulated this feeling when describing the excitement she felt when returning to Los Angeles: "I go back to L.A. and I feel at home. This is the place [where] I grew up. I know the little stores, the restaurants. They all bring back so many memories. People smile at me and remember my name."

The narratives of Pedro and Alexia demonstrate another important aspect of belonging—attachments extend in both directions. Their neighborhoods evoke vivid memories in undocumented young people, and in turn former neighbors, merchants, and assorted community members remember *them*. The recognition Pedro and Alexia received from others when they returned home validated them as part of the community.

Decades of research on childhood suggest that forming relationships outside the household allows children to envision themselves as part of a larger community.[25] For my respondents, connections with community members such as neighbors, postal carriers, crossing guards, and store clerks provided the mortar that cemented community ties. These relationships often developed slowly through exchanges that, taken separately, might be easily forgotten but that established patterns and familiarity when repeated over time: trips past a neighbor's house on the way to school, afternoon stops at the convenience store to buy candy, ongoing involvement in programs at community centers.

Presence, patterns, place, and relationships inscribed these young people in their communities, figuratively and sometimes even literally. Near the end of my tour with Elizabeth, she took me to an area about a block from her apartment where her name was written in the sidewalk. "I can't believe it's still there," she told me. "I still remember that day. That's so cool. It's like I left a little part of me there."

This sidewalk inscription was a powerful symbol of belonging. Writing in wet cement is a common rite of passage in many neighborhoods. But for young people like Elizabeth who ultimately have no legal claim on membership, it is especially meaningful. It proves physical evidence of their presence in and history with the community.

Assertions of Home

These respondents' strong attachments to place are *assertions of home.* To be sure, for most people, "home" does not have uniformly positive associations. This held true for my respondents as well. Their narratives reflected the tension between the negative and positive aspects of their communities. Just as they recalled parks and playgrounds with nostalgia, their narratives also evoked memories of vacant lots, police stations, or territory marked by gangs.

Sonny worked as an orderly at a retirement home. I met him through his mother, a street vendor I came to know. At 6'3" and about 240 pounds, Sonny looked like a linebacker. His stature was imposing to those who did not know his "softer side." As a teenager, he had been in a neighborhood "crew" and had experienced numerous unpleasant exchanges with police officers. At least six of his "associates" from the neighborhood had been killed by gang violence, including his best friend, Casper, whose death Sonny had witnessed. Nevertheless, Sonny felt a strong affinity for his Anaheim community.

When I met Sonny at his apartment, I noticed that he and his wife Rosie had matching tattoos with "714"—the area code of north Orange County—inscribed across their forearms. Sonny was also wearing an

Anaheim Angels T-shirt, another sign of his love for Orange County. I asked them to talk about their tattoos. Their answers gave me interesting insight into their affinity for where they lived.

> *Roberto:* Tell me a little about that [pointing to Sonny's forearms]. It looks like you both have matching tattoos.
>
> *Rosie:* Yeah, we got them together after our first son was born.
>
> *Roberto:* What do those numbers represent to you?
>
> *Sonny:* It's where we're from.
>
> *Roberto:* So, it's where you both grew up?
>
> *Sonny:* Yeah, but it's different from that. Maybe bigger. It's like who we are. It's the block we live on. It's our friends and family, our memories, the struggles we've gone through. Like how you feel about your favorite team or something. If you're loyal to that team, you stand by them even when they're losing. You feel proud of them. That's how you identify. It's the same. I have love for this place, always. For the cockroaches, the brown lawns, the jacked-up cars outside. We may not have much, you know, but you've got to have respect for who you are. We're Orange County.
>
> *Rosie:* You know, we both weren't born here, but this is our home, and we have pride about that.
>
> *Roberto:* Do you think your children will feel the same way?
>
> *Sonny:* It'll probably be different for them. But yeah, I think they will.

The narratives of my respondents suggest the need for more nuanced theories about undocumented life. By virtue of their early integration into American communities, undocumented children form attachments that parallel those of their American-born and legal peers.[26] Respondents reported connections that began in childhood as they explored their neighborhoods and attended local primary schools. They recalled various opportunities for integration and the development of a sense of belonging that tied them to their communities. They formed attachments to friends, teachers, and community spaces, and they enjoyed playing and spending time with other neighborhood children. Taken together, these experiences paint a richly textured picture of community belonging—not of the outsiderness that one might expect.

While these experiences highlight different types of membership that are connected not to legal citizenship but to the experience of belonging, we might ask if these forms are sufficient enough to be considered full membership. Feelings of belonging and the desire for inclusion in the broader community exist in a dialectical relationship with the larger society, which may or may not accept alternative claims of member-ship.[27] Nevertheless, these local manifestations remind us that in some spaces and during some historical moments, even when immigrants do not have formal legal citizenship or even a form of permanent resident status, they may find belonging at the local level.

CHAPTER 4

School as a Site of Belonging and Conflict

The American dream is a powerful ethos, shaping general beliefs and attitudes regarding hard work and opportunity. This ethos resonates with Americans of all stripes, but especially the working class and the newly arrived. Generations of immigrants have come to the United States believing that America will provide opportunities for them and especially for their children.

Many immigrant parents view the public school system as the ideal instrument to realize the American dream for their children. They believe, as Horace Mann did over 150 years ago, that "education . . . beyond all other devices of human origin, is the great equalizer of the conditions of men, the balance-wheel of the social machinery."[1] The belief that the education and assimilation of immigrant children are in the best interests of American democracy has been supported historically by efforts to mainstream these children through English language instruction and lessons in civics.[2] At the same time, however, American public schools are sites of stratification, often reinforcing and widening society's inequalities.[3] Still, most Americans view school as the primary means of producing a class of citizens ready to contribute to America's social, political, and economic life at all rungs of the mobility ladder.

ENVIRONMENTAL EFFECTS ON SCHOOL SUCCESS

Unsafe neighborhoods, multiple relocations, cramped living conditions, and overworked parents are common themes described by respondents and unavoidable aspects of undocumented life in the United States. In addition to their direct effects, these disadvantageous conditions indirectly harmed respondents by limiting their ability to do their best in school.

Most middle-class American children grow up with rooms of their own, with doors that shut and lock. They have their own desks, pens, staplers, art materials, bookshelves and books, computers, and televisions. My respondents lacked not only the financial resources to fill their worlds with these types of school-related enhancements but also the space to use and store them. The home environment Ana described was not conducive to homework.

> We really didn't have much and things were so crowded. It was like I had no space to breathe. It made it really hard to do homework sometimes. Like I didn't have, I couldn't, you know, ever get my homework done at home. I would try to study at the kitchen table, on the floor, anywhere I could find, but with so many people coming in and out, it was too noisy. It wasn't like I had headphones I could put on to drowned [sic] out the noise. Sometimes I went to the library to do my homework. It was nice and quiet. But then, I also had to take care of my two younger sisters, so that didn't work so well most of the time. I tried to bring them with me but they would get bored there.

Like Ana, many respondents lacked the time to do the hours of homework teachers expected. Their household responsibilities (e.g., cleaning, cooking, and babysitting siblings) kept them busy and took priority over schoolwork. Gloria described assuming a large share of household duties beginning at age eight.

> I always had big responsibilities. I don't think I would call them chores. It was just like what I was responsible for to help out, you know, around the house. My mom taught me to use the *plancha* (iron) when I was eight. I was cooking by nine. I used to help make breakfast for everyone. Then I'd have to get my younger brother and sister ready for school [when Gloria was nine, her brother was seven and her sister was five]. We would walk to school together, then I'd pick them up from their classrooms after school and we'd walk home together. From there, I'd make them a snack when we got home, and then I would start on dinner. I did this, I think, until I was sixteen, when I started working. That's when my sister, the younger one, started helping out more with cooking and cleaning.

Household duties often fell disproportionally on female respondents.[4] However, many male respondents were asked to begin work at early ages. Of the seventy-one male early exiters, fifty-eight had jobs before they were sixteen, and thirty-six were working before the age of fourteen.

Immigrant families frequently experience tension between parents' recognition of the value of education for their children and the economic necessity of employment for as many family members as possible. Most respondents' parents held education in high regard. However, the strains of poverty and undocumented status made acting on these values by providing children with environments conducive to academic achievement very difficult. For most respondents, heightened family responsibilities coupled with cramped and often chaotic home environments that severely curbed privacy restricted their ability to keep up with schoolwork and ultimately undercut their chances for academic success.

THE EARLY SCHOOL YEARS

In her work on school culture, sociologist Karolyn Tyson makes the important point that in the earlier school years a broader swath of the student population (students of color and white students, boys and girls) is oriented toward school participation and achievement and is deeply attached to the promise of the American dream.[5] Student bodies tend to fracture in the later years,[6] but in the lower grades students are more universally engaged because they have more opportunities to share common experiences (e.g., the daily Pledge of Allegiance, class explorations of state history and symbols, all-school assemblies, daily playground activities with classmates). School sorting practices based on the labeling of ability and behavior are also less common.

Integrative and Americanizing Influences

When reflecting on their experiences in the primary grades, my respondents highlighted schools as the principal mechanism in their integration and Americanization. Andrea, who had "many memorable moments" throughout her school years, told me that her years in primary school were probably the most notable:

> It's funny, but the things I remember the most from school [her entire educational experience] are the California history and geography unit we had in

the fourth grade. I really liked that. I remember, we learned, we had to draw a California map. I've always liked history and all the, but this was cool because in a way it was like my history right here. I don't know, but it had a special meaning because it was of my state. It really stuck. I chose to show [on a map] where all the missions were in the state because my mom once took us to the Mission San Juan Capistrano. I think my mom still has that [the map].

Many respondents noted that reciting the Pledge of Allegiance and singing patriotic songs planted early seeds of a "sense of we-ness." "You know what?" Lilia said to me. "They say go back to your country, but I don't even know the Mexican national anthem. It's kind of embarrassing around my cousins from Mexico, but I didn't grow up there. I sure do know all of our national songs, 'My Country, 'Tis of Thee,' 'America the Beautiful.' We learned them in school. It's like every American kid knows those songs because we learn them in school. I think that means something. It says something about me, where I'm from. It connects us."

Even many of my respondents who did not have positive high school experiences held fond memories of primary school. For example, though Sergio's relationships with teachers and school officials were antagonistic in his later years of schooling, his memories of elementary school involved the same feelings of inclusion and safety described by many college-goers: "I just always liked school," he told me. "No matter what was happening at home, I felt like I was safe and stable at school. Now, that changed once I had to change schools to go to seventh [grade], but I used to really like school." He laughed. "There was something about the familiarity, you know, the routine."

Many others recalled similar experiences that evoked a sense of belonging. Pedro described handball tournaments one of his teachers arranged for the children during their lunch period. Flor said that one of her favorite school rituals was the all-school assembly because "I always looked forward to those times when we all got together, cheering and feeling the school spirit."[7]

Benefits of Adult Support

Relationships with primary school teachers were particularly important for many respondents, giving them enough support to feel a sense of stability and comfort within their schools. Gloria described a relationship with a teacher that led her to return to her grade school "when things got bad" for her in later years:

I was in ESL and then I got mainstreamed in third grade. My third-grade teacher really helped me a lot. I mean she was just really warm. She created that kind of atmosphere in her class, and I have to say that I am still friends with four other girls from that class. Well, we were together for two years because [the teacher] moved up to fourth [grade] with us. I still visit her. Well, after fourth grade, I'd go to see her all the time until I left [moved on to seventh grade]. Then I would go back to her to talk. When I felt I had nowhere to turn, it felt good to know that she was there for me. I would say that she's like a second mom to me.

Unlike public middle schools and high schools, elementary schools are generally smaller and more neighborhood based. Many of the primary schools my respondents attended were financially strapped and lacked adequate resources, but the school setting positioned students to feel a part of the whole, to "belong." Every school day, young children were greeted by friendly faces and participated in the activities and rituals that embedded them in the school community; these people and activities allowed them to have a sense of belonging to the school and, by extension, to the nation. But by the time these same children entered high school, school sorting mechanisms were in full swing, creating starkly unequal distributions of most of the positive aspects of schooling. For many of those not fortunate enough to be labeled smart and/or deserving, school-based feelings of belonging did not persist. Whereas generally positive elementary school experiences made respondents' school histories mostly indistinguishable, their later middle school and high school years began to set them on distinct pathways toward college-going and early exits from school.

CULTIVATED BELONGING: THE SECONDARY SCHOOL EXPERIENCES OF COLLEGE-GOERS

Beginning in middle school and accelerating in high school, many public schools offer specialized classes or smaller learning environments designed to boost academic achievement among a select number of students. These pupils take the same classes and move through school together, often sheltered from the general student body. By the time they reach high school, they are prepared to compete for slots in gifted and talented programs, specialized academies, and honors and AP classes. Many college-goers were introduced to select school environments as early as fifth grade. Esmeralda, who went to school in San Bernardino (a city about sixty-five miles from Los Angeles), benefited very early in her schooling from this type of school sorting.[8] "Before we even moved on to high school, my teachers kind of already recommend[ed] certain classes," she recalled. ". . . From middle school to high school they had already chosen for me. 'You're my best student. I recommend you for this class or that one.'"

Particularly in large schools, the smaller environment provided by these programs can be more conducive to learning. It also separates students from many of the problems plaguing large urban schools such as gangs, apathy, and inadequate resources. Zulima, another college-goer, described her school and program:

> At the time, it was the second-largest high school in the nation. We had around, I think, 5,400 students. When I started, my class was like 2,200, but by the time I graduated, we were, I think, like 800. Within the school there are little minischools. I was in Odyssey Academy. You have the same classes with the same students, all four years. You have to apply to get in, and basically you have to take certain classes. I guess it's a division; it was more . . . like a tracking-like system. You saw which students were bound for college.

Similarly, JD, who lived in Camarillo (in Ventura County), experienced the benefits of being shielded from the broader population and from the additional resources allocated to her program:

> Every year someone got hurt. I mean, it was a safe place if you just hung out with the right crowd. I was placed into all honors courses from the beginning, so I was always secluded from all the, what they would call the CP kids, the college prep kids, which really were just kids that were tracked to not go to college. I would talk to my friends who were in the regular CP courses and they never got the presentations or the counselors coming in the way they did in my courses. In my courses, every time we would have a counselor come in and talk about colleges and applications are coming in. "You need to go check them out, you need to go do this and that." Counselors would call us in. I was pretty much tracked to go to college.

Another respondent, Irene, graduated from a competitive film program at California State University in 2008. In high school, she was part of a selective academy that accepted a small number of students each year. The students, who stayed together through graduation, developed close relationships with their teachers, were provided unique access to college counselors, and took yearly trips to visit university campuses. As Irene described it, "My academy was small. They tried to keep it very, very small. They wanted to make sure the program was for you. My teacher mentored me to make sure I was college material." Other college-goers similarly constructed self-narratives of success that reinforced their placement within the school's stratification system. They internalized the labels that teachers had assigned to them, such as "my best student," part of "the right crowd," and "college material," as evidence of their special talents or gifts.

The Role of Enhanced Resources

College-goers benefited from resources that were specifically associated with their smaller and more select school environments. Celina, for example, took part in a program at her high school in Orange County that prepared her for college and provided career mentorship. She was matched with a pediatrician whom she shadowed for two years. This experience exposed Celina to the world of medicine and facilitated a relationship that would pay great dividends in the years to come. Her mentor helped finance her university education and provided research opportunities throughout Celina's four years at the University of California.

College-goers were acutely aware of the relationship between getting into specialized programs or advanced tracks during high school and their future outcomes. Several talked about how they gained entrance to these programs. Sal (who graduated from the University of California in 2006 and began studying for a law degree two years later) described his high school experience this way:

> I was never tracked in AP until I began to fight with my counselor. I knew what honors were, but I never had them, you know, until I talked to my Spanish teacher. She was like, "What other honors classes are you taking? You're doing really good. Are you taking any other ones?" I was like, "No." She's like, "Well you should, and you should ask that you be put in AP and honors because you could do it. You have good grades in every other one of your classes. There's no reason why you shouldn't be doing it." My math teacher would tell me the same.

Sal was a strong student, but like many others who are shunted into lower tracks, he did not think to question his course placement.[9] A nudge in the right direction from an influential teacher helped Sal move up within the high school stratification system. As a result, he succeeded in getting into AP classes and was immersed in a culture that emphasized school success.

Many other college-goers benefited from the opportunities that smaller learning environments gave them for developing relationships of trust with teachers and counselors.

Daisy: I felt very strongly about their support. I have so many memories about my English teacher and my history teacher. . . . I'm gonna take [those memories] with me everywhere because they were just so motivating in their teaching style and in the way they showed their support to each student.

Irene: It was like a family. You just knew that people were looking out for you, and that felt good.

Luis: I had help from counselors, from teachers, from the principal. They were helpful; they were my mentors. Any resources, any help that I needed . . . those were the people that I would always go to. They had my back.

By segregating students from the broader student body, smaller learning environments provided certain students access to significant resources. Perhaps most importantly, the select environments were nurturing and offered opportunities to form a community with peers, teachers, and other school staff. Most of the college-goers believed they could count on their networks for any help they needed. Sociology of education scholars argue that networks like these give students advantages that are crucial for school success.[10]

The Role of Peer Networks

Within their peer networks, college-goers benefited from opportunities to support, teach, and compete with each other in ways that enhanced their intellectual development and advanced their academic pursuits. Many mentioned the benefits of having friends that pushed them to excel. Oscar recalled, "We had study nights or study days, and we would help each other and tutor each other. A lot of the students trusted me and knew that I knew the material already, so they would prefer to have me and other friends tutoring them."

College-goers also leveraged friendship groups to maximize their resources by sharing information. JD was the oldest of three girls. Her parents were very protective of their daughters and insisted that they come straight home after school (in fact, JD did not go to a movie theater by herself until she was twenty-four). Because her after-school activities were so closely monitored, JD learned to maximize her time and resources. She relied on her friends for information about academic opportunities. Together, they devised a system to compile and then share important information: "It was more of just a group of people helping. I mean, we were friends. My friend Amanda, she was one of us. She was the one that whenever she would get one piece of information or she heard something I wasn't aware off, she'd let me know, 'Hey, did you hear about this that's due?' 'No, I didn't.' Or we would help each other. There was someone from a different university coming in to talk. We would sign up and get information and give it each other."

For Scarlet, the transition to high school brought about a change in her peer group. During middle school and at the start of high school, she was more interested in "flirting and socializing" with her friends than in doing her schoolwork. However, when she started receiving positive attention from her teachers, she began to develop a sense of belonging tied to achievement. She slowly pulled away from her old friends.

> I was kind of in the popular crowd, and we were like into going out and talking to guys and hanging out and stuff like that. And then we got into an argument. They thought I was getting all big-headed because I was doing well in school. So I stopped talking to all of them and they stopped talking to me. So then I made new friends and the friends that I made were like the honors students. They were like more calm. They were into school. And I think in a way that kind of helped me. Because I think that if I would have stayed with the other crowd, I don't know if I would have done as good as I have. I don't know. I would probably, you know, would have gone the wrong way or something.

The Role of Extracurricular Activities

In addition to their beneficial relationships with teachers and high-achieving peers, some college-goers were able to extend networks through their participation in extracurricular activities. Celina, for instance, developed a passion for windsailing through an after-school program that introduced her to peers from backgrounds and environments different from her own. "My background is so different from my friends'. I basically try to keep my school life and family life separate, but I have brought my [high school] friends to my home. It really kind of freaks them out when they meet my parents. One of my friends said to me, 'I didn't realize you were Mexican. You just seem like one of us.' Yeah, I know, kind of messed up. But that's my world."

In some cases, teachers encouraged these extracurricular pursuits. Andrea initially dropped out of school at age thirteen, but when she returned two years later her teacher noticed that she was a leader among her classmates. Within a short time, Andrea was asked to take part in an initiative spearheaded by the vice-principal. For the next two years, she served on an advisory council that gave recommendations to the administration about how to address racial and ethnic tensions at the school. This experience served as a catalyst, prompting Andrea to later take leadership positions in college and her community. Her council position inspired what she referred to as a "feeling of ownership in my education and development."

Joining school-sponsored clubs also provided respondents important opportunities to work with teachers and community members. At her school, Alexia attended weekly meetings with the district superintendent. Students who participated in similar school-sponsored activities enjoyed school-sponsored field trips, university visits, and assistance with college applications.[11] Involvement in extracurricular activities was not the exception but the rule among college-goers. Most said they had been part of multiple school activities.

College-goers' narratives show that for a select group of young people schools cultivated a sense of belonging. Positive messages from teachers about being part of a group, being committed to hard work, adhering to the rules, and striving for high academic achievement were typically reinforced by peers, other school personnel, and community members. For most college-goers I spoke with, feeling integrated and developing a sense of belonging began early. They received various affirming messages about their abilities, and they were encouraged to internalize a culture of meritocracy. As their behavior was rewarded—with positive reinforcement from teachers, placement in small academies or advanced-level classes, and peers' respect and admiration—they begin to see themselves as part of a valuable whole composed of a close-knit group of peers, teachers, and staff. As Luis described it, "I really felt like they had my back. I mean, I felt supported and that was like, it meant a lot to me. 'Cause I didn't feel that way other places. And it just helped me feel like part of something, part of the crowd. You know, one of them."

OVERLOOKED OR PUSHED OUT: THE SECONDARY
SCHOOL EXPERIENCES OF EARLY EXITERS

Early departures from school were not the result of financial pressures alone. Early exiters and college-goers shared similar socioeconomic profiles: students in both groups came from the same communities, and their parents labored in the same kinds of jobs and confronted similarly high costs of living. The primary factor separating the late adolescent and early adult experiences of the two groups of respondents was access to school-based resources and support.

Most respondents attended large high schools in very large school districts, where the ratios of students to counselors were as high as 1,000 to 1.[12] In contrast to the small classes and specialized attention described by the college-goers, early exiters described classrooms with as many as forty students. Many early exiters reported few interactions with counselors; Juan never met with a college counselor until late in his junior year. Because an overwhelming majority of these students outpaced their parents in educational attainment, many were left without proper guidance about school. Juan recalled, "Not a lot of teachers focused on students. They were terrible. They wouldn't teach us. I wanted to go to college, but the counselors didn't let me know the requirements for four-year colleges. I tried to go to see them, but they didn't have time for me."

Many early exiters said that they did not receive any attention at all. They were left to succeed or fail on their own. When I asked about relationships with teachers and counselors, few early exiters could recall the name of even one helpful person. Their general track classes did not give them access to individualized attention from teachers, and school personnel did not give them the kind of encouragement college-goers described receiving.

The Implications of Isolation

Suzie was noticeably uncomfortable when talking about her high school experiences in the city of Alhambra. Describing high school as "the worst time in my life," Suzie recalled being a "shy and overweight" adolescent who received Cs and Ds in her classes. She was picked on by several classmates because of her demeanor and "Goodwill" style of dress. She had no close friends and no relationships with teachers or other school staff.

When Suzie experienced a family tragedy, she saw firsthand the implications of not having an advocate within the school.

Roberto: How come you were kicked out?

Suzie: 'Cause I wasn't up to the other students with the GPA.

Roberto: So you were kicked out because of your grades?

Suzie: Well, I wasn't going to school for my ninth grade [her teachers allowed her to do her coursework at home], but I went back in tenth grade and I finished my tenth. I was barely starting my eleventh, so I was actually catching up to everyone else, but I guess the assistant principal had it against all the Latinos and they didn't want us there. Well, the ones that don't look good for the school. Supposedly it was because of my grades, but my grades were doing okay at that time. I even went to summer school to get [them] raised up.

Roberto: What was happening during ninth grade when you didn't go to school?

Suzie: That year my grandmother died. I was supposed [to] go on to school, but I got depressed.

Roberto: So you just, you didn't want to deal with anything?

Suzie: I got counseling when I entered tenth grade.

Roberto: And so, even with counseling, they still kicked you out?

Suzie: Yeah.

Initially, Suzie's exit from high school might appear to have been caused by a lack of initiative. But her explanation suggests that she may have been deliberately "weeded out." The counseling she received in tenth grade indicates that school officials were aware of her family and emotional issues. Without anyone to advocate on her behalf when she was expelled, Suzie had little recourse to remain in school. Suzie's story is illustrative of the consequences of such practices that fail to address the full needs of students. For many other respondents, problems originating at home or due to undocumented status not only are unaddressed but also, because of misperceptions, can lead to negative treatment.

The Power of Labels

Sociologist Nilda Flores-Gonzalez argues that schools exacerbate divisions among students by reinforcing dichotomous identities.[13] These labels support tracking decisions, making systems of school stratification invisible, if not natural. In her study of a Chicago high school, she found that school officials gave students informal binary labels as "school kids" or "street kids." These labels were assigned to students during middle school and the early years of high school, usually based on subjective perceptions of their abilities and behaviors. Labels remain with students for years, shaping interactions with teachers and school staff and influencing how students see themselves. If, as with the college-goers, the labels are positive, they can enhance students' school experience and deepen their sense of belonging. If they are negative, as occurred frequently with the early exiters, labels can lead to dismal, alienating school experiences.

The negative labeling of students as unmotivated, incapable, or given to making trouble is often based on educators' personal, cultural, and institutional ideas and values. Labeling practices result in students, rather than their behaviors, being treated as the problem, and they deflect attention from the school environment, which may be at least partially responsible for academic and behavioral issues.[14] Acts of negative labeling also influence how students think of themselves and how they think others perceive them. These perceptions in turn affect their possibilities for success.[15]

On separate occasions, I spoke to two siblings, Blanca and Junior, who each experienced what they described as episodes of racism. Both felt that school officials in their predominantly white school in Newport treated them unfairly because they were Mexican. The two siblings recounted nearly identical troubles with school officials. Blanca explained that when she fell short of credits she was told she needed to enroll in a continuation program.

> *Blanca:* My junior year they recommended that I go to continuation school and they put me down a lot. They were awful. They said, "You aren't going to graduate. There is no way." So then, I went over there [continuation school] and I worked my butt off and I finished. I caught up and then I had like a lot of teachers that supported me, telling me to go back and graduate from my regular high school. My mom was begging me to graduate from a regular high school, so I caught up with what I needed, and when I went to an interview with them, they tried to reject me. They said, "You're short fifty credits, there is no way you are going to make it, that's not possible. No one has ever done it and I doubt you'll do it."
>
> *Roberto:* Why do you think they were so awful to you?
>
> *Blanca:* I think [it] was because I was Hispanic. That's how I take it.
>
> *Roberto:* Did other Hispanic students have a hard time at school, too?
>
> *Blanca:* My brother (Junior). They put him through the same thing.

Blanca did not graduate. In fact, she did not return to a school setting for another five years.

California's continuation high schools typically serve students who are missing a large number of course credits or who have specific educational or social needs.[16] At most continuation schools, students receive minimal instruction, work independently in workbooks, and move through the program at their own pace. The goal is to make up credit deficiencies to either graduate from the continuation school or return to traditional high school. Graduation requirements are the same for traditional and continuation schools, but scheduling is more flexible at continuation schools, potentially making it possible for students to earn credits at a quicker pace.

To be eligible for attendance at a continuation school, a student must be at least sixteen and deemed at risk of not completing his or her education.[17] A fraction of students independently choose a continuation school. The vast majority are referred by their high schools (most of these students function far below grade level and are at risk of falling further behind). According to the state's Legislative Analyst's Office, the overriding focus on improving test scores in California places enormous pressure on schools to push low-performing students into alternative schools as a way of evading accountability for them.[18] Granted, continuation schools are not the only option to recover missing credits. Students can make up for failed grades by retaking courses or through summer school, weekend school, and after-school programs. But many respondents felt as though they had been unfairly steered toward continuation schools.

As evident from Blanca's comments, many students viewed referral to a continuation school as a punishment, a stigma that signaled their deficiency. Blanca believed she had such a difficult time in school because school officials and teachers linked her ethnicity to a perceived inability to succeed. This belief was confirmed when Junior, Blanca's American-born citizen brother, had similarly negative experiences with the same school officials four years later. After failing more than one class, he was told to finish his education at the continuation school.

> *Junior:* I didn't like school. It was really, it was a lot of racial stuff with counselors, and even at the counselors' office. If anything went wrong at that school, it was because there were Mexicans. . . . My own counselor, too, I would ask her for help, but somehow she wouldn't be able to help me out. If you ask me, it sounds ridiculous, man.
>
> *Roberto:* So the counselor was the one that pushed you out?
>
> *Junior:* Yeah, 'cause when I came back, I had a chance to go back to my high school. I went back and she was giving me a hard time. She was telling me that I couldn't come back. She said I needed community service hours.

Junior did not have his sister's determination to fight the school system. After being denied re-entrance to his high school, he went back to the continuation school, where he received his diploma three years later.

Many other early exiters I spoke with were also referred to continuation schools. Some finished their diploma, but most did not.[19] There is a great deal of variation among these second-chance schools. They are typically housed on smaller campuses—at community colleges or within community-based organizations—and have low student-to-teacher ratios. These structural characteristics are generally associated with good academic outcomes. But, as with the public schools, the culture of these programs critically affects their success. I observed a handful of continuation programs that were impersonal and institutional. Students attended regularly but had minimal interactions during the school day. Several early exiters who went to continuation schools said they had tried several but did not stay. For these respondents, the most "successful" continuation schools were programs that encouraged student interaction and that had caring and supportive instructors and staff members.

The problems faced by Blanca and Junior at their predominantly white school were not uncommon. Several other early exiters struggled in schools where Latino students were in the minority. But most of my interviewees attended Latino-majority high schools. Tony, from Riverside, who went to a Latino-majority high school, reported that he had "bad relationships with teachers because they did not like my attitude." He told me that his teachers often talked negatively about him in his presence.

> *Tony:* I wouldn't really do anything either, you know. Like always, I would just sit there. At one point [the history teacher] called me "scum of the earth" and [said] that I was going to be a drug dealer when I got older, and that I was going to sell rock [cocaine], and that I was going to steal money, and I was just like, "Ahhh."
>
> *Roberto:* Why was he telling you this?
>
> *Tony:* Because I wasn't turning in work, and he just got all crazy and calling me all this stuff.

When I first spoke to Tony in 2007, he had been out of school for two years. At age nineteen, he was considering returning to school, but he had no concrete plan to do so. Like Junior, Tony believed that he had been unfairly labeled as a troublemaker and could not do anything to change that. For many young people, these labels, particularly the ones given to them by teachers and other adults, have particularly negative impacts on their self-image. They also tend to stick, following them for some time to come. Many early exiters told similar stories.

Sergio: It was unfair 'cause my brother had a reputation and many of the teachers knew we were related. So yeah, they didn't care too much for me.

Josue: I didn't like any of my teachers. It was just the attitude they had. Like, "I know you're bad and I'm gonna be a hardass on you."

Flor: I can't tell you if I was any more singled out than others, but I had one teacher who was always rude, like really rude, to me. If I was even five minutes late, she would send me to the office. It was like, "Wow, someone woke up on the wrong side of the bed." She was always like that, though.

Jorge, from East Los Angeles, was frequently in fights that landed him in the assistant principal's office. After an incident leading to his expulsion that Jorge described as the "last straw" for his mom, Jorge promised her that he would do his best to graduate from high school. He forced himself to stay inside to avoid distractions while at home and resolved to go to school every day. He described how much he wanted to put his energies into school and his future but said he did not know how to go about making these changes. Moreover, he discovered that it was very difficult to undo the stigma attached to his negative label at school. "Even though I had a bad background, I really tried to turn myself around. Teachers didn't care about me. The assistant principal didn't like me. . . . The counselor wasn't there for me. I didn't know what to do. I tried to go back to regular high school, but they wouldn't let me. They said that due to 'my kind,' I had to be at the continuation school. I even tried to go to the district, but they gave me the run-around."

The treatment that Jorge received from school personnel differed radically from the narratives of college-goers, who consistently benefited from teachers' positive attention. Many of the college-goers were explicitly encouraged to continue their education and were provided resources to do so. Jorge felt that no one at school wanted to help him. Eventually, he grew frustrated and dropped out.

Stigmatizing labels negatively shaped early exiters' relationships with teachers and school administrators. As with college-goers, these messages were reinforced by the broader community or peers, school personnel, and community members. They also had particularly debilitating consequences. When these young people required additional support, the negative labeling affected their ability to mobilize resources. Jorge actively worked to improve as a student, but because school personnel had an entrenched negative perception of him he received no support to take a new path. Jorge, like others, found himself structurally locked into a downward academic trajectory.

The Pull of Family Need and the Desire for Autonomy

Limited or inconsistent levels of motivation and troubled backgrounds contributed to respondents' exit decisions. Many early exiters simply were not interested in school and had no college aspirations; others chose to have children or engaged in illicit activities that altered their educational pathways. However, along with the push factors that moved early exiters out of school, there were also significant pull factors. Parental poverty was a major challenge for many respondents. Without positive school experiences to counterbalance the growing pressure—both internal and external—to help their struggling families, some early exiters left school to enter the workforce.[20]

Although parents were often supportive of their children's education, many could not provide the crucial help needed to offset the negative effects of tracking or to redirect their children into academic achievement. The vast majority of respondents were the children of parents whose educational attainment was low or whose work hours precluded their active involvement during the school day. For high school students not fortunate enough to form relationships with informed adults outside their families who were willing to provide guidance, these parental characteristics posed a real disadvantage.

For many early exiters, school was not necessarily a hostile environment, but neither was it welcoming. Karina maintained a B average in her general track classes. However, she was quiet and did not attract much attention (positive or negative) from her teachers. When it came time to apply to college, she was without any guidance. Unaware that California state law made it possible for her to attend school at in-state tuition rates, Karina opted not to go to college.

> I didn't know anything about A. B. 540. So the reason I didn't go to university, well, first of all, was because I was lacking the money, so even if I were, well, maybe if I knew the information, I could have gotten a scholarship or something. But I didn't know anything. I didn't even know we had A. B. 540. So I thought I was going to pay like twenty thousand [dollars]. So I was like, "No way I was going to pay that." So that's why I didn't go. Nobody told me anything. I don't know if my counselors knew, but they never told me anything.

Many other early exiters were like Karina. They did not go on to college although they had attended high school regularly and had earned decent grades. Not feeling welcomed or valued or even noticed, they simply fell through the cracks.

For early exiters, labeling and negative interactions with school personnel sent strong messages regarding their presence and participation in school. Labels stayed with them for years. Many also internalized teachers' negative perceptions of them as lazy or troublemakers. Being left out of the school community had broader consequences as well. It sharply reduced their ability to access resources critical to their school success. While this made their path after leaving high school difficult, it also limited their beliefs about what the future could hold.

Still, some, like Tony, preferred their own autonomy to the negative messages and continual punishment at school: "At least outside [school] I set the agenda. I don't have any clown [referring to his history teacher] telling me that I'm lazy or scum, like that. I get up when I want to. I do as I please. It's not what I want to be doing for the rest of my life, but I don't have to worry about people telling me what to do and pushing me around."

INTEGRATED INTO DIFFERENT TRACKS

Today, as immigrant children spend more hours in school than ever before, public schools are the principal institution for both educating these children and integrating them into the fabric of US society. Carola Suárez-Orozco and colleagues identify public schools' critical role in shaping immigrant youths' understanding of their place in society: "It is in school where, day in and day out, immigrant youth come to know teachers and peers from the majority culture as well as newcomers from other parts of the world. It is in schools that immigrant youth develop academic knowledge and, just as important, form perceptions of where they fit in the social reality and cultural imagination of their new nation."[21] Certainly, the academic role of public schools is crucial, as the returns on education have sharply increased over the past few decades. But public schools' socialization mechanisms are also powerful catalysts for the acculturation of the children of immigrants.

School is where the experiences of undocumented children first diverge from those of their parents. Through the institutions of school and work, undocumented children and adults are integrated into very different spheres of American life.[22] Adults are incorporated into the clandestine labor market, where they work alongside co-ethnics who face similar circumstances, speak the same language, and share similar cultural practices. They have few opportunities to enter into the American mainstream. Conditions for their children are quite different. School provides them with an experience of life outside the shadows. Their legal inclusion in public schools gives undocumented youth opportunities to receive an education, prepare for their futures, embed themselves in social networks, and become familiar with the norms and values of American culture.

Through daily lessons and regimented schedules, schools are powerful facilitators of the acculturation process, fostering among their students what Rubén G. Rumbaut calls a "unity of experiences and orientation."[23] In more nurturing school environments (e.g., smaller classes, schools within schools, specialized learning academies), these routines can aid in the development of a community of purpose and action. As primary social contacts, school peers can share traditions that promote feelings of togetherness and inclusion and bind them to a common experience.

Like their citizen peers, undocumented youth are incorporated into an educational system that grows increasingly stratified as students move into middle school and beyond. School sorting had profound implications for both college-goers and early exiters, shaping feelings of belonging, affecting identity formation, and determining access to resources. Schools structure feelings of belonging by slotting students into categories of "deserving" or "undeserving." As my respondents' narratives confirmed, these categories were reinforced by the actions and attitudes of school administrators, teachers, and peers. The small group deemed deserving felt increasingly "at home" in the school community while the larger pool of students labeled undeserving felt ever more excluded. The result was that the vast majority of undocumented high school students were left without the means to successfully move into adult life.

CHAPTER 5

Adolescence

Beginning the Transition to Illegality

In the fall of 2007 I received a cryptic e-mail from Misto, a twenty-one-year-old college-goer, asking if we could get together to talk. I called him right away and we agreed to meet at a café midway between our homes. I had not talked with him in over two months. He and I had first connected at a community group through one of Misto's community college friends, who told him about my study. His participation in the group had come to an abrupt, unexplained halt. Misto arrived more than a half hour late. His face was flushed and his brow beaded with sweat. I sensed that something was amiss when he explained that he had missed his bus transfer; during the six months I had known Misto, he was never without his car, a 1998 Toyota Camry he had bought used from a coworker who let him make payments. That morning, despite his carefully combed and gelled hair and his customary attire of baggy pants, polished white sneakers, and a loose-fitting polo-style shirt, he looked tired and older than his years.

> *Misto:* These damn buses. I don't know how anyone ever gets anywhere on the bus. Nothing is convenient. It's just a useless system. I'm really sorry to be so unprofessional.
>
> *Roberto:* It's good to see you. Is everything all right?
>
> *Misto:* Yeah. Well, I don't know. Things are really stressed right now. I feel like everything is caving in on me. Maybe it's not bad. I don't know. Yeah, I just don't know what to do.

Misto had not always been this open with me. It had taken me some time to gain his trust. However, over the course of our conversations, he had eventually begun to open up about some of the challenges he experienced at the large, Italian-themed franchise restaurant where, over the course of six years, he had worked his way up from dishwasher to busboy to server. I had learned that the job provided sufficient income to meet his basic needs, to save for college tuition, and to help with family bills. Misto contributed a staggering $850 a month to his household now that he had finished high school and his older brother had moved back to Mexico after jobs in the construction industry started to dwindle. He had attended community college for three years, and with the encouragement of a professor and a close friend he was planning to transfer to a four-year university. Those plans included clocking more than sixty hours a week at the restaurant. Meeting the demands of school and more than full-time work was starting to take a toll on his health, and it was cutting into time available for sleep.

Perhaps even more troubling than Misto's sleep deprivation was the uneasiness he felt at his workplace. His Greek manager, suspecting that many of the Latino staff did not have legal immigration status and would not complain for fear of losing their jobs, routinely berated them using racial epithets. Misto had grown tired of his manager's abuse. About two months earlier, he had returned the man's racial slurs with a few of his own. If not for the intervention of an upper manager who had taken a liking to Misto, he would have been fired. He was still worried. What if "the Greek" decided to call immigration? One of Misto's cousins had narrowly escaped a workplace raid the year before. That incident fueled Misto's worry, leading to chronic stress that eventually led to a gastric ulcer.

At the café, Misto sat down across from me, searching for the words to describe how he felt. Staring into his coffee mug, he appeared to be in shock. Eventually, he found a way to tell me what had prompted his request for a meeting, breaking the silence that had fallen between us.

> *Misto:* Beto, I don't know what to do. Things are really messed up right now.
>
> *Roberto:* Can you tell me what's going on?
>
> *Misto:* I don't think I'm going to be able to transfer now. All of that work has gone down the drain. I don't know why I thought things were gonna be different. But I really wanted this.

Misto explained that his father, Ivan, had been deported to Mexico the week before. As an experienced driver of delivery trucks who had traversed

California's streets and highways for nearly two decades, Ivan knew how to avoid trouble. However, a routine traffic stop became perilous when his work partner, sitting in the passenger seat of his truck, initiated an argument with a police officer. In an instant, the situation escalated, and as Ivan tried to calm his partner, the police officer turned his attention to him. Before he knew it, the officer had confiscated the long-expired driver's license that he had legally obtained in the early 1990s.[1] For Ivan, who lacked any other papers, the driver's license was his livelihood and security. He desperately needed to get it back. Instead, the incident led to his arrest for driving with an expired license, the towing of his truck, and a one-way trip back to Mexico. While Ivan was in jail, the police ran his record and found out he was living in the United States without a visa. They called Immigration and Customs Enforcement, and he was transferred to a detention center in Los Angeles. After two weeks without contact, Ivan phoned the house, telling his brother that he had been deported and would need money to pay a "coyote" to return.

Misto's family faced a critical dilemma. The money needed for Ivan's return would impose a tremendous burden on the family. However, the absence of their patriarch would take a huge emotional toll on everyone and also remove a stable source of household income. Seeing no other solution, Misto emptied his savings account and gave all $4,000 to his uncle, who would arrange for his father's return.

It had taken Misto more than two years to save that money. His eagerness to attend a four-year university had been the subject of many of our previous conversations. Now his entire first year's tuition was gone.

In order to transfer to a four-year university, Misto would have to start saving again from scratch. This would mean more hours at work and perhaps time off from community college. I listened to Misto as a barrage of emotions seemed to pour out of him about his circumstances. Talking in the café that day, Misto was caught in an endless loop of doubt and fear. He told me about all the hard work he had put into the last two years to save money, about his manager's ongoing abuse, and how his stomach was "tied up in knots." With a scared look on his face, he asked me, "How did I get here?"

Misto's question stayed with me for a long time. It was one that had an unsettling resonance with each of the young men and women I met over the course of my study. It struck me that Misto was not just referring to the incident with his father. He was taking stock of his present circumstances, an accumulation of status-related challenges—the difficulties of his low-wage job, family problems that had him taking three (or more) steps backward for every step he took forward, and the gauntlet of daily hurdles that were reminders of his limitations. He was measuring these conditions against what he had grown up believing his future would look like. Adult life was tough and unrelenting. Although Misto's childhood had not always been easy, it had held the promise of a better life. His transition from the world of youthful innocence—of school and friends, clubs, sports, and dances—to the tenuous circumstances of clandestine adult life was jarring. He felt confused, regretful, fearful, and angry.

Circumstances like Misto's and the emotions these conditions evoked are common among undocumented youth; as they move toward adulthood they are similarly forced to confront the meaning of their immigration status. This chapter discusses the liminal time of the transition between adolescence and young adulthood, examining respondents' often-traumatic experiences as they begin the simultaneous transition to illegality. Most young people find life-course changes challenging, but for undocumented youth these changes can be especially nightmarish. The condition of illegality, which is temporarily suspended during childhood and early adolescence, becomes a significant part of everyday life in adulthood. Adult freedoms and responsibilities collide with diminished legal options, resulting in lives stranded on the threshold to adulthood. At pivotal moments in their life histories, respondents struggled to find their footing in a landscape defined by legal limitations and stigma. As legal exclusions narrowed their options, stigma management shrank their worlds. The narratives of these college-goers and early exiters provide a window into this turbulent transitional period, demonstrating how different experiences of membership and belonging have shaped divergent responses to life-course changes.

"WAKING UP TO A NIGHTMARE"
Broken Rites of Passage

In US dominant culture, the transition from adolescence to adulthood is believed to entail moving from full-time schooling to full-time work and from financial dependence to financial independence, living independently, getting married, and starting a family of one's own. The movement into adulthood is typically associated with a normative time line—certain milestones should be achieved by a certain age. Recent hand-wringing about millennials' "failure to launch" in the media supports the normativity of this time line, regardless of whether it reflects an empirical reality.[2] Young people today are living with their parents longer than they were several decades ago, for example, and are delaying marriage and child rearing as well.[3]

For undocumented youth, the transition to adulthood is more complicated. As these young people leave adolescence, they enter the condition of illegality. This dramatic shift occurs because changes in the life course reposition the 1.5 generation, putting young adults into closer contact with legal exclusions. Life-course scholars refer to life events of critical importance as "turning points." These pivotal moments "knife off" the past from the present and restructure routine activities and life-course pathways.[4] The attainment of a college degree, for example, can serve as a catalyst for making important social connections and attaining better jobs. On the other hand, being arrested and serving jail time can negatively affect employment, wages, and the ability to vote. Turning points enable identity transitions and set into motion processes of cumulative advantage and/or disadvantage.[5] For undocumented youth, coming of age is itself a turning point: it begins the *transition to illegality*. Laws aimed at narrowing the rights of those unlawfully in the United States prevent these youths from participating in key adult rites of passage. The result is a stalling, detouring, and derailing of the life-course trajectories of thousands of young adults every year.

Many of my respondents' parents came to the United States in the wake of the IRCA legalization in 1986 and knew of people from their communities in Mexico who had adjusted their immigration status as a result. This knowledge, alongside their children's inclusion in the school system, gave many of them a false sense of security. They thought that by the time their children would face adult decisions, their immigration problem would have resolved itself. But time caught up with them quicker than expected.

Mounting Exclusions

As the circle of membership drawn around respondents by school and childhood experiences began to shrink, they confronted unexpected and unwanted changes. And as the terms of inclusion dwindled, everyday life became a challenge.

College-goers and early exiters uniformly described a jolting shift at around age sixteen, when their attempts to take steps into adult life were met by legal barriers. They spoke of stalled progress and abrupt separation from their previous way of life. Rodolfo, an early exiter from Long Beach, described his first experience of legal exclusion:

Rodolfo: I never actually felt like I wasn't born here. Because when I came I was like ten and a half. I went to school. I learned the language. I first felt like I was really out of place when I tried to get a job.

Roberto: Why was that?

Rodolfo: I didn't have a Social Security number. Well, I didn't even know what it meant. You know—Social Security, legal, illegal. I didn't even know what that was. But when I actually wanted to get a job, I couldn't because I didn't have a Social Security number.

Sergio was sixteen years old when he first experienced a similar shrinking of his rights. He had his heart set on buying a vintage 1957 Chevy owned by a retired postal carrier who lived a block away from his school. After much pleading from Sergio, the owner agreed to sell the car to him if he could come up with a $5,000 down payment. For the next two years, Sergio worked odd jobs to earn the money he needed. He was nearly halfway to his goal when he went to take the written exam for his driver's permit. That day, his world turned upside down. "I was told at the DMV that I needed a Social [Security number]. So I went home and my mom told me I didn't have one. I couldn't believe it. What was I going to tell my friends? That really sucked. I had been all like, 'I'm gonna get my car before all of you,' but I couldn't. How could I tell them now I can't, I can't drive? I can't get my license. It really messed me up."

Sergio's mother was actively involved in local advocacy work to pressure the California legislature to pass a bill granting driver's licenses to undocumented immigrants, so he was aware of the legal connection. However, he never suspected that he was undocumented and that his own circumstances would keep him from driving.

Incidents like the ones Rodolfo and Sergio described were many respondents' first encounters with the restrictions of their undocumented status. Until late adolescence, most had never been required to provide a Social Security number or other proof of legal residency. Their schools did not ask for such identification, and as youngsters most had little or no reason to provide proof of their immigration status. It was only as teenagers, when they attempted to participate in the same rites of passage as friends and peers—acquiring a driver's license, getting a job, or taking a trip out of town—that they suddenly found themselves facing barriers.

Some respondents learned about their undocumented status as young children. However, as college-goer Rosaura explained, that knowledge did not prepare them for the sudden experience of exclusion:

I knew since the age of six that I didn't have papers. I heard it a lot from my mom growing up. *"No tienes papeles"* [You don't have papers], she would say. But I didn't really understand what that meant until middle school. I heard about the GEAR UP program at my middle school. I was so excited when I took the application home, only to find out that I couldn't fill out the application because I didn't have nine digits. I felt sad, angry, confused. What made me different than the other students? Than my friends? That's when it hit me. If I'm not eligible to be part of a school program, what else am I going to be excluded from?

For early exiter Lorena, as for other respondents who entered the world of work early, the fact that she lacked "papers" was part of her everyday reality by the time she was twelve and joined her mother and sisters cleaning houses in the affluent neighborhoods of Yorba Linda. Even before she began working, her sisters often reminded her of her status. Still, "It only really hit home" when she was in high school and wanted to branch out to other work. When she began applying for jobs, she was asked for her Social Security number. "I thought it was time to do my own thing. I didn't realize how much I had been sort of shielded by family, though. I didn't have to talk to clients. I didn't have to show my paperwork. None of that. My mom handled everything, so I guess I was still kinda shielded. When I started applying for jobs I couldn't, I mean I didn't have my papers. I couldn't fill out the applications because I didn't have a Social Security number."

Prior knowledge of undocumented status differed by group (see table 2). More than half of the college-goers discovered their status when applying to college or seeking financial aid; almost one-third of the early exiters indicated knowing as children. This difference can be explained by many early exiters' premature entry into the labor market. As Art said, "You kinda realize it when you start working." Flor expanded on this point, recalling that when she started working at age fourteen, "Me and my brothers and sisters were told what to do in case anything ever happened. You know, like if there, if Immigration came. So, yeah, I knew I wasn't legal since then."

These narratives highlight an important aspect of the belonging-illegality continuum: being undocumented became salient only when respondents began to experience exclusion. Although they were undocumented as children, the experience of exclusion was not a tangible aspect of their childhoods. Even those who had some awareness of their undocumented status as youngsters did not comprehend the ramifications of illegality until much later, when they began to transition to

TABLE 2. STUDY PARTICIPANTS' DISCOVERY OF THEIR IMMIGRATION STATUS,
BY EDUCATIONAL ATTAINMENT (N = 150)

Discovery	Early Exiters	College-Goers	Total
Were told as children	21	7	28
Learned when applying for work	42	9	51
Learned when applying for driver's license	8	3	11
Learned when school activity involved travel	1	7	8
Learned when applying for college/ financial aid	0	46	46
Other	1	5	6
Total	71	79	150

adulthood. Blocked access to jobs, driver's licenses, and other important markers of independence prevented these young people from fully participating in adult life.

Dawning Awareness of the Implications of Undocumented Status

The new patterns and changed routines of respondents' daily lives gave them a glimpse into a future starkly different from the past. Janet (an early exiter) was still in school when she first realized how directly and inescapably her immigration status affected her life.

> I remember going to the [public] library to get books for a school report. When I went up to check out the books, I didn't have a library card. The person checking me out asked me for my ID. I froze. I didn't know what to say, what to do. I just started crying and left. This really changed things a lot. I remember my parents telling us what to say if we were ever asked where we lived and where we were born, but I always saw that as something we had to do so my parents wouldn't get deported. This was the first time I had to face the possibility that something might happen to me.

Early exiter Angelica said that by the time she was nineteen years old she could barely see any of her former life in her present activities. "Nothing was the same anymore. Everything I thought I was going to be, everything I did, totally different. It was like I was living some other person's life."

Once respondents began to grasp their evolving role as unsanctioned members of society, they had to find ways to adjust to this new state. This was not easy. Unlike their parents, they had experienced life on the other side. Experiences in their neighborhoods and school in tandem with the relationships they had formed along the way tempted them into believing that they belonged. Their exclusion felt like being cast out. They faced a painfully disorienting disconnect between their long-held sense of belonging and their present reality. The college-goers especially grew up believing that their successful acculturation and educational attainment ensured their social membership. Now they confronted increasingly frequent experiences of exclusion. Many described feeling unprepared for the dramatic limitations on their rights but learning to take precautions nonetheless.

> *Scarlet:* My school was taking a trip to Washington, D.C., and I had been wanting to go for the longest time. I knew some of the [students] who went the previous year and they really said they enjoyed it. So I was looking forward to going. Then I told my teacher I wasn't able to go. I think she thought less of me after that, like I was lazy or something. I was just so scared, like if something bad was going to happen to me. Like what if I got caught or something?

> *Misto:* I always felt like I was going to be better off than my parents. It was just that we were really struggling, and I had to, you know, I had to get a job. My friend told me about an opening at a rental car company. His uncle was the manager or something like that. He said that he [the uncle] could set me up with a job and everything. I didn't know what that, what I would need to do, but I got scared.

> *Esperanza:* I tried to keep it in the back of my mind. But when the whole college process started, it really affected me. I realized then that I wasn't gonna go [to my dream college]. I had to accept letting go of my dreams. Community college was just way below my standards at the time. It was really hard.

Liminal Lives

In his book *Shadowed Lives,* Leo Chavez employs Arnold van Gennep's rites-of-passage framework to describe a *territorial* passage migrants make as they transition from one society to another.[6] When migrants leave their former homes and social groups, Chavez suggests, they experience a separation from a way of life. But as they make the clandestine crossing into the United States, their newly acquired undocumented status presents several legal constraints that prohibit them from a successful legal incorporation. They remain in a liminal stage indefinitely.

Liminality refers to the ambiguous space individuals occupy as they move from one key point in their lives to the next. It is a "betwixt and between stage."[7] The concept of liminality accurately characterizes the late adolescent and early adult lives of many undocumented young people. As Cory described it, "I feel as though I've experienced this weird psychological and legal stunted growth. I'm stuck at sixteen, like a clock that has stopped ticking. My life has not changed at all since then. Although I'm twenty-two, I feel like a kid. I can't do anything adults do."

Among undocumented young people, the effects of liminality often appear first in the context of school and relationships. In her study of undocumented minors and young adults, sociologist Leisy J. Abrego draws attention to her subjects' emotional responses as they became aware of the mismatch between academic experiences and aspirations on the one hand and their diminishing opportunities on the other. She points out, "This can often create disillusionment for undocumented students, many of whom have already internalized US values that guarantee upward mobility for those who succeed academically."[8]

My respondents reacted similarly. They described the early stages of discovery as disorienting and debilitating. Suddenly coming face to face with the disjuncture between their dreams and the reality imposed by their immigration status negatively affected these young people's schoolwork and relationships. A loss of motivation was common; so, too, were more active responses—feelings of frustration and anger. Many started to lose hope.

Waning Enthusiasm

Respondents' blocked transitions were paired with feelings of helplessness and uncertainty—a sense of having no control over their lives. Confusion about the future constrained decisions regarding the present. Many respondents reported withdrawing from previous activities and losing interest in their schoolwork. For instance, Sandra (an early exiter) told me that her grades dropped dramatically during her senior year of high school after a chain of exclusions left her with few options "to feel normal." "I started getting Cs, which was unheard of [for me]. I just didn't care." Similarly, Lupita (a college-goer), who had received a certificate of recognition for perfect attendance from her school during her freshman and sophomore years, missed fourteen days of school during her junior year after a disappointing conversation with a high school guidance counselor who informed her that she was not eligible for financial aid.

Withdrawal from once-regular activities and patterns took respondents away from environments where they could spend time with friends and peers. Miguel (an early exiter) told me that when he stopped going to an after-school chess club he ceased talking to many of his friends. "I just felt unmotivated to do anything, and when I stopped going it was like that's where I mostly saw my friends. So, yeah, after a while I stopped seeing them." Likewise, Griselda (also an early exiter) stopped socializing after school and began going directly home every day. "It got to the point where I just didn't want to wear a mask anymore. I was really down and it got harder to hide my true feelings." Antonio, a college-goer, described the experience as a "living nightmare."

> *Antonio:* Everything I thought, everything I did, it totally changed. I felt like I was in this parallel universe, and I was looking at my own life in disbelief. I kept wanting to wake up. I finally realized that I had. This was my living nightmare.

> *Sandra:* I felt the world caving in on me. What was I going to do? I couldn't ask my parents. They didn't know about college or anything. I was kind of quiet in school, so I didn't really know my teachers. Besides, I was scared. What would they do if they knew? I was scared and alone.

> *Miguel:* During most of high school, I thought I had my next ten years laid out. College and law school were definitely in my plans. But when my mom told me I wasn't legal, everything was turned upside down. I didn't know what to do. I couldn't see my future anymore.

College-goers and early exiters alike described depressed aspirations. For many, the fear of getting caught motivated decisions not to participate. They chose not to take jobs, drive, or meet friends for social activities, but they also began to restructure normal routines. Griselda told me that her worries "took over all parts of my life. Nothing, nowhere felt safe." For example, "If you wanted to work, you were afraid of it. There's a lot of people that use fake things, but you're always afraid of what might happen or *si llega la Inmigración* [if Immigration comes]. I guess more than that, just being afraid of walking, of being in your city or outside your house and feeling that fear of what if I get caught right here in front of my house, you know."

Anger and Frustration

As respondents struggled to make sense of their new lives, a common sentiment was a feeling of having been lied to. They blamed teachers and parents and became increasingly distrustful of individuals and institutions as problem solvers. They also began to take out their frustrations on those around them. College-goer David put it this way: "I always thought I would have a place when I grew up. Teachers make you believe that. It's all a lie. A big lie."

As respondents withdrew from their normal routines and held back from pursuits that could jeopardize their safety and security, their dealings with parents and teachers grew strained. Cory locked herself in her bedroom for an entire week. "[My parents] thought that by the time I graduated I would have my green card. But they didn't stop to think that this is my life. . . . Everything I believed in was a big lie. Santa Claus was not coming down the chimney, and I wasn't going to just become legal. I really resented them."

When Cory finally emerged from her bedroom, she moved out of her parents' house, blaming them for "keeping me in the dark during childhood." While Cory and her parents have since made up, she has not returned to live with them.

I asked respondents if they could think of reasons why their parents might have withheld information about their immigration status. "They didn't want us saying anything at school," Carlos told me. Yuvi, a college-goer whose brother's early entry into work provided clues about her own status, explained: "It was not my parents' intention to inform me that I was illegal. They were too busy surviving. Plus, they did not want me to work. It [my status] was irrelevant at that point in time."

Carlos and Yuvi, now adults themselves, viewed their parents' actions as rational responses to difficult circumstances. But it took many other respondents several years to deal with feelings of anger and resentment.

As 1.5 generation immigrants, my respondents faced the dual challenges of acculturating to an American way of life and making important life-course transitions. These two processes are challenging for most immigrant youth, but they are especially out of sync for undocumented young people. The passage of time works against them. The important and defining pathways to adult roles and identities are littered with legal barriers that block their progress. For them, questions about identity and membership that most young adults wrestle with are recast from a cultural framework into a legal one. Finding their new lives governed by ever stricter exclusions, my respondents had to devise methods to reconcile their past lives with their new ones. And in the midst of this enormous personal upheaval, they also had to negotiate changes within their broader social worlds of peers, romantic partners, teachers, counselors, and administrators. Previous certainties—claims to cultural belonging and faith in their abilities to successfully navigate illegally inscribed lives—grew increasingly precarious.

STIGMA: UNDOING YEARS OF ATTACHMENTS

Until age prompted their unavoidable transition to illegality, undocumented youth spent much of their lives sitting side by side with American-born and legal migrant friends in classrooms, participating in the same social functions, playing on the same sports teams, and experiencing similar ups and downs at school. Contending with the practical problems of managing their legal exclusion, while difficult, was only part of their struggle. Undocumented young people also had to come to terms with the shift to a new, stigmatized identity—that of the "illegal immigrant."

Development of a Heightened Sense of Awareness

As respondents accumulated experiences of exclusion in their daily activities, they became intensely self-conscious. They began to change their habits and patterns. They spent less time in public spaces and ventured outside their communities less often. Some developed a heightened concern with appearance. Griselda told me that fear prompted her to more carefully scrutinize the clothes she wore. "I don't know why, but I was afraid of being seen as an immigrant. I told my mom that I needed new clothes. She couldn't understand. I didn't know how to explain it, but I started doubting myself a lot."

Griselda's compulsion to change her appearance highlights an important transition that was common among my respondents: their growing awareness of undocumented status made them afraid of being seen. The new perception of themselves as unwanted, as *not* belonging, was an additional contour of illegality, one uniquely shaped to the experiences of the 1.5 generation.

Respondents also reported worrying much more about what others thought of them. Miguel began to belabor simple decisions that previously required little thought. "I don't know why it mattered [to me] what music I listened to or what stuff I supported. You know, sports, politics, things like that. I didn't want to be seen as different. I mean, I wasn't different. I didn't change. But I felt like I had a big sign above my head."

Marked by Stigma

The self-consciousness that many respondents articulated reflected an awareness of stigma and a growing fear of how it marked their lives.

Erving Goffman's classic work on the management of stigma—that is, on the strategies people use to deal with socially discrediting attributes and behaviors—has been extended by others over the last several decades.[9] Social scientists use Goffman's insights to address the roles of social identity and social context in the lives of individuals belonging to politically or socially marginalized groups.[10] This research shows that to avoid rejection or disapproval many people with a stigmatized status attempt to pass as "normal" by hiding the markers of that status.[11] But hiding stigmatized characteristics or attributes can be difficult, especially for people who are members of several stigmatized groups at once.[12] This was true of my respondents, who faced both racialized stigma as Mexicans and the stigma attached to their undocumented status. These two sources of stigma were also linked under a politically charged discourse enacted in the streets, in the classroom, and on the playing field. It is worth noting again that both Griselda and Miguel alluded to an association between illegality and a personal appearance that was tied to physical traits routinely (and inaccurately) ascribed to all Mexicans.

The experiences of one of my respondents, Estefania (an early exiter), illustrate this powerful connection between race and physical appearance in the eyes of broader society. Her height (close to 5'9"), complexion (fair), and eye color (green) provide Estefania with a *phenotypic passport* that allowed her to cross—unchallenged—back and forth between the United States and Mexico through the border at Tijuana every month to visit her father and friends. Estefania told me that she estimated that she had crossed back and forth more than a dozen times.[13]

> *Estefania:* My mom would often send us [to Mexico] to stay with our dad. Like when I was in high school I had this boyfriend and I didn't want to go to school. So I would ditch a lot to be with my boyfriend. So, my mom said, "If you keep doing what you're doing I'm going to send you to Mexico with your dad." One day I came home and my bags were packed. She sent me to Mexico. I was there for like nine months and then I came back.
>
> *Roberto:* How were you able to come back?
>
> *Estefania:* I came back the same way with my school ID. Well, I'm light (laughs), so we would always cross back and forth, no problem.
>
> *Roberto:* Is your whole family really light?
>
> *Estefania:* My dad's side is. My mom is kind of *morenita* [brown skinned], but yeah, my brother is white. My twin sister is just like me, so we would

always just cross. Back then I had my school ID and I'd just talk like a Valley girl, like I lived in California. [At the border] they'd always ask, "Where were you born? Where do you go to school?" You know, we knew all the history from California so I could answer all of their questions. And I'd say, "Yeah, I go to this school." They would never think that I was actually living in Mexico. I didn't get caught once during that time. I mean it's much harder now. You're not going to be able to come back just like that.

Apparently, Estefania's looks, defying common stereotypes of Mexicans, led Border Patrol agents to assume that she was white and therefore a native-born American. She literally and metaphorically "passed" as a US citizen.

Among my respondents, Estefania was unique. In fact, I have never heard of anyone else who was able to cross national borders with such ease. Most of my subjects worried that their racialized features marked them as "illegal." Chuy, an early exiter who played sports throughout school, recalled that after he heard one of his white high school soccer teammates berate players on an opposing team as "wetbacks" and "illegals," he began to worry more about how *he* was being perceived. "I grew up with this guy," he told me. "We had classes together and played on the same team for like four years. But wow, I didn't know that [he was racist]. I don't know what he would say, what he would do, if he knew I was one of those wetbacks."

Chuy lived in a predominantly Mexican neighborhood and took classes with mostly Mexican peers. His participation in soccer opened up his social world to include others with different class and racial/ethnic backgrounds. His teammate's angry reference to "wetbacks" is a vivid reminder that the fates of undocumented Mexican youth are linked inexorably to the racialized history of Mexicans in the United States. This association, too, casts them as outsiders. The long-standing contradictions between US employers' desire for cheap labor and adjustments and revisions in federal immigration policies have contributed not only to a legal definition but also to a cultural construction of the "illegal" (Mexican) migrant.[14]

Constructed to Look Like a Threat

Since the 1980s, politicians, scholars, and the media have perpetuated a notion that Latinos, particularly Mexicans, are an "invading force."[15] This discourse depicts Latinos, by virtue of their many alleged negative behaviors, as engaged in a cultural takeover of the United States.[16] Central to this construction is the connection between illegality and criminality. Reactionary commentators and politicians routinely use *illegal* as a noun, as in "Illegals are taking over." This "enemies of the national body" rhetoric has become so pervasive that the terms *Mexican, immigrant,* and *illegal* are now each independently capable of conjuring fear and loathing among the general public.[17]

The negative discourse about Latino immigrants is especially powerful because it expresses both economic and cultural concerns. One set of arguments contends that there are not enough resources to go around and that Latino immigrants are taking more than their fair share.[18] Specifically, Latinos allegedly take jobs that otherwise would be filled by "real Americans." They also allegedly take unfair advantage of publicly available social services and drain taxpayers' monies. Equally forceful are arguments that cast Latino immigrants as cultural invaders threatening an American way of life. This position asserts the existence of a core "American" culture that is Anglo and Protestant and that is jeopardized by the presence of Mexicans. Writer Victor David Hanson, for example, argues that the Mexican invasion of California is leading to the destruction of the state.[19] Similarly, in a widely read essay in *Foreign Policy,* Harvard political science professor Samuel P. Huntington goes so far as to say that Latinos, and specifically, Mexicans, pose the greatest threat to "America's traditional identity": "Unlike past immigrant groups, Mexicans and other Latinos have not assimilated into mainstream US culture, forming instead their own political and linguistic enclaves—from Los Angeles to Miami—and rejecting the Anglo-Protestant values that built the American dream."[20]

This kind of political rhetoric has been tied to a growing pattern of physical violence against Latinos.[21] According to the Southern Poverty Law Center, hate crimes against people of Latin American origin rose steadily during the first decade of the twenty-first century. In November 2008, an Ecuadorian immigrant was stabbed to death by a group of Long Island teens who had decided to go "beaner hopping"—their euphemism for instigating violent attacks on Hispanics.[22] This incident is emblematic of recent anti-immigrant violence that claimed the lives of several Latinos, including Chilean exchange students in Florida, a Cuban-born immigrant in Arizona, and a Mexican immigrant who was beaten to death in Shenandoah, Pennsylvania.[23]

Vitriolic political discourse played out in public life takes a toll on the everyday routines and activities of immigrants and their children. As social scientist Genevieve Negrón-Gonzales persuasively argues, "Undocumented immigrant youth grow up not only exposed to this discourse but as individuals directly implicated within it."[24]

My respondents confirmed the impossibility of escaping the effects of the politically charged discourse on immigration that pervades daily life in the United States. As Sal (a college-goer) told me one day as we ate lunch at a food court in Santa Monica, when he and other young people like him are outside the confines of their own communities, the dominant, negative image of Mexicans reduces them to a stereotype; they are assumed to be good-for-nothing criminals: "When I'm in places like this, most places I'm in outside my neighborhood, people don't see me as someone who got straight As in high school, who is the first in my family to go to a four-year university. They don't see the awards on my walls. No, they see a Mexican. Straight up. I get followed in stores. The police always be giving me a hard time. They think I'm a criminal or what have you. So I have to dress extra nice, talk very proper."

Other male respondents said that they started growing out their hair midway through high school because police in their neighborhoods profiled young Latino men with bald or close-shaven heads. "It's just part of growing up in Santa Ana," Tony told me. "The police are deep in here, and they're always itching to give a beat down."

> *Eric:* It was more of a conscious decision to try to dress, look older. I don't want to say white, but yeah, not look like someone who gets profiled. It's really tough out there, with the cops I mean. They're always harassing us [Latino males]. It's more than just an inconvenience, though, 'cause you had better not be at the wrong place at the wrong time. They use any excuse to get jumpy.

> *Rafael:* I used to always get [my hair] cut short in the summer. Since I was little. Actually, my dad had clippers and he'd shave all of our [Rafael and his brothers] heads. I remember him telling me that maybe I would be better off keeping my hair longer because the police might think I'm one of the *pelones* [slang to refer to gang members, literally bald ones] dealing drugs. He thought maybe it would keep me out of trouble.

The recent deaths of African Americans and Latinos at the hands of the police in Ferguson, Missouri; New York City; Pasco, Washington; and other cities and towns across the country have raised old questions about the salience of race. They also compel us to examine the power of legal citizenship and to question its limits for certain groups.

The worlds of undocumented Mexican youth are framed by these widespread racial and cultural constructions of Mexicans as "illegals":

as criminals and unwelcome outsiders. As I explain below, the strategies college-goers devised for managing stigma involved trying to conceal undocumented status and working to assert counternarratives of themselves as educational achievers and community members. Ironically, though many reported feeling angry over having been lied to in childhood, they adopted lying as a daily survival strategy, making up excuses for their sudden withdrawals from school and/or peer activities.

College-Goers: Asserting Belonging amid Challenges to Group Standing

Most stigmatized individuals occupy two worlds: one, usually limited in scope, in which everyone knows of their stigma; and one, usually much larger, in which no one suspects their status.[25] Most respondents (early exiters and college-goers) kept their secret from most people in their lives. Interestingly, however, many college-goers found it useful to disclose their status to certain individuals within their networks. Choices regarding sharing were conditioned by perceived risks and rewards. With some teachers and counselors, potential rewards outweighed risks; among peers, the risks of disclosure often were judged too great. For many college-goers, the school setting provided opportunities to cultivate relationships of trust with teachers and counselors. Drawing on these relationships for support and access to resources, they more readily shared their fears about their future and sought out assistance in moving forward. As a result, many of them received financial help, guidance, and referrals to others who could assist them. But the stakes in peer relationships were different. Many college-goers worked very hard to belong. They saw being open with peers about their immigration status as possibly threatening their high standing in social groups at school and within the broader community.

Trust as a Source of Capital

As high school students, the college-goers had access to higher-quality academic resources and greater institutional support than was common among the early exiters. The college-goers' smaller learning environments (e.g., specialized academies within large public schools, honors and AP courses with caps on enrollment) allowed them to develop meaningful connections with school-based adults. Several college-goers recalled asking teachers or counselors for relationship advice, suggestions for dealing with family problems, and help with school matters.

> Rafael: I had this history teacher who always made time for us. He was in charge of this Explorers Club after school. We could always go to him with problems, like in school, with other teachers or [with] our other classes.

> Yuvi: My teacher was always there for me. I remember this one time when I was having trouble with my boyfriend. She took me and some other students out to like a girls' night out. I really felt like she understood me and that she cared. I don't know. It was the little things. I just knew I could trust her. And she never let me down.

Ricardo described a relationship with a guidance counselor who allowed him to feel comfortable enough to share details about his life no one else knew:

> There was this one counselor at my school. I used to go into his office and we'd talk about sports. He had all the MLB [Major League Baseball] replica helmets lined up on his shelf. He was really cool. So we kinda developed a friendship. He told me that I could come see him whenever I wanted to talk. It was just comfortable going to him. There were things I couldn't tell my friends, about my family and stuff like that. He made a space for me and that was cool.

Over time, the rapport Ricardo developed with this counselor grew into a bond of trust. He sought him out more frequently. During his sophomore year, Ricardo mustered up the courage to disclose that he was gay:

> I thought that if there was anyone I could tell, it would be him. But man was I scared. I didn't know how he was going to take it, if he would accept it. I mean, he was there for me, but this was something different. I had decided to do it though. I remember I was shaking when I went to his office. He was on a phone call, so I just sat there waiting. I just wanted to leave, like make up an excuse that I had to go, like leave and say I would be back later. When I came out to him, though, he was very understanding. He asked me a lot of questions, like about if my family knew and if I felt safe at school. And yeah, he actually thanked me for trusting him. He was the first one, well, you know, adult, I told. I don't think I told my parents until like four years later.

This affirming experience helped Ricardo when he started contemplating his second "coming out."[26] He felt confident his counselor would be supportive:

> I just went in there [his office] and told him that I, you know, didn't have papers and that I needed his help. It was more like I wasn't ashamed, you know, to tell him. But I was really messed up at the time and I didn't know

what I was going to do. He didn't understand at first, until I explained to him that I couldn't work and was [not] going to be able to get financial aid [for college]. He told me to come back in a few days so we could talk more. I just figured that he was really busy. When I [returned], he had all of this information for me. He really helped me out. I just feel like I owe a lot to that guy.

Ricardo's story exemplifies the benefits of trust. Facing multiple forms of stigma, he found someone with whom he could safely share his burden of secrets. After he made himself vulnerable by disclosing his sexuality to his counselor, his risk was rewarded by the counselor's acceptance. So when Ricardo began to experience the constraints of illegality, he knew where to turn. The trusting relationship he had built with his counselor gave Ricardo an important form of capital, which he leveraged to gain assistance. At a pivotal moment, there was an adult whom he had deliberately allowed into his life who ultimately shepherded him through high school and on to college.[27]

Many other college-goers also found that trusting relationships they developed with adults at school had far-reaching benefits. When it came time for them to apply for college, for example, they felt safe disclosing their status to these adults. That, in turn, removed significant barriers because these teachers and counselors who knew their status explored options for them. Rafael's experience is particularly illustrative:

When I went to the [community college] Admissions Office, they were asking for [my] Social [Security number] and I was like, "I don't have one." The lady at the administration said that I needed to apply for a student visa, which was going to be like, freaking expensive. So I went back to my school and [talked to] this guy who works in the office. I went with him and he said, "Okay, let me see what I can do." So he called [the Admissions Office] again and he said, "Well, I have this student, this really good student, and he's trying to apply there but he doesn't have a Social [Security number]." So they told him about A. B. 540. That was the first time I heard about it. The lady in administration didn't tell me anything.

With the help of mentors, college-goers were able to access important forms of financial aid and social and emotional support. Many of them received initial assistance from mentors while they were still high school students. Supportive teachers told them about small scholarships or suggested creative ways to raise money. Irene, from the Boyle Heights neighborhood of Los Angeles, was a third-year university student when we first met in 2006. She said her high school English teacher had been helping her ever since she began receiving college acceptance letters. This effort started when her teacher went to the teachers' lounge and took up a collection from her colleagues. "Yeah, she said she went in there and told the other teachers about me and started passing around a hat," Irene recalled. "My first year at Cal State was paid for because of all of her help."

During my time with respondents, I met many of the mentors who gave students continuing support throughout college.[28] Their help provided an invaluable boost that enabled students to stay in school. Such support made it possible for many college-goers to maintain positive attitudes about their futures.

College-goers' disclosure of their status did not mark them as outsiders or threaten their membership within the school community because their standing and their claims to belonging were based on their school participation and potential to be good citizens in the larger community. As long as they stayed inside the circle—by playing by the rules and getting good grades—their teachers and counselors were there to help them. These relationships allowed many college-goers to make seamless transitions from high school to college, thus moving from one legally permissible pursuit and semiprotected environment to another.

Strained Peer Networks, Challenged Membership

Within peer groups, college-goers felt much less secure about their standing. Many were embarrassed by their immigration status, and they worried about how their peers would perceive them if they knew about their lack of documentation. Most respondents went to high schools with sizable Latino student populations; in these schools most of the ethnic, racial, and class diversity was concentrated in the advanced classes. For example, Oscar described his honors classes as consisting mainly of "elite" Asian American students who overwhelmingly went on to attend college. These environments, while supportive, were also very competitive. Despite coming from struggling households, many college-goers worked hard throughout their school years to create narratives of academic achievement and to present themselves as indistinguishable from their peers.

> *Esperanza:* (Laughs) None of my friends knew. I mean, no one. I just felt embarrassed and shame.
>
> *Nimo:* I had really good relationships with my classmates, but I didn't know how much I could talk about my situation. I don't know. It was like something I thought that could really make things strained. Like, they saw me as one of them, but who knows how they might react.

Concerns like these led many college-goers to keep their undocumented status a secret even from close friends and romantic partners. This was not easy. To make their everyday life seem as normal as possible, they avoided activities and situations where they could be excluded.

> *Sal:* It was not such a big deal not driving to school. Like all of my friends took the bus. But it was like, it affected my social life. It's really hard to date. I couldn't go out with a girl and ask her to meet me there. So I think I missed out on a lot by just not even trying to date.

> *Dani:* You can't really do anything if you don't have papers. Like get a library card or rent a movie. I found out that the more I tried to hide my status, the deeper it got. I had to hide almost everything.

> *Nimo:* I couldn't even go to an R-rated movie without worrying about getting carded.

College-goers recounted numerous examples of manufacturing excuses for opting out of activities. Omar recalled lying when his senior class took a trip to Sea World in San Diego. Rather than explain that he could not risk going through the freeway immigration checkpoints, he told his friends that his parents would not allow him to go.

These kinds of incidents circumscribed peer interaction. Esperanza remembered how "terrible" she felt when her friends gathered to share their college acceptance letters. She did not want to tell them the real reason she could not go to her dream school. As an undocumented student, she was not eligible for financial aid and could not afford the tuition at a four-year university.

> Everyone was so excited. My friend got into Stanford and another was going to UCLA. I didn't say anything. I felt terrible. There wasn't A. B. 540 at that time and I didn't know what to do. I really had no clue what I was going to do. They asked, they asked me where I was going to go. I didn't want to go into the whole undocumented thing, so I told them I was going to community college to save money. They couldn't believe it. I mean, they told me that Stanford was giving them this much, and UCLA was giving them this much. I should be able to get financial aid, and besides, I shouldn't be going to community college. "You should be with us," they said. I didn't want to say anything, but I felt really bad. They were all happy and hugging each other, but I couldn't share in their excitement. I felt I had to hide. I was really embarrassed.[29]

Esperanza's story highlights a key aspect of stigma management among undocumented youth: concealment of disappointment. Even as she struggled to come to understand the effect of her status on her aspirations to go to a competitive university, Esperanza hid this internal struggle because she was unsure of how her friends would react to her status. Esperanza's friends were shocked by her decision to delay entrance into her dream school and instead go to community college, but Esperanza made herself appear happy about the decision.

For many respondents, acts of concealment became routine. As college-goers made successful transitions from their high schools to university campuses, they maintained double lives. Only a small number of family members and friends knew of their immigration status; everyone else was in the dark. However, these choices had consequences. Celina told me about the double life she had begun living when she started high school. In ninth grade, she earned entrance into a competitive magnet school. Many of her new friends took vacations abroad, and by tenth grade they were driving their own cars. This lifestyle appealed to her, and she took advantage of this opportunity to widen her social world. Celina, although dark-skinned, was tall and athletic. Her status in her school and social circles transformed her ethnic identity. Instead of being seen as Mexican, she was described by friends and strangers as having "an exotic look."

However, during her senior year of high school, the effort to preserve her double life became overwhelming. The number of activities that would have been risky for Celina increased precipitously that year. Lying to avoid these situations damaged Celina's social standing and strained or even ended many of her close relationships.

> I just stopped going out. I was tired of asking for a ride and coming up with excuses. And every time it was a hassle with my friends. They wouldn't let it go. They wouldn't let it go. So I just started telling them I was too busy with school. At first they didn't like that, but after a while they just stopped inviting me. I end up spending a lot of weekends by myself because most of my friends don't call me anymore. It's such a hassle to explain everything to people. And it has affected the way I am when I meet new people. I used to be very outgoing, but I try to keep my guard up [now], try not to get too close to people.

When Celina started college, she was hopeful that she could "start over." She began dating a young white man from an affluent family. He had grown up in coastal Orange County and was hoping to enter medical school after college. Celina liked the fact that in his world she could leave her problems behind.

I often saw Celina at community meetings, where I was repeatedly impressed by the way she facilitated dialogue between health care pro-

fessionals and community members. Her demeanor and her professional attire made her seem much more like the executive director of a
community agency than a university student. So I was unprepared for
the transformation I saw in Celina when I ran into her on her university
campus several weeks after a community meeting. I almost did not recognize her. She was wearing a sweatshirt and jeans. She looked as
though she had not slept in days and had recently been crying. We went
to a café to talk. She told me that her relationship with her boyfriend of
almost a year had just ended.

Celina explained that one Saturday morning when she and her boyfriend were having breakfast at her apartment, a segment on immigration aired on a cable news channel they were watching. "He started
going off about illegal immigrants, this and that. And how they should
be deported. It was disappointing. And I couldn't say anything because
he didn't know about me, about my situation, I mean. I couldn't accept
that or him anymore."

Celina's boyfriend knew nothing about her immigration status. She
had considered telling him, but fear held her back. The day after the
incident at her apartment, she told him that she had become very busy
with school and work and that she was having a difficult time balancing
everything. She needed some time to herself.

The narratives of college-goers like Celina drive home the extent to
which illegality penetrates the social lives of undocumented youth. Many
of these young people found a sense of comfort among teachers and
other adult mentors, but they perceived their standing within peer groups
as much more fragile. To preserve the status quo, college-goers frequently
chose to avoid potentially uncomfortable situations. Stigma management required constant effort. It was exhausting. For many respondents,
it also resulted in what they had been trying to avoid: it removed them
from their own social worlds. Ultimately, stigma management acted as a
secondary border in their lives, reinforcing legal exclusions.

Early Exiters: Coping with Outsiderness and Illegality

Early exiters and college-goers responded to transitions to illegality
with similar degrees of confusion, fear, and anxiety about their futures.
Their new awareness of their immigration status created a deep sense of
alienation. Both sets of respondents acted decisively to curtail activities
and relationships because others' awareness of their status carried the
dual threats of social rejection and physical danger. Like college-goers,

many early exiters hoped to avoid these consequences of stigma by withdrawing from normal activities and keeping their status secret. This approach was particularly costly for early exiters because, compared with college-goers, they were less integrated in their school communities, less likely to have trusting relationships with school personnel, and less likely to have strong adult advocates. For many of them, their friends and acquaintances were all the support they had, and to lose that would leave them vulnerable and alone.

Victor, a soft-spoken and fidgety early exiter, told me that he had not liked school. He was easily bored in class, and he resented being a target of "constant harassment" from school security guards. He and some other boys often ditched school to "drink 'forties' in the park." This routine lasted for several months of Victor's junior year. Then, one day he noticed ICE agents at the park. He recounted, "I got real scared. Started acting all jumpy when this guy Joe—he was this crazy white stoner guy—looks over at me and says, 'Look at the Mexican. He's about to shit his pants.' The thing is, I was scared. I'm not gonna lie. It's just that, well, I realized I was just about as scared of those guys [his peers] finding out about me. You know, what they would say. How they would treat me. So, I just stopped hanging out with them. That's about the time I left school for good."

Several other early exiters mentioned similar concerns about how their school peers perceived them.

> *Lorena:* I don't know. I just felt ashamed. Like, this is a part of me that I don't want you to know about. Everyone has their dark secrets. There are parts of us we are okay with sharing. That's the person they know. Then there are all these other things, you know, behind the scenes, that no one knows about that person.

> *Kathy:* It's definitely not something I would share with friends or even associates [acquaintances]. I mean, it's not really anyone's business. But you know how people do when they find out something incriminating about you.

Like Kathy, Manuel kept his status from his friends because he worried that they might use the information against him. He stated, "Even though some of them might've also been in my situation, I didn't want to have any of them use it against me for anything. People can turn on you in a minute. No way I was going to give someone ammunition to use against me."

In adolescence, when peers exert an especially strong influence over one another's decisions and actions, personal information can indeed be used like "ammunition." For undocumented students, however, adults' awareness of personal information can be even more consequential, especially in the absence of trusting relationships. As the previous chapter showed, students' position in the school hierarchy was important for accessing critical forms of support and capital. Placement in honors and AP classes strongly shaped college-goers' sense of belonging. It gave them solid claims to other identities—good student, high achiever, class president, valedictorian—that could provide a bulwark against pressures to leave school. Early exiters' placement in middle and lower tracks typically eliminated special relationships with teachers and classroom visits from counselors. Likewise, most early exiters were not encouraged to participate in school-sponsored trips to visit college campuses or urged to attend college and financial aid workshops.

Many early exiters were also disadvantaged by teachers' and administrators' perception of them as troublemakers. In some cases, their disruptive school behavior was rooted in frustrations tied directly to the barriers erected by their newly consequential but still secret undocumented status. For example, when legal limitations began to weigh heavily on Sergio, he started acting out at school. I asked him why he did not try to talk with a teacher or counselor. He replied, "I had problems with teachers. I didn't like them and they did not like me. I didn't like people telling me what to do, but at the same time I felt bad. I just felt like nobody there cared about me. I was a troublemaker, and that's all they wanted to see. Nobody knew me."

After a series of incidents, Sergio was expelled. Regardless of whether this outcome was justified, he was disadvantaged by a school culture that categorized troublemakers as beyond assistance. Sergio did not have positive relationships with adults at his school, so there was no one he could confide in or ask to advocate on his behalf. And because school personnel did not probe for the reasons underlying Sergio's behavior, the connection to his immigration-related problems went unnoted. Sergio had no idea how consequential these decisions would be, but they had the immediate effect of funneling him out of school and into a life of uncertainty where legal exclusions multiplied.

The troubles of many early exiters like Sergio went unaddressed because their status within their schools—either as troublemakers or, equally unfortunate, as invisible beings—provided no basis for forming relationships of trust or for eliciting the attention of sympathetic school personnel.

Unintended Effects of Enforced Secrecy

In addition to keeping secrets of their own, undocumented students bore the burden of family secrets. Parents hampered by jobs that paid too little to support their families and fearful of discovery and deportation often decreed that family secrets were to stay within the four walls of home. Many respondents grew up receiving subtle and not-so-subtle messages from their parents about what information they should keep to themselves.

> *Lina:* Yeah, I remember [my parents] telling [us] what we should say if we were ever actually asked about our, you know, information. Like my whole family had a different identity we would tell.
>
> *Juan:* There were just things we knew not to tell. I don't think my parents ever told us, but growing up, and I guess watching how they were, it was understood what kinds of things we didn't talk about.
>
> *Pedro:* One time my mom got really mad at me when I told my sixth-grade teacher that we were living in a living room. I guess she called my mom. She [mother] was very strict. . . . So I got punished for just talking about that to my teacher. . . . I learned not to say stuff.

Parent's efforts to enforce secrecy were a rational strategy to avoid trouble and to keep themselves and their children safe. But for adolescent children, keeping these secrets meant concealing large parts of their everyday lives and telling lies that were often hard to keep track of.

UNEQUAL TRANSITIONS

As the transition to illegality awakened college-goers and early exiters to a living nightmare, they came to understand that they would probably not realize the lives they had imagined for themselves. Awareness of the far-reaching implications of their immigration status came at a critical time. They were poised on the threshold of adulthood, ready and eager to move forward with their friends into fuller engagement with adult society. Indeed, their social relationships and years of public schooling provided respondents with both experiences and expectations of inclusion. But as they became aware of their lack of legal residency and what that meant for their membership in the larger community, they felt cast out. They experienced a trauma that destabilized their sense of self. They were forced to come to terms with what the condition of illegality meant for their lives and their futures, including being targeted by enforcement efforts and disciplinary practices and living in a narrowly circumscribed world of constrained mobility. As they awakened to the reality of their marked lives, these young people came to realize that their paths were diverging from those of their peers. Their growing awareness of this transformation into the stigmatized "other" led many to withdraw from friendships and to cut back on activities, thus making stigma a secondary, self-imposed border that reinforced legal exclusions. Keeping their status secret compelled them to lie about why they did not work, drive, go to college, or participate in nightlife. The lies were a constant reminder that they no longer belonged.

The diverging pathways of college-goers and early exiters described in this chapter reveal that the process of exclusion does not happen uniformly and that local and institutional contexts importantly mediate the transition to illegality. Largely because of supportive school environments, trusting relationships with teachers and other adults, and positive peer networks, college-goers developed the necessary social capital to counter some of the negative effects of family poverty and illegality. These advantages allowed them to transition from one legally permissible pursuit to another. In turn, moving seamlessly from high school to college provided the important opportunity to suspend many of the negative consequences of illegality, making it possible for college-goers to remain optimistic about their futures.

In contrast, a perfect storm of unfavorable conditions swept a more diverse group of young people, the early exiters, into untenable adult circumstances. Negative school experiences, resource-poor families, and the constraints of illegality strained these respondents' abilities to make successful school transitions. Many fell through the cracks or were pushed out of school. For many early exiters, leaving school led to early entry into low-wage work, a world they were left to navigate on their own because they lacked access to the networks of supportive adults the college-goers were able to rely on.

CHAPTER 6

Early Exiters

Learning to Live on the Margins

When I met Gabriel in 2003, he was twenty-two years old with little hope of ever joining mainstream society. Gabriel had moved to the United States at the age of seven with his mother and four of his older siblings, leaving four other siblings back in Puerto Vallarta, Mexico. He was expelled from his high school during sophomore year for excessive truancy and trouble with drugs, a coping strategy he used to reduce stress and anxiety. Out of school, Gabriel had difficulty navigating the clandestine low-skilled labor market, and a series of blocked opportunities left him frustrated and deflated. He was working only on weekends, and though he had earned his GED and started taking classes at a community college a year prior he was no longer enrolled because he could not afford tuition, fees, and books. To make matters worse, he was fired from his job when his employer received a no-match letter from the Social Security Administration.[1] The termination put him and his mother in a bind; they were unable to come up with enough money to cover the rent. Feeling like a burden to his mom, a single mother with meager income, Gabriel decided to find a place of his own. However, the no-match letter was an ominous indication of the dangers ahead if he continued to work. "I felt like a burden," he told me. "But I didn't know what to do. I mean, I don't know what would happen if I was actually caught. I love my mom and I want to help more, but I'm scared."

After being evicted, Gabriel lived separately from his mother, but he continued to provide her with financial support. Gabriel's mother moved in with her boyfriend, who was also undocumented and who worked as a dishwasher, but their combined income often did not cover their basic needs. A series of close calls with immigration agents several years earlier had left her scared and isolated. Instead of taking her chances with low-wage factory work, she remained an in-home domestic worker for over fifteen years.[2] Her work arrangement severely limited her social contacts; she had no coworkers and few friends to look to for support.

Even with the high school diploma he had earned at a local continuation school, Gabriel could not get ahead; he was no better off than his mother. Gabriel faced the cumulative disadvantages of illegality. His job options were limited to low-wage work that he might need to leave at a moment's notice. His high school degree and handful of college credits were no substitute for job experience, making it difficult to compete for open positions. He needed a steady source of income because he was responsible for his rent, utility and phone bills, and groceries in addition to the financial support he provided for his mother each month.

Sociologists measure intergenerational mobility by evaluating the gains made by subsequent generations in educational attainment and job mobility. For the children of undocumented immigrants, the bar is relatively low. Undocumented migrant laborers arrive with low levels of education, and because of their precarious immigration status they work for long periods in very undesirable, poorly paid jobs. Presumably, it does not take much for their children, educated in US schools, to fare better. However, most of their undocumented children, despite greater levels of education, end up in similar jobs making comparable wages because of limitations imposed by their own immigration status. Like their parents, the undocumented 1.5 generation faces strained financial circumstances, family need, and a lack of employment options.

This chapter probes more deeply into the condition of illegality, exploring the bleakness of the choices that confront undocumented young adults like Gabriel as they move into their twenties. Many early exiters feel marginalized in high school. Yet upon leaving, most discover that life outside school presents even greater challenges. Each passing year moves them deeper into the world of low-wage work, where they are repeatedly exposed to instances of exclusion, isolation, and stress. Early in their lives, youth of the 1.5 generation are easily distinguishable from their parents, but over time early exiters became indistinguishable from the larger pool of migrant workers. Adult life forces them to confront the daily dilemmas of working and driving illegally and the larger challenges of establishing a home under the threat of deportation. Still, many work hard to maintain dignity amid exclusionary encounters, poor working conditions, and harmful discourse casting them as criminals.

BOTTLING UP HOPE: LEARNING TO BE ILLEGAL

For many early exiters, "learning to be illegal" involved an even steeper learning curve than the one their parents faced. Like Eric, most had internalized enough of the American dream ideology to leave them unprepared for their new, curtailed identities as outsiders: "I had grown up thinking I was going to have a better life. I saw my older [American-born] cousins get good jobs. I mean, they're not lawyers or anything like that, but they're not in restaurants or mowing lawns. I thought, yeah, when I graduate from school, I can make some good money, maybe even go to college."

Respondents described their jobs as stressful and difficult. Simon, who had played piano throughout his childhood and adolescence, showed me calluses and cuts on his hands. "Can you believe this? I'm so far away from those days," he said. Many struggled to come to terms with the narrow range of bad job options their illegal status forced upon them. Janet told me that during the first two months she worked as a maid she needed to use a heating pad to relieve her lower back pain: "I can't believe this is my life. When I was in school, I never thought I'd be doing this. I mean, I was never an honors student, but I thought I would have a lot better job. It's really hard, you know. I make beds, I clean toilets. The sad thing is when I get paid. I work this hard for nothing."

Early exiters' youthful inexperience initially put them at a disadvantage in the low-wage labor market. They joined the same job pool as their parents and other migrant workers who had much less education but far more work experience. Many early exiters reported having trouble finding jobs of any kind. Others failed to stay in jobs after falling noticeably behind other workers. And still others were mistreated by employers who knew that these workers' lack of documentation left them with very few options.

By the time they reached their early to mid-twenties, most early exiters had left home and were settled into work and family routines. Their early entry into low-wage work meant that by this age they had accumulated the experience and knowledge to hold on to jobs for as long as possible. They also were now fully acquainted with the monotony and stress associated with the low-wage labor sector, and increases in their responsibilities to help out their parents and take care of themselves and loved ones kept them teetering at the edge of subsistence, no matter how long or hard they worked. Their earlier optimism was fading. Many had let go of aspirations for career mobility long ago, opting instead for security and stability in employment and housing.

Historically, for young adults in the United States, the move from school to work has been an important transition.[3] At the turn of the twentieth century, thanks to an expanding industrial economy, when young people left school they could expect to find blue-collar employment, job stability, and financial security. But today well-paid manufacturing jobs are largely relics of the past. Changes in the US economy and labor market have made educational attainment critically important for the social mobility of all young people.[4] Today's job applicants need a college degree to qualify for most positions that offer relatively good wages, benefits, and the possibility of advancement. For most of those who do not go on to college, entry into today's workforce involves intense competition for jobs that offer meager wages, limited security, few benefits, and insufficient opportunities for advancement. As a result, many modestly educated young people find themselves shut out of opportunities that could lift them out of poverty.

Scholars have long sought to understand the effects of economic and demographic shifts on the outlooks of young people growing up under conditions of disadvantage.[5] In classic works, Paul Willis (*Learning to Labor*) and Jay MacLeod (*Ain't No Makin' It*) probed deeply into the lives and attitudes of low-income, low-achieving youth as they developed theories to understand the ways in which working-class young people responded to the structural conditions framing their lives.[6] Willis understood the oppositional behavior of his study subjects as a response to their assessments that good grades and credentials would not be of much use for the factory jobs that awaited them.[7] MacLeod described this flattening of expectations and aspirations as "keeping a lid on hope."[8] While the young men in these studies assessed the opportunity structure in relation to their general experiences of discrimination and negative interactions in school, the chief structural barrier preventing both groups from leading successful adult lives was occupational mobility.

Early exiters shared these negative assessments of their prospects for work and chances for an improvement in their life circumstances. But their expectations were framed by a broader constellation of exclusions, limited options, and temporariness. Indeed, the experiences of early exiters provide unequivocal evidence that although educational attainment matters in the labor market, undocumented immigration status is the strongest factor limiting the possibilities of their lives.

The frustration Margarita expressed during a conversation we had at a Glendale mall food court in 2007 speaks directly to the link between illegality and the loss of opportunities for mobility. "I graduated from high school and have taken some college credits," she told me. "Neither of my parents made it past fourth grade, and they don't speak any English. But I'm right where they are. I mean, I work with my mom. I have the same job. I can't find anything else. It's kinda ridiculous, you know. Why did I even go to school? It should mean something. I mean, that should count, right? You would think. I thought. Well, here I am, cleaning houses."

When Flor and I talked in 2009, I asked her about her plans for the future. Her response was very much like Margarita's. At thirty-one, Flor had three children and a history of bad jobs. She had cleaned houses for seventeen years; during the last three of those, she was "looking for something better." Flor complained of back problems and occasionally wore a brace on her wrist. She hoped to find a job that was not so physically tiring and one she could "feel proud about." Instead, she moved through a long string of unfulfilling, and often temporary, jobs—waiting tables, babysitting, telemarketing, and working weekends at a swap meet. She could not regularize her immigration status because she had no one to sponsor her (her husband was also undocumented). When I asked Flor what she hoped her future would bring, she looked at me and laughed. But her laughter turned quickly into a frown and a sigh.

> *Flor:* It's really hard to move up in my position.
>
> *Roberto:* You mean your position at work?
>
> *Flor:* No. I mean my *situation.* My status. The best I can hope for is to get a job that's not so much physical labor. The kinds of jobs I get, there's no moving up, really. It's just maybe you can find a job that is not so [physically] hard.
>
> *Roberto:* So, in a way, it's kind of like the jobs you have also don't allow you to improve your salary or get promoted.
>
> *Flor:* Yeah, you could say that. But that's the thing. For people like me, there are no other kinds of jobs.
>
> *Roberto:* Sorry? People like you?
>
> *Flor:* Yeah, in my situation (looks down).

Flor was resigned to a life of limitation. She had once contemplated community college but found it hard to balance work, day care for her children, and school. She also found it difficult to envision education as a means to improve her limited options. She saw herself as different—marked by her immigration status and confined to a very narrow range of opportunities. But the limitations experienced by Flor encompassed more than just her job. For early exiters, the spatialized and racialized condition of illegality permeated nearly every aspect of everyday life. It narrowed the realm of the possible and circumscribed time to the immediate present. The condition of illegality subjected young adults to harassment and vulnerability, illustrating anthropologist Sarah Willen's observation that illegality is both produced and experienced.[9]

Finding Work

The range of job possibilities open to early exiters was narrow. Limited to situations in which employers paid cash or where the inspection of official documents was lax, early exiters generally took jobs in low-end, service sector work, light manufacturing, construction, and private businesses such as landscaping, housekeeping, and cleaning.

> *Art:* I've been doing landscaping for a long time. It's hard, very hard work, but it's very steady. I bought a truck a couple years ago. I've got all of my equipment, so I can go anywhere.
>
> *Miguel:* My brother got me a job at this restaurant where he used to work. Because of my English, I was able to move kinda quick from dishwasher to server.
>
> *Belinda:* I've had so many jobs, I can't even count. You name it, *las fabricas* [factories], restaurants, cosmetics, child care, the swap meet. Way too many to remember.

The industries where early exiters found work typically employed a disproportionate number of undocumented workers. Most positions did not offer benefits, opportunities to advance, or job security. Early exiters typically had little in common with their coworkers, mostly older adult immigrants who spoke little English and had attained only minimal levels of education.

> *Gabriel:* Barely anyone where I work speaks any English. Like, I'm the only one there who went to school here.
>
> *Daniel:* I don't really socialize with anyone [at work]. I mean, I don't cause trouble. I do my job. It's just that, there's like, well, it's a big difference between me and them. Besides, my Spanish isn't real good.

Entry into the labor market was a difficult transition for early exiters who found themselves in unfamiliar and uncomfortable settings. Many of the rights they grew up thinking they had did not exist at work. Moreover, many early exiters lacked the experience needed to keep up with a fast work pace. Others discovered that their English fluency and education were detriments rather than assets in the low-skilled labor force.

> *Josue:* Yeah, it's hard. Especially now, because they are looking for experience, not so much an educational background. They're looking for a more experienced person who knows how to work in the field.

> *Gabriel:* It's not easy getting those kinds of jobs. It's not because it's a good job, you know. It's that, you've got to be able to do a good job and you have to be fast. It's also, a lot of times they [the bosses] see you and say, "He's gonna be slow." Or, "He's gonna complain too much." It's not worth it to them when they have a lot of guys willing to do the job for almost nothing. The *paisas* [slang for Mexican immigrants] don't say anything when they don't get a break or they have to work on holidays. No, they want that. I've seen a lot of guys go in there who were raised [in the United States]. They don't last that long and they're always wanting something. I think that's the difference.

Navigating Precarious Work Environments

Even after they gained experience in the world of low-wage work, most early exiters found themselves in unstable, legally risky, dangerous jobs. At their work sites, many endured harassment, unsafe conditions, and harsh disciplinary practices. Josue told me he was fired from a factory job for going to the restroom without permission. Janet was let go from a hotel housekeeping job when she missed a day to take her mother to the hospital.

For many early exiters, workplace safety was a common issue. Given their limited options, they took jobs that exposed them to health hazards and other types of unsafe and physically harmful conditions. Pedro witnessed an accident with a nail gun by a young and inexperienced coworker who ultimately lost a finger as a result. Several early exiters were sent home at least once for injuries like concussions, deep cuts, bruising, and broken bones. In most cases, there was no guarantee that their jobs would still be available when they were ready to go back to work. In fact, many lost their jobs as a result. Early exiters also developed chronic health issues related to their jobs such as back pain, arthritis, carpal tunnel syndrome, asthma and other lung problems, joint strains, and skin exposure to toxic chemicals. More than half of all early exiters said they had missed work because of a workplace illness or injury. The dangerous work conditions early exiters described were typical of jobs employing undocumented workers. According to medical anthropologist Seth Holmes, "The structural violence of labor hierarchies in the United States organized around ethnicity and citizenship positions them [undocumented Mexican migrants] at the bottom with the most dangerous and backbreaking occupations and the worst accommodations."[10] That is, the legal, political, and social structures that constrain undocumented Mexican migrants' lives enact physical violence on their bodies through these workplace conditions.[11]

Early exiters' jobs are integral to the economy and to their communities, but they are not high status. Terms like *invisible* and *disposable* came up frequently in conversations about work lives. For several years Sonny worked as an orderly at a nursing home seven blocks from his apartment. His broad frame and dimpled smile served him well in a job that required lifting residents into and out of bed and helping them feel at ease while he provided assistance with personal tasks such as bathing and toileting. He enjoyed certain aspects of his job, especially "the chance to help make [the residents'] lives more comfortable." But his salary of $7.50 per hour was never enough to meet the mounting household expenses of raising two toddlers.[12] Even when he put in sixty-hour weeks, his take-home pay was little more than $1,200 a month. Without a Certified Nursing Assistant credential (unavailable to him because he was undocumented), Sonny was at the bottom of the pecking order, as his employer was quick to remind him:

> It's always something. She's [his employer] forever riding me about every little thing. Always telling me I'm too slow or [that] I'm lazy. That she'd fire me if she wasn't short-staffed. It used to really get to me. Ask my wife. I would come home frustrated every night. You kind of get used to, well, I am used to it by now. It just kinda sucks. Like, I really care about our residents. You know, this kind of job—you do a lot of, you get real close, let's say. There's no choice about that. I don't expect to be the employee of the month, or anything like that, but just don't make it so obvious that my job is so meaningless to you.

Sonny's sentiments were echoed by many other early exiters who also described feeling unappreciated by employers and customers, or worse, being treated with outright hostility. But few had any choice other than to remain in thankless jobs and carry on despite injury or illness. Not one of the seventy-three early exiters had health insurance, and most lacked savings to fall back on if they were out of work. Flor was an early exiter who kept working despite chronic work-related pain. "Look," she told me, "I've got kids to take care of and the world is not going to stop if I get sick. I've been working since, let's say more than half of my life, and I can't remember the last, the last time I wasn't in pain. My knees, my back, both of my wrists now. I don't see any way out, so I do what I have to do to make sure my kids have what they need."

Repeatedly Searching for Better Jobs

As early exiters transitioned into less-than-ideal work environments, finding and securing jobs typically required a combination of strategies: calling family and friends, visiting local churches, making appointments at community organizations, scouring local businesses for job postings, and even visiting pickup sites for day jobs.[13] For those with connections, the process was much shorter and smoother. But for others, long searches that did not yield stable employment led to frustration and disappointment.

During the summer of 2003, I spent several weeks tutoring Aldo, a twenty-one-year-old who had left high school at age sixteen. He attended the continuation school at a community organization to earn the remaining credits he needed for his high school diploma. He also used the organization's employment services, but he was eligible for few of the jobs they promoted. The staff job developer found him sporadic day jobs that paid cash and arranged semiregular employment for Aldo and a few other undocumented young men setting up and taking down carnival rides. At best, these jobs provided only ten to fifteen hours of work per week. Aldo needed more.

One day, Aldo returned to the classroom from the employment services office and entered into a heated exchange with his teacher over a math problem. Aldo stormed out of the room. From the hallway, I overheard the commotion and then saw Aldo. Behind him was Freddy, one of the staff members, who had followed him out of the classroom.

Aldo: I don't know how they expect me to do anything with these temp jobs.

Freddy: You're not able to find full-time work?

Aldo: That's all they're giving me. Some of the other guys are getting real jobs. Construction jobs that pay good. It just isn't fair.

Freddy: Is this because of your status? Your immigration status?

Aldo: Affirmative. I want to do something more. It's like I have nothing to do all day. I want to work. You know, I can work hard, I think, if I just had a chance. But this is ridiculous. I feel like a freeloader at home. Like what am I doing with my life? It sucks. It really sucks.

Aldo's frustration is understandable. Like other early exiters, he felt a growing restlessness born of the limitations presented by his undocumented status. His choices were limited to a narrow range of low-wage bad jobs without proper protections, but even within this range it was difficult to find employment.

Most of the early exiters had cycled through many jobs during the time I knew them. Their limited choices and the temporary nature of most of the jobs that came their way left these young women and men restless and dissatisfied. Hector, a twenty-year-old who was asked to leave high school during his senior year because he had missed too many classes, lived in Ventura and commuted thirty-five miles to Santa Barbara for work. He described his cycle of jobs:

Hector: I [recently] got let go from this landscaping job because a couple guys who were gone came back and they didn't need me no more. I was there for like a couple months. Before that I was delivering pizzas using a fake Social [Security number]. I was there for three weeks, but I quit because I heard they were checking them. Before that, I worked as a dishwasher at a restaurant, but I got injured there.

Roberto: What happened?

Hector: It's stupid. I was carrying a stack of pots over to my station and slipped on the floor. One of the pots fell on me and hit me right above my eye. I was bleeding like crazy and my cousin, who got me the job, told me that I have to leave because if it became like a big deal, he would get in trouble.

Roberto: Did you get any help?

Hector: Nah, I just left right then and went home. My eye was purple for like a week and a half and I had a big bump above it. It was pretty sick. I felt worse for losing my job.

As is evident in Hector's comments, early exiters experience not only the temporariness and instability of low-wage jobs but also the horrors of job sectors characterized by a lack of security and flexibility. Low-wage workers in the United States—those who care for our children and parents; clean our hotel rooms and offices; prepare our food and serve us in restaurants; harvest and process the meat, fruits, and vegetables we eat; mow our lawns and tend to our gardens; sew and clean the clothes we wear; and wait on us in restaurants and grocery stores—seldom have much job security, autonomy at their places of work, or flexibility to balance work and family needs.[14] These very workers constitute an invisible labor force that, while critical to the economy, is undervalued and unappreciated. Early exiters' entry into these jobs was a further awakening to their own marginality and limitations.

Adjusting to Limited Choices

American citizens and legal residents from disadvantaged communities with modest educational attainment face many structural barriers to securing decent jobs. But they do not have to worry about the lack of a Social Security number barring them from most formal employment, and they do not face a daily fear of identification leading to arrest, detention, and deportation. For their undocumented counterparts, legal exclusions not only constrict job opportunities but also narrowly circumscribe many other aspects of life.

Most traditional forms of support for low-income young adults are off limits to undocumented immigrants. Government-sponsored career preparation and development programs such as Job Corps offer young people with legal status vocational and academic training, as well as career planning, on-the-job training, job placement, basic health and dental care, and living and clothing allowances. These programs help low-income young adults gain a fresh start, accumulate skills, and position themselves to enter the job market at higher rungs.[15] The US military is also a long-standing source of opportunity for young men and women who want to start new lives, gain opportunities for steady employment, and increase their human capital.[16]

Noncitizens can enlist in the military, but in order to do so they must have a valid alien registration card (a "green card"). This means that permanent residents are eligible, but undocumented immigrants are not. The military's stance on the eligibility of immigrants is often misunderstood, apparently even by some recruiters.[17] Several early exiters indicated that they had been given false information about the military as a ticket to a green card.

> *Juan:* In high school, there were all of these recruiters at my school and they would talk to me about enlisting. Made it sound all nice. I was hanging around with the wrong crowd and I thought it might be good for a fresh start. I mean, to get out of town. Do something with my life. Then I was told I couldn't do it. I went in to the office and talked to like three or four different people, then the guy comes out and tells me I was not eligible to serve. It really brought me down.

> *Art:* I always thought it was an option, but it's not really for people in my situation.

Lupe: I was in the JROTC in high school, but I was told that I couldn't go further. A few of my friends served, but I couldn't. I just thought it was really messed up. They stress citizenship and ethics and make you feel proud to be a part of that, and I was. But I guess because I am not really a citizen, I couldn't go further.

Early exiters' outsider status was made clear to them at nearly every turn. In addition to their trouble accessing employment, entering the military, and enrolling in work-readiness programs, they were ineligible for health services, could not set up bank accounts, and could not apply for credit cards—limitations also experienced by their parents.[18] Early exiters' ineligibility for driver's licenses created ongoing tensions between obeying the law and carrying out the routine tasks that are necessary to daily life, such as traveling to and from work and taking children to school or to a relative's home for day care. For some early exiters, even imagining themselves as part of a world larger than the four or so square blocks of their neighborhoods grew challenging. For Blanca, legal exclusions and the grind of low-wage work had dramatically shrunk her everyday world. "My life has become really small, you know. All I do now is going [*sic*] to work and back. I barely have any time to go out with friends, and it's gotten really tough with my status. I used to drive, but now there are immigration checkpoints all around. My dad knows this guy who got stopped and they deported him. I don't know the bus routes too well, but it's not very convenient if I need to get somewhere fast or on time. I mostly just stay home."

Blanca's words poignantly describe an exile from mainstream life, a painful separation from a home she once knew. The experiences described by early exiters demonstrate the extent to which illegality restricts already limited worlds. As Jonathan explained, undocumented status seemed to close off every avenue for getting ahead:

> The way I look at it, it's like I'm playing a game at a disadvantage. There are those who have everything they need to win—good jobs, cars, parents with money, all that. But me, I've got all of these things in the way. I can't move one way because I don't have permission, and if I move this other way I could be in danger. Like I could be taken off the board [deported] like that [snaps his fingers]. It's a bunch of obstacles that keep me from being on an equal field with everyone. Given those odds, it's nearly impossible to win, to ever get ahead.

As Jonathan's explanation powerfully conveys, the transition to illegality dramatically chokes off a wide range of options most people take for granted. Previous studies of blocked mobility point to impenetrable labor markets or glass ceilings and human capital limitations as major causes. For early exiters, these challenges were severely compounded by their undocumented status.

Getting By with a Little Help

Finding jobs through networks is a well-documented employment strategy for most immigrants.[19] Early exiters faced unavoidable hardships that required them to turn to others for help locating jobs. Many early exiters relied on inside information about job openings provided by community organizations or employed family members, or they went to work in family businesses. These options allowed them easier access into the workforce.

> *Silvia:* It's kind of sad, you know. My parents came all the way here so I could have something better. Just last week, I started working with my *tía* [aunt] at this Mexican restaurant over near Santa Monica. I know it's hard for them, but we need the money.

> *Eloy:* At least I have work right now. I know some of my friends who are in the same situation who barely get part-time work. Of course I want something better. But I'm not really in a position to be too greedy with my job choices.

A few respondents pieced together additional hours by combining jobs they found through community organizations with opportunities found through family members or friends. For example, Jenny worked as an orderly at a retirement home, a job she had landed through her aunt, who was already on staff there. She supplemented the meager wages she made at the home by taking temporary weekend or evening jobs whenever her neighborhood organization's employment services staff could find them for her. Pedro was able to get weekend work through a local church and also engaged in entrepreneurial activity during the week, selling socks and lighters on the commuter train and an assortment of beauty care products around the neighborhood. As he told me, "If you can't hustle out here, you're gonna go nowhere fast."

In addition, friends and immediate and extended family members, some with legal status, provided sources of valid identification and the economic and social capital needed to buy cell phones, cash checks, and even apply for loans. Miguel told me, "I don't know what I would do without my uncle. He really helped me out a lot, especially early on. Neither of my parents have papers, so we're all on [sic] the same boat.

My dad's brother got his papers in the '90s [through IRCA], so he's now a citizen. He helps me with a lot of stuff. Like he put my cell phone in his name, and like little stuff, like a Netflix membership so I can get DVDs."

For some early exiters, family businesses provided the most direct and easy points of entry into the world of work, allowing them to minimize risks and bypass the job application process.

> *Belinda:* My family has a cleaning business. We do office buildings. Right now we have one that's eight floors, so we had to ask a couple of my cousins to help. I've been doing that since I was about fourteen. It's at night, so when I was in school it wasn't much of a problem. I'd be tired in class, but that was all right. . . . My mom has arthritis now, so I'm taking on a lot more of the responsibilities with the family business now.

> *Dora:* My *suegra* [mother-in-law] sells cosmetics. So, when we really need money, I go out with her. I can sell with her. It's kind of nice, 'cause she has lots of friends, and a lot of those ladies like the products. So I can make some money.

> *Art:* I got started in landscaping with my dad and my uncles. They've had their own business since my dad came here. They were here first, then my dad started working with them when he came. When I was in high school, I started with them. I got experience and then kinda branched out on my own. I still work with my dad sometimes, but he supports me having my own business.

The literature on adult transitions highlights the importance of family resources for allowing young people to delay independence and accumulate sufficient resources to make critical investments in human capital and lead successful lives.[20] However, the relationships described by early exiters point to something different, drawing attention to intersection of their life-course stage and undocumented status and their parents' limited resources and mounting needs.

While many young adult respondents utilized their parents' resources, their narratives suggested a more complex and interconnected web of support: from parents to their children, from children to parents, among extended family of different generations, and among extended family of the same generation. These bonds were cemented by undocumented status and the associated vulnerability and dependency. Reliance on family members was not so much a strategy as a necessity. It was at once a burden and a benefit. The successful completion of everyday tasks often required multiple bodies working together. But these interdependent relationships involved trade-offs, including stunting the growth of autonomy normally associated with adulthood.[21] Early exiters who worked with family members provide a poignant example. Relying on family for jobs and access to services made it possible for early exiters to accomplish mundane tasks but at the cost of undermining their sense of control over their own lives. Also, dependence on family kept early exiters' worlds local and small, limited their privacy, and reduced their opportunities for time away from family members. Kathy, whose family had lived in the same Carson neighborhood since migrating in the mid-1990s, longed for greater emotional and physical space: "Sometimes I just feel like I have no room to breathe. I love my family, but I'm with them all the time and it kinda depresses me. Like, okay, I work with my mom and sisters all day [cleaning houses]. That just makes me feel like I'm not doing anything with my life. Then I come home and our apartment is so crowded. Right now there's like ten of us in a two-bedroom. I have no space for myself."

Nevertheless, these arrangements provided benefits that spread out across the larger family unit. Many families with businesses pooled their wages or took their pay as a lump sum that was distributed to individual members only after the highest-priority expenses were met. Typically, pooled funds or lump sums were used first to pay rent and household bills, purchase groceries, and defray costs related to the business, leaving little money for family members' personal expenses. For example, Flor's family business cleaning houses in Orange County's coastal cities involved all family members of working age. The income generated by the business went primarily to household expenses, "and if there were leftovers [sic], we might get a little spending money, but that was rare 'cause things were always tight."

CREATING MEANINGFUL LIVES: THE AGENCY OF EARLY EXITERS

Early exiters have childhood experiences very different from those of adults who migrate in order to find work, but they end up in the same kinds of work arrangements. Their everyday lives powerfully illustrate the crushing force of illegality. However, it is important to emphasize that these young adults are more than the embodiment of an immigration status. Today's scholars have deliberately uncoupled community belonging from notions of formal citizenship to point out that immigrants often transcend the boundaries of territory and polity, carrying out their everyday lives in various social and political fields.[22] Beyond the formal legal and juridical frameworks that shape possibilities for immigrant belonging and exclusion are on-the-ground practices exhibited by immigrants and those who interact with them. For some, practices of belonging inhere in daily routines (e.g., taking children to the park, socializing with friends, or participating in a community celebration). For others, community membership entails advocating for the addition of a stop sign on a busy street, joining other parents in the community to demand changes within the neighborhood's schools, or taking a bus to the state capital to protest congressional inaction on immigration reform.

Addressing contradictions in his country's guest-worker program, the late Swiss writer Max Frisch poignantly proclaimed, "We asked for workers. We got people instead." In other words, immigrants, whether they are temporary workers or high-skilled visa holders, put down roots, form relationships, contribute to their communities, and ask to be treated with dignity. As Frisch's words acutely convey, migrants are full, not partial, human beings. They have needs, desires, interests, and emotions. And like other human beings, undocumented immigrants have multiple, overlapping identities. A worker may also be a spouse, parent, neighbor, teammate, and churchgoer.

Certainly, illegality permeated most facets of early exiters' early adulthood. However, it did not define the entirety of their experiences. Adult life was difficult, if not painful, most days. But early exiters did not passively give in to the forces that constrained them. To the contrary, most of them did what they could to push back against legal and institutional structures. With the deck stacked against them, they carried out their daily lives as best they could.

Italian sociologist Nando Sigona cautions against "construct[ing] undocumented migrants as passive and agencyless subjects overdetermined by structural conditions."[23] Too strongly emphasizing the force of legal and institutional structures can lead to ignoring individuals' full human capacity. The actions of early exiters contain evidence of resilience and resourcefulness, of measured risk and resistance. These acts of agency can be easy to miss because they do not fall into the traditional ways in which we view resistance. As I discuss in the next chapter, unlike college-goers who advocated on behalf of the DREAM Act or engaged in civil disobedience to draw attention to the disastrous effects of immigration enforcement practices, early exiters expressed their agency in more restrained ways. During the course of their everyday lives, they seized opportunities to resist and reject the barrage of actions and messages that cast them as outsiders.[24]

The Temporary Respite of Acts of Resistance

There is a large academic literature on school resistance, but it is framed by competing perspectives. The scholarship on segmented assimilation posits that youth living in minority neighborhoods are susceptible to negative influences by similarly poor minority peers who have internalized their limited chances of success.[25] An equally compelling body of work sees youth resistance as a rational response to unequal schools and to limited (and limiting) opportunities in the workforce for poor and minority youth.[26] As Paul Willis argues, working-class youth are aware that what will ultimately determine their fate is not the acquisition of skills or the choice of particular pursuits but the requirements of the low-skilled labor market. What I discovered from the narratives of early exiters was more subtle, yet equally powerful. Whether through delinquent acts or more mundane everyday life they endeavored to "feel normal."

For some early exiters, leaving school and steering clear of low-wage "immigrant jobs" were both deliberate choices that allowed them to exert some control over their everyday lives.

> *Pedro:* I had problems with school, but I preferred, you know, to not worry about it. I didn't need that, you know. I thought that I was cool, you know. I had my own money. I was selling drugs, and screw it, you know.

> *Luz:* It was like, what did I have to lose? I can have a better chance on my own. Like, that I didn't have anyone telling me I couldn't do this-and-that because I didn't have papers. Until it caught up to me, I had more fun going out and partying.

> *Flor:* I really looked a lot to my [lawful permanent resident] boyfriend back then. I thought that since he could take care of me and help me get my papers. I had my first son when I was seventeen. We were living with his parents, so I didn't have to worry about getting a job. I was happy just being a mom. But it was really hard.

Whether they sold drugs, joined gangs, had children, or partied with their friends, finding ways to exercise agency allowed some early exiters brief periods of respite during which their actions were not determined by their immigration status. Nevertheless, many of the decisions early exiters made as teenagers had long-term consequences.

Resistance to school and authority ultimately reinforced these respondents' disadvantaged social position and class oppression. Once they were out of school, their position was more, not less precarious. Most made early entries into the low-wage labor market. And in many cases, their exits from school went unnoticed by authorities. They simply joined a pool of anonymous dropouts. Few (if any) teachers or school administrators were aware of these early exiters' struggles with undocumented status, and it was rare for school-based adults to reach out to them after they left school.

Refusing to "Live in a Cage"

When common acts are rendered illegal, acting against the legal framework can be dangerous, with implications ranging from job loss to arrest and removal. However, as the narratives of early exiters convey, not doing anything can be emotionally and mentally numbing. As young adults, a small number of early exiters chose to avoid actions that could put them in legal peril. This kind of withdrawal from adult life became increasingly difficult as they moved through their twenties. The majority of early exiters risked their own security to leave their homes every day to support families and to participate in life around them. As Silvia told me, "I refuse to live in a cage. It's hard to breathe like that."

Work routines structured much of early exiters' time. Employment was a source of both livelihood and threat. Securing work and holding on to jobs was essential. But long work hours kept early exiters away from their families and generated constant stress. Would they suddenly lose their job? Would there be an ICE raid? Even under these conditions, early exiters worked hard to create identities that captured more than their undocumented immigration status. Hector, for example, put it this way: "I guess I am undocumented, or whatever you call it. But it's like I don't really consider myself an immigrant. It might sound a little funny to say it like that. Like I'm illegal, I don't have papers. But it's not how I think about myself. I don't know if that makes sense. I just don't think my [legal] situation should, you know, define me."

Many of these young men and women had little reason to trust the institutions and institutional actors in their lives to address their needs. Nevertheless, among more intimate contacts, they managed to form communities of belonging. For some, these relationships were forged early on and were based on common bonds with classmates or neighbors. Jonathan described his childhood friendships as an important source of trust and support: "I had some hard times when I was younger. There are two friends, well, two people I can really call friends, who have always had my back. They knew me when I was young, so by now they know everything, all my secrets. I know I can go to them with anything. I think I'd be lost without them. They're like my life support."

Aldo's comments draw attention to how the shared experience of being outside the circle of membership can provide opportunities for friendship: "Most of my friends I hang out with now I knew from school and my old neighborhood. They're kinda also having a hard time getting going with their life. You know, they didn't finish high school and they're either still living with their parents or couch surfing with friends or other random people they know. That's like me. All of them know about my situation. Some of them are also illegal."

Taking Risks

Early exiters are forced to confront the discomforts, frustrations, and real dangers associated with working illegally. They face difficult choices every day. The most mundane tasks put them in jeopardy of arrest and deportation. Many early exiters used aliases to get jobs, cash checks, and even drive. But this strategy had its own risks. After Pedro completed a day labor job in 2002, the employer gave him a check in payment for his work. When Pedro tried to cash the check, the teller at the local currency exchange called Pedro's employer to verify the check. The employer denied writing the check, and the police were summoned. They found multiple sets of identification on Pedro and arrested him. He spent eighteen days in jail and had to serve a three-year probation sentence.

Many early exiters learned similarly difficult lessons. Some tried to minimize potential contact with authorities by finding rides with coworkers or taking public transportation. I met several young women who used the bus each morning to take their children to day care and then to get themselves to work. They doggedly repeated this long commute in reverse at the end of each workday.

It is very difficult for undocumented young adults to avoid breaking the law. The majority of early exiters work clandestinely, and most also choose to drive without a license at least 50 percent of the time. Beyond legal exclusions from work and driving loom numerous other barriers. Many taken-for-granted activities, such as buying a cell phone, applying for a credit card, obtaining a library card, or renting a movie, require a state-issued form of identification. Without these legitimizing emblems of membership, it is difficult to carry out even simple pursuits without assistance from friends or family members. Many of my respondents felt they had no choice but to buy false documents.

Several early exiters maintained the hope of adjusting their status through family members. They were especially fearful of taking jobs or engaging in illegal activity that might jeopardize the process of changing their status. This kind of caution often led to feelings of paralysis, of an inability to move in any direction. In 2004, Sergio, whose stepfather (a lawful permanent resident) had filed the necessary paperwork to sponsor him, his brother, and their mother, discussed his situation with me. His three-year wait left him in limbo. "Once he [my brother] fixes his papers, he's gonna go back to school," he told me. ". . . He's married to a citizen but still it takes time. . . . Supposedly, I'm waiting for their approval, but you know, now everyone has told me once the approval comes, you have to wait six months being approved so I can get a work permit. I don't know what to do. I've been waiting for three years."

Sergio's long wait brought him ever nearer to his twenty-first birthday, when he would age out of eligibility for parental sponsorship. At twenty years old, he worked only occasionally, taking temporary jobs in catering or helping at parties for a day or weekend. He avoided all forms of ongoing employment: "The thing is that I've been offered jobs, but the thing is that it messes me up. There's ways around it, but let's say okay, there's a job I've been offered. If I get it, I have to buy fake papers. If I get caught with fake papers, that's a federal offense, so I'll be screwed. And I mean, I'm closer than I've ever been on getting my papers. I don't want to mess it up with something like that so I can't get it later on."

Sergio chose to take the safe route in hopes of someday being able to work without the burden of constant worry. Nevertheless, he was becoming frustrated with the wait. He felt stuck. He told me, "When you don't have papers you're not really motivated . . . you can't go anywhere."

In contrast, Luz's efforts to regularize her status failed twice. First, she aged out of eligibility before her mother could petition a green card for her. Then, her husband of six years, also a green-card holder at the time, was arrested for giving a ride to an undocumented coworker and was charged with alien smuggling. After his arrest, her husband was incarcerated and deported upon release. Luz's hopes for a change in her status dwindled. At twenty-four, she knew better than to count on good luck. She was raising three children by herself in a tiny apartment in Pomona. With few remaining options, Luz continued to work as a cashier at a neighborhood hamburger stand despite earning only minimum wage and enduring constant verbal harassment from her racist employer. She recognized her immigration status as the most salient barrier to success. But she saw little likelihood of change.

Respondents' narratives made it clear that they were fearful of the police and of ICE surveillance in and around their communities. They learned the safest routes to get from point A to point B, and they limited their social activity. With time, these routines began to feel increasingly constraining. Many respondents took risks so they could, as Eloy told me, "enjoy a life that wasn't determined by my status."

> For a while I kind of got used to staying in. I still live with my parents, and my dad is very protective. I mean, I don't blame him, but it's kind of hard. Like I don't want to feel like I'm in jail, you know. I used to basically go to work and then straight home. But I started to feel like, "Screw it. I want to have a life." So I started doing things I used to do, like going to movies and concerts. I go with friends sometimes, but I also go by myself. It used to feel like I was doing something wrong, but [now] it actually feels good, like I can actually have a life.

Silvia was even more amenable to taking chances. An early experience of disclosure gave her courage to battle against fear. She told me she did not want anything holding her back from fully participating in life:

> I try to not let my status keep me from doing the things I want to do. Probably the scariest thing I've done was coming out [as a lesbian] to my parents. Once I did that, I felt I could do anything. I don't want to regret things later on. Sure, I could be picked up by ICE just walking out my door, but I could also die from some random illness. That shouldn't stop me from having a full life. Besides, I don't want to give them [immigration authorities] the satisfaction of knowing they control me.

Silvia's narrative highlights the double closet occupied by many undocumented lesbian, gay, and transgender individuals. Their process of coming out, while dangerous, also provides some with a sense of liberation. Pulitzer Prize–winning journalist Jose Antonio Vargas described this process in his own life as difficult yet empowering.[27] Like Vargas, Silvia found that once she came out as a lesbian to her parents she was bolder about the choices she made to spend time in public spaces.

The Ongoing Importance of Early Friendships

Other early exiters sought out community supports for help with issues ranging from isolation to partner abuse. Blanca became involved with an older white man she met online. Shortly after they started dating, he became physically and emotionally abusive. He made several threats that he would report her to authorities if she reported the abuse.[28] She told me, "You know what's the worst thing about my status? It makes me vulnerable. I really liked this guy. I really poured out my heart to him. He was so soft and gentle in the beginning. Then he used it all against me, everything. First he told me that he was going to tell my boss if I ever broke up with him. Then he got kind of physically abusive too. I didn't have anywhere to turn. It was terrible."

Eventually, Blanca confided in a friend who referred her to a domestic violence clinic that helped her get back on her feet. "I felt completely powerless to do anything. They helped me get a new start, you can say. I was in a really bad place, and they showed me that I had the power to change things for me. I really appreciate that, and I think it's made me stronger."

Blanca's experience with domestic violence and a lack of power due to her undocumented status is similar to that of other undocumented women. Like other women in her situation, she had few avenues to seek help. Finding a friend she could trust provided her means to move beyond her perceived limitations.

Because work was central to the lives of most early exiters, the workplace was a common source of social contacts. Although some early exiters initially felt no affinity with their migrant coworkers, others recognized and responded to similarities, and others grew to recognize their common plight. In the world of low-wage work in factories, restaurants, housecleaning, and landscaping, many of their coworkers also lived on the margins. Jonathan explained: "I've met some cool people at my job. Most of them have only been here [in the United States] for a couple years. They don't speak much English, but my Spanish is okay. Like, I speak it at home with my parents. I can understand, you know, what they go through, their struggles living in this country. They're cool, you know. So, yeah, sometimes I hang out with them after work. Go get a beer or something like that."

Learning Solidarity with Other Undocumented Migrants

A common plight with other undocumented immigrants was an important basis for social connection. Over time, several early exiters began to look to their more experienced migrant coworkers for help. Despite differences of language and US experience, these first-generation peers had more experience with migrant life, were better connected, and were more adept at finding community resources. These relationships were an important source of support and of what Aldo called "on-the-job training."

> *Aldo:* My coworker was noticing I was wearing the same clothes all the time, and she approached me during our lunch break. And she was like, *"Tú no tienes papeles* [you don't have papers], right?" I said, "What, is it stamped on my forehead?" And she tells me about some resources [places that provide help regardless of legal status] over in Oxnard.
>
> *Aldo (different interview):* Actually, I've learned a lot from my coworkers. Like where I can go to receive help, like services I'm eligible for, places to avoid where they might have checkpoints set up, things like that. Many of my other friends don't know my status anyway; and besides, they have papers, so they don't know these kinds of things. It's been helpful to know others who are in my shoes. I feel like I can be myself too, not having to hide.

Belinda met an older woman at a garment factory who took her in, treating her like a daughter. She lived with this coworker for a few months after she broke up with her boyfriend. When I spoke to Belinda in 2009, she was living on her own, but she had remained in regular contact with this friend. "She calls me sometimes, tells me about jobs, like who's hiring, what I should avoid. You know, where they treat you like shit. I appreciate her advice."

Early exiters formed relationships in a variety of community spaces. Some relationships blossomed into romance. These unions counterbalanced some early exiters' fear that their lives had ended when they reached adulthood. Relationships made some respondents feel less alone and gave them confidence to engage more with the world around them. Silvia and her partner Rosie met in their midtwenties. They had been together for almost two years when I met Silvia. She recounted how they had met:

> I met my partner Rosie there. We had the same tutor and everyone was like, "Hey, she likes you." At first she didn't have any time for me. To be honest, I think she thought I was kind of an asshole. But we started hanging out. First at lunch with a few other students. We got along really good. We'd crack jokes about the other students and we'd share snacks and things. But I didn't think she, you know, liked women. Finally I got up the nerve to ask her after class. She says I worked my way in (laughs). . . . What I appreciate about Rosie is that I know she's got my back 110 percent. We've been through a lot already and she's just always there for me. It's hard to explain, but I feel that sense of security with her. People say I've changed a lot. It just feels right.

Using Community Organizations to Find and Connect with Peers

Many communities within the five-county Los Angeles metropolitan area are densely populated with community organizations like the ones where many early exiters found jobs. These centers offer community members much-needed opportunities to meet and engage with peers, receive information, and escape the fear and stigma attached to their undocumented identities. In addition to offering important services and resources, caring staff facilitated social activity and the formation of relationships. Many early exiters learned of these organizations through Internet searches, their parents' efforts, referrals from parish priests, and court mandates.

Early exiters also forged connections with peers in the GED classes or continuation schools that community centers hosted. Carla was reluctant to enroll in a continuation school after being out of school for a little over four years. But she reconsidered after she was let go by her employer. She found a school that was a short bus ride from her home in Whittier. She told me that she felt as though she benefited as much or more from the social atmosphere. "I like going there. It's a place that feels comfortable, and I've met a lot of the other students there and they understand me more than I think anyone else [does]. I don't have to explain things to them; it just clicks. And that feels like a big load off my back to not to have to hide who I am."

After conducting an informal survey, the staff at a community center in Riverside found that their students wanted to engage in social activity beyond their GED classes. So the staff started affinity and leadership groups aimed at fostering a sense of community and building skills. Josue, who participated in a men's support group, became the center's most vocal supporter, recruiting several other males to join the support group. "Before, I felt like no one really understood me. But here, it's like family, a family of social misfits (laughs). No, no, seriously, it's true. We're a group of banged-up and wounded individuals. Like they say, we leave drama at the door. I've made some really good friends here. We do a lot together outside of here, I mean. They're my homies."

Community organizations were also helpful as mental and emotional health resources.[29] While early exiters were ineligible for most forms of care and benefits, some local organizations reached out to community members regardless of immigration status. Manuel's priest told him about a community mental health clinic in Santa Ana. It took several weeks before he could bring himself to walk in the door, but he eventually started seeing a counselor at the clinic to talk about the feelings of anger and frustration he was experiencing. As he described it,

> It's been really helpful to have someone to talk to on a regular basis. I don't go every week, but it's cool to be able to have a sounding board to be able to talk about some of the things I'm thinking. I've only been to the group sessions they have a couple times, but I like talking to the counselors there. If you told me five years ago that I would be seeing a therapist, I would have laughed at you. It's just not something that especially men in my culture do. But I'm really thankful to have this service. It's helped me a lot.

Joining Clubs, Teams, and Artistic Groups "to Be Part of Something"

Early exiters also engaged in ongoing activities that, while increasing their risks of being apprehended, connected them more fully to their communities and expanded their social contacts. Several managed to find time, outside work and family commitments, to take part in informal groups or clubs. A few participated in sports leagues, community dance circles, drum groups, and other types of artistic expression

> *Blanca:* I might not be very successful. I'm surely not in the place I thought I would be when I was younger. But I'm more than just my status. They try to reduce you to that, an "illegal," and that really limits what you can do. But I'm a person. I don't know how to say it, but it's like I refuse to live in a box. I started going to this [community] center downtown where they play *son jarocho* music [Mexican folk music particular to Veracruz]. I've never had any real talent for music, but they explained to me that it wasn't important. They emphasized that what was most important [was] that I come and participate. That together we make up a community. I really liked that. I've learned how to play the *jarana* [guitar-shaped, fretted stringed instrument from the southern region of Veracruz] [a] little and I dance. It's really amazing when we throw fandangos and everyone is together, playing and dancing.[30] It's my community. It's really beautiful to be part of something so powerful.

> *Sonny:* I'm on a bowling league every Thursday. I guess that's my social activity every week. It's one place where I can put everything out of my mind. I can just be me, not any negative stereotype. I have a good time with my friends. We drink and just have fun. I'm also very competitive, so it's like a friendly competition, and our team is really good. That's also a positive aspect; I feel like I'm a part of something.

> *Jonathan:* I got invited by one of my coworkers to play on his soccer team. One of his teammates got hurt and I had told him that I used to play. It's a lot of fun. At first I didn't know if I would fit in. You know, it's kind of

all *paisas*. No one speaks English. But actually, I have more in common with them than [with] many of the people I went to school with.

In Jonathan's community, more than twelve thousand soccer players (mostly immigrants) at all competitive levels play in leagues every year. Most of Jonathan's teammates are immigrants, and most came to the United States as adults. As he and other early exiters found, participation in sports is enjoyed at the level of school and community by young and old, by immigrants and native born, by those who are legal and those who are undocumented.

Whether on a stage at the local community center or a field at the park, these activities provided brief opportunities for early exiters to leave their status behind. Some felt free to temporarily take on alternative identities. Joanna stated, "I play competitive fast pitch softball. No one on my team knows about my situation. I can be somebody else. I don't know if I'd ever tell them. For those two hours I'm not so-and-so the undocumented immigrant. I can be me, just me. It's a good outlet for all my stress."

Joanna's comments poignantly convey an important point: illegality does not go away, but neither does it have to overpower every facet of adult life. The efforts early exiters made to engage in community building and to carve out safe spaces offer useful reminders of their agency. These actions also make visible the moments in their days and the spaces in their worlds where their immigration status was less consequential. Many facets of their lives were indeed beyond their control. But by maximizing experiences in which immigration status could be temporarily set aside, they enlarged the opportunities to be active agents in their own lives.

Many early exiters' narratives highlight the personal significance of occasions when they felt free to be themselves. These respondents' determination to define themselves as more than their immigration status is important theoretically as well and should be addressed in discussions about illegality and belonging. Nevertheless, in the face of legal exclusions, backbreaking work, and the ever-present threat of removal, moments of freedom from the burden of undocumented status represented a very small part of early exiters' daily lives.

DIMINISHED HOPES

Eventually, early exiters lowered the threshold for the type of work they would accept. They stayed in jobs that posed risks to their health. They put up with supervisors who verbally abused them, using racial epithets and slurs. They put up with employers who physically abused them, requiring long hours on the job and no breaks. They labored in dangerous environments. And they ignored aches and pains. While many were initially appalled and angered by such circumstances, they gradually stopped complaining. Over time, most early exiters became accustomed to undocumented life. As Mario told me, they learned to "handle [their] own." But even as they gained skills and experience that made them more competitive in the job market and developed strategies to minimize the risks of being apprehended, learning to be illegal also moved them away from any semblance of their earlier American life and closer to the life of the undocumented laborer.

Along the way to their adult lives, many early exiters also lost sight of dreams of going to college, of holding better jobs, of living free from stress and fear. The daily grind of undocumented life left them expecting very little. Certainly, at younger ages they had much loftier visions of their futures. But many of their hopes flattened over time and their dreams died. Day-to-day struggles, stress, and the ever-present ceiling on opportunities forced them to acknowledge the distance between their prior aspirations and their present realities. The sense of hopelessness many expressed grew out of the confluence of legal limitations, a world shrunken by their station in life and the struggle to make ends meet.

Some of the difficulties of undocumented life were mitigated by relationships and by participation in activities and community life. But early exiters found it deeply frustrating to see documented and citizen friends, and sometimes family members, moving forward with their lives, even in very modest ways, while their own status kept them frozen in place. Ramon's trajectory provides a vivid example of this problem. He and his brother Jose had been very close growing up. Jose was sixteen months younger than Ramon and had been born in Los Angeles as a US citizen. Both Ramon and Jose had spent their early childhoods in Mexico with their maternal grandmother because their mother could not afford to take care of them during her first years in Los Angeles. By the time Ramon was ten years old, his mother had finally saved enough money to bring him and his brother Jose to the United States. She first sent for Jose using his birth certificate. Two weeks later, she used the same birth certificate to bring Ramon across the border.

In Los Angeles, Ramon and Jose went to the neighborhood public school, but neither stayed very long. Without adequate English skills and with no prior formal education in Mexico, they failed to adapt and felt alienated at school. They were also picked on by their classmates because of their clothes and their lack of English fluency. The harassment became so bad they left school. Both boys dropped out before they were sixteen and, with their mom at work, spent a lot of time in the streets. Eventually, Jose and Ramon formed a gang to protect themselves. Delinquent activity led to drug use and stealing. When Jose was ordered to serve time at a juvenile detention facility, he took it as a wake-up call. Upon his release, both brothers enrolled in a continuation school. This is where I met them. The staff noted that Jose worked hard to get his life on track. Over a period of a few years, he had his gang tattoos removed, made consistent progress in the continuation program, and finished all of the credits he needed to graduate. He also opened a bank account and obtained a driver's license. Jose's story was held up as an example for others to follow. It is an important attestation to the power of second chances.

Ramon was also enthusiastic when he entered the program. He enrolled in classes, made new friends, and established himself as a leader in his new setting. For a while, friends and family noticed him smiling much more frequently. Over time, however, Ramon was unable to keep pace with his brother. He became frustrated and disengaged. While he felt good about his progress, in the back of his mind he knew that without legal immigration status he could not qualify for a driver's license, open a bank account, or get a job. He stopped viewing educational attainment as a means of improving his circumstances. His record also followed him—he was told by a pro bono attorney that because of crimes he committed as a juvenile he would probably not be able to adjust his status. It was not fair. Why could he not shake his past when his brother seemed to be moving forward? His interest in doing schoolwork trailed off. He eventually dropped out of the continuation program and returned to selling drugs.

This glimpse into the lives of two modestly educated brothers with troubled childhoods offers a sense of how undocumented status changes the playing field. While Jose's accomplishments would do little to convince urban poverty scholars of his relative success, those same accomplishments dramatically underscore Ramon's failings. Jose struggled to keep his head above water, but he had access to a host of opportunities that were out of his brother's reach. In addition, Jose can legally move on from his transgressions, while Ramon's past will forever follow him. For Ramon and other early exiters like him, these empirical realities have deep and debilitating emotional effects.

LIMITATIONS ON MOBILITY

Most native-born and legal immigrant youngsters, even those from poor families, experience some level of intergenerational mobility. Most early exiters speak English with much greater ease than their parents, and most of them have exceeded their parents in educational attainment. But they and their parents expected much more for them. Because they are blocked from many of the opportunities available to their native-born peers and siblings, their adult lives look more like their parents', marked by a similar narrow range of options and numerous barriers to social and economic mobility.

Early exiters' resilience is a powerful testament to the ways in which they pushed back against the all-encompassing character of their immigration status. Their efforts to escape the grip of their status—even if only temporarily—were remarkable. They prioritized community and connection. They actively sought ways to belong by investing in relationships and by taking advantage of community spaces and activities. At the same time, they also came to realize that resistance required them to take risks (i.e., break the law) that their documented or native-born peers were free of. Overall, the challenges of being undocumented—the gauntlet of legal barriers, limited choices, and perilous environments— afforded them very few spaces unaffected by their illegality. In light of such risks, their daily choices were undertaken with the tacit acknowledgment of illegality as a master status.

CHAPTER 7

College-Goers

Managing the Distance between
Aspirations and Reality

It is a Friday evening and unseasonably cold for mid-November in Anaheim. A dozen students crowd into the small downtown office space
they rent from a local community group. The mood is serious, yet
upbeat. Four of the students are sitting on folding chairs grouped
around a small square table on which a large calendar rests. Another
three are more comfortably seated on a worn couch that has been res-
cued from a nearby alley. Cell phones out, the students on the couch
chat about school. Occasionally, they join the conversation going on at
the table, offering their opinions or answering questions about their
availability for scheduled activities. Several of the group's other members are hard at work making posters for a protest at University of
California Los Angeles. Poster boards, markers, crayons, scissors, and
wooden dowels are strewn across the floor. Lani, a small woman wearing a ribbed tank top, skinny jeans, and flip-flops, calls out, "Hey Esperanza, can you go with Tezca next week to a high school in Long Beach?
There's a group of moms who have organized a meeting with the principal and some of the counselors, and they want us to present on going
to college."

Esperanza, is hunched over a poster board in a hooded USC sweatshirt she has procured from the lost and found; a brown knitted beanie
covers her long, black hair. In blue and yellow marker, she traces the
words "Shame on you UC Regents! You're Squeezing Us Out!" Esperanza responds, "Sure, what day is it? I've got more time now since I lost

my job. I just might need a ride, though. Someone ran into my car last week and I don't have any money to get it fixed."

This is an important moment. It is perhaps the first time Esperanza has openly asked the group for help. With a wide smile, Tezca, who does not drive, pulls a bus card out of his wallet. "It might take us longer to get there, but you can use this. I've got another one." Tezca and others in the group empathize with Esperanza's troubles. Humor, especially that which makes light of their circumstances, is often the best way to give comfort. Esperanza smiles back and asks, "What time do we need to be there?"

It was 2009, and I was visiting a group of students I had spent several years interacting with during my earlier fieldwork. Esperanza and I had first met in 2002, during her first week at the University of California; at that time she was shy, but she seemed very hopeful.[1] She had graduated in 2006, and in the years since, she had been engaged in advocacy and community work, piecing together paid work when she could get it and living with her father in a small, one-bedroom apartment. After graduation, life had not been kind to Esperanza, but she told me she felt "at ease when doing work that matters."

Esperanza spent more than two years feeling isolated at her University of California campus, where she did not know anyone else who was undocumented. Although she tried to contact student groups and to get involved in DREAM Act work, she could not find anyone who wanted to devote time and resources to making the issues she cared about a priority. In addition to her social isolation, she worried constantly about paying for tuition and books. These worries consumed her thoughts and made it difficult for her to connect with other students. During her senior year she met Cesar, the cochair of a local undocumented student group. Unlike Esperanza at the time, Cesar was "out" about his undocumented status and had found that he could motivate other undocumented students by sharing his story. Inspired by his commitment to bringing about change and impressed by what she learned about his organization, Esperanza decided to join. She spent the next six years working more than full-time hours, actively involved in community education and advocacy. This work gave her a sense of purpose and enabled her to put her education and skills to use. "I have been in so many clubs and organizations, especially the ones where you are helping other people, but this one is special," she told me. "[Our group] is a mix of people affected and not. I can actually help myself and others. I can change others' lives as well as my own."

Esperanza went on to become a leader in the organization. She gave workshops at high schools and trained other group members on how to speak with the media, particularly during protests. During a conversation we had in 2008, she reflected on her role in the 2006 immigrant rights marches in Los Angeles: "It made me feel part of something big, you know. I was part of that whole, and not just as a participant—I mean, not just someone who shows up to support [the cause]. I was actually part of organizing it. I was involved behind the scenes. You know, to me it felt really good to actually be able to do that and to be responsible for training people. It was pretty cool to, like, share like everything I knew with them, to play a big part."

On that November evening in 2009, while Esperanza's future was no clearer to her than when she was in college, she had a community of peers and a higher purpose to buoy her against the tide of lost jobs and car troubles. Nevertheless, the difficulty and stress she experienced in college had lasting effects. She was often guarded with her emotions and was reluctant to talk about her personal troubles to friends. In this chapter, I turn from the stories of early exiters who, alongside other undocumented immigrants, confront experiences of illegality in the workplace to those of the college-goers and their experiences navigating the world of postsecondary education. Combining assistance from key mentors at their schools and communities and a determination to succeed, college-goers brought with them to college an impressive support system and a long list of achievements. For Esperanza and other college-goers, making that transition from high school to college allowed them to maintain hope for their futures and provided important proof that their hard work and determination were paying off. On college campuses most continued to benefit from key sources of support that mediated many of the constraints of illegality. They found assistance through caring and supportive staff at their universities and a network of similarly positioned undocumented peers. Several, like Esperanza, drew support from and found a personally fulfilling sense of purpose in community and/or campus-based advocacy networks.

Still, college-goers found that moving from high school to institutions of higher learning brought numerous new challenges and forced them to confront the limits of their belonging. Contemporary studies of immigration tend to focus on intergenerational mobility, providing insight into questions about group-level success and equality of opportunity.[2] But while much of the immigrant incorporation literature highlights what immigrants do to acclimate themselves to host societies' cultural and structural institutions, adaptation does not produce legal incorporation for undocumented immigrants. Adaptive decisions are circumscribed by larger contexts of exclusion that severely undercut efforts to belong. Thus, although many college-goers subscribed to narratives of meritocracy and positioned themselves to compete at selective colleges, graduate programs, and high-skilled jobs, their trajectories toward upward mobility had ceilings.

Drawing on the postsecondary experiences of the college-goers, this chapter makes clear that a lack of legal immigration status creates enduring hardships, even within the fairly insular world of college. Like Esperanza, many college-goers experienced feelings of isolation during their postsecondary educational pursuits, and they felt similarly constrained by financial, administrative, and legal constraints. New environments, much larger student populations, and a rigid bureaucratic structure left many feeling out of place.

Additionally, navigating the complicated web of bureaucracy on their campuses also proved to be difficult and frustrating. Interactions with college officials who lacked information about undocumented students' rights or who were outwardly hostile hindered college-goers' momentum and weakened their trust in administrators. On top of these challenges, several students described financial hardships, such as difficulty meeting rising tuition costs, purchasing books, and meeting other school-related expenses. These financial challenges necessitated hard decisions about how to balance school and work. Many respondents experienced college as a series of forced stops and starts.

NAVIGATING THE POSTSECONDARY LABYRINTH

For college-goers, stepping onto their college and university campuses for the first time was a dream come true, the culmination of years of hard work and perseverance. As Esperanza put it, "It felt so sweet to be at the university. The first one in my family. To know that all the sacrifices, everything, it was all worth it."

When she first entered the University of California in 2002, Esperanza projected the enthusiasm of someone who had been given a second chance. Her high school years had been the best of her life. She was popular among her peers, competed in sports, and was a member of the high school band. But in 2000 her plans for a university education were abruptly curtailed when she discovered that as an undocumented student she was ineligible both for the in-state tuition rate and for financial aid. With community college her only option, Esperanza felt like a failure. She decided to accompany her mother in a move to Wisconsin. Once there, to stay busy, she attended a local community college. When Esperanza moved back to California two years later, A. B. 540 was in place. She had earned enough college credits in Wisconsin to transfer with junior standing when she entered the University of California as an "A. B. 540 student."[3] Esperanza was elated and anxious to get back on the path that had been so affirming in high school.

Like Esperanza, most college-goers in the study were the first in their families to go to college. In fact, only seven college-goers had a sibling who had been to college, and all but nineteen had parents who did not even finish high school, much less college. For them, higher education was uncharted territory. Going to college was considered a major accomplishment and a source of pride for the entire family. For most college-goers, it also meant a temporary respite from their responsibility to work full time and regularly contribute significant sums of money to meet household expenses. Most parents of college-goers, while financially strapped, tried as best they could to help their children be successful in their educational pursuits.

In sharp contrast to early exiters, who left high school for routines of hard labor and risk, those pursuing postsecondary education had a chance to distance themselves from the everyday strains of illegality. While a small number of universities and postsecondary systems across the country have banned undocumented students, federal law does not expressly prohibit undocumented students from attending institutions of higher education. As a result, going to college is one of the very few activities legally available to undocumented young adults.

On their university campuses, college-goers like Esperanza spent significant shares of their time in the company of other upwardly mobile young people pursuing positive and legally permissible goals. They dove into their college classes. Life felt calm and unthreatening, at least during the hours in which they were on campus. They got lost in the world of ideas, not weighed down by fears of deportation. They participated in extracurricular activities and engaged in activism. They made new friends. And they encountered a range of different perspectives. Their worlds expanded with each passing day.

Leaving behind the crowded environments of their homes and communities, college-goers like Esperanza soaked up the intellectual life on campuses with sprawling expanses of land and gardens, elaborate facades patterned in brick and limestone, ocean views, cafés, and palm-tree-lined courtyards. Esperanza exclaimed, "I can say that I really love [the University of California]. Everything about it is nice. So calm and peaceful. I can actually think here. I have a lot of pride about this place. It's like a real university, you know. My parents never had a chance to go. I just feel really lucky to be here. Maybe not lucky, 'cause I worked really hard to get here. But it's like a real privilege to be able to go to school and to spend so much time in a place so beautiful."

The Influence of University Structures on Students' Sense of Belonging

California has been at the forefront of improving access to higher education for undocumented immigrant students. When legislators passed Assembly Bill 540 in 2001, California became the second state to offer in-state tuition to undocumented students attending public colleges and universities.[4] With higher education more financially feasible, college enrollment among undocumented students in California increased.[5] Nevertheless, undocumented students in California, particularly those of Latin American origin, face difficulties making successful transitions to college, persisting, and graduating. For example, annual statistics on the number of students receiving the A. B. 540 benefit within the University of California system point to disproportionately smaller number of Latino students taking advantage of the benefit compared to their undocumented Asian American counterparts.[6]

Moreover, the exclusion of all undocumented students from financial aid places these students at a distinct disadvantage all along the pipeline to and through college. Nearly 70 percent of all American students receive some form of financial aid. Despite coming from lower-income families than many of these students, undocumented students have limited access to this form of support.[7]

The Challenges of Going to College

The excitement Esperanza felt when she first arrived at the University of California did not last long. Before she met Cesar, Esperanza's time at the University of California was a struggle every step of the way. There was no organized group of undocumented students on her campus, so she did not have opportunities to meet and share stories with others in her predicament. This not only increased Esperanza's sense of isolation but also meant that she had no one with whom to share her frustration.

Unlike many of my respondents who benefited from student services staff, when she was seeking much-needed help Esperanza failed to connect with counselors or anyone else on campus whom she felt she could trust to help her penetrate the university's administrative bureaucracy. She became increasingly aware that she was different from her fellow students. Despite being in the insular world of college, Esperanza felt uneasy. She felt as though she did not belong.

Lacking access to financial aid put Esperanza in a tremendous bind. The cost of postsecondary education was dauntingly high.[8] Although paying tuition at in-state rates was a help, she had barely enough money to get through a full year. Like nearly every young person with whom I spoke, Esperanza could not rely on monetary support from her parents to offset legal exclusions from state-sponsored financial aid. An early decision not to work while going to college left her with very little other than the bare necessities. Given this difficult financial situation, she decided to cut corners as much as possible:

> I couldn't depend on my parents for [tuition] support. I mean, I was a burden enough, mooching off my dad. During my first year, tuition and fees were over $8,000. I had a few small scholarships, but it was hardly enough to get through the entire year. So I did everything I could just to stretch the little money I had. I didn't buy my books. I would check out all of the libraries in the area and I'd take the bus all around. Sometimes that took me two weeks, and I'd get behind in class.

Esperanza also decided to take public transportation, despite the inconvenience and time drain associated with bus travel in Los Angeles. These cost-saving strategies were not enough. It was not long before Esperanza joined the world of fast-food work, piecing together minimum-wage jobs over the next few years to pay for school. Annual tuition hikes forced her to repeatedly recalculate her budget. Over time, she accumulated a debt that slowed her down considerably. By her senior year, Esperanza had run out of answers. She took a leave of absence to work so she could pay off her debt and have enough money to carry her through to graduation. It took her two more years to graduate.

For Esperanza and many other college-goers, higher education presented several challenges. Even the brightest and most studious of the college-goers felt the ubiquitous constraints of illegality.

Most of the college-goers were still living at home. Unlike many of their middle-class native-born peers, this did not free them from financial concerns. Instead, they wrestled with the difficulties of balancing school expenses and time constraints against a responsibility to help their financially strapped parents. Parents' low wages and mounting expenses forced them to pass some of the household financial burden on to their children.

Transportation Constraints

Transportation was an ongoing struggle for most respondents. Until January 2015, undocumented immigrants in California could not purchase a car, buy insurance, or legally drive.[9] Without a car, getting to and from school or work can be a major problem. In the sprawling metropolitan area of Los Angeles, public transportation prospects are few, limiting options for school (and work) and extending commute times.

For respondents, transportation presented problems they could not fully surmount. Though some college-goers attended community colleges closer to their homes, most had to adjust to long commutes, some more than two hours each way. Grace lived only seven miles from school, but getting to and from campus involved three buses (each way) and consumed one and a half hours of her time. To make it to class on time, she got up at 5:00 a.m. most mornings. Carlos, who lived in Santa Ana, took three buses to his school in Long Beach, a one-way commute of a little more than two hours. "I waste a lot of time on the bus," he told me. "It's time that I can't get back [to do] something productive. I can't read because I get carsick; and besides, in the afternoon the buses are full. Sometimes I stand for the whole ride. I can't work, either. That's like a part-time job I lose."

Time Constraints

For undocumented youth, attending college requires time-consuming effort. College-goers like Enrique and Cesar lamented that they missed out on the college experience. In particular, tight schedules created by the necessity to work or the amount of time needed to commute by bus cut into their available time to attend study groups or professors' office hours.

> *Enrique:* Most of my classes were afternoon classes. They were the ones I could take because, you know, my schedule. But it was like, I was there for classes and that was it. I had to turn around and go right back home. Usually, in most classes, you know, for group projects, they wanted to get together at night, and I was either working or it was really far for me to get to. I usually had to do my part on my own. Explain to them I had no other choice. I really think that was a disadvantage for me.

Cesar: I definitely felt like a commuter while at [the University of California]. I went to my classes, to lectures and labs when I had them. After that, I would have to quickly drive to my tutoring job. I feel like I really missed out on the whole university experience. A lot of my friends had that. I wasn't in any clubs until my last year.

Cesar, whom I met in 2005, took the risk of driving. He told me that he carefully weighed the consequences of being stopped while driving against the time it would take him to get to campus using public transportation and the time (and money) he would lose by being in transit rather than working as a tutor.

Financial Balancing Acts: "It Feels Like I Can't Do Anything 100 Percent"

Many college-goers felt obligated to give back to their parents as a way of offsetting their loved ones' years of sacrifice. Others felt they had little choice. The money they provided their families, while burdensome, paled in comparison to what they would need in order to live on their own. In 2007 Scarlet was in her fourth year at California State University. When we spoke, she put the challenge of balancing adult independence with family obligations into real-life terms:

Because this is my last year at Cal State, my mom is worried that I'm going to get my own place. I can't do that right now. I mean, my job [at an ice cream parlor] pays me $7.50 an hour and I'm only getting about twenty, maybe twenty-five hours [a week]. I pay my mom $300, sometimes $400 a month. That's a lot of my check, I guess more than half. I used to complain a lot, 'cause I didn't have any money left over after giving it to her. Now I just see it as another bill.

Scarlet and her mother were in a situation of mutual dependence, each relying on the other's income to make ends meet. Their San Bernardino apartment, while small, met their needs. But the rent was a major expense for Scarlet. Compared to early exiters, however, college-goers contributed much less of their income to their parents. In most households, parents asked less from their college-going sons and daughters. Most respondents told me they were responsible for smaller household expenses, like phone bills or cable and Internet fees. But very few received any financial support for college tuition and related expenses, and only six of the seventy-seven college-goers received money directly from their parents.

Most of the college-goers tried to find reliable ways of raising money for tuition—usually through a combination of private scholarships and part-time jobs. Even when these efforts succeeded, the accumulated costs of tuition, books, transportation, food, and clothing strained their already limited budgets. Managing multiple roles, responsibilities, and needs required a careful balancing act, especially when legal exclusions hampered the accomplishment of even the most mundane tasks. Lacking a predictable set of responsibilities and a stable source of funding, many college-goers experienced higher education as a series of stops and starts. "Stopping out," or leaving college for a certain period of time with the intention of returning, is a growing, and concerning, trend among college students nationwide.[10]

In her sixth year at the University of California, Cory was little more than halfway through the coursework for her degree. Living on her own in Central Los Angeles, she worked to finance her tuition and living expenses. Going to school one term at a time, Cory found temporary jobs for the rest of the year to bank funds for the next term. Other undocumented students had different financial strategies. Carlos, a community college transfer student at a Cal State campus, spent a lot of time on small fund-raisers (raffles, bake sales, online donation requests) to meet the costs of school. His efforts were not always successful; budget shortfalls caused him to miss an entire semester. But his resolve to finish school allowed him to move past temporary setbacks.

Sometimes, despite their best efforts, when undocumented students come up short of funds, they must take time off from school to regroup. College-goers were remarkable in their optimism, but even they found difficulty contending with the barrage of barriers that impeded their everyday lives. Without the help of financial aid, coming up with money for tuition, fees, and books was no easy task. While some, like Cory and Carlos, were able to find their way back to school, others discovered the pull of family need and a regular check too strong. Many failed to get back on track.

Despite assistance from high school teachers and community mentors, only a small number of respondents managed to move through higher education without financial struggles or interruptions. Most moved back and forth between school and work commitments, and almost half (thirty-six) left without earning a degree.

For some, this balancing act led to disastrous results. During Pancho's first semester at community college, his savings from work allowed him to cover tuition as a full-time student. He also had enough money to pay for books and other related expenses. However, the next semester proved to be more challenging. While attending college full time, he could not make enough money to meet all of his costs. He cut back to half time at school and took a full-time job as a parking attendant in downtown Los Angeles. His grades dropped. It became harder to leave his full-time job after he began to depend upon a larger paycheck to cover his own expenses and to help his mother. Pancho missed the fall semester. When he tried to go back to school in the spring, he enrolled in only one course. Even that was too much: he missed three classes during the first month and had to drop the course.

Pancho and I had several conversations during this period (between 2003 and 2005). He sincerely wanted to continue his education, but his financial circumstances made it a very difficult pursuit. He lamented, "It feels like I can't do anything 100 percent. I mean, I'm doing everything myself. That's fine, but without any help, it's hard. The thing is, I'd like to be able to be a full-time student, but I can't afford that. So I have to work, and working takes me away from being able to go to college. Maybe later, like in a few years, I'll be able to be in a position to focus more on school."

Pancho never returned to college.[11] His trajectory is not unusual. Nationally, only about one in five community college students successfully transfers to a four-year university. In California, the community college system enrolls roughly two-thirds of all the state's college students (and nearly one-fourth of all community college students in the nation).[12] Growing numbers of undocumented young people are attending postsecondary institutions, but the vast majority of these begin at community colleges.[13] Like Pancho, many of these young people experience college as a revolving door.

Many college-goers who were competitive for the University of California chose to attend lower-tiered California State Universities. The Cal State campuses offered a college education for a fraction of the tuition at University of California schools. Some academically gifted college-goers avoided applying to UCs altogether, selecting only private schools with Cal States as a backup. When Scarlet was not accepted to Stanford, she was deeply saddened. But her disappointment grew when she was "forced to go" to Cal State:

> It really got me down. I mean, I had this English teacher who encouraged me to apply to Stanford. She said that if I got in I could get most of [the tuition] paid for in scholarships. I thought it was a long shot, but I said, "Why not?" I knew I couldn't get the same kind of deal at any of the UCs, so I only

applied to Cal States as a backup. When I didn't get it [to Stanford] I was stuck having to choose between Cal States. Don't get me wrong, I've had a good experience, but for a while I felt really down.

A Sense of Not Belonging: "I Kinda Felt Like a Ghost There"

Several other respondents began college eagerly, at either two- or four-year institutions, only to leave without finishing. Like Pancho, most left because they had trouble balancing multiple roles and responsibilities, but several others left college because they felt as though they did not fit in. Whether they attributed their uneasiness to their undocumented status or to perceptions about their race, they expressed feeling out of place on their large, impersonal college campuses.

> *Sofia:* It just felt weird. I can't really pin it down to one thing. Like I didn't belong there. And it started bugging me after a while. I didn't have any friends there. I tried to talk to some of the girls in my class, but they were all stuck-up.

> *Fernando:* I just feel like I lost confidence. [College] was a struggle, like financially and everything. Not just that, though. It was more the rude comments by some of the administrators. Like I wasn't supposed to be there because of my [undocumented] status.

> *Rogelio:* College was not for me. I'm not gonna lie. I halfway blame it on myself. You know, working all the time. I didn't really have any time to really be on the campus, like getting to know people, being comfortable with everything. I kinda felt like a ghost there. Basically, I just took classes, didn't talk to no one there. (Laughs) And no one missed me when I left.

A subset of the literature on belonging addresses young people's school experiences and the aspects of school environments that allow them to feel accepted, included, and supported in their school environments.[14] Much of this literature has focused on the problems of adolescents not feeling like they are a part of their high schools, but the findings apply to postsecondary experiences as well.[15] In particular, the observed links between lacking a sense of belonging and the predicted outcomes of diminished motivation, declining academic performance, alienation, feelings of disconnectedness, and ultimately withdrawal provide important clues for related experiences in institutions of higher learning.[16]

Most of the college-goers in my study had generally positive secondary and postsecondary school experiences. They were persistent and hardworking, and they benefited from a variety of resources that helped them move through high school and college. However, reflecting broader trends among undocumented students, the pool of college-goers in my study shrank over time. Like Pancho, many who started postsecondary schooling left before receiving degrees. Unfortunately, it is that kind of downward trajectory that most closely resembles the reality most undocumented young people experience.

Administrative Barriers: "Why Does It Have to Be So Hard?"

While measures such as A. B. 540 facilitate educational access, their provisions are not always implemented on college campuses in a clear or consistent manner. Students admitted to state schools under A. B. 540 are required to submit a Statement of Legal Residence to the campus residence deputy. In support of the Statement of Legal Residence, it is common for the campus residency deputy to ask students to provide documentation of in-state high school attendance and graduation (e.g., copies of high school transcripts, diploma).[17] Their financial challenges and precarious legal status thus engender circumstances that put them into more frequent and fraught interactions with campus bureaucrats than are typical of other students.[18]

Meeting A. B. 540 stipulations and deadlines in addition to general admissions requirements and deadline results in multiple trips to and from the campus registrar and residency offices. Typically, there is very little coordination between offices and staff. Moreover, students are seldom assigned to one particular person responsible for dealing with their case. As a result, they often receive contradictory information. Along with other students, they wait in long lines, taking their chances that the next available staff person will be familiar with the specific circumstances relevant to their case.

The physical environment that structures encounters between college staff and undocumented students matters for these encounters. Most interactions between students and administrative personnel take place across a counter, and often through a glass window. Administrative staff members sit in offices while students wait in lines that often snake through indoor waiting areas before spilling out doorways and onto sidewalks. At some institutions, particularly at the beginning of the school term, there can be as many as seventy-five to a hundred students waiting in line at any given time. While there is usually a short distance separating the counter/window from the first person waiting in line, conversations between administrators and students are often easily overheard by those waiting nearby.

Throughout the course of my study, I accompanied several respondents on campus visits as they attempted to complete their paperwork.[19] During these interactions, I found that many of the front-line administrative workers did not have direct knowledge of A. B. 540 and were not familiar with other rights of the undocumented students on their campus. This lack of knowledge forced students not only to have to explain the laws but also to tell their stories in embarrassing detail within earshot of others standing nearby. Receiving services from the registrar, cashier, and residency offices required in-person visits in which the students had to divulge personal details about their financial situation, legal status, and family history. Many experienced these situations as frustrating and humiliating; others received treatment that felt hostile and threatening, as employees staffing the front desks engaged in blatant forms of discrimination. Multiple trips meant time wasted on long bus rides to the university, and some students even had to ask their parents to take time away from work to accompany them. Unless they were fortunate enough to have a knowledgeable companion, respondents navigated this complex bureaucratic process on their own.

Wendy, who started college in 2006, was one of the many college-goers who voiced their frustration over having to make multiple trips back and forth between the admissions and residency offices:

> I think I talked with like five different people. I don't understand why they can't talk to each other. The last time I was there I was told that I needed another form. The time before I asked the woman if I needed the form and she told me I could do it online. But the man said that he couldn't do anything about my registration until I brought back the form. The same lady was standing behind him. I told him what she told me, but he didn't even bother to ask her. I couldn't help it, I started crying right there. Why does it have to be so hard? I don't understand.

During Tezca's sophomore year, he was told by a university official that as an A. B. 540 student he was eligible to make tuition and fee payments in installments throughout the semester (a financial arrangement that had been agreed upon at a meeting of university officials the week before). However, when Tezca went to the business office, the employee at the window handling payments brusquely informed him that there was no such policy. "He told me that I wasn't going to be able to register until I paid my full tuition. I tried to explain, but he wouldn't listen to me. So I got back in line and saw another person. She told me the same thing. I got in line a third time, and finally the guy told me I had to go to the next window, just ten feet away."

Similarly, Vicente was turned away four times by staff at the residency office on his campus. On each occasion, he was told that he was missing a required form. He was later told that he did not need the form if he registered online. Each trip to the university required Vicente to take time off from his job and forego a whole day's pay. "I don't mind," he told me. "I mean, I'm excited that I am able to transfer to the university. I've worked very hard for this. But you know, they make you feel as though you don't belong. I'm going to give them everything they ask for. I'm not going to let this stop me."

In 2007, during a meeting of an undocumented student group in Camarillo that I regularly attended, Priscilla, a twenty-year-old undocumented community college student, shared with her peers a harrowing experience that almost caused her not to pursue college. When she was looking for a part-time summer job, a potential employer asked her for her California ID and Social Security number. Priscilla, who lacked both, was discouraged by her inability to get a job. She was going to abandon her plans to apply to college. Her mom and sister, however, persuaded her not to give up. "You have to go to school. You have to prove [people] wrong," they said. But when Priscilla tried to access her application through the online system she was notified that there was a hold on her registration because of questions regarding her residency status.

> When I went, some girl attended me and she said, "We'll take it off. We just have to prove that you have papers." She went to the back and made me wait for a long time, and some other lady came and said, "What's the problem?" And I said, "I'm just trying to get my hold off so I can register for classes," and she just started being mean. She's like, "Are you legal?" And I said, "Yeah." And she's like, "Did you come here illegally?" And I just stared at her, and I was like, "What kinds of questions are those?" And she asked me, "Do you have a border pass? Do you have a border ID? How did you get here? How much did you pay for the coyote to come over here?" And I was just, I felt bad because I was gonna go to school and she was putting me down. I came to school happy and I came out really sad.

This humiliating incident kept Priscilla out of school for an entire year. The bureaucratic structure of the college's administration, which left little room for a humanizing approach, is partially to blame. But the communication of anti-immigrant sentiments from front-line staff also played a role. Tezca, the student who used information obtained through his positive relationship with a university official to advocate for himself at the business office, recognized that negative experiences with front-line staff were harmful for many of his peers: "It's really unfortunate. The system has turned away a lot of A. B. 540 students because many of them are too scared to advocate [for] themselves or they don't know how to challenge these acts of discrimination. It gives them the message that they're not supposed to be here."

Young people recently out of high school are generally unfamiliar with the complicated and decentralized bureaucratic systems common at most institutions of higher learning. Given the stigma that attached to immigration status, this lack of familiarity translated to embarrassment, anxiety, and fear among students who had to account for themselves at multiple bureaucratic offices. Seemingly minor challenges at crucial entry points sent an unwelcoming message and slowed, stalled, or in some cases even fully derailed undocumented students' college plans.

Immigration laws prohibited undocumented students' participation in a host of college pursuits, including study abroad. In other cases, program requirements posed barriers to entry. Some internships and service-learning programs required applicants to submit a valid Social Security number and agree to a background check with fingerprints; credentialing and certification programs often required that students possess a state-issued form of identification and pass a state exam. College-goers therefore approached academic and extracurricular opportunities with trepidation.

Respondents' experiences in higher education shed some light on the university as a place that on one hand buffers illegality but on the other hand forces students to confront their legal limitations. Increasing numbers of undocumented immigrant students are making their way through college and thinking about postbaccalaureate options. However, it can be difficult for them to determine which postbaccalaureate education and training programs will be open to their participation. In this context, their experiences while on college campuses take on tremendous significance. It is clear that for some students university structures have aided and derailed students' career pursuits, as well as facilitated and closed off spaces of belonging.

THE CULTIVATION AND ASSERTION OF CULTURAL CITIZENSHIP

Despite bureaucratic, financial, and legal barriers to their postsecondary plans, many college-goers found ways to persist. After all, the alternative—to be toiling in low-wage jobs, risking deportation and worsening their future outlook—was enough to make them work even harder. Central to their resolve was a belief that they belonged there. They staked their claims to belonging in their cultural citizenship.

The concept of *cultural citizenship*, first introduced by anthropologist Renato Rosaldo, recognizes the agency of immigrant communities and the potential of immigrants as political subjects despite their limited access to formal political participation.[20] The term offers an alternative to the exclusionary nature of the dominant discourse of who "belongs," or who qualifies as "American" and highlights local, informal articulations of membership that take into account the broad range of activities and relationships in everyday life through which disadvantaged groups claim space, and eventually rights, in society.[21] For college-goers, evidence of their cultural citizenship and their right to belong was apparent in their various interactions on campus and the ways in which they leveraged sources of support to secure greater levels of access.

Getting Assistance from Student Services Offices

Indeed, the bureaucratic structure of postsecondary education is large, decentralized, and difficult to navigate. Many undocumented students forged relationships with college staff and administrators (especially those in student services) who provided them with the know-how needed to master the bureaucratic complexities of their institutions. Like some of their teachers and counselors in high school, student services staff helped these students access privately administered pots of money, provided them with key information, and advocated on their behalf.

On most college and university campuses, student services offices are oriented toward retaining students by improving their chances of success.[22] In addition to helping the student body at large, these staff members provide aid targeted to special needs, traditionally underrepresented, low-income, and first-generation students. Student services offices are often designed to encourage students to drop in, sit down, and meet with staff without restrictive barriers. These settings tend to be more intimate than the open counters and office cubicles common in other parts of university clerical and financial administration; a closed door offers students some level of privacy.

I noticed that in these offices students and staff alike often were on a first-name basis with one another and sustained long-term relationships.

Student services workers found creative ways to provide undocumented students on their campuses with internship opportunities and private scholarships. This was extremely helpful because prior to 2011, when state laws were finally revised, undocumented students were not eligible for any form of public financial aid. Staff members also helped college-goers surmount barriers that arose during their interactions with personnel in other campus administrative offices.

Tezca was ultimately able to make arrangements to pay his tuition in installments because he learned about the policy through his relationship with a key student services administrator. Armed with this knowledge, he did not accept the first roadblock presented by an ill-informed worker but instead persisted from a position of empowerment until he found someone who could help him.

Similarly, when Oscar had troubles with the residency office, he approached a staff member of his university's Educational Opportunity Program (EOP) to ask for assistance. "They were really cool about it. Yeah, two people from the office assisted me. Basically they went in there and explained everything to them. It saved me a lot of time."

As Enrique discovered, a lack of clear guidelines sometimes worked in the student's favor. Despite being told by an administrator within the teacher credentialing program at his California State University campus that he could not enroll in the program, Enrique, with help from a student services employee, was able to successfully complete the background check and pass the California Basic Educational Skills Test (CBEST). He relayed to me, "We recently had discussions with the directors of the [credentialing] program during their open forums. A year ago they were appalled to learn that I had gone through the preliminary test [CBEST] and to learn that I was able to put my fingerprints through. Now they are deterring students from applying by insisting that without a Social [Security number] they won't be able to fulfill the preliminary requirements."

Through his campus's undocumented student support group, Enrique met two other students who were also in the process of obtaining their teaching credentials. All three students, along with the student services employee, met as a group to share information. They also went together—for mutual support—to meetings with university officials. They discovered on their own that no official policy stipulated that a teaching credential should be denied to an applicant without a Social Security number.

Rosalba was also able to complete her teaching credential with the help of a strong network of university employees and administrators.

The staff in the student services office at her university helped her to pore over the requirements for the state exams. And, with the help of the vice president of student affairs, Rosalba had her fingerprints taken at her university without being subjected to invasive questions about her lack of a Social Security number.

Though college-goers faced difficulty navigating the bureaucratic structure of their universities, they also benefited from student service offices developed to assist low-income and first-generation students. This kind of support bolstered their feelings of belonging and claims to membership.

Advocacy and the Extension of Citizenship Claims

Student services offices also benefited undocumented students by providing opportunities for these students to meet one another. In California, beginning in the mid-1980s, many college and university officials in counseling centers and admissions offices started to identify undocumented students and bring them together.[23] Indeed, much of the early activism on behalf of undocumented students was carried out by university officials. From these efforts, coalitions like the Leticia A. Network in California began to push for policy change, in-state tuition policies were crafted, and campus support groups began to take shape.[24]

As advocacy efforts in California began to pick up, gradually, students began to stand up for themselves.[25] Since the early 2000s, undocumented immigrant college and university students in California have organized local campus and community-based groups to provide mutual support, share resources, and advocate for inclusive changes in state and federal laws.[26] Following the immigrant rights marches of 2006, the number of these groups grew significantly.

Accompanying this growth was an increased visibility of undocumented students' plight and a growing sense of their political power nationwide. By 2009, they had compelled elected officials, university presidents, organized labor, the business community, and city councils across the country to cheer them on, provide public endorsements of their cause, and become better informed about their predicament. Several of these entities have publicly endorsed the DREAM Act.

I witnessed this growth in activism throughout the United States—in traditional immigrant-receiving cities like Miami and Chicago and in new destination areas like rural Georgia and suburban Colorado. In Southern California, during the later stages of my fieldwork, I observed a pronounced increase in activity on community college, Cal State, and University of California campuses as once-isolated undocumented immigrant students began to find one another and form groups. These young people strategically used spaces of contradiction to claim social membership while also demanding expanded rights and formal membership. It was not long before they grew into a potent political force. Many college-goers had grown deeply frustrated with the limitations in their daily lives. They wanted to do something to bring about change, even at the risk of drawing public attention to themselves. Aided by immigrant rights organizations and elected officials, these groups formed a statewide coalition, partnered with California state legislators, and used diverse media sources to tell their stories.

Many of these young people made it clear that they were dissatisfied with the legislative process and had grown tired of waiting as others debated their futures. This restlessness, coupled with an increasingly clear vision of life without the protections and benefits of membership, motivated many to take actions they might otherwise have been unwilling to take. As Andrea explained in 2006: "This is our struggle. It's time for undocumented students to stand up for ourselves, and if we do not do it for ourselves, we will have lost everything we're fighting for."

Asserting Belonging through Advocacy

No single path led the college-goers into advocacy work. Neither was there only one reason for becoming involved. Many expressed the need for a community of support. Others said they wanted to take control over their lives. Over time, however, many of those who were involved began to realize their own capacity as agents of change and the importance of the space they were creating, not only for themselves but also for other community members. In their community and political practices, they began to exercise important forms of cultural citizenship.

These students' more public acts of protest generated the most attention to their cause. Equally important to these efforts was targeted outreach aimed at educating community members—teachers, counselors, parents, and students—not only about the challenges facing undocumented students but also about their rights.

Rosalba, an aspiring teacher when I met her, saw a great void among educators. Her weekly participation in school workshops was driven by a desire to change those "who are in a position to change lives." She reasoned, "I would like to raise awareness in the community because it's really missing among educators in particular. There are a lot of good, really good, teachers that just don't have the information kids and families need, and that causes a lot of misinformation and missed opportunities. So that's why I participate. I would like to donate my story and be able to help out."

Many of the other college-goers publicly acknowledged what they referred to as privilege (i.e., being in college and not having to hold full-time jobs while in school). They tried to support other, particularly younger, students. Take Nimo, for example. As the beneficiary of a full scholarship from a sponsor who took care of all college-related expenses, Nimo was aware of his unique circumstances. Not needing to work to help his mom also freed up a great deal of his time. He kept his good fortune constantly in mind. People often were surprised by Nimo's level of optimism, something he used to educate and inspire others. He told me, "I believe that since I'm in this situation [I can] educate other people about the injustices that happen around the world. I think that it is a good way to change people's minds for the better and so there is a peace and justice in the world."

To be sure, these young people faced steep barriers to traditional forms of political participation. Historically, marginalized groups who have been denied access to traditional political power or whose interests have been shut out of traditional political channels have found extrainstitutional avenues to articulate their interests and seek change. These avenues include street protests, acts of civil disobedience, rallies, and marches.[27] College-goers engaged in political participation embraced similar methods. They held bake sales, car washes, and banquets to raise money for scholarships. They staged mock graduations to bring awareness to their plight. And they engaged in hunger strikes, sit-ins, and other acts of civil disobedience to escalate their battle for inclusive rights. These efforts, often tactics used as a larger national strategy, make them one of the most impressive social movements of the times.

While their actions may seem to others a foolish risk of their futures, many college-goers took a different view. They saw their activism as a way to stake claim to a political world long the exclusive domain of citizens. Marco explained his own and others' activism this way: "We've given a lot to this country. The youth, their parents, our community. We are not asking for special consideration, no handouts, nothing like that. But we demand respect, to be treated as equal members of this country. When we see parents separated from their children because of deportation, when we see our neighbors detained for making a questionable lane change, when we see kids afraid to go to school, that's what motivates us to keep going. And we will."

The politically active college-goers articulated a sense of hope rooted in the ideals underpinning the educational system and based on a belief that, despite exclusion from the formal political system, they had the potential to change policy through their claims to membership as insiders.[28] By asserting their degrees and high grade point averages as well as their ties to their community, they demonstrated their merit as productive and contributing members. Even though invisibility is a defining characteristic of the undocumented experience, college-goers risked associations with visibility in order to assert claims of belonging on their college campuses and in the broader community. Growing numbers of undocumented immigrant students are moving through the educational pipeline, gaining exposure to a more inclusive world, and deliberately coming out of the shadows. Like early exiters, college-goers bring their agency to bear in their attempts to overcome isolation, loneliness, and other hurdles erected by their undocumented status.

The Mixed Blessings of Broadened Horizons

The notion of cultural citizenship provides social scientists and advocates alike with a model for understanding and asserting how individuals who are formally deemed outside the law can be recognized as legitimate political subjects claiming rights for themselves on the basis of their economic and cultural contributions.[29] It functions as a belief system and as a means through which those marginalized from formal membership, or whose formal membership is deemed of lesser value, are able to recognize their contributions and root their rights claims in social, economic, and political contributions.[30]

Cultural citizenship was the grounds upon which college-goers claimed membership based on years of accumulated Americanizing experiences and on their educational attainment.

Most college-goers included in their self-narratives examples that located them inside a culturally drawn circle of membership and community. Many tried to minimize the effects of legal outsiderness by elaborating on the aspects of their lives that allowed them to actualize cultural membership. They emphasized their good grades and academic achievements. They doubled their efforts in their communities, giving workshops to parents and working with educators to help them better work with their immigrant students. They drew attention to elements of their everyday lives—shared cultural experiences common to their generation of American-raised young millennials—that resembled those of their native-born peers. And they sought out opportunities to extend college life.

For example, some, like Cesar and his brother Oscar, pursued work opportunities that allowed them to replicate their lives on campus. Their tutoring business, which connected college students to low-income Mexican children throughout Riverside County, was so successful they were able to offer an eight-week science academy in the summer. Classes were held on a California State University campus with the support of one of Cesar's mentors, the vice president of student affairs.

Cesar was frequently invited to speak about key community topics.[31] I accompanied him to several community meetings where he was treated as an equal by adult community leaders. His perspective always seemed to be held in high esteem. As a group of us were driving back from a meeting where Cesar had spoken about the DREAM Act to a group of more than two hundred community members, a younger student expressed her surprise at the way in which Cesar carried himself during the meeting:

Linda: You're the man around here, aren't you?

Cesar: (Laughing) I don't know about that.

Linda: I mean, you're just like them. It's like your situation doesn't even get in your way.

Cesar: I try not to let my situation get me down. Don't get me wrong. I've really struggled, but I try to put that out of my mind. I'm always looking for opportunities to feel normal. You know, to shut out that side of my life. Most people are surprised when they find out I'm undocumented because I actually have a position of importance in the community. I may not be able to do everything they can do, but no one doubts that I should be at the table.

Cesar's attempts to "shut out" the aspects of his life that made him feel like an outsider was a strategy many college-goers used to maintain positive outlooks regarding their present lives and future possibilities. But Andrea adapted a somewhat different strategy for dealing with the stresses of undocumented life.

When we met, Andrea was the cochair of a campus organization for undocumented students. I was impressed by her leadership style—she was inclusive, but she also was a firm, no-nonsense leader. Largely through her leadership, her group participated in high-level discussions within their community and city government, conversations historically reserved for established groups.

Andrea held her position as cochair for a little over two years. When she graduated from college, she was hired by a local not-for-profit group that found a way to support her position as an organizer by paying her as an independent contractor. I was taken aback when she left her job only months after starting. I was even more surprised when she began selling cosmetics. But within a few months she was managing a team of women selling cosmetics. The rationale for her decisions made sense:

> *Andrea:* I feel like I'm finally putting my [sociology] degree to work. I'm successful at what I do, and I'm empowering other women just like me. Most of these women don't even speak English, and about 80 percent don't have papers. But they get to dress up to go to work, just like the women who work in offices, and they can be successful entrepreneurs.

> *Roberto:* Yeah, that makes sense. But didn't you feel like you were doing that at your last job and with the [student group]?

> *Andrea:* I don't know. Maybe. It's just that I never felt like we were, I was getting anywhere. It's like running into a wall over and over. And that got really tir[ing], you know. Last year was really bad for my health. I had to go to the emergency room twice because I thought I was having a heart attack. I realized that that work, I mean it's important, but it was time to pass it on to someone else. I was always thinking about my status. Every day. In my work, my personal life, at home. I needed to get away from it.

> *Roberto:* And now?

> *Andrea:* Now I can be a successful woman and kind of give some of that other stuff a break, at least for now. I feel much happier and healthier, like a big weight has been lifted.

While barriers related to their immigration status, economic limitations, and complicated college bureaucracies were often difficult to overcome, many respondents met legal obstacles with an optimism born of accumulated experiences of inclusion and success. The compulsion of many of these young people to engage in such activity in the first place merits further attention. Most college-goers entered college with the support of teachers, counselors, administrators, and other mentors. Their high school and college opportunities also provided them with powerful, horizon-expanding experiences, affirming their beliefs in American achievement ideology. Many used these experiences as leverage to assert identities that countered those of undocumented immigrants. And they consolidated small victories—full days or weeks of feeling normal, the successful navigation of campus barriers, and gains made for undocumented students on campus or through legislation—into a portrait of their inclusion.

But for many, the desire to lead a normal life, coupled with the necessity to support themselves and take care of family members, overshadowed activist pursuits. By minimizing daily reminders of their undocumented status and normalizing everyday routines, they were able to assert some control over their circumstances, spend more time in regular pursuits, and reduce stress. During my time in the field I met many college-goers who cycled in and out of activist and advocacy groups, leaving when other aspects of their lives (e.g., paying bills, supporting family members, taking care of their health) took precedence. Nevertheless, returning to normal after years of inclusion and the excitement of activist pursuits was not something for which many were prepared.

In one conversation I had with Luis and a few of his friends after a campus meeting, Luis spoke in a frank and emotionally charged way about his fears of the future. He had no other plans but to return to his old neighborhood after finishing college. I followed up on some of the issues he raised. His response shed light on how large his world had become.

> *Roberto:* What exactly about finishing college worries you the most?
>
> *Luis:* To be honest, it's going home. Going back to my neighborhood. That's what gets me down. Don't get me wrong, I love my family and would do anything for them. It's just that in my time here at [California State University] I've grown a lot and done some really special things. Like my work with the counseling center. I've worked with a lot of the administrators. Earlier this year, I attended a luncheon put on by Student Affairs and sat at the same table as our [university] president. Last spring I got to go down to Louisiana with [a campus group] to help hurricane victims. I feel like things are really starting to happen for me right now in my life, and I know it's not going to be the same when I go back home.

Luis's comments reflect a sentiment common among young people who have left home. In fact, the theme that inspired Thomas Wolfe's posthumously published novel *You Can't Go Home Again* has entered the American lexicon as a shorthand reference to the difficulty of returning home after being away and seeing the world.[32] In addition to making clear the many ways in which college had altered his life, Luis's response clearly illustrates the extent to which colleges acted as spaces of inclusion and opportunity for undocumented students. But his concerns point to another, much darker, reality. Even after completing a college education and earning a degree, many college-goers are bound to return "home," to illegality, a regressive slide into a life of limited choices and the ever-present threat of removal.

Open Doors and Closed Windows

The post–high school trajectories of the college-goers offer important evidence of the benefits of making it to college. The transition from high school to college is an important one for American students. College offers young people the opportunity to make important investments in their futures. For undocumented college-goers, this transition provided a buffer against the condition of illegality, although many college-goers shouldered heavy work responsibilities.

The postsecondary experiences of college-goers tell a mixed story. On one hand, many of these young people moved successfully through college and earned degrees—no small feat given the legal context that frames their adult lives. Along the way they found support from caring student services counselors who helped them navigate the difficult bureaucracy of their institutions. Many also formed connections with other undocumented students in similar circumstances. These relationships allowed them to share information about scholarship funds and campus resources as well as provide academic and emotional support. The support they received from college staff and undocumented peers enabled many to combat the damaging stigma that limited high school social and educational pursuits and to become more assertive in their claims of membership and belonging. Realizing their collective agency, they became a powerful political force.

An equally powerful counterstory also emerges from these narratives—a story of the university as a place of discrimination and difficulty for undocumented students. This story is often lost in popular narratives but is just as much a part of the undocumented experience. For many college-goers, financing their education and related expenses was a struggle at every step of the process. Restricted access to financial aid, work-study, and other key sources of financial and academic support severely handicapped their progress. Many college-goers felt as though forces beyond their control hindered their ability to leave college before completing their degrees, and many more received the message that they did not belong. Those who found support from student services staff were able to access spaces of belonging. However, many others experienced their campuses as cold and impersonal. While the experiences of college-goers appeared to diverge sharply their early-exiter counterparts, as the two groups moved farther into adulthood the differences between them began to disappear. As the next chapter vividly illustrates, for early exiters and college-goers alike, illegality is a master status for undocumented adults.

College-going undocumented young adults have become the face of the immigrant rights movement. By pointing out the very real legal barriers to upward mobility, college-goers appeal to ideals of deservingness traditionally tied to merit and achievement. The framing of undocumented youth as innocent children or as truly American has proven such a successful strategy for the promotion of their deservingness that it has become the basis for this group's full legal inclusion. In his book *We Are Americans: Undocumented Students Pursuing the American Dream*, William Perez argues, "They have grown up 'American' in every way possible; their dominant language is English, they proclaim an American identity, and they live an American lifestyle."[33]

In many ways the college-goers are different from early exiters, who cannot as easily be portrayed as "deserving." Many of the aspects of merit and achievement that have been used to define their deservingness also separate them from their own siblings and other family and community members. Many indeed "grew up American." However, their everyday adult lives remind us that, like early exiters, they too are stigmatized, excluded, and offered only partial access to the American dream. For both groups their lack of formal permission to be in the United States challenges claims of deservingness that rely on false dichotomies.

CHAPTER 8

Adulthood

*How Immigration Status Becomes
a Master Status*

As I ask Ricardo to describe his experience working on the assembly line, he pauses to wipe the sweat off his designer glasses. His coworker Jonathan, sitting across the table from me, arms folded, interrupts before Ricardo can reply. "This is his worst nightmare. He shouldn't even be here."

We are sitting at the end of a long lunchroom table, within earshot of more than a dozen other immigrant workers crowded together on cafeteria-style benches, eating lunches brought from home. The lunchroom is abuzz. The chatter seems likely to drown out the details of our conversation. "Don't worry," Jonathan tells me. "No one speaks English here."

Jonathan—built like a fireplug and given to devilish smiles—breaks into laughter and wraps his thick, calloused fingers around the back of Ricardo's lanky neck. Ricardo—tall, wiry, and pedantic-looking—snaps, "This is precisely where I should be." But despite his smock, gloves, and work boots, Ricardo clearly looks out of place. His boyish face and slight build defy his attempts to fit in with his mostly immigrant coworkers.

Jonathan's words are not intentionally provocative. They are born out of a frustration at seeing friends and family members stymied by their lack of papers. Ricardo's reaction, on the other hand, is in response to a growing accumulation of negative adult experiences, of coming to always expect something bad to happen. As he elaborates, he explains why an assembly line is where he is "supposed to be":

You see, this right here is right where I'm supposed to be. It's probably where I'll be in five years. Well, maybe not this job exactly, but doing this, working with my hands so somebody else can get rich. [We're] invisible to most of society because they can't see us. Because they don't want to see us. Hey, I'm the same kid who sat in class with your children, who played soccer with your son and took your daughter to prom. But now I can only watch. It's like being in a bubble. I can't touch. And you don't see me.

It was the summer of 2011, and these two young men—a study in contrasts—had known each other for almost two years as they worked together assembling auto parts. The factory work was difficult and mind-numbingly tedious, but it allowed them to pay their bills. The job paid wages in cash and did not require a Social Security number—attractive features for both Ricardo and Jonathan as undocumented immigrants.

When Jonathan was younger, he never envisioned his adult life would be so difficult. He had a small group of close friends who came from families similar to his own. He recalled his childhood as a generally happy time. But at the large Los Angeles high school he attended, Jonathan failed to stand out or to gain the attention of his teachers and counselors. He lost all motivation to stay in school during his junior year, when he came to the stinging realization that his immigration status was going to keep him from working, driving, and taking part in many other activities. Once he left school, his options were limited. His economically strapped parents needed his help, so he went to work mowing lawns with his father and uncles. He found the work difficult at first; his pace was noticeably slower than that of his mostly immigrant coworkers. Every night he came home feeling as though he had been beaten up. His hands were cut and bruised and his back burned from bending over all day.

In the ten years after he left school, Jonathan took more than his share of poorly paid jobs. Work was not always steady, but over time he accumulated a great deal of experience in factories and restaurants, in construction, and in landscaping. Back pain was now part of his everyday life, and his hands were permanently calloused. Adulthood amounted to much less than he had hoped for. He spoke readily about his disappointment, but he also worked to accept his life of limitation.

In contrast, Ricardo had not settled into his present circumstances. His experience in the low-wage labor force was much less extensive than Jonathan's because he had attended school much longer. School had always been easy for Ricardo, and he had dreamed of running for political office. When he was a high school senior, his stellar academic record provided him with a broad range of postsecondary options. He decided to attend the University of California, where he majored in political science. He did well. His success gave him hope that he could eventually overcome his unauthorized status.

He made friends with a group of students who were also undocumented and committed most of his free time to DREAM (Development, Relief, and Education for Alien Minors) Act advocacy.[1] Although the constraints of his undocumented status were a source of constant stress, Ricardo found ways around them. During college, he supplemented his private scholarship by working at a friend's café and living with friends to minimize costs. These arrangements allowed him to pursue additional education. After graduation, he enrolled in a management program at California State University, where he earned a master's degree in one year.

In 2011, over two years out of school, Ricardo had been unable to put his impressive education to use. Doors stopped opening after he left his master's program. His living expenses had more than doubled, and his parents were counting on him for financial support. Passage of the DREAM Act, which would permit Ricardo to change his immigration status, had stalled once again. Meanwhile, every day spent in legal limbo saw his talents go to waste.

Both Jonathan and Ricardo had reached dead ends. Lacking a high school diploma, Jonathan resembled other modestly educated young adults from low-income backgrounds who face a narrow range of employment options and little or no job security. But Jonathan's undocumented status provided an additional layer of difficulty. His American-born high school buddies, despite also having left school without graduating, had many more choices available to them. And Ricardo, with two postsecondary degrees, would have had his choice of attractive job possibilities if he had been a citizen. But lacking legal status, he could not pursue a career in which his education would position him as highly competitive and able to make immediate contributions in the workplace.

During my visits with Jonathan and Ricardo over the years, I observed changes in their lives—different partners, new jobs, accumulated debt, and flattened aspirations. I was often surprised by the ways in which they responded to these changes. These two men had starkly different educational trajectories, but by the end of their twenties both viewed illegality as the most salient feature of their lives, trumping their achievements and overwhelming almost all of their other roles and identities. When Ricardo predicted that in five years he would be in the same situation, he was acknowledging the stranglehold his undocumented status had on him. Although both he and Jonathan found ways to establish meaningful social relationships and to engage in nonwork activities that they enjoyed, illegality defined both men's lives.

This chapter returns to the broad question that frames this book: How did the transition from childhood to adulthood and the shift from belonging to marginalization shape the lives of the undocumented 1.5 generation? This simultaneous shift in statuses undermined childhood attachments to place and community, processes of acculturation, and Americanizing experiences that allowed many respondents to make claims to membership. The stories of college-goers and early exiters show that immigrant adaptation is not a uniform and unidirectional process. Instead, the impact of illegality becomes stronger and more consequential at key transitional points in time. For undocumented youth, assimilation is segmented not only across generations, as proposed by Alejandro Portes and colleagues, but also within an individual's life course.

COMPLETING THE TRANSITION TO ILLEGALITY

In his work on globalization, postcolonial scholar Homi K. Bhabha wrote, "The globe shrinks for those who own it; for the displaced or dispossessed, the migrant or refugee, no distance is more awesome than the few feet across borders or frontiers."[2] Bhabha's words evoke the experiences of displacement, loss, and risk common to migrants worldwide. For 1.5 generation undocumented young adults in the United States, his observation also vividly underscores the life-course implications of being on the wrong side of politically drawn boundaries. By their late twenties, both college-goers and early exiters found that doors had stopped opening. As their options dwindled to a limited number of undesirable choices, illegality became the most consequential feature of their adult lives. It was now a *master status*.

By the time the Deferred Action for Childhood Arrivals (DACA) program was announced in June of 2012, most of my respondents were in their late twenties and early thirties. A few had entered their forties. Following many of the study participants for twelve years gave me a chance to observe the ways in which they experienced both belonging and illegality and to chart the various turns in their lives. Many had children; several married, including three whose marriages brought them legal status. Another six became legal permanent residents, having endured very long waits to adjust their status, four through family sponsorship and two through U-visas.[3] For the majority of my respondents, however, their life outcomes fell far short of their hopes and expectations. Five were deported, including two who served prison time before leaving the country. Several others had seen parents, loved ones, or other family members leave the United States voluntarily or through deportation—for most of them, parents and other family members continued to struggle in low-wage jobs and in lives deflated by their immigration status. And, tragically, three respondents have passed away.

While DACA offered important legal access to jobs and driver's licenses, many respondents believed it had come too late for them; they felt ambivalent. Time and the strains of navigating exclusions and bad jobs while avoiding law enforcement had taken their toll on respondents' minds and bodies. A lack of education or job experience was also a deterrent, as was the $465 application fee. Several were advised by attorneys not to apply because crimes they committed in their past made them not only ineligible but also deportable. A small handful applied, but the vast majority of my respondents did not.

With the exception of the few who found a path to permanent residence or citizenship, illegality was the most salient feature of day-to-day life for all respondents. This represented an especially dramatic change for the college-goers. During their late adolescent and early adult years, these respondents had vaulted ahead of early exiters, enjoying the pursuit of higher education and opportunities for inclusion in the worlds of their high-achieving peers. However, in their mid- to late twenties, most college-goers were out of school and learning that despite having attained advanced degrees they had few legal employment options. They faced the same narrow range of jobs and broad reach of legal exclusions that the early exiters had begun contending with years earlier.

As both groups of respondents completed the transition to illegality, it was the early exiters who were better adjusted. Since leaving school, they had spent many years in low-wage jobs, accumulating experience and improving their human capital. Many had let go of hopes for career mobility long before, opting instead for security and stability. They were settled into work routines and in adulthood. Many were in long-term relationships and several had children. While housing instability was a chronic problem for most early exiters, they were accustomed to squeezing all they could out of their paychecks to pay rent and their monthly bills. The college-goers were still trying to cope with the staggering mismatch between the new reality and their high educational attainment and aspirations for the future.

The everyday experiences of my respondents bore little resemblance to those of their native-born peers. But their lives were now much more like those of their parents. The overriding need to make ends meet forced them to make difficult choices, many of which involved taking risks. They were also far more dependent on others to accomplish even the most commonplace tasks.

Early Exiters: Settling into Routines of Illegality

As adults, early exiters settled into lives of limitation. They obtained fake identification to obtain unstable low-wage jobs, through which they eventually gained work experience, bought cars, and established homes. They achieved modest success by limiting their vision to basic life goals. Many who even into their early twenties had resisted low-wage and clandestine jobs to avoid abusive employers and unsafe and demanding work environments eventually capitulated. With mounting financial responsibilities and a growing realization that work options were sharply limited by their undocumented status, they curbed their expectations and lowered their standards regarding the kind of job they would accept.

Many moved from job to job after they left high school. Aldo, for example, refused to accept the limitations of what he called "immigrant jobs." Over time, though, he came to realize that he would not find the kind of work environment he hoped for. When I spoke with him in 2012, he was working in a factory. He had been on the job for six months. I asked him to reflect on his work experiences. He responded, "I tried to find something better, but it was always like there just weren't the kinds of jobs I thought were up to my level. I had to, you know, set my expectations lower. It's really depressing realizing that the only jobs you can do are the ones at the bottom."

In other cases, respondents who opted out of low-wage work in favor of more illicit and dangerous opportunities that allowed them greater levels of autonomy and freedom gradually grew to desire a less risky lifestyle and a steadier income. This was true for Josue, who stopped selling drugs when life on the streets became too dangerous. "I had to grow up," he told me." I was out there doing stupid things and it just got tiring getting into fights and harassed all the time by cops. For what? I was barely making minimum wage."

In 2012, Josue was thirty years old. Time had not been kind to him. He was struggling to make ends meet at his full-time job at a fast-food restaurant chain, and his ever-thinning hair had given way to baldness. He looked ten to fifteen years older than his age.

Job Stability

Marriage and parenthood and the accompanying need to provide for growing families compelled other respondents to seek steady forms of employment. By 2012, fifty-four early exiters were living on their own, and another eleven had parents or other family members living in their homes. Forty-eight were married or cohabiting, and forty-one had children. Dora was thirty-one when I spoke to her in 2013. When we had first met nine years earlier, she was a stay-at-home mother with two children. When the housing market crashed, Dora's husband, who had previously been steadily employed in construction, had to find alternative employment. Dora needed to find work as well to make up for the drop in the family's income.[4] After initial difficulty, she found a job through a friend cleaning rooms at a motel. When we spoke, Dora had been working for four years. She estimated that during that time, cleaning ten to fourteen rooms a day, she had made more than fifteen thousand beds and cleaned almost as many toilets.

The years they spent in low-wage work provided early exiters with the social and human capital they needed to find and keep jobs. Over time, they learned skills in areas such as landscaping, garment making, housekeeping, and drywalling. Their bodies grew accustomed to long hours of physical labor.

For example, in 2004, after three years of low-wage work, Mario told me, "At first when I started it was hard. 'Cause it was a lot to learn and I was kinda slow. Not slow, but I guess I wasn't at their pace. But now I'm used to the job. I can handle my own." By 2012, Mario had been working eleven years in various "immigrant jobs" and had developed a broad skill set from jobs in food service, landscaping, and cabinetry.

Little by little, early exiters transitioned from inexperienced young adults to undocumented immigrant workers—cheap and expendable sources of labor in the low-wage economy. For those who had begun working as teenagers, this process started much earlier. Nevertheless, many continued to hope for some change in their lives throughout their young adult years. But by their late twenties and early thirties, early exiters had accepted that everyday routines of work and survival constituted their reality.

Holding low expectations for the future is a predictable result of cumulative years of severely restricted choices. For some, consciously letting go of previous expectations proved beneficial. Gabriel, for example, had had no income and no prospects when we first met in 2003. He was frustrated and scared. When I ran into him in 2008, he was twenty-six years old. He seemed to be at ease with his life. He was working in a factory where his coworkers were also immigrants, and he was participating in a community dance group. He told me he was "not as uptight" as he had once been: "I just stopped letting it [undocumented status] define me. Work is only part of my life. I've got a girlfriend now. We have our own place. I'm part of a dance circle, and it's really cool. Obviously, my situation holds me back from doing a lot of things, but I've got to live my life. I just get sick of being controlled by the lack of nine digits."

Four years later, in 2012, Gabriel was a father. His girlfriend, a college graduate, was a positive influence, and for his daughter's first year and a half he was a stay-at-home dad. But after bouts with drug use, he decided it would be best to leave. By 2015 he was back on his feet again. He had "cleaned up [his] act" enough to see his daughter, and he and her mom were on good terms. Gabriel was still in factory work, and he had started teaching Aztec dance at a community center near his apartment and was devoting large shares of his time to a community garden. Undoubtedly, Gabriel would have preferred greater stability in his life. But he had reconciled himself to his limitations, focusing instead on relationships and activities that were tangible and accessible.

As early exiters made the unavoidable transition to being undocumented immigrant laborers, they enlarged the pool of cheap, flexible, and disposable labor. Their work experience and the many pressures of undocumented adult life taught early exiters how to be "illegal." Pedro, whose story of getting caught with multiple sets of identification was highlighted in chapter 2, was now much more comfortable negotiating work situations and monetary transactions. In 2010, he was thirty-two. He told me that he had "learned so much since then": "It was really scary, bro. But what can I say? I messed up. I would never do anything that stupid now. I ask for cash now and I always keep my paperwork straight. I was just young and inexperienced then."

Pedro called himself a "hustler." For him, this term was not a direct reference to dealing drugs, although some hard times over the years had necessitated such endeavors. Rather, Pedro prided himself on his adaptive ability to "make it out there in the world." He used his brains, street smarts, charm, and smile to make money, and he was "always looking for that next dollar." In 2014, he was working semiregularly with a friend installing carpets and working as a DJ hosting karaoke nights at local bars on the side. Problems with his health—high blood pressure and diabetes—had started to slow him down.

By age thirty, Ramon too seemed more settled. Over the previous few years, he had become a father and a provider for his family. He had stopped hanging out with his old friends; he was now a familiar face at his wife Maria's church.[5] Ramon's brother Jose (a US citizen) and his family had achieved important milestones and lived more comfortably, but Ramon's and Maria's pathways remained blocked, and they felt powerless to change their broader circumstances.

Exclusions and fear limited participation in everyday life. These conditions gave early exiters the message that they no longer belonged to the country they had long considered home. Ramon reflected, "I don't know, it's just really messed up. In my heart, I feel like I'm part of this country. It's the only country I know. It's my home. But it don't accept me. And it's getting to where I feel [like I'm] on the outside. I used to feel good about things, like I could have that better life. But how could I, when there are all of these things I can't do, places that make it clear that I don't belong."

Illegality and Deportability

Enforcement activity—whether through DUI checkpoints, targeted activity in public spaces, or raids of homes—was stepped up in the mid-2000s, leaving little room for debate that the belonging of these young men and women was in serious question. Nicholas De Genova argues that deportability is a central aspect of undocumented life. In 2002 he wrote, "Migrant 'illegality' is lived through a palpable sense of deportability . . . [of] the possibility of being removed from the space of the nation-state. . . . What makes deportability so decisive in the legal production of migrant 'illegality' and the militarized policing of nation-state borders is that some are deported in order that most may remain (un-deported)—as workers, whose particular migrant status may thus be rendered 'illegal.'"[6] Today, this observation carries even greater weight. Legal scholar Daniel Kanstroom argues that while deportation has long been a legal tool to control immigrants' lives, it is now used with increasing crudeness.[7] The immigration dragnet in operation since the mid-1990s has swept up, detained, and eventually deported millions of individuals, increasing levels of anxiety and separating families.[8] Between 1997 and 2012, the US government carried out more than 4.2 million deportations—twice the total number of *all* deportations from the United States prior to 1997.[9] In fiscal year 2013, DHS removed 438,421 foreign nationals.[10]

Despite a stated policy of prioritizing criminals, Immigration and Customs Enforcement met annual deportation quotas of four hundred thousand by targeting, arresting, and deporting low-priority immigrants.[11] In 2012, nearly half of all immigrants deported had no criminal record. Roundups of noncriminals were achieved through searches of state driver's license records for information about foreign-born applicants, the assistance of ICE agents at traffic safety checkpoints manned by local police departments, and stepped-up processing of undocumented immigrants who had been arrested for low-level offenses and booked into local jails. These efforts snare immigrants guilty of very minor offenses—driving without licenses, making improper lane changes—as well as those who, innocent of any wrongdoing, have their personal information entered into databases when they witness crimes and report them to the police, or are victims of theft, or are in vehicles involved in traffic accidents.[12] These practices have heightened immigrants' vulnerability and have made them too scared to involve law enforcement even when they have been victimized.

The growing trend toward indiscriminate roundups by law enforcement has occurred in conjunction with federal measures to restrict rights of due process.[13] Unlike citizens, immigrants facing deportation do not have the right to a trial by jury or to an appointed counsel, calling into question whether a fair and balanced hearing is even possible. Both the increased numbers of immigrants deported and changes in due process highlight another important aspect of deportability: the threat of deportation serves to sustain immigrants' vulnerability and tractability.

Many of the early exiters confronted the very real prospect that their lives could change in an instant. Carla faced especially difficult circumstances. In an incident similar to what happened to another early exiter, Luz, Arizona police stopped Carla's husband (who, as a green-card holder, was a legal resident) in 2005 and charged him with transporting an undocumented immigrant (he was giving a friend a ride). With her husband in custody, Carla was left to care for their two children by herself and to assume all responsibility for the family's expenses. The last time I saw her was in 2007. She was preparing to take her children to Mexico to live with a relative temporarily while she waited to be reunited with her husband. His green card had been revoked, and he was scheduled to be deported. After struggling by herself for more than two years, Carla had run out of options to remain in the United States at age twenty-seven. "It's been hard doing it alone," she told me.

> I mean, life has been real tough. After my husband was arrested, I fell behind on the rent and we got evicted. This was terrible. We were living in our car until the shelter had space for us. Then we lived [in the shelter] for a few months. And that was really hard because I had to work. But then a friend I used to work with told me she had an extra room we could rent for cheap, and so we've been living there for just about eight months. . . . My kids need their dad, and I can't do this for much longer.

Carla and her family have been living in Mexico ever since, joining the hundreds of thousands of Mexican migrants and their family members who have left the United States to live in Mexico. Included in this collateral damage are spouses, American-born children, and other family members. According to Mexican census figures, between 2005 and 2010, 1.4 million Mexicans—including about 300,000 children born in the United States—moved to Mexico.[14]

As early exiters grew older and the chances of discovery and arrest increased, the threat of deportation clarified their feelings about belonging and about illegality as a juridical status. As one respondent told me, "Being illegal means that everything you do is illegal." For respondents and their families, the consequences of illegality are very serious. To survive, early exiters had to work and drive. But doing so increased the chances of their being arrested, detained, and deported. Very few had the luxury of not working, driving, or taking care of themselves; and all felt obligated to help their struggling family members.

In 2004 when I first met Sergio at age twenty, he felt conflicted about his undocumented status and identity. He loved all things Mexican—music, food, art, sports teams. He told me that once he almost got a very large Aztec calendar tattooed on his back. But he lamented that he really did not know the country of his birth. "I know I'm Mexican 100 percent," he told me. "But I haven't been there since I was a kid. They'd make fun of me if I went down there—call me a *pocho* [Mexican slang for someone who speaks Spanish poorly], things like that. But right now, I can't go because of my status. It's so frustrating."

Between 2004 and 2007, Sergio's life changed significantly. First, his girlfriend became pregnant and he felt compelled to assume greater financial responsibility to support his new family. Then he took a full-time job at a factory and carpooled with a coworker, a white man with tattoos covering his bald head. One evening after work, local police pulled them over and searched his coworker's vehicle. In addition to finding a small amount of drugs in the car, they found a homemade explosive device. Although Sergio had been unaware of the contents of the car, he was nevertheless charged as an accomplice to a federal crime and ordered to serve a three-year prison term.[15] In 2009, after he finished his prison time, he was deported. At age twenty-five, he was living in a country he had not visited since he left as a young boy.[16] Nostalgia for a homeland he never really knew had quickly turned on its head as he faced the difficulty of starting again.

Sergio spent two and a half years in Tijuana, doing "odd jobs" while renting out a room in an apartment above a loud bar. He returned to Los Angeles in 2012. He was vague about the details of his return, and he was now even more cautious of authorities. He did his best to stay "under the radar," living close to his job so that he could walk to work. Avoiding arrest and deportation was even more important now that he had two children.

Sergio's dilemma—being undocumented but also needing to make ends meet—brings to light another important tension. The undocumented 1.5 generation can make strong claims to social or cultural citizenship based on longtime presence in the United States and attachments to people, places, and institutions. However, the reality that they can be stopped, detained, and removed from the country strongly underscores the salience of the law as the ultimate determinant of their outsider status.

For my respondents, driving without licenses throughout their adolescent and adult lives increased their chances of being deported.[17] Taking buses presented other risks. Through my fieldwork, I heard about numerous sightings of ICE agents at bus stations. Sonny told me about a cousin who had been waiting with his girlfriend at a bus stop near Huntington Beach when local police stopped him and asked for his papers. When he was unable to produce them, they drove him a hundred miles to Tijuana and dropped him off. Since he had very little money with him and no familiarity with Tijuana, Sonny's cousin had a difficult time coping with this abrupt life change. When I spoke with Sonny again in 2009, his cousin had been in Mexico for almost two years. His family had been unable to come up with sufficient funds to bring him back to the United States.

Extending De Genova's work on deportability, sociologists Cecilia Menjívar and Leisy J. Abrego argue that the increased raids, apprehensions, detentions, and deportations associated with recent immigration enforcement efforts inflict "legal violence" upon individuals and families.[18] This reading of the consequences of heightened enforcement measures is related to my own and Leo Chavez's use of the concept of "abjectivity," drawing attention to those most vulnerable to the practices of power.[19] These processes are manifested in the deteriorating economic, physical, emotional, and psychological well-being of immigrants as they navigate their shrunken worlds. Important is the toll taken by the *fear* of these state-sponsored actions. In addition to individuals' direct experiences with immigration officials, stories shared by family members, neighbors, and the Spanish-speaking media detailing near misses, arrests, detentions, and deportations regularly spread in waves across communities, amplifying concern and elevating levels of fear.

In adulthood, as spaces of inclusion became less accessible and adult responsibilities multiplied respondents' legal exclusions, my respondents learned to police themselves, restricting their own actions and routines to avoid potential trouble. And as reports of family members, friends, and neighbors being swept up in the immigration dragnet became more commonplace, the sense of safety established in their childhoods became increasingly fragile. That is, pathways to adulthood increasingly and dramatically drew experiences of legal violence into their everyday worlds.

Over time, early exiters became better accustomed to living in the shadows. Although heightened levels of enforcement within their communities and parks, on streets and highways, and at bus stations provoked constant stress and worry, they developed survival skills and learned to navigate precarious work arrangements. This ability to accommodate to their changing circumstances was aided by their early entry into illegality, which had gradually provided them with a baseline set of tools and expectations that college-goers lacked.

Living in the Moment

Early exiters' dim view of the future stemmed from the cumulative effects of illegality and the seemingly insurmountable barriers framing their lives. Confrontations with their legal limitations and threats of apprehension and deportation underscored the stark reality that at any moment their lives could change. For early exiters like Luz, living in the moment was not a choice but an imposed state of being: "If you don't have papers and you do own something, the day that something happens, it just all goes away. Like if you get deported or something, everything that you worked for is gonna be gone. . . . I think maybe I'm gonna work hard for it, and have it, and then like, all of a sudden, you know, my dream [is] just shattered. And I think if I had papers, and I got ahead, and I know it would be mine and nobody could take them away."

Luz's hyperawareness of her precarious status was grounded in real-life experience. When Luz was stopped by the police for a minor traffic violation, the incident quickly escalated into an emergency. In California, driving without a license can result in a hefty fine and in the car being towed and impounded for thirty days.[20] When the police had Luz's car towed, she and her children were left stranded on the side of the road.

> I was coming from an appointment, and my, my son took off his seatbelt in the tantrum that he was throwing, and the cop passed by us and saw him without a seatbelt. And I couldn't pull aside to put his seatbelt back on because it was traffic time, and we were like in the middle of the road. The cop stopped me and he gave me a ticket for not having a license and they took the car. [Fortunately,] I still have it. I got it back. I got [the car] back because it's under my mom's [name]. And I look at it, and it's like, "Oh my God." The money I paid to get it out, I could [have] given it as a payment.

For Luz, this incident put into sharp focus the fact that at any moment her life could change. She grew fearful of everyday situations and reluctant to call anything her own.

I heard variations on these themes from several respondents. When Sergio and his brother were on the receiving end of a fender bender at a stoplight, they had no choice but to pay for the damage out of their own pockets. While the incident was not their fault, they were uninsured. They offered to pay the other driver $500 in cash if he would bypass an insurance claim. Shortly after that, Sergio traded in his souped-up Impala for a 1987 Chevy Cavalier, for which he paid $900. Loosening his grip on material possessions was one of many survival strategies Sergio and other undocumented youth learned over time. He reasoned that if he lost the car he would not be out very much money.

Early exiters like Luz and Sergio knew that nothing in their worlds was permanent. Like many other undocumented immigrants, they conditioned themselves not to make long-term plans or invest too much in their jobs, friends, or material possessions. They lived only in the present because doing so was a requirement for survival.

The lives of early exiters were pushed to the margins. Compared to college-goers, they had a heightened awareness of limitations and an inability (or perhaps an unwillingness) to envision the future. College-goers also inhabited a world narrowly circumscribed by their legal limitations, but these limitations were temporarily eclipsed by a pervasive sense of promise and optimism. Freed from burdensome family responsibilities and the need to take on full-time jobs, college-goers were less threatened than early exiters by the worries of daily survival and possible apprehension. Their world extended farther, reaching outward to their college campuses and into the lives of teachers, mentors, professors, and a diverse group of peers. In early adulthood, college-goers' lives reflected a sense of belonging cultivated much earlier in childhood that provided them with a longer view into the future and a stronger belief in possibility.

College-Goers: When Doors Stop Opening

On February 14, 2007, Rosalba received a Valentine's gift that would change her life. Her father, a migrant worker who had received his green card as a result of IRCA-based legalization in the late 1980s, had initiated the process to sponsor Rosalba and her sister for legal status more than twelve years earlier. Her younger sister was able to obtain legal residency by her fourth year of college, but Rosalba turned twenty-one during the process, "aging out" of eligibility to be sponsored by her father. She had to start over. During her long wait, she accumulated multiple degrees: an associate's degree from her community college and a bachelor's and a master's degree in mathematics. By 2007, she had also met all of California's requirements for a teaching credential. On Valentine's Day Rosalba's work permit arrived in the mail, and her green card arrived shortly after. She sent an e-mail to share the good news with friends and mentors who had supported her over the years. By the end of the week, three local high schools had offered her a position teaching math. She took a job that spring as a temporary math instructor at a high school near her home, and by fall she had a permanent teaching position at the high school. With her combination of advanced degrees and legal status, she had become a vital contributing member of her community, doing work she loved. By 2012, she had been teaching for five years.

Rosalba's story points to what might have been for many of her college-going counterparts if immigration policies had allowed for their regularization. The initiation of the Deferred Action for Childhood Arrivals (DACA) program on August 15, 2012, sought to remedy some of the problems associated with their undocumented status, but for many of my respondents (as I discuss in the final chapter) the lack of a pathway to legalization was a deterrent to apply. Moreover, the temporary and partial nature of the program was not sufficient to pull many of these young people significantly away from the margins.

Before the initiation of the DACA program on August 15, twenty-nine respondents held bachelor's degrees. An additional twelve had finished graduate programs. For nearly all of these young men and women, a combination of hard work and assisted opportunities had allowed successful transitions from high school to college. Their progress gave them hope for a better future and seemed to confirm the often-cited relationship between hard work and material success.

Prior to DACA—and even after, for some respondents—college-goers' high levels of educational attainment and strong beliefs in a system of meritocracy were losing their power. These seemingly successful young men and women were crashing headlong into the limits of belonging. The reality of their legal circumstances defied the dreams that years of accumulated Americanizing experiences had inspired, leaving them frustrated and often angry. Many of their high-achieving legal peers benefited from paid internships, experienced a larger world through travel, and embarked on careers in high-skilled work sectors. Meanwhile, aside from the few like Rosalba who were able to adjust their immigration status, not one of the remaining undocumented college-going respondents had been able to legally pursue an occupation that made use of his or her educational credentials or professional preparation. Instead, as adults (most in their late twenties and early thirties), they were on downward trajectories. Once-open doors had firmly closed. For them, adult life represented a steep fall from their earlier experiences and lifestyles. Finding that their hard work and talent no longer brought success was disorienting and deeply distressing.

Life after College

For most college-goers, leaving postsecondary education was more of a challenge than their transition out of high school. For them, as for many of their legal peers, the exit from institutions of higher education was the first time they were without a clear guide for what to do next.

I followed Scarlet as she progressed through college and then through a two-year master's program in counseling. I knew that along the way she had faced some tough decisions about school, work, personal relationships, and family responsibilities. Nevertheless, she was able to reconcile these tensions in order to make a seamless transition from college to graduate school. She persuaded her mother to let her live at home for the two years of her master's program, and because her boss liked her she was able to retain her part-time job. These arrangements allowed her the time and resources needed to attend school full time.

Scarlet, like many others, had hoped that in pursuing postcollege education she would buy the time needed for the DREAM Act to finally become law. But Congress remained stalled and Scarlet had to face the inevitable. She found herself confronting the same old dilemmas. Her mother gave her a choice: either find a place to live on her own or substantially increase her monthly contributions to the household. Her mother reasoned that Scarlet would be working full-time hours and should be able to find a job that paid her well, given her many years in school. But Scarlet's job options were as limited as always.

When we met at an educators' conference in 2010, Scarlet had been out of graduate school for several months. She was trying to retain her professional identity and outlook, but the increased demand for income compelled her to work more hours at her job while she looked for something better. The $9.50 an hour she was making, though adequate to help her mom when Scarlet had been a full-time student, was not enough to meet her current needs. But she did not expect to find a job in her field.

> All of my life, the decision has been really made for me. I haven't had to think too much about it. I've just known that I will be in school after the summer. When I finished my master's program last spring, I didn't know what I was going to do. You know that empty feeling in your stomach? I didn't have a job waiting for me. I couldn't really even look. My friends were looking for jobs and working on their résumés. I couldn't spend any more money to stay in school and my mom was pushing me to help out. It really felt scary.

Scarlet's dilemmas were not uncommon among college-goers as they headed into an uncertain future. Graduation signaled to them and to their families that it was time to take on greater levels of responsibility and participation in the workforce. It also marked a time of tremendous disappointment as long-held dreams went unrealized. By 2012, she had an office job answering phones for a startup company in Los Angeles, a job she had gotten through a friend of a friend. The work gave her full-time hours and enough money to better help her mom, but it was not where she wanted to be—especially after earning two degrees.

Dreams Denied

Higher education provided college-goers with an increased range of opportunities. As students, they enlarged their networks and gained important skills and experience. They also received a greater level of exposure to a world of opportunity. In 2006, Ramona, who interned at her university's career center, told me, "If you take advantage of every-thing, the resources are definitely there for you." However, over time, Ramona found that many attractive possibilities ultimately were beyond her reach. She and other college-goers found themselves having to turn down job offers, invitations to travel, and other exciting, potentially life-changing opportunities. These incidents began to highlight what sociologist Richard Alba refers to as the "bright boundaries" between these young adults and the full membership that they sought.[21]

When Cesar finished college, his years of struggle and persistence were rewarded: he was offered exactly the job he had most wanted, a position analyzing chromosomes in a cytogenetics lab. Over the years, he had worked hard to ready himself for this kind of step. To get to col-lege in the first place, he had to overcome several obstacles. After real-izing he could not afford the tuition at his dream school in Northern California, Cesar enrolled in a community college closer to home.[22] Meanwhile, he put aside the money he made through the tutoring busi-ness he started with his brother. In two years, he successfully completed his transfer requirements with a 3.8 grade point average and honors. Help from his parents, combined with his own savings, allowed Cesar to transfer to a prestigious public university in Los Angeles just as A. B. 540 passed in 2001. Cesar excelled at his studies; a number of his biol-ogy professors soon identified him as having great promise. He spent his remaining two years gaining valuable experience working in their labs.

Upon graduation, one of his professors offered him a job in the lab. None of his peers or mentors was surprised by the offer. Cesar knew that thanks to his diligent work he was well prepared for this experi-ence. But he also knew that he could not take it. His immigration status required that he turn down the job he wanted most.

Cesar's story of denial stayed with me a long time. Over the years, however, I heard similar stories from many of the degreed college-goers whose efforts garnered them praise and recognition from their professors and potential employers. Their advanced degrees and extensive networks positioned them well for career opportunities, but as they began to finish their educational pursuits and exit semilegal spaces, the obstacles in their path became progressively pervasive and strong—a disturbing reminder of their legal limits.

Several college-goers tried hard to resist the transition to illegality. They may have been in denial regarding the life awaiting them; or they may have become too accustomed to lives that could not be sustained. In either case, these young men and women inevitably found themselves in uncomfortable situations, trying to negotiate non-negotiable legal barriers.

Irene also tried and failed to resist the transition to illegality. As an undergraduate in a highly competitive film program at California State University, she landed an internship with a large, Spanish-speaking national television network. She loved the experience and the access to "an unimaginable network of contacts." Near the end of her senior year (2008), I met with Irene on her university campus. Over lunch, we discussed one of her film projects. After our meeting, as we were saying goodbye, she broke down in tears. She explained that she had been keeping a major disappointment to herself for two weeks and needed to tell someone about it. The producer who was supervising her internship had been so impressed with her work that he had invited her to join his film crew in Mexico City, where they would be shooting a television series. She would be gone for three months. He told her that he had booked a flight; the crew would be leaving shortly.

Without thinking, Irene excitedly accepted. She told me that though she knew she would not be able to travel, she "wanted to hold on to the good feeling for a little longer." She added, "This hurts a lot and it shouldn't. This should be the most exciting time in my life. I should be out right now shopping for the trip, buying myself some new outfits. You know, the stuff you do. Here it is right in front of me, and I can't do anything about it. I've got to, I can't go forward. I don't want to face that reality. I can't tell him. I feel ashamed to tell him the truth." Eventually she had to tell him something. She told me that she felt so sad lying about it. It just was not fair.

Irene continued to stay active in the arts community. She volunteered as a stage manager for a theater space in Boyle Heights for several years.

And in 2012, she cofounded a multiarts production company, where she assumed the position of creative director. This new venture opened up doors for Irene, and she maintained a positive outlook. But her group did not have enough capital to purchase the expensive cameras and editing equipment they needed, and Irene's position did not pay her full-time wages. She had no choice but to continue to live with her family—all five crammed into a two bedroom apartment—because the little money she made was not sufficient for financial independence.

Competing Needs

Even as they faced the increasingly thick boundary being drawn around them, college-goers had to confront another unsettling experience. Now that they had passed their midtwenties, the tension between their limited rights and their expanding financial and personal responsibilities was acute. Pushing the bounds of what was recently termed "adultolescence," the college-goers had an immediate and urgent need to earn money. They could no longer justify being out of the labor market and dependent on their parents.[23] In their families, no one had the luxury of not contributing to the household. Many college-goers had taken part-time jobs earlier in their lives to help their families and pay their own expenses. Exits from higher education, however, marked the beginning of another, very different phase. Olivia described to me the mismatch between her expectations and the hard reality of "undocumented life without a net": "During college, I worked part time at a friend's café. The arrangement was real convenient for me. I basically made my own hours, and if I got busy with school, like during finals week or something, I could work less. It was also nice because I could study there. After I graduated, I stayed on for a little longer, but I needed full-time work and my friend couldn't afford to pay me full time. That was a rude awakening for me. It was hard to find jobs that paid what I needed. I think I also had too high expectations."

Similarly, Nimo, who was for many years the most optimistic of all my respondents, experienced a dramatic fall when he was forced to confront life as an undocumented immigrant. After he had lived several years in his aunt's apartment, Nimo's mother decided it was time for her and her two children to find an apartment of their own. However, this new arrangement required Nimo to take on considerably more responsibility for helping out with rent and monthly expenses. He found a full-time job at a fast-food restaurant. Work was hard and a harsh wake-up call for him. Having finished schooling, he no longer had the daily affirmations of an upwardly mobile life to counter his negative experiences. Life became very different.

Other college-goers were fortunate to find positions working with youth or as part of community organizing campaigns in sympathetic community organizations offering wages through stipends or in-kind donations. These kinds of jobs made it possible to continue their activist pursuits and provided some continuity in their postcollege lives. These community groups were able to support a small number of "DREAM activists" after college. Other recent graduates were drawn to the independent options of selling cosmetics or plasticware as an alternative to taking "immigrant jobs."

Cesar and Oscar's tutoring business provided both young men with a productive pursuit once they left college. After adjusting to the increasing likelihood that his chances of becoming a scientist were fading, Cesar invested more time in the tutoring business. Over the years, they took on a greater number of higher-income clients. But the money coming in was not enough to allow either brother to move out of their parents' home. Still, much like the organization of DREAM Act advocates that Cesar co-chaired, the brothers' business gave them opportunities to continue to engage in a world where, as Cesar said, they felt as though they were "doing something positive." By 2012, Cesar had adjusted his immigration status through marriage to his long-time girlfriend, but Oscar remained undocumented.

Jobs with local community groups or working as independent contractors gave respondents a chance to pursue early career pathways related or at least parallel to their student lives and allowed them the luxury of continuity. Most of these options were neither long lived nor well paid, however. Ultimately, they did little more than delay college-goers' inevitable entry into low-wage work, and they kept them in dependent relationships with parents or other family members. Indeed, most college-goers were powerless to escape the strong pull of bad jobs—washing dishes, doing landscaping or construction, cleaning offices, taking care of other people's children, washing cars, working on assembly lines, or doing fast-food service work.

Adulthood was a restless time for many recently graduated college-goers. Several respondents moved through job after job, not staying more than six months in any one. Dissatisfied with meager wages and generally uneasy about their treatment by employers, they left because they felt entitled to something better. But each new job proved no better than last. Over time, they began to realize that they had few choices other than physical labor.

Respondents spoke frankly about how hard it was for them to come to terms with the bad options that illegality forced on them. As time created distance between the present and their differently spent college days, the harshness of their new reality began to erase the remaining traces of those earlier worlds. Working forty- to fifty-hour weeks, they developed routines that crowded out previous activities and pursuits. They saw less of their old school friends and more of their coworkers. Time available for activities other than work dwindled considerably.

"A Sinking Feeling in My Gut"

Over time, as adult college-goers came to grips with the new meanings of undocumented status, they began to view and define themselves differently. They began to explore the various meanings of "life as an 'illegal' immigrant."

Since I first met Esperanza in 2002, I had witnessed her change from an outwardly confident, wide-eyed, university student with "big plans for the future" to a socially withdrawn, inwardly focused adult who seemed to have the weight of the world on her shoulders. For many years, activism had buoyed her hopes, but her late twenties hit her hard and she began to lose hope. When I spoke to her by phone in 2007 I sensed the transformation. "My world seems upside down," she told me. "I have grown up, but I feel like I'm moving backwards. And I can't do anything about it. I had much more freedom in school. Like, I had rights, you know. Now I can't do anything by myself and it makes me feel so helpless."

As we talked, I could sense her frustration. She used metaphors to describe her feelings and at one point told me that she "couldn't breathe." But later in the conversation, she put into very clear terms the level of restriction that circumscribed her daily world:

> I know I can do so much more, but I can't because I can't live wherever. I can't choose where I live. I can't choose where I work. And the worst thing is that I can't choose my friends. In high school I was able to do that. I can't anymore. I can't even hang out with my high school friends anymore and that hurts a lot. Yeah, they want to do grown-up stuff. I can't do anything that is eighteen and over. I can't do anything. I can only hang out where little kids hang out. I can't hang out with them. I can't travel with them. I can't go out to dinner with them. I can't go to Vegas with them. If I want to go to a bar, I don't even have a drink. If they want to go to San Diego [a trip that involves passing through immigration checkpoints], if they want to go visit

museums down there, if they want to go to Sea World, I can't go with them. I can't go to any clubs in L.A. because after the marches [in spring 2006], they don't accept *matrículas* [identification provided by the Mexican government] anywhere.

This extreme and sudden narrowing of worlds left college-goers like Esperanza incensed. They described their worlds as a "jail" or a "cage." Several respondents told me they felt like "birds without wings." Significantly, they experienced these changes as something that stunted their development, unable to do anything "eighteen and older," as Esperanza so aptly described. Instead of allowing them to catch up, time seemed to move them backward.

As the condition of illegality came to define their daily routines and restrict their choice of identity, college-goers finally accepted that their immigration status—not their dreams—would shape most of their future plans. As Esperanza described it, "I just feel like this is now my life. I can't depend on other people to solve my problems. Like, look how long it has taken to pass immigration [legislation]. I just have this sinking feeling in my gut that things are going to stay this way for me."

Even as they tried to move on with their newly limited lives, however, some college-goers continued to actively resist their circumstances. Activism kept many busy and allowed them to take an active role in their attempts to change their legal circumstances. But these young people also needed to find jobs to take care of themselves. As I witnessed these now-adult respondents adjusting their lifestyles, I also observed their growing restlessness and frustration. In 2011, during a conversation I had with Esperanza about her employment status, she revealed her sense of hopelessness. She had been trying to move out of her father's apartment in order to be more independent, but she was unable to accumulate enough money. Unstable work arrangements forced her to hunt for new jobs every two or three months. When we spoke, she had been looking for work for a little over three weeks. She told me, "I just need a job. It's become about survival. If it used to be a choice, it is not a choice anymore. I am to the point where yes, I will clean somebody's home. I will take care of them. I will clean up somebody's saliva. More and more, it is getting to the point where I don't care."

In 2012, Esperanza moved to Wisconsin to join her mom and sisters. She soon found work as a late-shift receptionist at a hotel and gave birth to a baby girl. Now with extra responsibilities, she told me she had set aside many of the "big dreams" she had held onto in an earlier and more idealistic period of her life. Now, she just wanted to be a "responsible adult" and to do what she could to support her child and to help her mom and younger sisters have a better life.

THE EXPERIENTIAL DIMENSION OF ILLEGALITY AS A MASTER STATUS

On November 25, 2011, eighteen-year-old Joaquin Luna Jr. of Mission, Texas, a teen who had come to the United States as a six-month-old infant, took his own life. Despairing that his undocumented status would block his ability to achieve his dreams to go to college, he drafted goodbye letters to relatives, friends, and teachers. In a letter addressed to Jesus Christ, he wrote, "I've realized that I have no chance in becoming a civil engineer the ways I've always dreamed of here . . . so I'm planning on going to you."[24] Joaquin's suicide highlights the psychological distress, surprisingly strong among nearly all of my respondents, that undocumented status can generate.

As undocumented young adults transition to adulthood, their lives are increasingly marked by illegality: as a juridical status and as a sociopolitical condition that carries exclusionary and stigmatizing consequences. When they were children, important spaces and relationships—accessed largely but not exclusively through legal participation in school—mitigated the effects of undocumented status. The importance of these "legally safe" spaces was apparent in the childhood and early adolescent worlds of respondents, when legal immigration status was less consequential to their everyday lives. In late adolescence and early adulthood, the importance of these spaces became even more apparent as early exiters entered low-skilled labor markets and encountered a dramatically greater number of legal exclusions, while college-goers enjoyed legally unrestricted inclusion in their central pursuit, higher education. These uneven experiences highlighted the significance of institutional and community mediators that offset, delayed, and accelerated the impact of illegality. In adulthood, my respondents experienced little doubt about the consequential nature of immigration status. Both college-goers and early exiters experienced illegality as the most dominant force in their adult lives.

The adult lives of my respondents provide strong evidence for the claim that illegality is a master status. Whereas earlier experiences of inclusion and belonging provided some legitimate cause to question the overriding importance of illegality, in adulthood exclusions far outnumbered inclusions. The young men and women in my study, all of whom spent most of their adolescent and adult lives in the United States, ultimately found that they were outsiders. They could legally attend school but not work; they could form friendships and attachments with peers and romantic partners, but they could not join their peers as they began to drive, vote, and meet friends after work; and although they could plant roots in the broader community through local attachments and participation in organizations and institutions, they could never be full members. These experiences highlight the empirical reality that, as adults, undocumented members of the 1.5 generation were as limited as their parents.

Respondents' narratives draw attention to the *experiential* aspect of illegality. Their stories not only provide ample evidence of the effects of exclusion but reveal *how* policies and practices dramatically frame their lives. The anthropologist Sarah Willen argues that the scholarship that has drawn attention to illegality as a juridical status and as a sociopolitical condition is missing this experiential dimension. Drawing on fieldwork with undocumented immigrants in Tel Aviv, she observes that the complicated realities of illegality do more than narrowly circumscribe everyday life. They also frame migrants' individual and collective experiences of being in the world.[25] Daily perceptions of danger and the threat of deportation produce specific kinds of fear, anxiety, and suffering. Willen's subjects describe their constant vigilance against being apprehended by police and immigration authorities, their efforts to hide their skin and their bodies, and their struggles to contain stress and worry that invade even their nonwaking hours. Local configurations of migrant illegality, she argues, can extend their reach literally into undocumented migrants' "inner parts" by profoundly shaping their subjective experiences of time, space, embodiment, sociality, and self.[26]

My respondents' narratives speak to the nature of their vulnerability to this condition of illegality. That is, earlier experiences of inclusion left them mentally and physically defenseless, unsuspecting of the kinds of experiences that awaited them in adulthood. But as time passed, and they grew up, their experiences changed. Adult lives brought experiences of exclusion, stress, stigma, expulsion. This accumulation of experiences took its toll on their emotional and physical well-being.

Over the twelve years I have been in contact with young men and women for this study, I have been shocked by the magnitude of their pain and suffering and at how frequently they spoke to me of their anxieties, chronic sadness, depression, over- or undereating, difficulty sleeping, and desire to "not start the day." They also talked about the exacerbation of chronic ailments like high blood pressure, headaches, toothaches, and ulcers.[27] The more time I spent with respondents, the more clearly I recognized that the range of problems they detailed were those typically linked to unresolved grief.[28] Ramon told me that his wife Maria had "been sick for over a year" because of stress, but she had not seen a doctor. Neither Maria nor Ramon had medical insurance, and some months they did not make enough to fully cover their regular expenses. Other respondents mentioned similarly physical manifestations of stress. Misto developed an ulcer; Andrea made two trips to the ER because she felt as if she was having a heart attack and had to miss several days of work and school after experiencing chronic fatigue and recurrent headaches that required frequent trips to her community clinic. There were days when Esperanza could not go to school or work because, as she told me, "Sometimes I can't even get out of bed."

Most respondents did not have access to health care and could not afford to seek professional help. Many felt unable to communicate their problems to friends and loved ones. This led to misunderstandings, especially when symptoms were perceived by others as expressions of indifference or laziness. Early exiter Manuel told me that he felt as though nobody understood him: "It really made me mad. Nobody understood. I know I didn't let them in, but it just frustrated me. You know, get off my back. And it would really make me mad when they assumed I was being lazy." Shaking his head, he added, "If only they knew."

For some, stress and worry led to other types of acting out. Several respondents, including early exiter Geraldo, increased their alcohol consumption and started taking drugs, common strategies for self-medicating. Geraldo's friends started to notice he was drinking excessively, often during daytime hours. This led to arguments with his girlfriend and, in time, to his mother asking him to leave her home because his behavior frightened her. When I spoke to Geraldo in 2011, he had been living on his own for several weeks. He was sleeping on a coworker's couch and regretting some of his choices: "I don't know what is wrong with me. It's like watching myself from the outside. I don't like what I am doing, but I can't stop myself. At a point it just became, I didn't care. I was like, 'Screw it, it doesn't really matter anyway.' I just felt numb. At the same time, I can see that I am hurting a lot of people around me."

In addition to these better-known causes of stress and anxiety, my respondents contended with several others. As members of households that included undocumented members, many grew up understanding the consequences of living "outside the law."[29] As children, they witnessed numerous expressions of fear and stress among family members. They also saw relatives and community members detained and deported. Undoubtedly, these experiences shaped their sense of risk and insecurity.

It is not surprising that the scholarship seeking to draw connections between immigration experiences and health outcomes is growing, particularly as limitations on health care access have dramatically limited available care.[30] But the experiences of my respondents illustrate something new. To be sure, their bodies bore the injuries and sickness doled out by their low-wage jobs. And the stress of worry about being undocumented undoubtedly manifested in their mental and physical health. But it was their experiences of shattered dreams and expulsion that stung the most.

For many of my respondents, persistent stress gave way to a crippling inability to take control of their lives. As their problem-solving strategies faltered, the mounting stress progressively reduced their functionality. The message that emerges from their individual accounts is unequivocal: being undocumented is bad for one's health. However, a lack of legal immigration status alone does not necessarily generate the suffering these respondents described. Indeed, in some neighborhood and institutional spaces and stages of the life course, their lack of formal immigration status had a relatively small impact on respondents' everyday lives. However, as their life course progressed, these spaces shrank as a constellation of laws and practices mobilized around formal and informal efforts to exclude and expel undocumented immigrants sowed fear, anxiety, and suffering in their worlds. It was a fate many could not escape.

DACA'S LIMITED REACH

On August 15, 2012, the US Immigration and Customs Enforcement (USCIS) initiated the Deferred Action for Childhood Arrivals (DACA) program. An estimated 1.2 million young immigrants were eligible for immediate enrollment in DACA at the time.

After the implementation of DACA, I heard many stories of new jobs and new lives, of widened access, and of the newly acquired ability to pursue dreams and help family members.[31] It is too early to tell what effect this will have on many of my older respondents, but several college-goers who were under the age of thirty-one as of June 15, 2012, had already begun utilizing DACA to continue their education and get better jobs. Cory was finally able to take a campus job that allowed her to finish college and had begun working as a freelance journalist. Irene was accepted into a PhD program that had recently changed its policy to admit DACA beneficiaries. And in 2015 Tezca, who had managed to stay connected with mentors and to remain engaged in campus life, thus holding on to a positive outlook, landed a job as a special education teacher in Los Angeles. At thirty-one years old and married, he had received an opportunity that was a game changer—a chance to finally have a little breathing room financially while he began a professional career.

At age thirty in 2012, Esperanza just made the age cutoff. In 2013 she was happy, hopeful, optimistic. "You have no idea how thankful I felt that I got included into that. I remember the day, I logged into Facebook at the library and [my friend messaged me], and she congratulated me on barely making it. She sent me the memo to make me believe it. And when Obama finally made the announcement after taking forever, I was watching, still incredulous that I had made it in."

Prior to that day Esperanza's plan was to move to Wisconsin with her dog and live there for a year. Her plan was to spend time with her mom and sisters and then leave the country after her thirty-first birthday: "I had heard of [California friends] who had moved to Canada while I was still in college, though I never really met them or confirmed anything, and I had made up my mind that I did not want to live my thirties with chains and that by then I would have the courage to leave."

However, she told me that since the DACA announcement her life had been hanging by a thread. She had been fired from a telemarketing job and faced eviction from her apartment. She had sent her dog to California to be "pet-sat" while she got back on her feet. But the costs of the DACA application delayed her time line to get into a new apartment. That week she was also stopped by the police and given a ticket for driving without a license. She completed her biometrics for DACA, hoping she could be approved and get a driver's license before having to go to court. That day she was hospitalized and told she could have preeclampsia, a pregnancy complication characterized by high blood pressure and signs of organ damage. Left untreated, it could lead to serious, even fatal, complications. "That meant that I would have a preemie, though my biggest worry was how I was going to pay for my apartment and my ticket and keep up with my bills and still be able to afford to bring my dog back if I was not going to be able to work for six weeks. And of course I work in a minimum-wage job with no benefits."

Esperanza somehow managed. She did not receive her work permit as fast as she had expected and was not able to bring her dog back as soon as she wanted (in the waiting, he poisoned himself and died shortly before Esperanza went back to work). Her baby spent sixty-seven days in the neonatal intensive care unit. But being in Wisconsin, Esperanza had her younger sister there to "help make sure she had everything she needed to start her life at home." Esperanza also received help from nonprofits and food pantries, which provided her with a crib, a car seat, a dining table, and a microwave. And with the help of friends, WIC, and visiting nurse services things started to turn around for Esperanza and her daughter.

It took Esperanza several months to get back on her feet. In January of 2014 she was working at a bank, a job she obtained through a temporary agency. She did not feel as though this was a job that matched her degree. She had earned a college degree from a prestigious university, but her résumé was unimpressive and she lacked the skills accumulated by legal residents of her age. And while she had worked for several years, Esperanza lacked job experience in professional positions. But since she had such a difficult time finding a job after receiving DACA she was reluctant to let this one go in order to begin a new search. "I learned that recruiters do not look for potential when hiring but for work experience and previous job length. They ask situational questions about your last job, that prove your capabilities."

Esperanza now has a job, a credit card, and a driver's license. She told me that she had stopped having panic attacks when driving but that the "post-traumatic stress," as she called it, had lingered for a long time. She had also mustered up the courage to apply for a car loan and to buy a new car.

> Seriously, it had gotten to the point where I would look over my shoulder constantly and shake uncontrollably if I would spot anything that looked like a police or sheriff's vehicle. Along with credit come new opportunities, like not so much job security, but I no longer feel constrained as far as housing goes. Like I no longer have to worry about whether the place I want to live in will require a Social or not. I no longer have to worry about needing a cosigner for my lease, my car registration, or my utility bills.

Esperanza's relationship with her son's father did not work out. As of our last contact in January of 2015, she was a single mom and trying to provide a good life for her baby.

Among the early-exiter respondents, to my knowledge only two have applied to DACA. Several were ineligible for the program because of crimes they had committed as youths. Others found the prospect of working legally and receiving a stay of deportation attractive, but they could not afford the program's application fee. Most struggle each month to simply keep up with normal expenses. In addition, several told me that DACA status would not improve their financial prospects significantly given their education levels and job experience. They may be right.

After several months of saving for the fee, Ramon's wife Maria sent in her DACA paperwork. With Ramon out of work for an entire year because of a workplace injury, their family that now included four children needed a financial boost. Initially, both Ramon and Maria were going to apply. But after a consultation with a pro bono attorney who told them that because of past crimes Ramon would be at risk for deportation if he submitted documents to the government, Ramon decided not to apply. While he has worked very hard to make up for his troubled past and to overcome the numerous barriers of his undocumented status, he cannot shake off the troubling implications of his past. The belief that individuals are capable of atoning for past transgressions is the cornerstone of most modern societies. But for most immigrants a slight slip-up can have lifelong consequences. Ramon has spent several years living a modest life, trying to be a good husband and father. He has done everything in his power to get his life back on track. But current immigration laws fail to take rehabilitation into account. Someone with an old DUI, even from decades ago, can still be flagged as an enforcement priority and denied adjustment of status even if he or she has done nothing wrong for many years.

Coming up with the application fee for Maria was no easy feat. In 2012 the family was living check to check, unable to meet expenses most months, and Ramon had fallen into a deep depression. In addition to her savings Maria borrowed money from her mother, sister, and a local lending agency.

In 2014, although she had held a work permit for more than a year, Maria had not been able to find a better job. She was still in the same low-paying job that she held for almost two years prior to applying.

DISCARDABLE LIVES

For most respondents, reaching their late twenties marked their full transition into a life stage whereby exclusions overshadowed points of access. Although early exiters and college-goers both reached the same dead end, each group got there by a different route and at different ages. Many college-goers spent their early and midtwenties improving their writing and building the analytic skills needed for high-skilled jobs. Early exiters became more savvy navigating exclusions and the world of low-wage work, and they more regularly took the risks necessary for everyday survival. They also grew more apt to provisionally accept some of the limitations of their lives, while becoming more determined to make the most of the few opportunities they had for making connections, relaxing, and enjoying themselves.

For college-goers, completing the transition to illegality was much more jarring and abrupt. As they accumulated bachelor's and postbaccalaureate degrees, they felt that their hard work and educational investments included them in an increasingly more elite group that would have better access to good jobs and a bigger slice of the American pie. Free-falling from that world into the life of an "illegal" and taking on the status of the quintessential lawbreaker and outsider created mental and emotional upheaval. College-goers had to discard previously held beliefs and prepare their minds and their bodies for daily lives of limitation. And they had to learn the ropes quickly in order to seize the few choices available to them.

These processes did more than detour and derail their plans; they also changed the tenor of their lives. Bit by bit, both early exiters and college-goers became the "stranger," the "illegal immigrant." As adults they transitioned fully into lives of illegality. As their narratives make painfully clear, they were doing their best to avoid notice and to accept and settle into worlds shrunken by legal exclusions and state controls. But perhaps the most important aspect of their adult lives is one typically unacknowledged by scholars and policy makers: for undocumented members of the 1.5 generation, illegality extends far beyond legal boundaries. It reaches into their bodies, minds, and hearts. It saps their energy, consumes their dreams, and crushes their spirits.

As adults, college-goers and early exiters both concentrated on the task of learning to be illegal, and both groups found that illegality consumed larger proportions of their worlds and defined most aspects of their lives. Elevated levels of enforcement ratcheted up fear and raised the consequences of being outside the law. Dreams and goals faded. The two groups continued to display instances of resilience, courage, and resistance, but these attitudes and actions often were trumped by the condition of illegality and the high physical and emotional costs it exacted.

When DACA was announced in 2012 it was hailed by many as a positive step for undocumented young people. This may be true, especially for younger immigrants. But for college-goers and early exiters who came of age in the late 1990s it may have been too little, too late. While many were the intended targets of DREAM Act legislation in the early 2000s, years of grueling work, heartbreak and disappointment, and exclusion from opportunities that could have helped them get ahead have worn down their spirits and have left them disadvantaged in their ability to capitalize on its benefits.

CHAPTER 9

Conclusion

Managing Lives in Limbo

In 2015, when Esperanza, after graduating from the University of California in 2006, was working as a receptionist and taking care of her baby girl, I asked her, "What do you think your life would be like now if you had received your papers ten years ago?" She responded,

> I would have taken the job working at a lab at the University of California instead of dismissing the opportunity because I was quietly undocumented. I would have applied for the undergraduate research program at my university and the [Washington, D.C.] Academic Internship program. I might even have stayed an extra year [in college] and minored in sociology or gotten a second BA in order to get my grades up—it would have made a huge difference in my GPA. After college I would have taken the job I was offered as an underwriter at an insurance company, instead of making up a story about why I could not give my ID number over the phone and saying that I would call them back and never actually calling back. After working for four years there, I would have gone on to law school. Can you imagine? I would have been young and extraordinary. I would have been the walking truth instead of a walking shadow.
>
> Maybe then my [older] sister would have gone on to a university and my cousins would have surpassed my educational accomplishments instead of dismissing them. And today, in 2015, my two teenage sisters would not be so nonchalant about school. No matter how much I tell them to go to college and go as far as the wind will take them, they always come back at me with "Well, what degree do you have? Do you need a university degree to work where you are at? How much do you make? I can make that without going to college, have good credit, and get a nice car [because they are US citizens]." My US citizen friends who graduated with me have jobs they adore. They are living the life.

For young people like Esperanza, and the other young people I have come to know these last twelve years, questions of "What if?" consume their everyday thoughts. What if Sergio had become legalized through his stepfather during his early twenties when he still had a positive outlook on school and his future? What if Irene had been able to accept the offer of an internship with the television film crew in Mexico City? What if Ramon had been eligible for DACA despite the mistakes he made as a teenager? What if Gabriel, Scarlet, and Nimo had had the financial means to give themselves and their families a respite from worry? Would these young people have better lives than the ones they have now? One can only speculate. What is certain, though, is that the lives they have led these last twelve years epitomize Langston Hughes's "dream deferred." Their lives are a testament to the effects of a dysfunctional immigration system and Congress's failure to fix it.

Despite some early momentum, the first fifteen years of the twentieth century brought no progress in the creation of a more coherent immigration policy. In 2001, George W. Bush's first year in office, immigration reform was a key agenda item for the former Texas governor, and both chambers of Congress signaled a willingness to pass significant immigration legislation. By the fall, three key pieces of legislation were moving forward: a pair of agricultural bills, each introduced with bipartisan support; extensions (approved by the House and Senate) to an existing provision that allowed undocumented immigrants who were otherwise eligible for green cards to adjust to lawful permanent residency without leaving the country and bills backed by bipartisan groups in both chambers that would provide a pathway to citizenship for young immigrants.[1]

Moreover, there was growing momentum to advance a bill that would legalize immigrants brought to the country as children. Early in 2001, Senator Richard Durbin (D-IL) met a high school student named Thereza Lee who had been accepted to the Julliard School of Music—a dream come true for her.[2] The music director at Ms. Lee's school contacted Durbin's office when she found out that this student's immigration status would prevent her from being able to attend Julliard. An honors student and concert pianist, Ms. Lee had come to Chicago as a toddler, but because her parents failed to file her immigration paperwork she had no legal residency status. Durbin, moved by her story, helped champion what would later be proposed as the DREAM Act, a bill that would provide conditional permanent residency to certain immigrants of good moral character who graduated from US high schools, had arrived as minors, and had lived in the country continuously for at least five years prior to the bill's enactment.[3]

Throughout 2001, President Bush and Mexican president Vicente Fox spent considerable time negotiating a bilateral agreement on immigration policies and programs that would benefit Mexican migrants and their families.[4] On September 6, 2001, the two leaders formally endorsed a framework agreement on immigration and publicly committed to completing the deal by the end of the year. Finally, real immigration reform appeared certain.

However, a few short days later, the terrorist attacks on the World Trade Center and the Pentagon occurred. In the wake of the tragic events of 9/11, immigration reform negotiations collapsed. Since the attacks were carried out by individuals who were in the United States with visas, immigration measures and border security immediately became central topics of concern. On September 12, Thereza Lee had been scheduled to give a special performance in Washington, D.C., in which she and other undocumented students would make their case for the DREAM Act. Instead, all flights were cancelled that day, and it would be a long time before the DREAM Act and other immigration issues would return to the fore.

Almost four years later, in May 2005, in an attempt to revive immigration discussions, Senators John McCain (R-AZ) and Ted Kennedy (D-MA) introduced S. 1033, the Secure America and Orderly Immigration Act, more commonly known as "McCain-Kennedy." This bill, which incorporated legalization, guest worker programs, and border enforcement components, was the first comprehensive immigration reform package to be introduced since the early 2000s. Although the bill never came to a vote in the Senate, subsequent bills were drafted on the basis of its framework.[5] During this time, the DREAM Act was attached to various bills (including McCain-Kennedy) and was proposed as an amendment to the 2008 Department of Defense Authorization Bill (S. 2919). None of these efforts succeeded. On October 18, 2007, Durbin, along with Republican cosponsors Charles Hagel (R-NE) and Richard Lugar (R-IN), introduced the DREAM Act as S. 2205. But the bill ultimately failed a cloture attempt and did not make it to the Senate floor.[6] Despite bipartisan support, several more years passed before the DREAM Act again came up for debate.

During the years in which the DREAM Act remained stalled, stories like Thereza Lee's multiplied. In 2006, the *Wall Street Journal* reported the dilemma of Princeton salutatorian Dan-el Padilla Peralta, who faced the daunting prospect of not being able to return to the United States if he accepted a two-year scholarship to attend Oxford University in the United Kingdom. A chorus of high-level supporters, including Senator Hillary Clinton and the deans of Harvard Law School and Princeton's Woodrow Wilson School of Public and International Affairs, pressed Citizenship and Immigration Services officials to issue Padilla Peralta a visa, arguing that this high achiever (who delivered his salutatorian speech in Latin) should not be punished for a crime he did not commit.[7] Four years later, the *Boston Globe* reported the arrest and detention of nineteen-year-old Harvard biology student Eric Balderas as he tried to board a plane back to Boston after visiting his mother in San Antonio. When Balderas was granted a temporary visa to stay in the United States, his high school history teacher exclaimed, "It's like somebody up there understands the situation and that he's really a great person and the kind of people we want here in this country."[8]

In a lame-duck session of Congress in December 2010, an eleventh-hour attempt came very close to producing passage of the DREAM Act. After a strong push by President Obama and top congressional Democrats, the act was debated on the floor of the House. To the elation of its supporters, the Democratically controlled House passed the bill by a vote of 216–198. A week later, hopes were dashed when a cloture motion in the Senate was rejected by a margin of five votes, killing the bill and effectively stalling momentum.[9]

The defeat of the DREAM Act in the House meant that undocumented immigrant youth and young adults would have to wait longer. It also suggested that the stories being told by and about hardworking, successful "DREAMers" were failing to sway a segment of Congress. By that time many Americans had come to know hundreds of undocumented valedictorians, class presidents, and model community members through stories told on the floor of Congress, by advocates on college campuses and communities, and on the pages of media outlets throughout the country. These narratives of wasted talent are a heartbreaking illustration of a dysfunctional immigration system that persistently denies the futures of aspiring teachers, doctors, engineers, and architects. The stories also provide ample ammunition in the fight for immigrants' rights. Nevertheless, instead of incorporating these young people, Congress has blocked their progress.

Blocked access to higher education and high-skilled jobs is a serious problem. Legal barriers to the mechanism most Americans try to use to get ahead have grave consequences for undocumented young people, their families, and their communities. When these young people have what it takes to fill the gaps in our highly skilled workforce, this denial is also costly to society as a whole. The theme of wasted talent used by many advocates resonates with many Americans. It is important to recognize, however, that this is only one aspect of the ruinous consequences of current immigration laws. The political debate that has undoubtedly swayed public opinion, prompted more state legislatures to pass bills that improve college access for undocumented students, and moved business leaders, university presidents, and city councils to join their cause, while successful in these terms, has nevertheless obscured many of the realities this book has sought to uncover.

The narrative of the hardworking, academically successful undocumented immigrant student, while helpful in gaining public support, does not address the deeper and more far-reaching consequences of being undocumented: living in poverty, having parents and family members who also bear the burdens of being undocumented, watching friends moving forward but being unable to join them, watching opportunities pass you by, navigating a world of exclusions while constantly looking over your shoulder, and living in fear of deportation. The academically successful make up a small portion of any demographic group and an even smaller fraction of poor, immigrant, and minority youth. Though some undocumented youth become academic high achievers but are barred by immigration laws from obtaining employment at the level of their education and skills, a far larger number encounter, even earlier, obstacles that hamper their ability to succeed in school. A focus on high achievers tends to obscure the struggles of the many other undocumented young people who have fallen from view.[10]

By the time I was finishing this book in the summer of 2015, exactly fourteen years had passed since the initial introduction of the DREAM Act—for my respondents, fourteen years of lost opportunities, diminishing hopes, balked efforts, and grinding stress. Congress's failure to pass legislation to address the untenable circumstances of undocumented immigrant young people has left more than two million children and young adults in a legal limbo.

TIME AND THE TRANSITION TO ILLEGALITY

For undocumented young people, the passage of time is the force that first suspends and later catalyzes the transition to illegality. While familial decisions to migrate are often out of children's control, the timing of a family's migration determines the institutions through which children will enter the host country's society: day care, primary or secondary school, or perhaps the labor market.

During childhood, time is a friendly, slow-moving companion. It encourages a child's attachment to neighborhood spaces and nurtures the development of relationships. Through these experiences, children develop an understanding of their place in the world around them. The accumulation of experiences over time transforms their new surroundings into home. This change is apparent in the way they think, speak, dress, and interact with others.

The childhood and adolescent experiences of my respondents provide compelling evidence that links membership to a set of activities a person engages in as part of a national community and to formal and informal community participation.[11] In this view, community belonging is tied to group membership, but people can belong in many different ways and to different kinds of groups. For children, peers exert a great influence over their lives and thus are an important part of their primary community.

Laws frame immigrants' integration and determine their opportunities for work, their access to political participation, and their eligibility for a range of social benefits.[12] Regardless of the extent of their social participation and economic contribution, immigrants who lack legal status are excluded from full membership. My findings, which document illegality as a *master status*, uphold this observation.

As my respondents entered adolescence, they confronted new requirements of membership and participated in different types of institutions. And as they began to confront glass ceilings in adolescence and early adulthood they came to realize the strict limits to their belonging. Their exclusion from a range of experiences open to their friends tore them out of affirming and nurturing peer networks and drove them toward outsider status. Being undocumented carried a stigma that compelled them to keep secrets even from their closest friends. Instead of explaining why they could not drive or join friends for drinks after work, many respondents began to drop out of peer activities. Stigma management functioned as a *secondary border* by inducing them to withdraw from peer activities in order to hide their immigration status. Over time concealment became routine. These actions not only reduced their participation but also made them coconspirators in the narrowing of their own worlds.

Unable to participate on an equal footing with their peers, my respondents found themselves on the outside of the circle looking in.

This new and painful perspective did not stop them from experiencing their surroundings as home. To the contrary, everyday spaces of inclusion were a powerful reminder of what they could not fully have. The American dream is seductive; children grow up believing that their participation, hard work, and achievement will garner material success and the recognition of formal citizenship. This is perhaps the most devastating aspect of illegality for the 1.5 generation. Everyday life offers daily glimpses of hope—the possibility of friendly exchanges with familiar faces and opportunities to participate in community events. But for undocumented youth these moments are ultimately tainted by the larger frame of exclusion and their growing realization that full membership can be achieved only through formal citizenship.

Inexorably, time caught up with my respondents. As in other societies, the United States has cultural norms specifying age-appropriate behaviors, responsibilities, and rites of passage that shepherd each new generation of youth into adult roles. But for undocumented youth, the transition to adulthood is akin to a *waking nightmare*. As my respondents reached significant points of transition (acquisition of a driver's license, a first paycheck, a senior class trip), their movement toward adulthood was suddenly and irrevocably blocked by immigration status. Because the accumulated experiences of inclusion during their childhood and adolescent years had solidified their sense of integration and membership, this transition to illegality was shocking and debilitating. It represented a fundamental loss of footing that required them to rethink their own identities and their place in the social worlds they inhabited.

The *transition to illegality*—changes in rules concerning undocumented status that took effect in respondents' late adolescence and early adulthood, shifting the meaning and implications of that status—caused respondents to fall dramatically far behind their native-born peers. As their life responsibilities grew, their legal options shrank. They were unable to carry out many adult tasks (working, driving, voting), even though they were just as eager to do so as their friends and classmates. Finding themselves out of step with peers was painful and disorienting, but this was not their only concern. Growing obligations to help out their families and to take responsibility for their own economic needs pushed them increasingly into activities for which they lacked the legal permission to participate. Immigration restrictions stunted their normal adult growth at the same time that family poverty kept them from lingering in adolescence.

Those undocumented youth who enjoyed some combination of reduced family responsibilities, the ability to avoid or postpone entry into the job market, and legally permissible opportunities such as higher education were able to avoid some of the more damaging effects of illegality during their early life transitions. As the experiences of the college-goers illustrate, a successful and seamless transition from K-12 schooling to higher education preserved important support networks and gave respondents a viable and productive pursuit, while also reducing their contact with illicit spaces.

Life course scholars note a recent shift in Western societies with respect to the timing of traditional adult transitions. Economic changes that privilege postgraduate education prompt young people whose families can finance postsecondary schooling to delay their entry into the workforce and marriage. These young people are able to spend their late adolescence and early adulthood gaining a competitive edge in today's high-skilled labor market by developing skills, building résumés, and earning advanced degrees.

For the young adults I interviewed, however, the dominant culture's frame of reference was often less salient than the frames of reference that they had grown up with in their families and communities. They seemed to worry, not that they were staying home too long to help out their families, but that they were unable to help out as much as they wished because of work instability. Ultimately, though, they were concerned that the paths to adulthood that they had chosen—paths influenced both by family loyalties and by cultural expectations—were being blocked by their undocumented status.

As respondents grew into adulthood, a chasm opened up between their stressful, precarious present and a happy, more inclusive past, between illegality and belonging. Early exiters began the transition to illegality as teenagers through everyday behaviors that solidified into narrow, unvarying routines. As opportunities passed them by, lives of illegality became the norm. Most became accustomed to lives of limitation, learning the skills and attitudes necessary to succeed in truncated worlds. Although college-goers were able to delay this transition, time eventually caught up to them. They had come so far, but they continued to face barriers that limited their opportunities to accumulate relevant work experience, build résumés, and challenge their sense of belonging and their own physical and psychological capacities.

These powerful forces of time and the law channeled these undocumented young adults into a stream of bad options. Their work opportunities were limited to grueling low-wage jobs, and working exposed them to many other negative aspects of undocumented life. They needed to recalibrate their expectations for the future while simultaneously learning new survival skills to avoid being caught in Immigration and Customs Enforcement (ICE) raids at work or being arrested, detained, and deported on their daily commute.

Time was distorted in adulthood. Family need forced many respondents to enter the low-wage labor force early, accelerating their transitions to adulthood and illegality. However, exclusions from work, driving, and adult activities prohibited them from crossing important thresholds into adulthood. All the while, under the crushing weight of illegality—of low-wage work, of family responsibilities, and of the everyday struggle to make ends meet—time stopped. Future outlooks began to dim. Deferred dreams began to die. The lofty goals of adolescence faded into the realm of impossibility. And day-to-day worries about getting home safely, coping with stressful and unfulfilling jobs, and balancing rising expenses against uncertain income forced respondents' attention to remain fixed on the present. This stopping of time is also evident in the trajectories of those who made mistakes in their past but were unable to put previous charges behind them—despite years of rehabilitation and good behavior.

Much of the recent scholarship on migration has moved away from an exclusive focus on individual immigrants to a more nuanced interplay between individual-level characteristics and the larger structural forces— immigration law, the educational system, the labor market, and communities—that shape opportunities and barriers.[13] My respondents' experiences support claims that the key problem to be studied is not undocumented young people per se but the laws and structures that frame their lives. Immigration laws do more than set the parameters for inclusion and exclusion. Increasingly, by transforming normal activities into illicit acts, they also shape the terrain on which immigrants carry out their daily lives. In addition to arresting, detaining, and removing migrants, the state has many other mechanisms to modify migrants' actions. Practices such as establishing immigration checkpoints, deploying immigration agents to public spaces like parks, recreation centers, and bus stations, and recruiting a wide range of community and institutional actors for immigration enforcement duties severely curtail undocumented migrants' ability to pursue the normal activities of everyday life.

Empirical studies demonstrate that the conditions created by these legal structures have pervasive effects on embodied, subjective experiences of illegality in everyday life.[14] However, for my respondents, the experience of being an "illegal subject" varied across the life course, with a brutal disruption occurring in late adolescence. This variation is consistent with recent theorizing about the inadequacy of a stark "legal"/"illegal" dichotomy to describe the status of the many migrants globally who are 'trapped in legal ambiguity.'"[15] However, while this research recognizes gray areas between legal and illegal statuses, it fails to describe the experiences of transitioning between these categories that were so disruptive and life-changing for my respondents.

The experiences of undocumented youth growing up in the United States highlight these contradictions and can help scholars expand the framework for understanding processes of illegality. In particular, the experience of being first included and then, as they come of age, legally and socially excluded—cast out of the circle—sets the 1.5 generation apart from first-generation undocumented migrants. To theorize illegality, then, we need a theoretical perspective that not only accounts for the contradictions between laws and practices and lived experiences but also moves beyond a general framework that addresses the vulnerabilities of adult migrants to one with enough flexibility to capture their diverse experiences in their families and their communities. This general, yet nuanced, framework is especially visible in young people's experiences. To be sure, the deportability of the 1.5 generation remains a critical dimension of their condition of illegality. However, their exclusion from the normal activities of daily American life is perhaps even more consequential. For American-raised young people who pay close attention to the progress and achievements of their peers, this exclusion represents the ultimate denial of their personhood and the revocation of their status as members of the society they thought was theirs. It threatens them with a loss of connection to home.

Following Cecilia Menjívar, it is important for me to acknowledge that my focus on the legal aspect of membership in this book does not imply monocausality.[16] In nearly every society, experiences of belonging are patterned by a constellation of factors. My respondents live in a racialized culture that has produced and legitimated forms of discrimination against persons of Mexican descent for several generations. Their parents' and eventually their own quests for work within a low-wage economy were also part of a longer history of labor migration and the formation of a flexible workforce. Thus multiple processes of racialization, labor formation, and immigration restriction worked in tandem to constrain my respondents' participation and belonging. However, even as these other processes mattered a great deal to my respondents' lives, illegality dominated most situations and interactions.

THE SLIPPERY SLOPE OF "DESERVINGNESS"

Just as the pendulum appeared to be swinging in the direction of immigrant integration, on February 16, 2015, a day before the president's DAPA and expanded DACA programs were to take effect, a US district court judge, hearing a Texas case that included twenty-six states challenging Obama's administrative actions, issued an injunction stopping them from being carried out.[17] The president's plans took another hit in May when a federal appeals court denied a request from Justice Department lawyers to allow the president's actions to go into effect pending appeal. As of late July, neither DAPA nor the DACA expansion was moving forward.

Then, on July 1, 2015, an undocumented Mexican laborer released from a San Francisco city jail stood accused in the fatal shooting of a thirty-two-year-old Pleasanton woman on the city's waterfront.[18] The alleged shooter, Juan Francisco Lopez-Sanchez, whose criminal record included several felony drug and criminal reentry convictions, had been previously deported from the United States five times, raising questions about why he was in the United States in the first place.

The case added fuel to an already incendiary debate for which the flames had been recently fanned by Republican presidential candidate Donald J. Trump, who, in his campaign kickoff event in Manhattan two weeks prior to the incident, had targeted Mexican immigrants as a central problem facing the country. "When Mexico sends its people," he asserted, "they're not sending their best. They're sending people that have lots of problems, and they're bringing those problems with us. They're bringing drugs. They're bringing crime. They're rapists."[19]

In the wake of the San Francisco incident, Trump pointed to the crime as "yet another example of why [the United States] must secure our border immediately." Several congressional leaders called on the city and several other so-called sanctuary cities across the country to restore cooperation with the US Immigration and Customs Enforcement in enforcing immigration laws. And Republican lawmakers proposed legislation to cut off federal funding from local governments that have policies prohibiting law enforcement officers from questioning a person's immigration status. Once again, a chorus of immigration restrictionists were advocating for measures that would paint immigrants with a broad brush.

This book's focus on the 1.5 generation helps us see more clearly the dangers of political discourse that promotes binaries of deserving and undeserving. For many immigration restrictionists, "Illegal is illegal" and there should be no shades of gray. But as immigration debates have heated up and legislative attempts have stalled, advocates have resorted to rhetorical measures and the promotion of policies that draw attention to two types of immigrants: those who deserve to be in the United States and those who do not. This strategy was evident in President Obama's speech on November 20, 2014, when he drew bright lines between "felons" and "families," "criminals" and "children," "gang members" and "hardworking moms." However, as long as there is an "undeserving" category, there is always a risk that a random event or a change in the political tide can shift the discourse to cast all immigrants as undeserving.

The American dream ethos has long tied deservingness to the ideals of hard work and achievement. The United States prides itself as a country that helps those who help themselves. The struggle to be considered deserving has been interwoven into the country's policies, political agendas, and public discourse for more than a century. And the lives of many poor youth have been bound up in this dichotomy of deserving and undeserving. Historically, the public as well as lawmakers have been more sympathetic when the roots of poverty have derived from uncontrollable external factors—natural disasters, the closure of large factories and massive layoffs, and debilitating injuries, for example. On the other hand, when unfortunate circumstances have been seen to be the result of individual actions (or a lack thereof), the public has handed out considerably less sympathy. Those deemed undeserving tend to be tied to the negative stereotypes of criminals, welfare abusers, and the lazy—in other words, those who want a free and easy ride with no strings attached.

Since the late 1990s the "illegal" Mexican immigrant has replaced the "welfare queen" as the country's persona non grata.[20] Though immigration violations are actually a civil offense, the federal government has increasingly chosen to criminally prosecute individuals who enter the United States without legal documentation.[21] In doing so it has contributed to the public misperception that residing in the country without legal residency status constitutes a crime, thereby making undocumented immigrants an accepted target of punitive enforcement practices. It also categorically casts undocumented immigrants as lawbreakers, deserving of expulsion and exclusion and undeserving of citizenship.

Current immigration policy has been shaped by such stereotypes, and immigrants are increasingly being defined as threats. Many classes of crimes have been newly defined as "felonies" when they apply specifically to immigrants. And deportation has become a punishment for even minor offenses. Despite a large body of evidence revealing that immigrants are less likely to commit serious crimes or to be behind bars than the native born, they cannot shake the stigma of "criminality."[22]

Proponents of immigrant labor have attempted to win over the American public by appealing to core values of hard work as a justification for their inclusion. Advocates highlight the economic contributions made by undocumented workers as an engine that has strengthened communities and the nation. They argue that "they take jobs Americans are not willing to do."

This book has focused on the experiences of a group of young people, for whom advocates have rallied to draw distinctions from their migrant parents. During a time of unprecedented nativism and restrictionism and concerns about national security and terrorism, the presence of these children is seen as less consequential than the "original sin" of their parents' clandestine crossing.[23] The refrain "Don't punish children for the sins of their parents" has become a commonly used trope in the immigration debates. Proponents of the DREAM Act have held up examples of high-achieving undocumented students—class presidents, valedictorians, and star athletes—as evidence of their deservingness.

But this strategy is vulnerable to slippage. Indeed, it is easy to draw sympathy for innocent children. But children grow up. Historically, the public school system has integrated the children of immigrants into the fabric of society. Because of the *Plyler* ruling, undocumented immigrant children have been afforded the same opportunities. But research on school inequality has underscored a simple truth: school is not a meritocracy. This is borne out in the hard empirical realities confronting low-income, minority, and immigrant children. Poor kids who do everything right do not achieve more than rich kids who do everything wrong.[24] And undocumented immigrant students who play by the rules and earn good grades are not rewarded with citizenship.

There is another equally important, yet more nuanced, argument. When the children of Mexican migrants arrive in the United States, they inherit the conditions of life in impoverished households headed by undocumented adults—cramped dwellings, neighborhood violence, and low-performing schools. But they also enter American society with a different orientation than their parents. Whereas undocumented adults are shut out of the formal labor market, the primary institution incorporating children—public schooling—opens its doors to them. Schools provide a window of opportunity and a set of lessons through which undocumented youth develop identities of successful Americans.

I was struck by how many of the college-goers told me that because of their positive school experiences they believed that everything would turn out okay—that their problems would be solved by the time they were to be consequential. This thinking was the engine that propelled them to persist, to continue to dedicate time and hard work to school and career pursuits. Undocumented children's legal inclusion in the public school system allows them to access a broader social world and to avoid the barriers associated with their immigration status. They experience similar environments and develop identities and aspirations similar to those of their American-born peers.

Nevertheless, the young people in this book encountered numerous barriers to school success. Many were pulled out of school to work and contribute to their families. Others held tremendous responsibilities for the care of their younger siblings. Cramped conditions at home provided little time or privacy to do homework. Family fears promoted secrecy over disclosure. Coming to terms with the disappointment of a future that would not be what popular culture and teachers told them was demoralizing. Countless examples within their narratives shed important light on the ways in which undocumented children start considerably behind the starting line.

Since the 1990s schools have become testing hubs that increasingly disempower students of color. They have also been sites of inequality where low-income and minority youth are harshly punished under zero-tolerance policies.[25] Decades of disinvestment have left schools lacking in the resources fundamental for preparing their students for an increasingly competitive global economy.

In California, the Proposition 98 guarantee, designed to ensure a minimum level of funding for California's schools and community colleges, has not prevented significant cuts to the resources available to schools.[26] Strained state budgets have led to repeated cuts, leaving California lagging behind most states in K-12 spending. California has more students per school staff than the rest of the United States, ranking last or near the bottom with respect to the number of students per teacher, the number of students per counselor, the number of students per librarian, and the number of students per administrator.[27] The vast majority of students in these schools do not receive adequate attention.

The experiences of early exiters and college-goers show that illegality crushes hopes and derails futures. But they also provide important insight into the ways in which a lack of support from teachers and counselors at a critical time in one's schooling shrinks options for the future and the ways negative labels stay with young people. A lack of individualized attention from teachers and the application of stigmatizing labels such as "troublemaker" or "delinquent" pushed many early exiters to the margins of their schools, thereby accelerating their transition to illegality. It was difficult for many of their parents to counteract the damage done to their children by the combined effects of negative school experiences, run-ins with truant officers and the police, and stigmatizing labels given by teachers and counselors.[28] Those who did not have supportive relationships with adult mentors to provide guidance and advocacy were less likely to feel that they belonged and more likely to make early transitions to the workforce and the condition of illegality. Access to help from teachers, college counseling, and relationships with caring adults can mean the difference between a seamless transition to college and an early exit from school and an entry into adult life constricted by barriers and exclusions.

In the modern era, schools have masked the underlying structural reasons for inequality. By expending school resources on those deemed deserving and by highlighting the failings of the larger student body, schools hold up success as the result of individual actions while hiding the structural dimensions underlying school failure.

My respondents' narratives underscore an empirical reality that being undocumented has long-lasting effects. Indeed, schools fundamentally shape where and how undocumented youth enter adulthood. But in the survival of the fittest, far too many young adults begin to fall off as they make adult transitions. Many of my respondents who began college eventually made multiple stop-outs or left higher education altogether. Growing needs to earn money funneled respondents out of their college classrooms and into low-wage jobs. For those who managed to complete postsecondary education, the earning of advanced degrees brought them no closer to legal status. One by one, even the talented and hopeful college-goers could not outrun time. Without a change in their immigration status, many of the educational and social advantages that college-goers accrued from delaying the transition to illegality eventually dissolved. For them, this transition was as debilitating as it was spirit-crushing.

Learning to be "illegal" is a tragic consequence of an unfair system. By transforming everyday mundane actions into criminal acts our laws force young adults into difficult decisions that hinge on breaking the law. Given the turn toward immigration enforcement during the first decade and a half of the twenty-first century, a wide range of minor infractions—an improper lane change, for example—have become crimes that are punishable by jail time and deportation. Since the late 1990s these measures have disproportionately targeted men of color, especially Mexicans.[29] During a time in which the United States has made significant progress on reintegrating the formerly incarcerated into American communities, many immigrants are being denied the right to remain with their families and to reintegrate into their communities.[30] The longer college-goers and early exiters have lived under the condition of illegality, under grueling and exclusionary circumstances, the more vulnerable they have become to being snared by law enforcement.

Over time, college-goers become indistinguishable from early exiters and other undocumented adult immigrants. Many of the markers that once set them apart—their youthfulness, their innocence, their lofty ambitions, and their unworn hands and bodies—have undergone significant transformations. Diplomas and awards mean less in their daily routines, and lives of illegality have forced them into decisions that have compromised their innocence. Whereas they once benefited from false dichotomies that cast them as meritorious and deserving, they now find themselves on the other end of these binaries.

Despite my grouping of respondents into contrasting categories of educational attainment, they are ultimately more similar than they are different. Regardless of childhood and adolescent experiences of belonging, and despite where most of my respondents began their transitions to illegality, most now face the same kinds of problems. During childhood their experiences were markedly different from those of their parents; adulthood has brought them closer to parents' struggles. Whereas in childhood most of these young people may have elicited the sympathy of the American public as innocent and deserving "Americans in waiting," by 2015 many of them were in the political crosshairs, with their standing threatened in the country where they grew up.

THE MEDIATING INFLUENCE OF LOCAL CONTEXTS

Congress's failure to devise a consistent and ethical system of immigration laws has forced state and county governments to come up with their own solutions to immigrant integration. Scores of laws have been passed at the state, county, and municipal levels, and hundreds more have been proposed. These local laws run the gamut from immigrant integration bills providing in-state tuition and access to health care to punitive laws that deny immigrants access to housing, health care, jobs, and education. Where an undocumented immigrant lives matters a great deal.

Over the last decade, a growing number of studies have sought to understand the effects of what geographer Matthew Coleman has called a "complex landscape" of uneven immigration policies and enforcement practices across the United States.[31] As state and county policies move in diverging directions, experiences of illegality and of belonging vary according to place.[32] Hence, an undocumented young person living in Manhattan may have access to a vast and affordable public higher education system and extensive public transportation options, yet be negatively affected by competition for a limited number of adult education seats. A similarly situated young person living Atlanta may be negatively affected by exclusions from medical care and postsecondary education and by increased integration between police activities and federal Immigration and Customs Enforcement (ICE) agents but may benefit from a strong network of community organizations.

According to sociologists Alejandro Portes and Rubén G. Rumbaut, the distinct pathways of immigrants' incorporation are determined by a combination of positive and negative contexts.[33] In Los Angeles, where one out of every three persons is foreign born and where the number of undocumented residents is higher than anywhere else in the country, immigrants and their children experience a mixed set of conditions framing their everyday lives.[34]

Until the recent economic downturn, jobs in the area were plentiful in most economic sectors. Los Angeles also has strong ethnic communities anchored by hundreds of community institutions to assist children and immigrant families. Since 2012 the state has taken great strides toward restricting enforcement practices and better integrating undocumented immigrants.[35] It has enacted legislation making undocumented immigrant young people eligible for health care, driver's licenses, professional licenses, and state financial aid. It has taken strides to protect workers' rights. And it has effectively limited cooperation between local law enforcement and ICE.

While these recent efforts may have taken too long (or have come too late) for many of my respondents, the state is in a good position to provide a significant boost to a generation of undocumented children and adolescents who are making adolescent and adult transitions today. Nevertheless, these young people will face challenges.

Immigrants in California, especially Mexican males, have borne the brunt of national enforcement efforts.[36] They also continue to struggle financially, as many job sectors that have traditionally hired immigrants were hurt by the country's economic downturn. Existing jobs are often a great distance from where immigrants live, creating long commutes. Meanwhile the cost of living in the state has steadily increased, as has tuition at California colleges and universities. Families in Los Angeles today are paying more for their children's college tuition while the value of the dollar in the metropolis is shrinking. Los Angeles residents have also felt the effects of reductions in tax dollars to support struggling K-12 school districts. Poor and minority neighborhoods have been hit the hardest. Families face an unfavorable mix of de facto segregation, overcrowding, and a lack of resources necessary to prepare children to make successful transitions to postsecondary schooling and decent jobs.

While Los Angeles may be a model of immigrant integration, it has also weakened or broken many rungs of the ladder to upward mobility for poor and immigrant families. And its progressive slate of recent immigrant integration policies are, nevertheless, undercut by a lack of federal reforms.

CONTEMPORARY IMMIGRATION POLICY AND UNDOCUMENTED YOUNG PEOPLE

Until the late 1980s, the experience of illegality was shorter in duration and affected fewer family members.[37] Today, illegality affects entire families and is a much more long-term status. Undocumented children's life chances are tied to the fates of their parents and other adult family members. Yet their lives in the United States are distinct from their parents'. Inclusive institutional practices permit undocumented children to enjoy childhoods with few restrictions and to dream of brighter futures. However, laws promoting their personhood conflict with those that delimit their rights as noncitizens. Taken together, these laws prevent continuity along the life course as children become adults.

The number of people living in the United States in an unauthorized residency status has increased sixfold since the 1986 IRCA (Immigration Reform and Control Act) legalization. Nevertheless, Congress has failed to create a legal pathway for them despite their long-term presence. Moreover, a growing number of restrictions, coupled with ramped-up enforcement efforts, drastically narrow the worlds of undocumented youth as they enter adulthood.

The Benefits and Limitations of the Deferred Action for Childhood Arrivals Program

As of March 31, 2015, over two and a half years after the initiation of DACA, over 664,000 cases had been approved and almost 244,000 renewals had been granted.[38] DACA has provided an opportunity for a segment of the undocumented immigrant population to remain in the country without fear of deportation, allowed them to apply for work permits, and increased their opportunities for economic and social incorporation. DACA beneficiaries have experienced a pronounced increase in economic opportunities and have become more integrated into the nation's economic and social institutions. They have started new jobs and paid internships, increased their earnings, opened bank accounts and obtained credit cards, and enrolled in health care programs and obtained driver's licenses.[39] These benefits appear to be the strongest for those connected to community organizations, those attending four-year colleges, and those with college degrees.[40]

For many highly educated DACA-eligible individuals, the program has provided an opportunity to make the most of their postsecondary degrees; for college-bound youth and students currently enrolled in postsecondary institutions, DACA has provided an additional incentive to invest in education and skills. However, of those potentially eligible for the program, more than half have not applied.[41] Explanations vary. Many older individuals may not have been aware that community organizations were able to assist them with the application process; older individuals also may have had more difficulty proving their continuous residence, given that they arrived in the United States earlier and had been out of school for many years.[42] The low uptake rates by DACA-eligible youth might also be attributable to educational barriers. An earlier analysis of the potential effects of legislation aimed at legalizing undocumented immigrant young people concluded that barriers to education, especially family poverty and the costs of pursuing postsecondary education, would lead as many as 62 percent of those eligible to apply not to do so.[43]

DACA enrollment rates also seem to be influenced by where eligible individuals live.[44] California joins Texas and Florida in having the most DACA applicants. There are many fewer enrollees among residents of

East Coast states.[45] In California, connections with key institutional actors such as teachers, counselors, and youth workers have enabled many young people to receive assistance critical to filling out and submitting DACA applications and taking advantage of its benefits.[46] Moreover, even as DACA has widened access for hundreds of thousands of youth and young adults, its effectiveness has been undercut by state policies. This effect supports the notion that the uneven geography of local enforcement and educational access in the United States profoundly shapes the number and kind of impediments and opportunities undocumented immigrant young people experience.

DACA has increased undocumented access to work, higher education, and other attainments of adulthood, but this is not enough. As an executive memorandum that shifts bureaucratic practice in US Customs and Border Protection (CBP), US Citizenship and Immigration Services (USCIS), and US Immigration and Customs Enforcement (ICE), DACA has limited inclusionary power. The program is temporary in duration and partial in coverage. Most importantly, it offers no pathway to legalization for its beneficiaries. DACA status does not confer the right to vote, travel freely, or qualify for federal financial aid.[47] Despite the program's two-year reprieve from the threat of deportation, enrollees can still be removed in the future. DACA offers its beneficiaries no respite from long-term uncertainty and the possibility of legal limbo. And, given the large numbers of undocumented young people who have not enrolled, even those limited benefits have yet to reach a sizable portion of the eligible population.

A Legislative and Administrative Commitment to Enforcement

Over the last twenty years, efforts aimed at stripping immigrants' rights and patrolling immigrant communities have radically restricted the worlds of millions of immigrants. The centrality of undocumented migration in the larger immigration agenda has perpetuated the notion that our immigration problems are best solved by increased levels of enforcement.[48] Since the 1990s Congress has passed no laws to integrate long-term immigrants and their families; instead it has expanded the categories of immigrants subject to deportation, increased the number of deportable offenses, and limited immigrants' ability to appeal deportations. This federal legislation has been accompanied by the administrative expansion of enforcement activity as the Department of Homeland Security has extended its efforts from the border to the interior.

Under the Bush administration, high-profile workplace raids and neighborhood sweeps to round up undocumented migrants increased in visibility and frequency. During the Obama administration, agreements between ICE and local law enforcement have multiplied.[49] These practices became national in scope under the Secure Communities program, according to which state and local police checked the fingerprints of individuals they were booking into jail against DHS immigration databases and ICE was notified automatically if a match occurred, regardless of whether the person being booked had been convicted of any crime. Individuals were then transferred to ICE for deportation.[50] The Priority Enforcement Program that replaced Secure Communities in July 2015 has narrowed the range of activities for which undocumented immigrants can be targeted for deportation but continues the immigration database-matching and ICE notification practices of the former program and thus still entangles ICE's interests of immigrant deportation with the priorities of local law enforcement to protect people's welfare.[51] Miscommunication among ICE, the FBI, and local law enforcement could prove to be a problem, and implementation across ICE jurisdictions may be unevenly applied. Moreover, ICE has not reduced its annual removal quota of 400,000. And although the Department of Homeland Security has revised its priorities for the "apprehension, detention, and removal of undocumented immigrants," among the top tier are any undocumented immigrants apprehended at the border while attempting to unlawfully enter the United States—so, in addition to terrorists, convicted felons, and gang members, parents and their children who do not qualify for asylum or other forms of relief remain a top priority for deportation.[52] Many undocumented individuals with social membership in American communities are left out of these new programs, including many of my respondents who committed infractions such as DUIs, who were gang-involved at a younger age, or who simply found themselves in the wrong place at the wrong time. Thus, despite the implementation of the DACA program, the Department of Homeland Security's focus on enforcement continues to generate problems for undocumented immigrant youth and young adults.

While Congress has effectively limited the everyday lives of undocumented immigrants through laws aimed at curbing their access to social institutions and resources, immigration enforcement efforts have created a chilling effect, altering the daily routines and practices of millions of immigrants. This narrowing of worlds is not only harmful to immigrants; it also affects Americans more generally. Undocumented immigrants live in American communities, they participate in our social, religious, and economic institutions, and through their everyday involvements they have ties to neighbors, teachers, employers, and community stakeholders. Laws that restrict their participation hinder employers' opportunities to hire them, disadvantage teachers wanting to educate them, and impinge on the freedoms of those who have relationships with them.

By creating opportunities for their socioeconomic advancement and social integration, the United States is poised to offer a model of social prosperity through the many contributions immigrants can make. We like to hold up the success stories of those who could become doctors or lawyers. Indeed, making the case for these folks is much easier. But many others will become agricultural workers, caretakers, members of churches and PTAs. These young men and women will make important contributions too.

POLICY RECOMMENDATIONS

This book does not aim to solve the problems that riddle our nation's immigration policy, nor is it intended to promote specific legislation. In fact, I have found that even some of the most supportive advocacy efforts obscure much of the pain and suffering that my research has uncovered. Policy and advocacy frames aim to simplify what are typically messy problems—matters of immigration are no exception. Nevertheless, the findings presented in this book do have significant policy implications. While I do not subscribe to arguments about deservingness or merit that create hierarchies within the larger immigrant population, I cannot overlook the reality that the circumstances of the 1.5 generation are not the same as those of migrants who come to the United States as adults. Yet in current immigration discourse and policy proposals there has been an increasingly troubling trend of legislating deservingness—that is, tying legal citizenship to educational attainment and inadmissibility and deportation to past offenses without taking into account any rehabilitation that has taken place. On the surface, this seems like an issue without controversy—after all, it is sensible to encourage an educated public. But the drawing of these distinctions serves to alienate and marginalize large portions of the population driven deeper into the shadows.

The needs and concerns of all immigrants as well as the American public must be carefully considered. One-size-fits-all policies are likely to be too general to have any meaningful impact.

The Case for Legalization

The 1.5 generation is a sizable and vulnerable subset of the nation's immigrant population. Without immediate intervention, this group is at risk of becoming a disenfranchised underclass. Ultimately, it is only through a pathway to legalization that these young people will be able to participate fully in the world in which they are already social and cultural members. Legalization will help lift them out of poverty, integrate them into adult society, and increase their opportunities for more education and better jobs. This is not to say that, once legalized, undocumented youths and young adults will uniformly experience upward mobility. Historically, persons of Mexican origin in the United States have faced disadvantages in the labor market and in access to housing. Moreover, Mexican children continue to face structural barriers that cause them to lag behind in educational attainment. However, for hundreds of thousands of currently undocumented Mexican youth, legalization could further bolster their academic aspirations and give teachers and counselors greater incentive to push them through.

When allowed to regularize their status, undocumented immigrants have experienced substantial upward mobility. For instance, those who received legal status under the IRCA found significantly better jobs over time and increased their wages.[53] Given the opportunity to receive additional education and training and move into better-paying jobs, legalized immigrants pay more in taxes and have more money to spend and invest. It is therefore likely that if currently undocumented youth and young adults were granted a pathway to legalization they would improve their circumstances and be in a better position to contribute to the US economy as well as to their families and local communities.

Legalization also would undo the disastrous effects of exclusion. Giving undocumented young people legal access to the blocked resources of their adult worlds (e.g., working, driving, voting, and attending college) would permit them to participate in common rites of passage with their peers. While DACA granted access to some of these pursuits to more than 664,000 young people, the benefits could easily be undone through a change in administration. Moreover, a sizable portion of the eligible population has yet to apply for DACA. Legalization could significantly reduce stigma, improve the overall health and well-being of the undocumented 1.5 generation, and free them from the strains associated with their liminal lives.

While the president's deferred action programs provide temporary relief from deportations for some undocumented immigrants, more permanent solutions are needed that cover larger portions of the population. With two million removals during its first six years, the Obama administration holds the disturbing distinction of deporting people at a scale unmatched by *any* prior administration. Detention quotas set at more than thirty-four thousand people per day have produced problems of unconscionable proportions. The *New York Times* recently reported that two-thirds of those who have been deported either have committed minor infractions, including traffic violations, or have no criminal record at all.[54] Ending Secure Communities is a step in the right direction. But discontinuing deportation quotas is a must. Those who have ties to this country, who have children, and who do not pose criminal threats should be spared the constant worry and physical danger of deportation.

The debate between those who support legal residency with citizenship and those who favor a legal permission to work without citizenship is a long-standing one.[55] The argument, at least from the perspective of those favoring immigration restrictions, usually hinges on the question of whether those who have broken the rules should be entitled to special consideration. But a deeper question lies at the heart of this debate: Does legal citizenship matter? The findings in this book support the fundamental importance of legal citizenship. Without it, immigrants have only second-class membership. Noncitizen immigrants are far more vulnerable to exclusion and deportation, and the denial of their memberships in the broader US society is a source of major psychological pain. If, as I have argued in this book, illegality is indeed a master status, its only undoing is legal citizenship.

Additionally, Congress must reward immigrants who have rehabilitated themselves and have paid the price for transgressions committed years ago. Undoing the reclassification of misdemeanors as aggravated felonies would be a step in the right direction. There is growing support for criminal justice reform in the United States. The president, along with leaders from both parties, has advocated for structural change: measures to restore voting rights to felons who have served their sentences, efforts to make it easier for people with criminal records to get jobs, and a reduction in long mandatory minimum sentences. While there is little dispute that those who commit crimes owe a debt to society, there is growing consensus that it should not be a life sentence.[56] Similarly, young people like Ramon should not be required to serve life sentences in exile.

Congress should also recognize the broader potential of young immigrants beyond their contributions to the high-skilled labor force. Not every young immigrant will become a doctor, lawyer, or engineer. But many may become x-ray technicians, certified nursing assistants, dental hygienists, paralegals, Web developers, and teacher's aides. Many more may find jobs in the trades, as electrical technicians, construction machine operators, or as mechanics or hairstylists. All of the young immigrants I have met want to work. They come from families and communities that value hard work. Congress can reward those efforts. Moreover, young immigrants value their communities and contribute in myriad ways. The United States should build on this engagement.

The Need for State and Local Interventions to Support Undocumented Youth

It is not clear when Congress will act on immigration reform. Given the history of legislative inaction, the problems undocumented young people confront on a daily basis beg for changes in federal administrative policies and local-level practices. An estimated one million undocumented children will make the transition to adulthood over the next ten years. While we cannot slow time, we can take measures to ensure that their transitions will be smoother. Relief from enforcement activity is needed; so is a comprehensive set of strategies aimed at providing more immediate support and assistance.

The material conditions of undocumented immigrant youth place them at risk as they are growing up,[57] but many of the most pressing problems they confront have their onset in late adolescence and early adulthood, when the world that was largely accessible to them in childhood and through their participation in K-12 schools starts to shrink. Current policies leave these youngsters without many options and ramp up their levels of fear and anxiety. While legalization would remedy many troubles, it is not the only solution to a complex and interconnected web of problems. In the absence of federal legislation that would put these young people on a pathway to legal inclusion, many local-level measures and community efforts would be helpful. For example, barring school personnel, health care officials, social service providers, and community police from performing immigration enforcement duties would increase levels of trust and establish and preserve relationships with adults who could help keep undocumented youth productive and motivated. At the state level, access to driver's licenses, in-state tuition, financial aid, and health care, measures that are now in place in California, would increase safety, reduce stress-related illness, make treatment available for chronic injuries, and offset some of the financial barriers to higher education. In addition, states should devote more funding to adult education and literacy classes. By allowing immigrants to more fully integrate, the United States can provide the right opportunities to better position them to contribute to their families, communities, and the American economy. Access to day care and workforce development programs would also provide young people with the kinds of building blocks they need for successful careers.

Schools can also do a better job of meeting the needs of their undocumented student population. This book has demonstrated that the longer undocumented youth stay out of school, the more susceptible they are to the negative aspects of illegality and the less likely they are to return to school. Supportive school environments, positive peer groups, adult mentors, and extracurricular involvement contribute significantly to successful postsecondary outcomes. Positive school-based relationships can provide undocumented students with access to information about college, much-needed support, and assistance in applying for college.[58] Schools can improve the campus climate by offering awareness and sensitivity training for staff and teachers. Further, by modeling college "Dream" resource centers and identifying staff liaisons, K–12 schools can offer safe spaces and identify trusted adults who can work directly with undocumented students and build better bridges from high school to college. Several schools around the country have begun to encourage and establish student support groups for undocumented students to connect with one another and receive some targeted assistance from school personnel. These efforts can be replicated and multiplied. Schools can also facilitate the creation of visible networks of teachers, counselors, staff, and community partners to provide internship and work opportunities for students to give them job experience in their fields of interest while they are in school. School-based efforts to connect undocumented high school students with peers who share their experiences and with college mentors who understand the legal and financial hurdles they face could also yield a big payoff in helping them manage college transitions.

Chambers of commerce, police districts, community service agencies, schools, and other neighborhood institutions can play a vital role by expanding the menu of community-level activities in which undocumented young people may legally participate—job training programs, internships, community service opportunities, leadership development workshops, and recreational programs, to name a few.[59] These local efforts would not only broaden the range of productive activity for undocumented youth but also allow them to build the work experience they need to ensure their competitiveness in the workforce should some form of legalization be granted.

While DACA has certainly widened the access of its beneficiaries, it leaves many other issues unaddressed. In particular, undocumented students remain locked out of opportunities to receive financial aid and are ineligible for federal work-study jobs. To expand relief for youth, the United States must address the restrictions that prevent undocumented young adults from obtaining financial aid. Given the soaring costs of college, and given that the majority of American students receive some form of federal or state financial aid, restrictions will continue to disadvantage undocumented students, particularly those from low-income families. This problem could be remedied by opening eligibility to Pell Grants to undocumented students. College access, retention, and completion are crucial. But in order to be successful undocumented students require the same level of access to aid as their documented and citizen peers. A growing number of scholarships are now available to undocumented students. Latino DACA beneficiaries are now eligible to apply for a Hispanic Scholarship Fund General Scholarship, and TheDream. US scholarship fund has raised more than $80 million for scholarships for undocumented students. In addition, Educators for Fair Consideration (E4FC) in the Bay Area recently initiated a matching grant program to support local scholarship funds across the United States. In 2014, it awarded $250,000 in matching grants. Several private universities have also begun offering private need-based financial aid to undocumented students, and in March of 2015 students at Loyola University in Chicago voted to endow a scholarship for undocumented students. Former *Washington Post* owner Donald Graham doubled their efforts when he donated matching funds to support the scholarship. These efforts are important. But until undocumented students are eligible for state and federal financial aid, economic need will outpace existing resources.

Attention must also be paid to the individual-level mental and physical health consequences of legal exclusion. Adolescence is a difficult time for many young people, but the need for support is especially urgent among undocumented youth confronted with the condition of illegality. Schools must train counselors and teachers on the unique challenges facing undocumented immigrant students. Schools must also commit resources to hire mental health professionals who are sensitive to the unique circumstances and needs of undocumented students. Finally, schools can work with community mental health professionals to develop guides that are informative and accessible.[60] Schools can support these efforts by instituting training for teachers and counselors.

Undocumented youth and young adults have lived in the United States most of their lives and long to be recognized as full members. What they urgently need is policies and programs that will allow them to be recognized as full Americans. But these young people are also members of families and communities that lack important forms of access, suffer economic hardships, and are vulnerable to the threat of deportations and victimization because of their undocumented status. Their ability to lead successful lives depends greatly on the options available to their parents, siblings, and neighbors. Addressing the untenable circumstances of the eleven million undocumented immigrants (young and old) living in this country is the best way to ensure that the investment made in the lives of these young people will realize its full potential.

The pattern of contemporary immigration is not the same as it was a century ago. Across the country, there are many more undocumented immigrants living in families. These settled populations will not go away anytime soon. Implementing legislation that would provide them opportunities to more fully and meaningfully participate in everyday life would not only be good for them. It would benefit us all.

Notes

PREFACE

1. Langston Hughes's poem "Harlem" would later inspire playwright Lorraine Hansberry to write *A Raisin in the Sun,* taking the title from Hughes's first stanza. Hansberry's play about an African American family living on the South Side of Chicago debuted at the Ethel Barrymore Theatre in New York City on March 11, 1959. It has since been made into a musical, and there have been at least three film adaptations.

2. I left these community centers in 1999 but stayed in the neighborhood and continued having contact with youth and their families.

3. Like all other names in this book, "Alex" is a pseudonym I have given to protect the family's confidentiality.

4. Chavez (1998).

5. Hagan (1994).

6. Mills (1959).

7. Bob Dylan, "It's Alright Ma (I'm Only Bleeding)," Warner Bros., Inc., 1965.

1. CONTESTED MEMBERSHIP OVER TIME

1. In this book, I use the terms *undocumented* and *unauthorized* interchangeably. I use the term *undocumented* more frequently because this was the term used by the young adults I studied (in both English and Spanish) to characterize their circumstances.

Neither the exercise of prosecutorial discretion nor the granting of deferred action is a recent development. For as long as Congress has placed limits on who may enter or remain in the United States, authorities have possessed discretion to prioritize the removal of some immigrants over others. Since at least the

1970s, the federal government has formally designated certain immigrants (including John Lennon) as nonpriorities for removal.

2. The DREAM Act was first introduced in the Senate on August 1, 2001, as S. 1291 by Richard Durbin (IL) and Orrin Hatch (UT) to provide a pathway to legal residency status for young people who were born abroad but raised and educated in the United States. The act proposes that students who live in the United States for at least five years, graduate from US high schools or the equivalent, and maintain "good moral character" (by US government standards) become eligible to apply for six-year conditional resident status. This status could become permanent after they complete two years of college or military service. While DREAM Act proposals have been regularly reintroduced since 2001 and have gained increased support, no version has yet become law. See Olivas (2012, 2011).

3. All names in this book are pseudonyms, and all references to respondents' educational status, unless otherwise noted, are as of 2012. In addition, specific details about families, schools, workplaces, and in some cases, neighborhoods have been modified to ensure anonymity.

4. Contemporary immigration policies generate intense debate over who should be admitted to the United States and what steps should be required to achieve citizenship. According to legal scholar Hiroshi Motomura, for over 150 years immigration was assumed to be a transition to citizenship, with immigrants essentially being "Americans in waiting." This view of immigration, once central to US law and policy, has been radically revised. Historian Mae Ngai argues that immigration restrictions, particularly national-origin and numerical quotas, remapped the United States both by creating new categories of racial difference and by emphasizing the nation's contiguous land borders and their patrol. As a result, the "illegal alien" became the central problem in US immigration policy, an "impossible subject." See Motomura (2006) and Ngai (2004).

5. Bosniak (2006).

6. See, for example, Thorpe (2011); Cleave (2010); Díaz (2007); Eggers (2006); Nazario (2005); Urrea (2004); and Lahiri (2003).

7. Levinson (2005: 336), emphasis added.

8. Bosniak (2006); Benhabib (2004); Ong (1999); Soysal (1994).

9. Inda (2006); De Genova (2002).

10. Sigona and Hughes (2010).

11. A recent report focusing on nine European countries found that basic social rights for undocumented children are few and that access is rife with barriers. A strong response by NGOs and human rights organizations prompted movement toward greater inclusion for these minors (Platform for International Cooperation on Undocumented Migrants 2008).

12. In 1996 two pieces of legislation, the Illegal Immigration Reform and Immigrant Responsibility Act (IIRAIRA) and the Personal Responsibility and Work Opportunity Reconciliation Act (PRWORA), directly and indirectly restricted access to social welfare programs for noncitizens in the United States. Driven by a widely held belief that immigrants were drawn to the United States to access state benefits, PRWORA restricted legal immigrants' access to cash transfer programs such as welfare and to other social safety net programs such

as food stamps and health insurance. Today, undocumented immigrants are still denied assistance, except for short-term disaster relief and emergency medical care. The law also endows states with independent authority to deny benefits to noncitizens, significantly curbing immigrant integration policies while bolstering immigrant enforcement efforts. See Fix (2009).

13. R. G. Rumbaut (2004); R. Smith (2006). Immigrants who arrive in the United States in their late teens or as adults are generally designated as first generation; those who come as children are considered 1.5 generation, and those born in the United States to at least one immigrant parent are second generation. While there is some general overlap in definitions, in this book I use age twelve as a cutoff point to define the 1.5 generation. Distinct from other research, this study focuses on the *undocumented* 1.5 generation.

14. The number of undocumented youth is an estimate drawn from Batalova and McHugh (2010).

15. Batalova and McHugh (2010).

16. Gans (1992).

17. Alba and Nee (2003: 282).

18. Chavez (1994). See also Gordon (1964).

19. Zuñiga (2012: 277).

20. Bloemraad, Voss, and Lee (2011: 18).

21. Van Gennep (1960).

22. Turner (1967: 95).

23. Menjívar (2006).

24. Settersten, Furstenberg, and Rumbaut (2005).

25. R. G. Rumbaut and Komaie (2010); Fuligni and Pedersen (2002).

26. Fuligni and Pedersen (2002); Suárez-Orozco and Suárez-Orozco (1995).

27. Gleeson and Gonzales (2012).

28. Moss (2009).

29. Hallinan (1994); Kilgore (1991); Oakes (1985); Schafer and Olexa (1971).

30. Lucas and Berends (2002); Oakes (1985).

31. Alba and Nee (2003); Portes and Rumbaut (2001); Telles and Ortiz (2008).

32. Tyson (2011).

33. Conchas (2001); Gándara (1995).

34. Gándara (2002); Suárez-Orozco and Suárez-Orozco (2001).

35. Stanton-Salazar (2001).

36. Apple (1982).

37. Hughes (1945).

38. Feagin and Feagin (1993).

39. Becker (1963).

40. Robert Courtney Smith's study of Mexicans living in New York began several years earlier than mine. See R. Smith (2006, 2008). While Smith's sample includes many undocumented young people, undocumented status is not the sole focus of his study.

41. Snowball sampling is a nonprobability sampling technique where existing study subjects recruit future subjects from among their acquaintances. This

sampling technique is often used in populations that are difficult for researchers to access.

42. Bourgois (1995: 13). Extra effort is needed to develop relationships of trust with vulnerable populations (see Dreby 2010).

43. Portes and Fernandez-Kelly (2008).

44. Youth under age twenty-one are considered family dependents who receive priority for relative-sponsored legalization. At twenty-one, immigrants "age out" of this priority status, and longer wait times attach to their applications for legal admission into the United States. Other targeted regularization efforts set other limits regarding age and eligibility. For instance, DACA originally excluded undocumented residents who were over thirty-one at the time of the policy's enactment in 2012.

45. Batalova and McHugh (2010) produced the most detailed estimate to date of the DREAM Act–eligible population.

46. The Mexican Farm Labor Program, or Bracero Program, ran from 1942 to 1964 and sponsored some 4.5 million border crossings of guest workers from Mexico to work in the US agricultural industry. See Calavita (1992).

47. Once they arrived in the United States, the doctors, nurses, and engineers covered by the skilled-worker category applied for permanent resident status and eventually citizenship. Beginning in the 1970s, professional-class immigrants were accompanied by several waves of refugees from Vietnam, Cambodia, and Laos eligible for the full range of federal means-tested benefits. Each of these migration streams and refugee inflows brought secondary waves as many took advantage of the family reunification preferences to bring over spouses, children, and other family members.

48. Massey and Pren (2012).

49. Because of their proximity to the United States, Mexico and Canada were initially given quotas of forty thousand.

50. Many growers were recruiting migrant laborers outside legal channels well before the initiation of quotas and restrictions.

51. Massey, Durand, and Malone (2002).

52. Escobar Latapí, Bean, and Weintraub (1999).

53. Chavez (2008).

54. Nevins (2010); Inda (2006).

55. See Cornelius and Lewis (2006); Massey, Durand, and Malone (2002); Hondagneu-Sotelo (1994).

56. Passel (2006).

57. These bars to reentry are found in the Immigration and Nationality Act (INA), § 212(a)(9)(B) and INA § 212(a)(9)(C).

58. A provision of the 1965 Immigration and Nationality Act (INA), section 245(i) allowed people to adjust their residency status if they paid a $1,000 penalty. They were able to stay in the country by applying through a consular process. In 2000, Congress temporarily extended section 245(i) (as part of the Legal Immigration Family Equity [LIFE] Act). This extension allowed people to be grandfathered if they were included on any petition initiated by a relative before April 30, 2001.

59. Passel and Cohn (2008); Passel (2006); Passel and Suro (2005). This trend accelerated during the 1990s and the first half of the following decade as annual flows increased from 575,000 to 850,000.

60. Passel (2005); Massey, Durand, and Malone (2002).

61. Because of several issues, including a slowing of the US economy and the buildup in security along the border, immigration from Mexico began to slow around 2007. See Passel, Cohn, and Gonzalez-Barrera (2012).

62. See Hagan, Castro, and Rodriguez (2010). IIRAIRA and the Antiterrorism and Effective Death Penalty Act (AEDPA), also enacted in 1996, work in tandem to expand the categories of immigrants subject to deportation, restrict the ability of immigrants to appeal deportation, and widen the range of crimes for which immigrants may be deported. And in 2001, in the wake of the terrorist attacks, Congress enacted the USA PATRIOT Act, which created new grounds for detention and deportation, ratcheting up the level of fears within immigrant communities and heightening anxieties of immigrant children and families.

63. Pub. L. No. 104–132, 110 Stat. 1214 (1996) and Pub. L. No. 104–208, 110 Stat. 3009–546 (1996), respectively.

64. Prior to the passage of AEDPA and IIRIRA, § 212(c) of the Immigration and Nationality Act had provided discretionary relief from exclusion and deportation for certain noncitizens ("§ 212(c) relief"). Under § 212(c), lawful permanent residents who had lived in the United States for seven continuous years were eligible for the relief. Even permanent residents who had been convicted of an aggravated felony were eligible, as long as the term of imprisonment served was less than five years. AEDPA rendered noncitizens convicted of aggravated felonies ineligible for discretionary relief from deportation under § 212(c). Effective April 1, 1997, IIRAIRA § 304(b) repealed INA § 212(c) altogether and eliminated all possibility of relief under the old rule. IIRAIRA provided for a form of discretionary relief available to a small group of noncitizens that did not include noncitizens convicted of an aggravated felony, regardless of the length of sentence served.

65. Massey and Sanchez (2010).

66. Stumpf (2006); Seghetti, Viña, and Ester (2004).

67. US Department of Homeland Security (2013). See also Golash-Boza (in press).

68. Mexican American Legal and Education Defense Fund (2014).

69. Golash-Boza and Hondagneu-Sotelo (2013).

70. Thompson and Cohen (2014).

71. TRAC Immigration (2014).

72. National Conference of State Legislatures (2012).

73. In 2012, after a two-year court battle, a federal court judge approved implementation of the "Show me your papers" provision of S. B. 1070. See Santos (2012).

74. The National Immigration Law Center (n.d.) compiles a running list of anti-immigrant legislation and its status in state legislatures and in the courts.

75. Johnson (2011).

76. Robinson and Preston (2012).

77. Walker and Leitner (2011).

78. For a detailed summary of state action regarding undocumented immigrant students, see National Conference of State Legislatures (2014).

79. In North Carolina, the community college system has reversed its policy four times since 2001. As of 2012, they were permitted entry.

80. Menjívar and Rumbaut (2008). See also Menjívar and Abrego (2012); Gonzales and Chavez (2012).

81. Lopez, Morin, and Taylor (2010).

82. Olivas (2007); cf. Menjívar and Rumbaut (2008).

83. Ono and Sloop (2002).

84. McGreevy (2013).

85. The licenses, which became available January 2015, carry a special designation on the front and a notice stating that the license is not official federal identification and cannot be used to prove eligibility for employment or public benefits.

86. DACA application statistics from USCIS (2015b).

87. Svajlenka and Singer (2014).

88. DACA beneficiaries fall under a benefit eligibility category called "Permanently Residing in the United States Under Color of Law (PRUCOL)," which makes them eligible for Medi-Cal and other health programs. Under Medi-Cal, recipients are eligible for ambulatory patient services, emergency services, hospitalization, maternity and newborn care, mental health and substance use disorder treatment, dental care, vision care, and long-term care and supports.

89. Singer and Svajlenka (2013).

90. Batalova and McHugh (2010).

91. During this time, the following states passed bills allowing in-state tuition rates for undocumented students: Texas, California, Utah, Oklahoma, Illinois, Washington, New York, Kansas, New Mexico, Nebraska, Wisconsin, Connecticut, Rhode Island, Maryland (for community colleges only), Minnesota, New Jersey, Oregon, Colorado, and Florida. In most states, there is a vast difference between in-state and out-of-state tuition rates. Such laws benefit those students who attend high school in a state for a specified number of years, graduate, and meet certain other criteria, regardless of the students' immigration status.

92. In 2014 Washington became the fifth state to offer state financial aid to undocumented immigrants when Governor Jay Inslee signed into law the Real Hope Act, which will extend State Need Grant money to undocumented students.

93. Ewing, Martinez, and Rumbaut (2015: 2, 4).

94. Chavez (2008).

95. This study also included twenty-four second-generation young adults who had at least one undocumented parent.

96. It is also difficult to obtain survey data from undocumented populations because of their relatively small numbers, legal vulnerability, and low-income backgrounds. See Bloch (2007). Surveying them through random dialing meth-

ods, respondent-driven sampling, or other types of probability sampling can be quite costly, and sometimes cost-prohibitive, especially on a national scale.

97. Foner (2003: 26–27).

98. Kubal (2013: 20). See also Foucault (1992); De Certeau (1984: xiv).

99. Anthropologist Clifford Geertz coined this term. See Geertz (1973).

100. Cebulko (2014); Enriquez (2011); Perez (2009, 2012); F. Contreras (2009); Abrego (2006, 2008).

101. Writer Chimamanda Ngozi Adichie (2009) warns that if we hear only a single story about another person or country we risk a critical misunderstanding.

102. R. Smith (2008).

103. See also R. Contreras (2012).

104. Bourgois (1995: 11).

2. UNDOCUMENTED YOUNG ADULTS IN LOS ANGELES

1. Between 1960 and 2005, Los Angeles went from having the smallest proportion of immigrants of any American city (8 percent) to hosting the largest ethnic minority population in the country, the overwhelming majority of whom are of foreign birth or foreign parentage. In 2007, the total population of Los Angeles County was 10 million; 7.1 million, or 71 percent of these residents, were members of ethnic minorities. The other four counties that make up the Los Angeles metropolitan area—Orange, Riverside, San Bernardino, and Ventura—are also "majority-minority," with populations of more than 50 percent minority residents. See R. G. Rumbaut (2008).

2. R. G. Rumbaut (2004).

3. Waldinger and Bozorgmehr (1996: 5).

4. Gonzalez-Barrera and Lopez (2013).

5. Gonzalez-Barrera and Lopez (2013). Between the 1980s and 2000, Mexican migration was the largest driver in population growth among Mexicans in the United States. However, in the decade from 2000 to 2010, births surpassed immigration as the main source of growth in the US Mexican-origin population.

6. Passel and Cohn (2009).

7. Passel and Cohn (2010); Hoefer, Rytina, and Baker (2011).

8. Fortuny, Capps, and Passel (2007).

9. Hill and Johnson (2011).

10. Findings from recent studies show residential segregation is increasing along class lines. Dreier, Mollenkopf, and Swanstrom (2011).

11. Orfield and Ee (2014).

12. California Department of Education (2015b).

13. Reed, Rueben, and Barbour (2006). During the 2004–5 school year, 9 percent of all teachers and about 28 percent of newly hired teachers did not have a full credential in high-poverty districts.

14. In 2013–14, these were the ten largest districts (majority-majority districts in *italics*): (1) LAUSD; (2) San Diego USD; (3) Long Beach USD; (4) Fresno USD; (5) *Elk Grove USD*; (6) San Francisco USD; (7) Santa Ana USD; (8)

Capistrano USD; (9) San Bernardino City USD; and (10) Corona-Norco USD (California Department of Education 2013).

15. The high school graduation rate in 2013 for Latinos in was 75.7 percent, approximately 12 percentage points lower than for whites. However, Latinos, like African Americans and American Indian or Alaskan Natives, show a 9 percentage-point gender variation in graduation favoring females over males.

16. The California Master Plan, formally titled the Donahoe Higher Education Act (now located at Part 40 of Division 3 of Title 3 of the California Education Code), was created in 1960.

17. California's public postsecondary education system consists of three tiers, comprising nine University of California campuses, twenty-three California State University campuses and eight off-campus centers, and 112 California Community Colleges.

18. Pew Research Center (2015).

19. Fortuny, Capps, and Passel (2007). In 2004, undocumented migrants represented more than a quarter of all workers in production, construction, and service occupations.

20. Fortuny, Capps, and Passel (2007).

21. Portes and Rumbaut (2006); Bean and Stevens (2003).

22. De Genova (2002: 427) is drawing on Susan Coutin's concept of "legal non-existence" (1993) and Donald Carter's concept of "the revocability of the promise of the future" (1997: 196).

23. Coutin (1993: 98); cf. Chavez (1998: 158–65); Hagan (1994: 94, 129, 160).

24. The Social Security Administration routinely notifies employers when the Social Security numbers they submit for employees do not match the names in SSA records. A mismatch can arise from clerical error or a legitimate name change and thus does not necessarily indicate a lack of authorized work status. In most cases though, employers terminate an employee named in a mismatch letter rather than risk being investigated for hiring undocumented workers.

25. Kasinitz et al. (2008); Portes and Rumbaut (2001, 2006); Waters (1999); Zhou and Bankston (1998); Kao and Tienda (1995); Suárez-Orozco and Suárez-Orozco (1995); Suárez-Orozco, Suárez-Orozco, and Todorova (2008).

26. Conchas (2006); Pizarro (2005); Osterman (2000, 1998).

27. Croninger and Lee (2001).

28. Gibson Gándara, and Peterson-Koyama (2004).

29. Unlike classic studies that contrast smaller friendship groups (see Willis 1977 and MacLeod 1995), college-goers and early exiters are broad categories I created to contrast educational and work experiences.

30. Agius Vallejo (2012); R.G. Rumbaut and Komaie (2010); Agius Vallejo and Lee (2009).

31. This nickname is tied to the DREAM Act. Media stories linked to DREAM Act advocacy efforts have profiled high-achieving undocumented immigrant youth—valedictorians, star athletes, Ivy League students—whose talents are wasted because current laws do not allow them to pursue their dream careers. See, for example, Tobar (2010); Sacchetti (2010).

32. Espiritu (2003); Angela Valenzuela (1999); Adler, Kless, and Adler (1992); Lever (1976); Eder and Parker (1987); J. Coleman (1961).

33. Sociologist Robert C. Smith (2006) refers to these as "lockdown girls." Outside school hours they are not allowed to leave home without an older relative.

34. See D. Carter (1997: 196).

3. CHILDHOOD

1. Yuval-Davis (2006). Yuval-Davis also includes feeling safe as a component of belonging. See also Ignatieff (2001).

2. Yuval-Davis (2006).

3. Portes and Rumbaut (2001).

4. De Genova (2002); see also Coutin (2000).

5. R.D. Rumbaut and Rumbaut (2005).

6. Piore (1979).

7. R.G. Rumbaut and Ima (1988).

8. For a detailed account of families "divided by borders," see Abrego (2014); Dreby (2012).

9. Fortuny, Capps, and Passel (2007).

10. Menjívar and Abrego (2009); Rodriguez and Hagan (2004); Hagan, Rodriguez, and Castro (2011).

11. Duncan, Ziol-Guest, and Kalil (2010); Yoshikawa and Kalil (2011).

12. The Department of Health and Human Services has defined housing instability as high housing costs in proportion to income, poor housing quality, unstable neighborhoods, overcrowding, or homelessness. See Johnson and Meckstroth (1998).

13. Chavez (1998); Hondagneu-Sotelo (1994); Zlolniski (2006).

14. Capps, Fix, and Murray (2005).

15. Passel (2006).

16. Chavez (1998).

17. Crowley (2003).

18. For studies examining household density among immigrants in the United States more generally, see Zlolniski (2006); Standish et al. (2008); Schill, Friedman, and Rosenbaum (1998).

19. Many Mexican immigrants in the greater Los Angeles area find single rooms to rent through ads at local supermarkets and *carnicerías* (meat markets). During my fieldwork, I saw scores of these ads, often scribbled in pen on small scraps of paper posted on community boards. By providing a cost-free marketplace for households looking for renters who would supply some extra income or day care assistance, these community boards serve the needs of individuals and families low on capital and credit.

20. Romero (2011); Hondagneu-Sotelo (2007).

21. Family separation, while a defining experience for children, is beyond the scope of this discussion. See Dreby (2010) for a rich account of family separation and its consequences.

22. Berndt (1996); Bronfenbrenner (1979).
23. Tuan (1977: 159).
24. Tuan (1977: 183–84).
25. Eccles and Appleton Gootman (2002); Crosnoe (2000); Rhodes (1994); Greenberg, Siegel, and Leitch (1983).
26. Suárez-Orozco, Suárez-Orozco, and Todorova (2008).
27. Chavez (2008: 14).

4. SCHOOL AS A SITE OF BELONGING AND CONFLICT

1. Cremin (1957: 79–80, 84–97).
2. Abbot (1910: 379).
3. Donato (1997); G. Gonzalez (1990).
4. See Espiritu (1999); Hondagneu-Sotelo (1994); Glenn (1992).
5. Tyson (2011).
6. Bowles and Gintis (1976).
7. Émile Durkheim ([1903] 1995) called this kind of feeling "collective effervescence." He associated it with the break from profane and menial tasks that occurs when members of a group come together to share a sacred experience. A high energy develops among the group that bonds individuals to one another.
8. Esmeralda, Zulima, and JD legalized their immigration status before I interviewed them. But each was undocumented through high school graduation.
9. Tyson (2011).
10. Conchas (2006); P. Carter (2005); Gibson, Gándara, and Peterson-Koyama (2004); Stanton-Salazar (2001).
11. The Puente Project is an academic preparation program targeting California's educationally disadvantaged students. The project's mission is to increase the number of educationally disadvantaged students who enroll in four-year colleges, receive college degrees, and return to their communities as mentors. The program was launched in 1991 as a grassroots initiative to address the low rate of academic achievement among Mexican American and Latino students. The Puente model consists of three components: language arts instruction, sustained academic counseling, and mentoring by community members. Currently the program is in fifty-nine community colleges throughout California.
12. California Department of Education (2015b).
13. Flores-Gonzalez (2002).
14. Osterman (2000).
15. Noguera (2003a, 2003b); Flores-Gonzales (2002); Deschenes, Cuban, and Tyack (2001); Ferguson (2001); Skiba (2000).
16. Continuation schools are part of a larger network of Alternative Schools Accountability Model (ASAM) schools. The California Public Schools Accountability Act of 1999 established ASAM, which provides school-level accountability for alternative schools serving highly mobile and at-risk students. "California's school districts and county offices operate the largest and most complex alternative education system in the United States. Designed to provide specialized assistance to students who are failing in a traditional school setting due to

academic or behavioral problems, the system is unique nationally in terms of both size and scope" (WestEd 2009: 3).

17. California Department of Education (2015a). In October 2010, there were 499 continuation high schools reporting an enrollment of 69,510 students. However, CDE demographic reports from prior school years indicate that the total number of students served by these schools over the entire year averaged over 116,500.

18. See Warren (2007).

19. In the school year 2005–6, California's nontraditional high schools enrolled only 12 percent of the state's high school students but accounted for half of all dropouts in the state (Rumberger 2008: 5).

20. R.G. Rumbaut and Komaie (2010); Fuligni and Pedersen (2002); Suárez-Orozco and Suárez-Orozco (1995).

21. Suárez-Orozco, Suárez-Orozco, and Todorova (2008: 2–3).

22. Gleeson and Gonzales (2012).

23. R.G. Rumbaut (1997: 944–45). See also Park and Burgess (1921).

5. ADOLESCENCE

1. Before passage of S. B. 976 in 1993, California drivers did not have to provide proof of citizenship to obtain a license. S. B. 976 required residents to provide a Social Security number and proof that their presence in California was "authorized under federal law." A. B. 60, passed in 2013, permits licenses for undocumented residents.

2. Silva (2012); Berlin, Furstenberg, and Waters (2010); R.G. Rumbaut and Komaie (2010).

3. Furstenberg et al. (2002).

4. Elder (1998: 966).

5. R.G. Rumbaut (2005).

6. Chavez (1991: 258); Van Gennep (1960). See chapter 1 for a discussion of van Gennep's work, particularly his concept of liminality.

7. Van Gennep (1960); Chavez (1998); Menjívar (2006).

8. Abrego (2006: 223).

9. Goffman (1963).

10. LeBel (2008).

11. Link and Phelan (2001); Crocker (1999); Leary and Schreindorfer (1998: 15); Herman (1993); Link, Mirotznik, and Cullen (1991); Jones, Scott, and Markus (1984).

12. LeBel (2008).

13. This was before 2004, when US citizens were required to present passports in order to cross.

14. Ruiz (1998); Romo (1983); Barrera (1979); Camarillo (1979); Galarza (1977). Also, see chapter 1 for an overview of contemporary Mexican migration and immigration policies.

15. Chavez (2008, 2001).

16. Huntington (2004); Hanson (2007); Brimelow (1995); Lamm and Imhoff (1985).

17. Ono and Sloop (2002).
18. Negrón-Gonzales (2009).
19. Hanson (2007).
20. Huntington (2004: 30).
21. Massey and Sanchez (2010).
22. See Fernandez (2010).
23. Mize and Peña Delgado (2012: 2).
24. Negrón-Gonzales (2009: 29).
25. Herman (1993); Link, Mirotznik, and Cullen (1991); Jones, Scott, and Markus (1984).
26. Pulitzer Prize–winning journalist Jose Antonio Vargas describes his experiences coming out as gay and as undocumented in a *New York Times Magazine* piece, published June 22, 2011.
27. Espinoza (2011).
28. I did not formally interview any of the respondents' mentors, though I had several informal conversations with many of them, triangulating what respondents told me and helping me assess these relationships.
29. Esperanza graduated from high school in 2000, before the passage of A. B. 540. Facing the prospect of nonresidency tuition at three to five times the in-state rates, Esperanza realized that her only choice was to enroll in community college because tuition was more affordable.

6. EARLY EXITERS

1. Each year, employers file a Wage and Tax Statement (Form W-2) with the Social Security Administration (SSA) and the Internal Revenue Service to report how much they paid their employees and the amount of taxes deducted from their wages. The SSA sends a "no-match" letter when the names or Social Security numbers listed on an employer's Form W-2 do not match the SSA's records. The purpose of the letter is to notify workers and employers of the discrepancy and to alert workers that they are not receiving proper credit for their earnings, which can affect future retirement or disability benefits administered by the SSA. The letter does not indicate whether the worker is undocumented. But some employers use the letter against workers who have been injured on the job or who complain of labor violations.
2. For more on immigrant women who do domestic work, see Hondagneu-Sotelo (2007); Romero (1992).
3. Furstenberg et al. (2002); Elder (1987, 1998); Rindfuss (1991).
4. The link between school outcomes and future success among immigrant youth is well documented. See Kasinitz et al. (2008); Portes and Rumbaut (2001, 2006); Suárez-Orozco and Suárez-Orozco (1995); Suárez-Orozco, Suárez-Orozco, and Todorova (2008); Waters (1999); Zhou and Bankston (1998).
5. R. Contreras (2012); Rios (2011); Wacquant (2004); Newman (2009); Fine and Weis (1998); Willis (1977).
6. For more nuanced views, please see Prudence Carter's (2005) theorizing of the influence of social identities on school engagement patterns among low-income black and Latino youth and Angela Valenzuela's (1999) "subtractive

schooling" concept that draws attention to the ways schools erode Mexican students' social capital by dismissing their definition of education and by enforcing assimilationist policies and practices.

7. Willis (1977: 14).

8. MacLeod (1995: 61).

9. According to anthropologist Sarah Willen (2007), daily perceptions of uncertainty, danger, and the threat of deportation produce specific kinds of fear and anxiety that have physical as well as emotional effects—what Willen aptly terms the "embodiment" of illegality. The complicated realities of everyday life in the shadows have tremendous implications for physical and mental well-being.

10. Holmes (2013: 109).

11. See, for example, Seth Holmes's (2013) description of the suffering experienced by Mexican migrant farmworkers, and related work on undocumented Latino day laborers (Walter, Bourgois, and Loinaz 2004; Walter et al. 2002).

12. In 2009, the minimum wage in California was $8.00 an hour. It increased to $9.00 an hour on July 1, 2014, and effective January 1, 2016, it will increase to $10.00 an hour. However, many undocumented immigrants settle for jobs that pay far less than the standard minimum wage.

13. Purser (2009); Theodore, Valenzuela, and Meléndez (2006); Theodore (2000); Valenzuela (1999).

14. Capps et al. (2003); Griffith, Stull, and Broadway (1995); Sassen-Koob (1984); Portes (1981).

15. Job Corps is the centerpiece of this government outreach. Initiated as the core program of the Johnson Administration's Great Society social reforms and administered by the US Department of Labor, Job Corps offers a broad menu of programs for young people between the ages of sixteen and twenty-four. Undocumented immigrants cannot enroll.

16. In addition, the military offers active-duty members and veterans a variety of health benefits and assistance with rent and mortgage, business loans, and college tuition.

17. Amid the misinformation regarding undocumented immigrants' participation in the military, there is one certainty: the federal government cannot petition on behalf of an undocumented immigrant to grant legal status for enlistment. See Air Force Information (2015).

18. Contemporary policies and practices have constructed and subsequently modified categories of exclusion, deepening the division between undocumented immigrants and their legal counterparts. See Bosniak (2006); Ngai (2004); De Genova (2002); Coutin (2000); Hagan (1994).

19. Hagan (1998); Waldinger (1996); Boyd (1989); Massey et al. (1987); Rodriguez (1987).

20. Rindfuss (1991).

21. See Arnett (2000) on emerging adulthood and the prolonged period of independent role exploration during the late teens and twenties.

22. Coutin (2003).

23. Sigona (2012: 51).

24. Das (2006); cf. Sigona (2012).

25. Portes and Rumbaut (2006, 2001); Portes and Zhou (1993); Gans (1992).

26. MacLeod (1987); Willis (1977); Bowles and Gintis (1976).

27. See Vargas (2011).

28. See Menjívar and Salcido (2002) for a review of the literature on domestic violence among immigrant women. See also Parson et al. (2014) further exploration of Spanish-speaking immigrant women's experiences of partner violence.

29. See Gonzales, Suárez-Orozco, and Dedios-Sanguineti (2013).

30. Many Chicano and Mexican communities in California and throughout the United States have recently engaged with communities in Veracruz to use fandango as a means of community building and social justice. See M. Gonzalez (2011, 2009).

7. COLLEGE-GOERS

1. Our first meeting took place several months before I started this study.

2. Some scholars counter that this focus has limited our ability to uncover the more immediate barriers to everyday life immigrants face and to recognize the patterns that promote immigrants' upward or downward mobility. See Portes and Fernandez-Kelly (2008).

3. Abrego (2008) argues that the passage of California's Assembly Bill 540 immediately relieved stigma among undocumented immigrant students because it provided a socially acceptable identity and label little known to most others on college campuses.

4. As noted in chapter 1, A. B. 540 provides the in-state tuition provision to all students meeting California residency requirements regardless of immigration status or nativity. Growth among undocumented student campus groups following the 2006 immigrant rights marches resulted in more emotional and financial support for these students and more opportunities to be involved in advocacy work. See Gonzales (2008).

5. Kaushal (2008).

6. Between 2002 and 2012, the percentage of undocumented students receiving the A. B. 540 exemption who were Latinos was 48 percent, while Asian students represented 45 percent. While Mexicans made up a slightly larger portion of this group, their numbers in California are close to ten times greater. See University of California, Office of the President (2013).

7. Baum and Payea (2013). As mentioned in chapter 1, undocumented college students became eligible for state financial aid in January 2012.

8. With the exception of only six respondents, the college-goers did not rely on their parents for financial assistance, and none had any significant savings of their own. Several started at more affordable community colleges, hoping to save money and then transfer to four-year universities. Others applied to the less expensive California State University system.

9. This change in state legislation went into effect while this book was going to press. During the time period of my study, this was not the reality for most of my respondents (through their late twenties and early thirties).

10. Hoyt and Winn (2004).

11. My last contact with Pancho was early in 2012. At that time he was working in a convenience store owned by his neighbor.

12. Campaign for College Opportunity (2012).

13. Flores (2010).

14. Dockett and Perry (2001); Goodenow and Grady (1993).

15. Gibson, Gándara, and Peterson-Koyama (2004); Battistich and Hom (1997); Deci et al. (1991); Finn (1989).

16. There is also an ever-growing interdisciplinary literature that specifically addresses postsecondary transitions. This literature links the problems of alienation and the sense of not fitting in among students from a range of backgrounds to problems persisting in and graduating from college. See Trent et al. (2007) and other articles from the *Teachers College Record* special issue (vol. 9, no. 10) on disciplinary- and field-based research on youth transitions into and through college.

17. See, for example, the University of California policy on the A. B. 540 nonresident exemption (University of California Admissions Office 2014).

18. Lipsky (2010).

19. Initially, I observed these interactions. However, after seeing patterns, I began to take on a participant-observer role, often attempting to intervene by asking questions of university officials and encouraging students to assert themselves.

20. See Rosaldo (1994).

21. Rosaldo and Flores (1997); Rosaldo (1997, 1994).

22. Aragon and Perez (2006).

23. Seif (2004).

24. Rincon (2008).

25. McGray (2006).

26. See Gonzales (2008); Rincon (2008); Seif (2004).

27. Voss and Bloemraad (2011).

28. For an elaboration of this argument, see Gonzales, Heredia, and Negrón-Gonzales (2013: 174–78).

29. Stephen (2003).

30. Silvestrini (1997: 43).

31. Cesar never charged a fee for these appearances and never accepted honoraria.

32. Wolfe (1940).

33. Perez (2009: xii).

8. ADULTHOOD

1. The act was first introduced in Congress by Senators Orrin Hatch (R-UT) and Richard Durbin (D-IL) in 2001 to provide a pathway to legal residency status for young people who were born abroad but raised and educated in the United States. The act proposed that students who lived in the United States for at least five years, graduated from US high schools or the equivalent, and maintained "good moral character" (by US government standards) would become

eligible to apply for six-year conditional resident status. This status could become permanent after they completed two years of college or military service. While DREAM Act proposals have been regularly reintroduced since 2001 and have gained increased support, no version has yet become law. See Olivas (2012, 2009).

2. Bhabha (1992: 321).

3. U nonimmigrant visas are set aside for victims of certain crimes who have suffered mental or physical abuse and are helpful to law enforcement or government officials in the investigation or prosecution of criminal activity. Congress created the U nonimmigrant visa with the passage of the Victims of Trafficking and Violence Protection Act (including the Battered Immigrant Women's Protection Act) in October 2000. See US Citizenship and Immigration Services (2014).

4. The credit crisis resulting from the bursting of the housing bubble is credited as the primary cause of the 2007–9 recession in the United States. While housing prices peaked in early 2006, they began to decline by late 2006, a trend that continued into 2007. As a result, construction on new houses slowed nearly to a halt, affecting hundreds of thousands of workers. See Byun (2010).

5. Despite receiving legal advice not to marry, Ramon and Maria finally did so in 2011. Marriage between two undocumented persons cuts off a potential avenue to family sponsorship because neither spouse can legally sponsor the other.

6. De Genova (2002: 439).

7. Kanstroom (2010).

8. Dreby (2012); Hagan (2008); Golash-Boza (2009).

9. Golash-Boza and Hondagneu-Sotelo (2013).

10. Simanski (2013).

11. Heath (2013).

12. Mexican American Legal and Education Defense Fund (2014).

13. Golash-Boza (2012).

14. Cave (2012).

15. Under the Uniting and Strengthening America by Providing Appropriate Tools Required to Intercept and Obstruct Terrorism, or USA PATRIOT Act of 2001, Public Law 107–56, the possession of explosives is punishable by mandatory prison time.

16. By law, when immigrants are arrested, they must face the US justice system before dealing with any related immigration violations. They are tried, and if found guilty, they are sentenced to prison. Those who are undocumented are deported after serving prison time. Several kinds of criminal offenses merit loss of lawful permanent status. Green-card holders can be removed for engaging in any act included as punishable by deportation under Section 237 of the Immigration and Nationality Act (e.g., immigration fraud, criminal activity, or abandonment).

17. On October 3, 2013, California governor Jerry Brown signed into law a bill allowing undocumented immigrants to apply for driver's licenses. The law, which went into effect January 2015, replaces earlier state legislation that granted driver's licenses to DACA beneficiaries. However, this was not part of my respondents' experiences during the twelve years of this study.

18. Menjívar and Abrego (2012).

19. Gonzales and Chavez (2012).

20. Alterations in California's car-towing and impounding policies, effective January 1, 2012, permit an unlicensed driver to have a licensed driver take his or her car home.

21. Alba (2005).

22. Cesar was ready to enter college before the passage of A. B. 540. To attend his dream school, he would have had to pay nonresident tuition, which was nearly three times the in-state rate.

23. Chatzky (2006).

24. Joaquin Luna's suicide was covered in many national media outlets. See, for example, Fernandez (2011).

25. Willen (2007).

26. Willen (2007: 10). See also Holmes (2013).

27. Symptoms such as these also have been experienced by highly accultur- ated immigrants with chronic stress. See Bui et al. (2011); Hacker et al. (2011); Viruell-Fuentes (2007).

28. Lannen et al. (2008).

29. Motomura (2008).

30. On immigration experiences and health outcomes, see Messias, McE- wen, and Clark (2014); Holmes (2013); Chavez (2012); Willen (2012, 2007); Marrow (2012); Willen, Mulligan, and Castañeda (2011). On limitations to health care access, see Castañeda and Melo (2014).

31. In 2012, I formed a research team, first at the University of Chicago and then at Harvard University, to study the impact of DACA on the lives of eligible young adults. See Gonzales, Terriquez, and Ruszczyk (2014). In 2013 we reached 2,684 young people, and in 2015 we began carrying out in-depth interviews in Arizona, California, Georgia, New York, Illinois, and South Carolina.

9. CONCLUSION

1. The agricultural bills were the Republican-backed Agricultural Job Opportunity Benefits and Security (AgJOBS) Act of 2001 (S. 1161), introduced by Sen. Larry Craig (R-ID) on July 10, 2001, and the Democratic H-2A Reform and Agricultural Worker Adjustment Act (H. R. 2736), introduced during the 107th Congress by Rep. Howard Berman (D-CA) on August 2, 2001. The extensions were a four-month extension of Section 245(i) passed by the House by a vote of 336–43 in May, and a one-year extension approved by the Senate by unanimous consent in September. The bills for a pathway to citizenship were H. R. 1918, sponsored in the House by Rep. Chris Cannon (R-UT) and sixty- two bipartisan cosponsors, and S. 1291, sponsored in the Senate by Sen. Orrin Hatch (R-UT) and eighteen bipartisan cosponsors. See H. R. 1918, Student Adjustment Act of 2001, 107th Cong., 1st sess.; and S. 1291, Development, Relief, and Education for Alien Minors Act, 107th Cong., 2nd sess.

2. Here and other places in the chapter I use the proper names of undocu- mented young people whose stories were chronicled in the public record.

254 | Notes to Chapter 9

3. Durbin was a cosponsor of the Development, Relief, and Education for Alien Minors Act that Sen. Hatch introduced in 2001 (as S. 1291).

4. Rosenblum (2011).

5. The Comprehensive Immigration Reform Act of 2006 (S. 2611) and the bipartisan Comprehensive Immigration Reform Act of 2007 (S. 1348).

6. Cloture is the "only procedure by which the Senate can vote to place a time limit on consideration of a bill or other matter and thereby overcome a filibuster. Under the cloture rule (Rule XXII), the Senate may limit consideration of a pending matter to 30 additional hours, but only by vote of three-fifths of the full Senate, normally 60 votes." See US Senate (n.d.), s.v. "cloture."

7. Jordan (2006); Lau (2006).

8. Sacchetti (2010).

9. Preston (2010).

10. Portes and Fernandez-Kelly (2008).

11. Soysal (2000, 1994); Jacobson (1996).

12. Aleinikoff (2001: 267).

13. Willen (2007); De Genova (2004, 2002); Ngai (2004); Coutin (1999).

14. Gonzales, Suárez-Orozco, and Dedios-Sanguineti (2013); Willen (2012, 2007); Holmes (2013); Quesada, Hart, and Bourgois (2011); Castañeda (2009).

15. Kubal (2013: 555); Goldring, Berinstein, and Bernhard (2007); Menjívar (2006).

16. Menjívar (2006).

17. Judge Andrew Hanen argued that the president's actions violated something called the 1946 Administrative Procedure Act, which Hanen interpreted as specifying the president should have formally posted a public notice in the *Federal Register* about the action and held a public comment period before enacting it. See Electronic Privacy Information Center (n.d.).

18. Preston (2015).

19. Miller (2015).

20. Chavez (2008).

21. Jones-Correa and de Graauw (2013).

22. Ewing, Martinez, and Rumbaut (2015).

23. Olivas (2011).

24. Duncan and Murnane (2011).

25. Giroux (2009).

26. California's Proposition 98, also called the Classroom Instructional Improvement and Accountability Act, amended the California Constitution to mandate a minimum percentage of the state budget to be spent on K-12 education.

27. California Budget and Policy Center (2011).

28. Rios (2011).

29. Golash-Boza and Hondagneu-Sotelo (2013).

30. Signed into law on April 9, 2008, the Second Chance Act (P.L. 110–199) was designed to improve outcomes for people returning to communities after incarceration. The Second Chance Act authorizes federal grants to government agencies and nonprofit organizations to provide support strategies and services designed to reduce recidivism by improving outcomes for people returning from prisons, jails, and juvenile facilities.

31. M. Coleman (2012: 181).
32. Gonzales and Ruiz (2014).
33. Portes and Rumbaut (2006).
34. The size of the Mexican population in Los Angeles is second only to that of Mexico City.
35. McGreevy (2013).
36. Golash-Boza (2012).
37. Cornelius and Lewis (2006); Massey, Durand, and Malone (2002); Hondagneu-Sotelo (1994); Massey et al. (1987).
38. U.S. Citizenship and Immigration Services (2015). The status is conditional on eligibility and is good for two years. USCIS has urged beneficiaries to submit renewal requests about 120 days before the period of deferred action will expire.
39. Gonzales and Bautista-Chavez (2014).
40. Gonzales, Terriquez, and Ruszczyk (2014).
41. Batalova, Hooker, and Capps (2014).
42. Singer and Svajlenka (2012).
43. Batalova and McHugh (2010).
44. Singer and Svajlenka (2013).
45. According to Singer and Svajlenka (2013), California, Texas, New York, Illinois, and Florida had the most DACA applicants through March 22, 2013. Among all applicants, nearly 75 percent were born in Mexico. While the majority of applicants residing in western, midwestern, and most southern states were also born in Mexico, East Coast states have a more diverse composition.
46. Gonzales, Terriquez, and Ruszczyk (2014).
47. DACA's benefits derive from the legal distinction between lawful presence and lawful status. Normally when one has unlawful status, one accrues unlawful presence. Although DACA recipients have lawful presence, interpreted as a temporary authorization by the Department of Homeland Security to be in the United States that avails access to certain privileges, DACA does not confer a lawful status, which would allow access to federal financial aid.
48. Jones-Correa and De Grauw (2013); Dreby (2012); Golash-Boza (2012).
49. ICE ACCESS (Agreements of Cooperation in Communities to Enhance Safety and Security) section 287(g) permits the delegation of immigration enforcement authority to state and/or local law enforcement agents. See US Immigration and Customs Enforcement (n.d.-a).
50. US Immigration and Customs Enforcement (n.d.-b).
51. US Immigration and Customs Enforcement (n.d.-b).
52. US Department of Homeland Security (2014).
53. Powers, Kraly, and Seltzer (2004); Kossoudji and Cobb-Clark (2000); S. Smith, Kramer, and Singer (1996).
54. Thompson and Cohen (2014).
55. This debate was renewed in 2013. When House Republicans indicated that they would not support a pathway to citizenship for the nation's more than eleven million undocumented immigrants, many advocates responded that immigration reform that did not include citizenship would not be a deal-breaker.
56. Rhodan (2015).

57. Dreby (2015).

58. Under United We Dream (UWD), the DREAM Educational Empowerment Program (DEEP) works with students, parents, and educators to engage in local efforts to improve educational equity for undocumented immigrant students. Also, under the Illinois DREAM Act, high school counselors are required to receive training to better understand undocumented students and to learn about postsecondary options so as to help their students.

59. UCLA's Dream Summer National Internship Program is one example of how local organizations can help undocumented young people gain work experience and develop relevant skills. Chicago has created over five hundred volunteer positions and internship opportunities for undocumented high school and college students; and nationwide, UndocuNation events promote and celebrate art produced by undocumented young people.

60. Efforts such as the National Immigrant Youth Alliance's Undocuhealth, the UCLA Labor Center's CIRCLE Project, and the University of Washington's Purple Group have provided important spaces for undocumented youth to discuss and seek support to mitigate the stresses stemming from growing up without legal immigration status.

References

Abbott, Grace. 1910. "The Education of Foreigners in American Citizenship." In *Proceedings of the Buffalo Conference for Good City Government and the 16th Annual Meeting of the National Municipal League,* 375–84. Philadelphia: National Municipal League.

Abrego, Leisy J. 2006. "I Can't Go to College Because I Don't Have Papers: Incorporation Patterns of Undocumented Latino Youth." *Latino Studies* 4:212–31.

———. 2008. "Legitimacy, Social Identity and the Mobilization of Law: The Effects of Assembly Bill 540 on Undocumented Students in California." *Law and Social Inquiry* 33 (3): 709–34.

———. 2014. *Sacrificing Families: Navigating Laws, Labor and Love across Borders.* Palo Alto, CA: Stanford University Press.

Adichie, Chimamanda Ngozi. 2009. "The Danger of a Single Story." TEDGlobal. www.ted.com/talks/chimamanda_adichie_the_danger_of_a_single_story.

Adler, Patricia A., Steven J. Kless, and Peter Adler. 1992. "Socialization to Gender Roles: Popularity among Elementary School Boys and Girls." *Sociology of Education* 65 (3): 169–87.

Agius Vallejo, Jody. 2012. "Socially Mobile Mexican Americans and the Minority Culture of Mobility." *American Behavioral Scientist* 56:666–81.

Agius Vallejo, Jody, and Jennifer Lee. 2009. "Brown Picket Fences: The Immigrant Narrative and Patterns of Giving Back among the Mexican Origin Middle-Class in Los Angeles." *Ethnicities* 9 (1): 5–23.

Air Force Information. 2015. "Citizenship." http://airforce.army.com/info/citizenship.

Alba, Richard. 2005. "Bright vs. Blurred Boundaries: Second-Generation Assimilation and Exclusion in France, Germany, and the United States." *Ethnic and Racial Studies* 28 (1): 20–49.

Alba, Richard, and Victor Nee. 2003. *Remaking the American Mainstream: Assimilation and Contemporary Immigration.* Cambridge, MA: Harvard University Press.

Aleinikoff, T. Alexander. 2001. "Policing Boundaries: Migration, Citizenship, and the State." In *E Pluribus Unum? Contemporary and Historical Perspectives on Immigrant Political Incorporation,* edited by Gary Gerstle and John Mollenkopf, 267–91. New York: Russell Sage Foundation.

Apple, Michael. 1982. *Education and Power.* Boston: Ark Paperbacks.

Aragon, Steven R., and Mario Rios Perez. 2006. "Increasing Retention and Success of Students of Color at Research-Extensive Universities." *New Directions for Student Services* 2006 (114): 81–91.

Arnett, Jeffrey J. 2000. "Emerging Adulthood: A Theory of Development from Late Teens through the Twenties." *American Psychologist* 55:469–80.

Barrera, Mario. 1979. *Race and Class in the Southwest: A Theory of Racial Inequality.* South Bend, IN: University of Notre Dame Press.

Batalova, Jeanne, Sarah Hooker, and Randy Capps. 2014. *DACA at the Two-Year Mark: A National and State Profile of Youth Eligible and Applying for Deferred Action.* Washington, DC: Migration Policy Institute. http://www.migrationpolicy.org/research/daca-two-year-mark-national-and-state-profile-youth-eligible-and-applying-deferred-action.

Batalova, Jeanne, and Margie McHugh. 2010. "DREAM vs. Reality: An Analysis of Potential DREAM Act Beneficiaries." Washington, DC: Migration Policy Institute. www.migrationpolicy.org/pubs/DREAMInsight-July2010.pdf.

Battistich, Victor, and Allen Hom. 1997. "The Relationship between Students' Sense of Their School as a Community and Their Involvement in Problem Behaviors." *American Journal of Public Health* 87 (12): 1997–2001.

Baum, Sandy, and Kathleen Payea. 2013. *Trends in Student Aid 2013.* College Board: Trends in Education Series. http://trends.collegeboard.org/sites/default/files/student-aid-2013-full-report.pdf.

Bean, Frank D., and Gillian Stevens. 2003. *America's Newcomers and the Dynamics of Diversity.* New York: Russell Sage Foundation.1Becker, Howard S. 1963. *Outsiders: Studies in the Sociology of Deviance.* Ann Arbor: University of Michigan Press.

Benhabib, Seyla. 2004. *The Rights of Others.* Cambridge: Cambridge University Press.

Berlin, Gordon, Frank F. Furstenberg Jr., and Mary C. Waters. 2010. "Introducing the Issue." *Future of Children* 20 (1): 3–18.

Berndt, Thomas J. 1996. "Exploring the Effects of Friendship Quality on Social Development." In *The Company They Keep: Friendship in Childhood and Adolescence,* edited by W. M. Bukowski, A. F. Newcomb, and W. W. Hartup, 346–65. New York: Cambridge University Press.

Bhabha, Homi K. 1992. "Double Visions." *Artforum* 30 (5): 85–59.

Bloch, Alice. 2007. "Methodological Challenges for National and Multi-sited Comparative Survey Research." *Journal of Refugee Studies* 20 (2): 230–47.

Bloemraad, Irene, Kim Voss, and Taeku Lee. 2011. "The Protests of 2006: What Were They, How Do We Understand Them, Where Do We Go?" In

Rallying for Immigrant Rights: The Fight for Inclusion in 21st Century America, edited by Kim Voss and Irene Bloemraad, 3–43. Berkeley: University of California Press.

Bosniak, Linda. 2006. *The Citizen and the Alien: Dilemmas of Contemporary Membership*. Princeton, NJ: Princeton University Press.

Bourgois, Philippe. 1995. *In Search of Respect: Selling Crack in El Barrio*. Cambridge: Cambridge University Press.

Bowles, Samuel, and Herbert Gintis. 1976. *Schooling in Capitalist America: Educational Reform and the Contradictions of Economic Life*. New York: Basic Books.

Boyd, Monica. 1989. "Family and Personal Networks in International Migration: Recent Developments and New Agendas." *International Migration Review* 23 (3): 638–70.

Brimelow, Peter. 1995. *Alien Nation: Common Sense about America's Immigration Disaster*. New York: Random House.

Bronfenbrenner, Urie. 1979. "Contexts of Child Rearing: Problems and Prospects." *American Psychologist* 34 (10): 844.

Bui, Quynh, Mark Doescher, David Takeuchi, and Vicky Taylor. 2011. "Immigration, Acculturation and Chronic Back and Neck Problems among Latino-Americans." *Journal of Immigrant and Minority Health* 13 (2): 194–201.

Byun, Kathryn J. 2010. "The U.S. Housing Bubble and Bust: Impacts on Employment." *Monthly Labor Review*, December, 3–17.

Calavita, Kitty. 1992. *Inside the State: The Bracero Program, Immigration, and the INS*. New Orleans, LA: Quid Pro Books.

California Budget and Policy Center. 2011. "A Decade of Disinvestment: California Education Spending Nears the Bottom." Report, California Budget Project, School Finance Facts, October. http://calbudgetcenter.org/wp-content/uploads/111012_Decade_of_Disinvestment_%20SFF.pdf.

California Department of Education. 2013. "Data Quest." Accessed January 14, 2015. http://dq.cde.ca.gov/dataquest/.

———. 2015a. "Continuation Education: CalEdFacts." Last updated June 8. www.cde.ca.gov/sp/eo/ce/cefcontinuationed.asp.

———. 2015b. "Research on School Counseling Effectiveness." Last updated May 5. www.cde.ca.gov/ls/cg/rh/counseffective.asp.

Camarillo, Albert. 1979. *Chicanos in a Changing Society: From Mexican Pueblos to American Barrios in Santa Barbara and Southern California, 1848–1930*. Cambridge, MA: Harvard University Press.

Campaign for College Opportunity. 2012. "Meeting Compliance, but Missing the Mark: A Progress Report on the Implementation of Historic Transfer Reform for Students from Community Colleges to the California State University via Senate Bill 1440." November. http://collegecampaign.org/portfolio/november-2012-meeting-compliance-but-missing-the-mark-a-progress-report-on-the-implementation-of-historic-transfer-reform/.

Capps, Randolph, Michael Fix, and Julie Murray. 2005. "The New Demography of America's Schools: Immigration and the No Child Left Behind Act." Washington, DC: Urban Institute.

Capps, Randolph, Michael E. Fix, Jeffrey S. Passel, Jason Ost, and Dan Perez-Lopez. 2003. "A Profile of the Low-Wage Immigrant Workforce." Immigrant Families and Workers: Facts and Perspectives, Brief No. 4, Urban Institute, Washington, DC. http://webarchive.urban.org/UploadedPDF/310880_lowwage_immig_wkfc.pdf.

Carter, Donald M. 1997. States of Grace: Senegalese in Italy and the New European Immigration. Minneapolis: University of Minnesota Press.

Carter, Prudence L. 2005. Keepin' It Real: School Success beyond Black and White. New York: Oxford University Press.

Castañeda, Heide. 2009. "Illegality as Risk Factor: A Survey of Unauthorized Migrant Patients in a Berlin Clinic." Social Science and Medicine 68 (8): 1552–60.

Castañeda, Heide, and Milena Andrea Melo. 2014. "Health Care Access for Latino Mixed-Status Families Barriers, Strategies, and Implications for Reform." American Behavioral Scientist 58 (14): 1891–1909.

Cave, Damien. 2012. "American Children, Now Struggling to Adjust to Life in Mexico." New York Times, June 18.

Cebulko, Kara. 2014. "Documented, Undocumented, and Liminally Legal: Legal Status during the Transition to Adulthood for 1.5-Generation Brazilian Immigrants." Sociological Quarterly 55 (1): 143–67.

Chatzky, Jean. 2006. "Your Adult Kids Are Back. Now What? Two of Three Grads Return Home Today. Skip the You-Got-It-Good Jokes and Get Set for a New Stage of Parenting." Money Magazine, December 29.

Chavez, Leo R. 1991. "Outside the Imagined Community: Undocumented Settlers and Experiences of Incorporation." American Ethnologist 18: 257–78.

———. 1994. "The Power of the Imagined Community: The Settlement of Undocumented Mexicans and Central Americans in the United States." American Anthropologist 96 (1): 52–73.

———. 1998. Shadowed Lives: Undocumented Immigrants in American Society. Fort Worth, TX: Harcourt Brace College.

———. 2001. Covering Immigration: Popular Images and the Politics of the Nation. Berkeley: University of California Press.

———. 2008. The Latino Threat: Constructing Immigrants, Citizens, and the Nation. Stanford, CA: Stanford University Press.

———. 2012. "Undocumented Immigrants and Their Use of Medical Services in Orange County, California." Social Science and Medicine 74 (6): 887–93.

Cleave, Chris. 2010. Little Bee: A Novel. New York: Simon and Schuster.

Coleman, James. 1961. The Adolescent Society. Glencoe, IL: Free Press.

Coleman, Mathew. 2012. "Immigrant Il-legality: Geopolitical and Legal Borders in the US, 1882–Present." Geopolitics 17 (2): 402–22.

Conchas, Gilberto Q. 2001. "Structuring Failure and Success: Understanding the Variability in Latino School Engagement." Harvard Educational Review 71:475–504.

———. 2006. The Color of Success: Race and High-Achieving Urban Youth. New York: Teachers College Press.

Contreras, Frances. 2009. "Sin Papeles y Rompiendo Barreras: Latino Students and the Challenges of Persisting in College." *Harvard Educational Review* 79 (4): 610–32.

Contreras, Randol. 2012. *The Stickup Kids: Race, Drugs, Violence, and the American Dream.* Berkeley: University of California Press.

Cornelius, Wayne A., and Jessa M. Lewis, eds. 2006. *Impacts of Border Enforcement on Mexican Migration: The View from Sending Communities.* Boulder, CO: Lynne Rienner; San Diego: Center for Comparative Immigration Studies, University of California, San Diego.

Coutin, Susan B. 1993. *The Culture of Protest: Religious Activism and the US Sanctuary Movement.* Boulder, CO: Westview Press.

———. 1999. "Denationalization, Inclusion, and Exclusion: Negotiating the Boundaries of Belonging." *Indiana Journal of Global Legal Studies* 7:585–93.

———. 2000. *Legalizing Moves: Salvadoran Immigrants' Struggle for U.S. Residency.* Ann Arbor: University of Michigan Press.

———. 2003. "Borderlands, Illegality and the Spaces of Non-existence." In *Globalization under Construction: Governmentality, Law, and Identity,* edited by Richard Perry and Bill Maurer, 171–202. Minneapolis: University of Minnesota Press.

Cremin, Lawrence A., ed. 1957. *The Republic and the School: Horace Mann on the Education of Free Men.* New York: Teachers College Press.

Crocker, Jennifer. 1999. "Social Stigma and Self-Esteem: Situational Construction of Self-Worth." *Journal of Experimental Social Psychology* 35 (1): 89–107.

Croninger, Robert G., and Valerie E. Lee. 2001. "Social Capital and Dropping Out of High School: Benefits to At-Risk Students of Teachers' Support and Guidance." *Teachers College Record* 103 (4): 548–81.

Crosnoe, Robert. 2000. "Friendship in Childhood and Adolescence: The Life Course and New Directions." *Social Psychology Quarterly* 63 (4): 377–91.

Crowley, Sheila. 2003. "The Affordable Housing Crisis: Residential Mobility of Poor Families and School Mobility of Poor Children." *Journal of Negro Education* 72 (1): 22–38.

Das, Veena. 2006. *Life and Words: Violence and the Descent into the Ordinary.* Berkeley: University of California Press.

De Certeau, Michael. 1984. *The Practice of Everyday Life.* Berkeley: University of California Press.

Deci, Edward L., Robert J. Vallerand, Luc G. Pelletier, and Richard M. Ryan. 1991. "Motivation and Education: The Self-Determination Perspective." *Educational Psychologist* 26 (3–4): 325–46.

De Genova, Nicolas. 2002. "Migrant 'Illegality' and Deportability in Everyday Life." *Annual Review of Anthropology* 31:419–47.

———. 2004. "The Legal Production of Mexican/Migrant 'Illegality.'" *Latino Studies* 2 (2): 160–85.

Deschenes, Sarah, Larry Cuban, and David Tyack. 2001. "Mismatch: Historical Perspectives on Schools and Students Who Don't Fit Them." *Teachers College Record* 103 (4): 525–47.

Díaz, Junot. 2007. *The Brief Wondrous Life of Oscar Wao*. New York: River-head Trade.

Dockett, Susan, and Bob Perry. 2001. "Starting School: Effective Transitions." *Early Childhood Research and Practice* 3 (2). http://ecrp.uiuc.edu/v3n2/dockett.html.

Donato, Ruben. 1997. *The Other Struggle for Equal Schools: Mexican Americans during the Civil Rights Era*. Albany: State University of New York Press.

Dreby, Joanna. 2010. *Divided by Borders: Mexican Migrants and Their Children*. Berkeley: University of California Press.

———. 2012. "The Burden of Deportation on Children in Mexican Immigrant Families." *Journal of Marriage and Family* 74 (4): 829–45.

———. 2015. *Everyday Illegal: When Policies Undermine Immigrant Families*. Berkeley: University of California Press.

Dreier, Peter, John Mollenkopf, and Todd Swanstrom. 2011. *Place Matters: Metropolitics for the 21st Century*. Lawrence: University Press of Kansas.

Duncan, Greg J., and Richard J. Murnane, eds. 2011. *Whither Opportunity? Rising Inequality, Schools, and Children's Life Chances*. New York: Russell Sage Foundation.

Duncan, Greg J., Kathleen Ziol-Guest, and Ariel Kalil. 2010. "Early Childhood Poverty and Adult Attainment, Behavior, and Health." *Child Development* 81:292–311.

Durkheim, Émile. [1903] 1995. *The Elementary Forms of Religious Life, a New Translation by Karen E. Fields*. London: George Allen and Unwin.

Eccles, Jacquelynne S., and Jennifer Appleton Gootman, eds. 2002. *Community Programs to Promote Youth Development*. Washington, DC: National Academy Press.

Eder, Donna, and Stephen Parker. 1987. "The Cultural Production and Reproduction of Gender: The Effect of Extracurricular Activities on Peer-Group Culture." *Sociology of Education* 60 (3): 200–213.

Eggers, Dave. 2006. *What Is the What?* New York: Vintage.

Elder, Glen H. 1987. "War Mobilization and the Life Course: A Cohort of World War II Veterans." *Sociological Forum* 2 (3): 449–72.

———. 1998. "The Life Course as Developmental Theory." *Child Development* 69 (1): 1–12.

Electronic Privacy Information Center. n.d. "The Administrative Procedure Act (APA)." https://epic.org/open_gov/Administrative-Procedure-Act.html. Accessed July 31, 2015.

Enriquez, Laura. 2011. "'Because We Feel the Pressure and We Also Feel the Support': Examining the Educational Success of Undocumented Immigrant Latina/o Students." *Harvard Educational Review* 81 (3): 476–500.

Escobar Latapí, Agustín, Frank D. Bean, and Sidney Weintraub. 1999. *La dinámica de la emigración mexicana*. Mexico City: Centro de Investigaciones y Estudios Superiores en Antropología Social.

Espinoza, Roberta. 2011. *Pivotal Moments: How Educators Can Put All Students on the Path to College*. Cambridge, MA: Harvard Education Press.

Espiritu, Yen Le. 1999. "Gender and Labor in Asian Immigrant Families." *American Behavioral Scientist* 42 (4): 628–47.

———. 2003. *Home Bound: Filipino American Lives across Cultures, Communities, and Countries*. Berkeley: University of California Press.

Ewing, Walter A., Daniel E. Martinez, and Rubén G. Rumbaut. 2015. "The Criminalization of Immigration in the United States." Special Report, American Immigration Council, Washington, DC. http://immigrationpolicy.org /special-reports/criminalization-immigration-united-states.

Feagin, Joe R., and Clairece Booher Feagin. 1993. *Racial and Ethnic Relations*. 4th ed. Upper Saddle River, NJ: Prentice Hall, 1993.

Ferguson, Ann Arnett. 2001. *Bad Boys: Public Schools in the Making of Black Masculinity*. Ann Arbor: University of Michigan Press.

Fernandez, Manny. 2010. "Teenager Testifies about Attacking Latinos for Sport." *New York Times*, March 29.

———. 2011. "Disillusioned Young Immigrant Kills Himself, Starting an Emotional Debate." *New York Times*, December 10.

Fine, Michelle, and Lois Weis. 1998. *The Unknown City: Lives of Poor and Working Class Young Adults*. Boston: Beacon Press.

Finn, Jeremy D. 1989. "Withdrawing from School." *Review of Educational Research* 59 (2): 117–42.

Fix, Michael E., ed. 2009. *Immigrants and Welfare: The Impact of Welfare Reform on America's Newcomers*. New York: Russell Sage Foundation.

Flores, Stella M. 2010. "State Dream Acts: The Effect of In-State Resident Tuition Policies and Undocumented Latino Students." *Review of Higher Education* 33:239–83.

Flores-Gonzalez, Nilda. 2002. *School Kids/Street Kids: Identity Development in Latino Students*. New York: Teachers College Press.

Foner, Nancy. 2003. *American Arrivals: Anthropology Engages the New Immigration*. Santa Fe, NM: School of American Research Press.

Fortuny, Karina, Randolph Capps, and Jeffrey Passel. 2007. *The Characteristics of Unauthorized Immigrants in California, Los Angeles County, and the United States*. Washington, DC: Urban Institute. www.urban.org /UploadedPDF/411425_Characteristics_Immigrants.pdf.

Foucault, Michael. 1992. *Discipline and Punish: The Birth of the Prison*. New York: Vintage.

Fuligni, Andrew J., and Sara Pedersen. 2002. "Family Obligation and the Transition to Young Adulthood." *Developmental Psychology* 38:856–68.

Furstenberg, Frank, Thomas Cook, Robert Sampson, and Gail Slap. 2002. "Early Adulthood in Cross National Perspective." *Annals of the American Academy of Political and Social Science* 580:6–15.

Galarza, Ernesto. 1977. *Farm Workers and Agri-Business in California, 1947–1960*. South Bend, IN: University of Notre Dame Press.

Gándara, Patricia. 1995. *Over the Ivy Walls: The Educational Mobility of Low-Income Chicanos*. Albany: State University of New York Press.

———. 2002. "A Study of High School Puente: What We Have Learned about Preparing Latino Youth for Postsecondary Education." *Educational Policy* 16 (4): 474–95.

Gans, Herbert J. 1992. "Second Generation Decline: Scenarios for the Economic and Ethnic Futures of the Post-1965 American Immigrants." *Ethnic and Racial Studies* 15:173–92.

Geertz, Clifford. 1973. "Thick Description: Toward an Interpretative Theory of Culture." In *The Interpretation of Cultures: Selected Essays*, 3–30. New York: Basic Books.

Gibson, Margaret A., Patricia Gándara, and Jill Peterson-Koyama. 2004. *School Connections: U.S. Mexican Youth, Peers, and School Achievement*. New York: Teachers College Press.

Giroux, Henry A. 2009. *Youth in a Suspect Society*. London: Palgrave Macmillan.

Gleeson, Shannon, and Roberto G. Gonzales. 2012. "When Do Papers Matter? An Institutional Analysis of Undocumented Life in the United States." *International Migration* 50 (4): 1–19.

Glenn, Evelyn Nakano. "From Servitude to Service Work: Historical Continuities in the Racial Division of Paid Reproductive Labor." *Signs* 18 (1): 1–43.

Goffman, Erving. 1963. *Stigma: On the Management of Spoiled Identity*. Englewood Cliffs, NJ: Prentice-Hall.

Golash-Boza, Tanya M. 2009. "The Immigration Industrial Complex: Why We Enforce Immigration Policies Destined to Fail." *Sociology Compass* 3 (2): 295–309.

———. 2012. *Immigration Nation: Raids, Detentions, and Deportations in Post- 9/11 America*. Boulder, CO: Paradigm.

———. In press. *Deported: Policing Immigrants, Disposable Labor and Global Capitalism*. New York: New York University Press.

Golash-Boza, Tanya, and Pierrette Hondagneu-Sotelo. 2013. "Latino Immigrant Men and the Deportation Crisis: A Gendered Racial Removal Program." *Latino Studies* 11 (3): 271–92.

Goldring, Luin, Carolina Berinstein, and Judith Bernhard 2007. "Institutionalizing Precarious Immigration Status in Canada." *Early Childhood Education Publications and Research,* Paper 4, Digital Commons @ Ryerson. digitalcommons.ryerson.ca//islandora/search/institutionalizing%20precarious%20immigration%20status?type=dismax.

Gonzales, Roberto G. 2008. "Left Out but Not Shut Down: Political Activism and the Undocumented Student Movement." *Northwestern Journal of Law and Social Policy* 3:219–45.

Gonzales, Roberto G., and Angie M. Bautista-Chavez. 2014. "Two Years and Counting: Assessing the Growing Power of DACA." Special Report, American Immigration Council, Washington, DC. www.immigrationpolicy.org /sites/default/files/docs/two_years_and_counting_assessing_the_growing_ power_of_daca_final.pdf.

Gonzales, Roberto G., and Leo R. Chavez. 2012. "'Awakening to a Nightmare': Abjectivity and Illegality in the Lives of Undocumented 1.5 Generation Latino Immigrants in the United States." *Current Anthropology* 53 (3): 255–81.

Gonzales, Roberto G., Luisa Laura Heredia, and Genevieve Negrón-Gonzales. 2013. "Challenging the Transition to New Illegalities: Undocumented Young

Adults and the Shifting Boundaries of Inclusion." In *Constructing Immigrant "Illegality": Critiques, Experiences, and Responses,* edited by Cecelia Menjívar and Daniel Kanstroom, 161–80. Cambridge: Cambridge University Press.

Gonzales, Roberto G., and Ariel G. Ruiz. 2014. "Dreaming beyond the Fields: Undocumented Youth, Rural Realities and a Constellation of Disadvantage." *Latino Studies* 12 (2): 194–216.

Gonzales, Roberto G., Carola Suárez-Orozco, and Maria Cecilia Dedios-Sanguineti. 2013. "No Place to Belong: Contextualizing Concepts of Mental Health among Undocumented Immigrant Youth in the United States." *American Behavioral Scientist* 57 (8): 1174–99.

Gonzales, Roberto G., Veronica Terriquez, and Stephen Ruszczyk. 2014. "Becoming DACAmented: Assessing the Short-Term Benefits of Deferred Action for Childhood Arrivals (DACA)." *American Behavioral Scientist* 58 (14): 1852–72.

Gonzalez, Gilbert G. 1990. *Chicago Education in the Era of Segregation.* Philadelphia: Balch Institute Press.

Gonzalez, Martha. 2009. "Zapateado Afro-Chicana Fandango Style: Self-Reflective Moments in Zapateado." In *Dancing across Borders: Danzas y Bailes Mexicanos,* edited by Olga Nájera-Ramírez, Norma Cantú, and Brenda Romero, 359–78. Chicago: University of Illinois Press.

———. 2011. "Sonic (Trans) Migration of Son Jarocho Zapateado: Rhythmic Intention, Metamorphosis and Manifestation in Fandango and Performance." In *Cornbread and Cuchifritos: Ethnic Identity Politics, Transnationalization, and Transculturation in American Urban Popular Music: Inter-American Perspectives,* edited by Wilfried Raussert and Michelle Habell-Pallan, 59–72. Trier: Wissenschaftlicher Verlag Trier; Tempe, AZ: Bilingual Press.

Gonzalez-Barrera, Ana, and Mark Hugo Lopez. 2013. *A Demographic Portrait of Mexican-Origin Hispanics in the United States.* Washington, DC: Pew Hispanic Center. www.pewhispanic.org/2013/05/01/a-demographic-portrait-of-mexican-origin-hispanics-in-the-united-states/.

Goodenow, Carol, and Kathleen E. Grady. 1993. "The Relationship of School Belonging and Friends' Values to Academic Motivation among Urban Adolescent Students." *Journal of Experimental Education* 62 (1): 60–71.

Gordon, Milton M. 1964. *Assimilation in American Life: The Role of Race, Religion and National Origins.* New York: Oxford University Press.

Greenberg, Mark T., Judith M. Siegel, and Cynthia J. Leitch. 1983. "The Nature and Importance of Attachment Relationships to Parents and Peers during Adolescence." *Journal of Youth and Adolescence* 12 (5): 373–86.

Griffith, David, Donald D. Stull, and Michael J. Broadway. 1995. "Hay Trabajo: Poultry Processing, Rural Industrialization, and the Latinization of Low-Wage Labor." In *Any Way You Cut It: Meat Processing and Small-Town America,* edited by Donald D. Stull, Michael J. Broadway, and David Griffith, 129–51. Lawrence: University of Kansas Press.

Hacker, Karen, Jocelyn Chu, Carolyn Leung, Robert Marra, Alex Pirie, Mohamed Brahimi, Margaret English, Joshua Beckmann, Dolores Acevedo-Garcia, and

Robert P. Marlin. 2011. "The Impact of Immigration and Customs Enforcement on Immigrant Health: Perceptions of Immigrants in Everett, Massachusetts, USA." *Social Science and Medicine* 73 (4): 586–94.

Hagan, Jacqueline Maria. 1994. *Deciding to Be Legal: A Maya Community in Houston.* Philadelphia: Temple University Press.

———. 1998. "Social Networks, Gender, and Immigrant Incorporation: Resources and Constraints." *American Sociological Review* 63 (1): 55–67.

———. 2008. *Migration Miracle: Faith, Hope, and Meaning on the Undocumented Journey.* Cambridge: Harvard University Press.

Hagan, Jacqueline M., Brianna Castro, and Nestor Rodriguez. 2010. "The Effects of U.S. Deportation Policies on Immigrant Families and Communities: Cross-border Perspectives." *North Carolina Law Review* 28:1799–1824.

Hagan, Jacqueline Maria, Nestor Rodriguez, and Brianna Castro. 2011. "Social Effects of Mass Deportations by the United States Government, 2000–10." *Ethnic and Racial Studies* 34 (8): 1374–91.

Hallinan, Maureen T. 1994. "Tracking: From Theory to Practice." *Sociology of Education* 67 (2): 79–84.

Hanson, Victor Davis. 2007. *Mexifornia: A State of Becoming.* San Francisco: Encounter Books.

Heath, Brad. 2013. "Immigration Tactics Aimed at Boosting Deportations." *USA Today,* February 17.

Herman, Nancy J. 1993. "Return to Sender: Reintegrative Stigma-Management Strategies of Ex-psychiatric Patients." *Journal of Contemporary Ethnography* 22 (3): 295–330.

Hill, Laura E., and Hans P. Johnson. 2011. *Unauthorized Immigrants in California.* Sacramento: Public Policy Institute of California. www.ppic.org /main/publication.asp?i=986.

Hoefer, Michael, Nancy Rytina, and Bryan C. Baker. 2011. *Estimates of the Unauthorized Immigrant Population Residing in the United States: January 2011.* Population Estimates, Office of Immigration Statistics, Department of Homeland Security. www.dhs.gov/estimates-unauthorized-immigrant-population-residing-united-states-january-2011.

Holmes, Seth. 2013. *Fresh Fruit, Broken Bodies: Migrant Farmworkers in the United States.* Berkeley: University of California Press.

Hondagneu-Sotelo, Pierrette. 1994. *Gendered Transitions: Mexican Experiences of Immigration.* Berkeley: University of California Press.

———. 2007. *Doméstica: Immigrant Workers Cleaning and Caring in the Shadows of Affluence.* Berkeley: University of California Press.

Hoyt, Jeff E., and Bradley A. Winn. 2004. "Understanding Retention and College Student Bodies: Differences between Drop-outs, Stop-outs, Opt-outs, and Transfer-outs." *NASPA Journal* 41 (3): 395–417.

Hughes, Everett Cherrington. 1945. "Dilemmas and Contradictions of Status." *American Journal of Sociology* 50:353–59.

Huntington, Samuel P. 2004. *Who Are We? The Challenges to America's National Identity.* New York: Simon and Schuster.

Ignatieff, Michael. 2001. *Human Rights as Politics and Idolatry.* Princeton, NJ: Princeton University Press.

Inda, Jonathan X. 2006. *Targeting Immigrants: Government, Technology, and Ethics*. Malden, MA: Blackwell.

Jacobson, David. 1996. *Rights across Borders: Immigration and the Decline of Citizenship*. Baltimore: Johns Hopkins University Press.

Johnson, Amy, and Alicia Meckstroth. 1998. "Ancillary Services to Support Welfare to Work." Project report to US Department of Health and Human Services, June 22. http://aspe.hhs.gov/hsp/isp/ancillary/front.htm.

Johnson, Kevin. 2011. "Sweet Home Alabama? Immigration and Civil Rights in the 'New' South." *Stanford Law Review Online* 64:22–28.

Jones, Edward E., Robert A. Scott, and Hazel Markus. 1984. *Social Stigma: The Psychology of Marked Relationships*. New York: W.H. Freeman.

Jones-Correa, Michael, and Els de Graauw. 2013. "The Illegality Trap: The Politics of Immigration and the Lens of Illegality." *Daedalus* 142 (3): 185–98.

Jordan, Miriam. 2006. "Illegal at Princeton." *Wall Street Journal*, April 15.

Kanstroom, Daniel. 2010. *Deportation Nation: Outsiders in American History*. Cambridge, MA: Harvard University Press.

Kao, Grace, and Marta Tienda. 1995. "Optimism and Achievement: The Educational Performance of Immigrant Youth." *Social Science Quarterly* 76:1–19.

Kasinitz, Philip, John H. Mollenkopf, Mary C. Waters, and Jennifer Holdaway. 2008. *Inheriting the City: The Children of Immigrants Come of Age*. Cambridge, MA: Harvard University Press.

Kaushal, Neeraj. 2008. "In-State Tuition for the Undocumented: Education Effects on Mexican Young Adults." *Journal of Policy Analysis and Management* 27 (4): 771–92.

Kilgore, Sally B. 1991. "The Organizational Context of Tracking in Schools." *American Sociological Review* 56:189–203.

Kossoudji, Sherrie A., and Deborah A. Cobb-Clark. 2000. "IRCA's Impact on the Occupational Concentration and Mobility of Newly-Legalized Mexican Men." *Journal of Population Economics* 13 (1) (2000): 81–98.

Kubal, Agnieszka. 2013. "Conceptualizing Semi-legality in Migration Research." *Law and Society Review* 47 (3): 555–87.

Lahiri, Jhunpa. 2003. *The Namesake: A Novel*. Boston: Houghton Mifflin Harcourt.

Lamm, Richard D., and Gary Imhoff. 1985. *The Immigration Time Bomb: The Fragmenting of America*. New York: Dutton Adult.

Lannen, Patrizia K., Joanne Wolfe, Holly G. Prigerson, Erik Onelov, and Ulrika C. Kreicbergs. 2008. "Unresolved Grief in a National Sample of Bereaved Parents: Impaired Mental and Physical Health 4 to 9 Years Later." *Journal of Clinical Oncology* 26 (36): 5870–76.

Lau, Tatiana. 2006. "Padilla's Future Remains Uncertain: Sachs Scholar Leaves for Oxford, Still an Illegal." *Daily Princetonian*, September 15.

Leary, Mark R., and Lisa S. Schreindorfer. 1998. "The Stigmatization of HIV and AIDS: Rubbing Salt in the Wound." In *HIV and Social Interaction*, edited by Valerian J. Derlega and Anita P. Barbee, 12–29. Thousand Oaks, CA: Sage Publications.

LeBel, Thomas P. 2008. "Perceptions of and Responses to Stigma." *Sociology Compass* 2 (2): 409–32.

Lever, Janet. 1976. "Sex Differences in the Games Children Play." *Social Problems* 23:478–87.

Levinson, Bradley. 2005. "Citizenship, Identity, Democracy: Engaging the Political in the Anthropology of Education." *Anthropology and Education Quarterly* 36 (4): 329–40.

Link, Bruce G., Jerrold Mirotznik, and Francis T. Cullen. 1991. "The Effectiveness of Stigma Coping Orientations: Can Negative Consequences of Mental Illness Labeling Be Avoided?" *Journal of Health and Social Behavior* 32 (3): 302–20.

Link, Bruce G., and Jo C. Phelan. 2001. "Conceptualizing Stigma." *Annual Review of Sociology* 27:363–85.

Lipsky, Michael. 2010. *Street-Level Bureaucracy, 30th Anniversary Edition: Dilemmas of the Individual in Public Service.* New York: Russell Sage Foundation.

Lopez, Mark Hugo, Rich Morin, and Paul Taylor. 2010. *Illegal Immigration Backlash Worries, Divides Latinos.* Washington, DC: Pew Hispanic Center.

Lucas, Samuel R., and Mark Berends. 2002. "Sociodemographic Diversity, Correlated Achievement, and De Facto Tracking." *Sociology of Education* 75 (4): 328–48.

MacLeod, Jay. 1995. *Ain't No Makin' It: Aspirations and Attainment in a Low-Income Neighborhood.* Boulder, CO: Westview Press.

Marrow, Helen B. 2012. "Deserving to a Point: Unauthorized Migrants in San Francisco's Universal Access Healthcare Model." *Social Science and Medicine* 74 (6): 846–54.

Massey, Douglas, Rafael Alarcón, Jorge Durand, and Humberto González. 1987. *Return to Aztlán: The Social Process of International Migration from Western Mexico.* Berkeley: University of California Press.

Massey, Douglas S., Jorge Durand, and Nolan J. Malone. 2002. *Beyond Smoke and Mirrors: Mexican Immigration in an Era of Economic Integration.* New York: Russell Sage Foundation.

Massey, Douglas S., and Karen A. Pren. 2012. "Unintended Consequences of U.S. Immigration Policy: Explaining the Post-1965 Surge from Latin America." *Population and Development Review* 38 (1): 1–29.

Massey, Douglas S., and Magaly R. Sanchez. 2010. *Brokered Boundaries: Creating Immigrant Identity in Anti-immigrant Times.* New York: Russell Sage Foundation.

McGray, Douglas. 2006. "The Invisibles." *Los Angeles Times Magazine,* April 23.

McGreevy, Patrick. 2013. "Signing Trust Act Is Another Illegal-Immigration Milestone for Brown." *Los Angeles Times,* October 5.

Menjívar, Cecilia. 2006. "Liminal Legality: Salvadoran and Guatemalan Immigrants' Lives in the United States." *American Journal of Sociology* 111:999–1037.

Menjívar, Cecilia, and Leisy Abrego. 2009. "Parents and Children across Borders: Legal Instability and Intergenerational Relations in Guatemalan and

Salvadoran Families." In *Across Generations: Immigrant Families in America*, edited by Nancy Foner, 160–89. New York: New York University Press.
———. 2012. "Legal Violence: Immigration Law and the Lives of Central American Immigrants." *American Journal of Sociology* 117 (5): 1380–1421.

Menjívar, Cecilia, and Rubén Rumbaut. 2008. "Rights of Ethnic Minorities and Migrants: Between Rhetoric and Reality." In *The Leading Rogue State: The United States and Human Rights*, edited by Judith Blau, David L. Brunsma, Alberto Moncada, and Catherine Zimmer, pp. 60–74. Boulder, CO: Paradigm.

Menjívar, Cecilia, and Olivia Salcido. 2002. "Immigrant Women and Domestic Violence: Common Experiences in Different Countries." *Gender and Society* 16 (6): 898–920.

Messias, DeAnne K. Hilfinger, Marylyn Morris McEwen, and Lauren Clark. 2014. "The Impact and Implications of Undocumented Immigration on Individual and Collective Health in the United States." *Nursing Outlook* 63 (1), epub. November 22. doi:10.1016/j.outlook.2014.11.004.

Mexican American Legal and Education Defense Fund. 2014. *Detention, Deportation, and Devastation: The Disproportionate Effect of Deportation on the Latino Community.* Los Angeles: Mexican American Legal and Education Defense Fund. www.maldef.org/assets/pdf/DDD_050614.pdf.

Miller, Jake. 2015. "Donald Trump Is Running for President in 2016." *CBS News*, June 16.

Mills, C. Wright. 1959. *The Sociological Imagination.* New York: Oxford University Press.

Mize, Ronald L., and Grace Peña Delgado. 2012. *Latino Immigrants in the United States.* Cambridge: Polity Press.

Moss, Hilary J. 2009. *Schooling Citizens: The Struggle for African American Education in Antebellum America.* Chicago: University of Chicago Press.

Motomura, Hiroshi. 2006. *Americans in Waiting: The Lost Story of Immigration and Citizenship.* Oxford: Oxford University Press.

———. 2008. "Immigration outside the Law." *Columbia Law Review* 108 (8): 2037–97.

National Conference of State Legislatures. 2012. "Immigration-Related Laws, Bills and Resolutions in the States: Jan. 1–March 31, 2012." www.ncsl.org /research/immigration/2012-immigration-laws-bills-and-resolutions.aspx.

———. 2014. "Undocumented Student Tuition: State Action." June 12. www .ncsl.org/research/education/undocumented-student-tuition-state-action .aspx.

National Immigration Law Center. n.d. "Laws, Legislation and Resolutions." www.nilc.org/legres.html.

Nazario, Sonia. 2005. *Enrique's Journey.* New York: Random House.

Negrón-Gonzales, Genevieve. 2009. "Hegemony, Ideology and Oppositional Consciousness: Undocumented Youth and the Personal-Political Struggle for Educational Justice." ISSC Working Papers Series, Institute for the Study of Social Change, Berkeley.

Nevins, Joseph. 2010. *Operation Gatekeeper and Beyond: The War on "Illegals" and the Remaking of the U.S.-Mexico Boundary.* New York: Routledge.

Newman, Katherine S. 2009. *No Shame in My Game: The Working Poor in the Inner City*. New York: Random House.

Ngai, Mae. 2004. *Impossible Subjects: Illegal Aliens and the Making of Modern America*. Princeton, NJ: Princeton University Press.

Noguera, Pedro A. 2003a. "Schools, Prisons, and Social Implications of Punishment: Rethinking Disciplinary Practices." *Theory into Practice* 42 (4): 341–50.

———. 2003b. "The Trouble with Black Boys: The Role and Influence of Environmental and Cultural Factors on the Academic Performance of African American Males." *Urban Education* 38 (4): 431–59.

Oakes, Jeannie. 1985. *Keeping Track: How Schools Structure Inequality*. New Haven, CT: Yale University Press.

Olivas, Michael A. 2007. "Immigration-Related State and Local Ordinances: Preemption, Prejudice, and the Proper Role for Enforcement." *University of Chicago Legal Forum*, 27–56.

———. 2009. "The Political Economy of the Dream Act and the Legislative Process: A Case Study of Comprehensive Immigration Reform." *Wayne Law Review* 55 (4): 1757–1810.

———. 2011. "*Plyler's* Political Efficacy." *UC-Davis Law Review* 45:1–26.

———. 2012. *No Undocumented Child Left Behind: Plyler v. Doe and the Education of Undocumented Schoolchildren*. New York: New York University Press.

Ong, Aihwa. 1999. "Cultural Citizenship as Subject-Making: Immigrants Negotiate Racial and Cultural Boundaries in the United States." *Current Anthropology* 37 (5): 737–62.

Ono, Kent A., and John M. Sloop. 2002. *Shifting Borders: Rhetoric, Immigration, and California's Proposition 187*. Philadelphia: Temple University Press.

Orfield, Gary, and Jongyeon Ee. 2014. *Segregating California's Future: Inequality and Its Alternative 60 Years after Brown v. Board of Education*. Los Angeles: Civil Rights Project. http://civilrightsproject.ucla.edu/research/k-12-education/integration-and-diversity/segregating-california2019s-future-inequality-and-its-alternative-60-years-after-brown-v.-board-of-education.

Osterman, Karen F. 1998. "Hostile Kids—Try a Little Tenderness." *Newsday*, March 26.

———. 2000. "Students' Need for Belonging in the School Community." *Review of Educational Research* 70:323–67.

Park, Robert E., and Ernest W. Burgess. 1921. *Introduction to the Science of Sociology*. Chicago: University of Chicago Press.

Parson, Nia, Rebecca Escobar, Mariam Merced, and Anna Trautwein. 2014. "Health at the Intersections of Precarious Documentation Status and Gender-Based Partner Violence." *Violence Against Women*, August 21. doi: 10.1177/1077801214545023.

Passel, Jeffrey S. 2005. "Unauthorized Migrants: Numbers and Characteristics." Report, June 14, Pew Hispanic Center, Washington, DC. www.pewtrusts.org/en/research-and-analysis/reports/2005/06/15/unauthorized-migrants-numbers-and-characteristics.

———. 2006. "Size and Characteristics of the Unauthorized Migrant Population in the U.S.: Estimates Based on the March 2005 Current Population Survey." Hispanic Trends, March 7, Pew Hispanic Center, Washington, DC. www.pewhispanic.org/2006/03/07/size-and-characteristics-of-the-unauthorized-migrant-population-in-the-us/.

Passel, Jeffrey S., and D'Vera Cohn. 2008. "Trends in Unauthorized Immigration: Undocumented Inflow Now Trails Legal Inflow." Hispanic Trends, October, Pew Hispanic Center, Washington, DC. www.pewhispanic.org/2008/10/02/trends-in-unauthorized-immigration/.

———. 2009. *A Portrait of the Unauthorized Migrants in the United States.* Washington, DC: Pew Hispanic Center. http://pewhispanic.org/files/reports/107.pdf.

———. 2010. *U.S. Unauthorized Immigration Flows Are Down Sharply since Mid-decade.* Washington, DC: Pew Hispanic Center. http://pewhispanic.org/files/reports/126.pdf.

Passel, Jeffrey S., D'Vera Cohn, and Ana Gonzalez-Barrera. 2012. *Net Migration from Mexico Falls to Zero--and Perhaps Less.* Washington, DC: Pew Research Center. www.pewhispanic.org/2012/04/23/net-migration-from-mexico-falls-to-zero-and-perhaps-less/.

Passel, Jeffrey S., and Roberto Suro. 2005. *Rise, Peak and Decline: Trends in U.S. Immigration, 1992–2004.* Washington, DC: Pew Hispanic Center.

Perez, William. 2009. *We Are Americans: Undocumented Students Pursuing the American Dream.* Sterling, VA: Stylus.

———. 2012. *Americans by Heart: Undocumented Latino Students and the Promise of Higher Education.* New York: Teachers College Press.

Pew Research Center. 2015. "Unauthorized Immigrants: Who They Are and What the Public Thinks." January 15. www.pewresearch.org/key-data-points/immigration/.

Piore, Michael J. 1979. *Birds of Passage: Migrant Labor and Industrial Societies.* Cambridge: Cambridge University Press.

Pizarro, Marcos. 2005. *Chicanos in School: Racial Profiling, Identity Battles, and Empowerment.* Austin: University of Texas Press.

Platform for International Cooperation on Undocumented Migrants. 2008. *Undocumented Children in Europe: Invisible Victims of Immigration Restrictions.* Brussels: PICUM.

Portes, Alejandro. 1981. "Modes of Structural Incorporation and Present Theories of Labor Immigration." In *Global Trends in Migration: Theory and Research on International Population Movements,* edited by Mary M. Kritz, Charles B. Keely, and Silvano M. Tomasi, 279–97. Staten Island: Center for Migration Studies of New York.

Portes, Alejandro, and Patricia Fernandez-Kelly. 2008. "No Margin for Error: Educational and Occupational Achievement among Disadvantaged Children of Immigrants." *Annals of the American Academy of Political and Social Science* 620:12–36.

Portes, Alejandro, and Rubén G. Rumbaut. 2001. *Legacies: The Story of the Immigrant Second Generation.* Berkeley: University of California Press.

———. 2006. *Immigrant America: A Portrait.* 3rd ed. Berkeley: University of California Press.

Portes, Alejandro, and Min Zhou. 1993. "The New Second Generation: Segmented Assimilation and Its Variants." *Annals of the American Academy of Political and Social Science* 530:74–96.

Powers, Mary G., Ellen Percy Kraly, and William Seltzer. 2004. "IRCA: Lessons of the Last US Legalization Program." *Migration Information Source,* July 1, 81–98. www.migrationpolicy.org/article/irca-lessons-last-us-legalization-program.

Preston, Julia. 2010. "Immigration Bill Fails in the Senate." *New York Times,* December 17.

———. 2015. "San Francisco Murder Case Exposes Lapses in Immigration Enforcement." *New York Times,* July 7.

Purser, Gretchen. 2009. "The Dignity of Job-Seeking Men: Boundary Work among Immigrant Day Laborers." *Journal of Contemporary Ethnography* 38 (1): 117–39.

Quesada, James, Laurie Kain Hart, and Philippe Bourgois. 2011. "Structural Vulnerability and Health: Latino Migrant Laborers in the United States." *Medical Anthropology* 30 (4): 339–62.

Reed, Deborah, Kim S. Rueben, and Elisa Barbour. 2006. *Retention of New Teachers in California.* San Francisco: Public Policy Institute of California. www.ppic.org/content/pubs/report/R_206DRR.pdf.

Rhodan, Maya. 2015. "Obama Calls for Sweeping Criminal Justice Reforms in NAACP Speech." *Time,* July 14.

Rhodes, Jean E. 1994. "Older and Wiser: Mentoring Relationships in Childhood and Adolescence." *Journal of Primary Prevention* 14 (3): 187–96.

Rincon, Alejandra. 2008. *Undocumented Immigrants and Higher Education: Sí Se Puede!* New York: LFB Scholarly Publications.

Rindfuss, Ronald R. 1991. "The Young Adult Years: Diversity, Structural Change and Fertility." *Demography* 28:493–512.

Rios, Victor M. 2011. *Punished: Policing the Lives of Black and Latino Boys.* New York: NYU Press.

Robinson, Campbell, and Julia Preston. 2012. "Appeals Court Draws Boundaries on Alabama's Immigration Law." *New York Times,* August 21.

Rodriguez, Nestor. 1987. "Undocumented Central Americans in Houston: Diverse Populations." *International Migration Review* 21 (Spring): 4–25.

Rodriguez, Nestor, and Jacqueline Maria Hagan. 2004. "Fractured Families and Communities: Effects of Immigration Reform in Texas, Mexico, and El Salvador." *Latino Studies* 2 (3): 328–51.

Romero, Mary. 2002. *Maid in the USA.* New York: Routledge.

———. 2011. *The Maid's Daughter: Living inside and outside the American Dream.* New York: NYU Press.

Romo, Ricardo. 1983. *East Los Angeles: History of a Barrio.* Austin: University of Texas Press.

Rosaldo, Renato. 1994. "Cultural Citizenship and Educational Democracy." *Cultural Anthropology* 9 (3): 402–11.

———. 1997. "Cultural Citizenship, Inequality, and Multiculturalism." In *Race, Identity, and Citizenship: A Reader*, edited by Rodolfo D. Torres, Louis F. Mirón, and Jonathan X. Inda. Malden, MA: Blackwell.

Rosaldo, Renato, and William V. Flores. 1997. "Identity, Conflict, and Evolving Latino Communities: Cultural Citizenship in San Jose, California." In *Latino Cultural Citizenship: Claiming Identity, Space, and Rights*, edited by William V. Flores and Rina Benmayor, 57–96. Boston: Beacon Press.

Rosenblum, Marc R. 2011. *US Immigration Policy since 9/11: Understanding the Stalemate over Comprehensive Immigration Reform*. Washington, DC: Migration Policy Institute.

Ruiz, Vicki. 1998. "Shaping Public Space/Enunciating Gender: A Multiracial Historiography of the Women's West, 1995–2000." *Frontiers: A Journal of Women Studies* 22 (3): 22–25.

Rumbaut, Rubén D., and Rubén G. Rumbaut. 2005. "Self and Circumstance: Journeys and Visions of Exile." in *The Dispossessed: An Anatomy of Exile*, edited by Peter I. Rose, 331–55. Amherst: University of Massachusetts Press, 2005. (Originally presented as two papers on May 8, 1976, at the annual meeting of the American Society for Adolescent Psychiatry, Miami Beach, FL. Reproduced in their original form.)

Rumbaut, Rubén G. 1997. "Assimilation and Its Discontents: Between Rhetoric and Reality." *International Migration Review* 31:923–60.

———. 2004. "Ages, Life Stages, and Generational Cohorts: Decomposing the Immigrant First and Second Generations in the United States." *International Migration Review* 38:1160–1205.

———. 2005. "Turning Points in the Transition to Adulthood: Determinants of Educational Attainment, Incarceration, and Early Childbearing among Children of Immigrants." *Ethnic and Racial Studies* 28:1041–86.

———. 2008. "The Coming of the Second Generation: Immigration and Ethnic Mobility in Southern California." *Annals of the American Academy of Political and Social Science* 620:196–236.

Rumbaut, Rubén G., and Kenji Ima. 1988. *The Adaptation of Southwest Asian Refugee Youth: A Comparative Study*. Washington, DC: US Office of Refugee Resettlement.

Rumbaut, Rubén G., and Golnaz Komaie. 2010. "Immigration and Adult Transitions." *Future of Children* 20:39–63.

Rumbaut, Rubén G., and Alejandro Portes, eds. 2001. *Ethnicities: Children of Immigrants in America*. Berkeley: University of California Press.

Rumberger, Russell W. 2008. *Solving California's Dropout Crisis*. California Dropout Research Project Committee Report. February. www.cdrp.ucsb .edu/dropouts/pubs_policyreport.htm.

Sacchetti, Maria. 2010. "Harvard Student Won't Face Deportation." *Boston Globe*, June 19.

Santos, Fernanda. 2012. "Arizona Immigration Law Survives Ruling." *New York Times*, September 6.

Sassen-Koob, Saskia. 1984. "Notes on the Incorporation of Third World Women into Wage- Labor through Immigration and Off-shore Production." *International Migration Review* 18 (4): 1144–67.

Schafer, Walter E., and Carol Olexa. 1971. *Tracking and Opportunity: The Locking-Out Process and Beyond.* Scranton, PA: Chandler.

Schill, M., S. Friedman, and E. Rosenbaum. 1998. "The Housing Conditions of Immigrants in New York City." *Journal of Housing Research* 9:201–3.

Seghetti, Lisa M., Stephen R. Viña, and Karma Ester. 2004. *Enforcing Immigration Law: The Role of State and Local Law Enforcement.* Washington, DC: Congressional Research Service, Library of Congress.

Seif, Hinda. 2004. "'Wise Up!' Undocumented Latino Youth, Mexican-American Legislators, and the Struggle for Higher Education Access." *Latino Studies* 2 (2): 210–30.

Settersten, Richard A., Jr., Frank F. Furstenberg, and Rubén G. Rumbaut. 2005. *On the Frontier of Adulthood: Theory, Research, and Public Policy.* Chicago: University of Chicago Press.

Sigona, Nando. 2012. "'I've Too Much Baggage': The Impact of Legal Status on the Social Worlds of Irregular Migrants." *Social Anthropology/Anthropologie Sociale* 20 (1): 50–65.

Sigona, Nando, and Vanessa Hughes. 2012. *No Way Out, No Way In: Irregular Migrant Children and Families in the UK.* Oxford: COMPAS.

Silva, Jennifer M. 2012. "Constructing Adulthood in an Age of Uncertainty." *American Sociological Review* 77 (4): 505–22.

Silvestrini, Blanca G. 1997. "'The World We Enter When Claiming Rights': Latinos and Their Quest for Culture." In *Latino Cultural Citizenship: Claiming Identity, Space, and Rights,* edited by William V. Flores and Rina Benmayor, 39–53. Boston: Beacon Press.

Simanski, John F. 2014. *Immigration Enforcement Actions: 2013.* Washington, DC: United States Department of Homeland Security, September. www.dhs .gov/sites/default/files/publications/ois_enforcement_ar_2013.pdf.

Singer, Audrey, and Nicole Prchal Svajlenka. 2013. "Immigration Facts: Deferred Action for Childhood Arrivals (DACA)." Report, Immigration Facts Series, August 14, Brookings Institution, Washington, DC. www .brookings.edu/research/reports/2013/08/14-daca-immigration-singer.

Skiba, Russell, J. 2000. *Zero Tolerance, Zero Evidence: An Analysis of School Disciplinary Practice.* Bloomington: Indiana University Education Policy Center.

Smith, Robert Courtney. 2006. *Mexican New York: Transnational Lives of New Immigrants.* Berkeley: University of California Press.

———. 2008. "Horatio Alger Lives in Brooklyn: Extrafamily Support, Intrafamily Dynamics, and Socially Neutral Operating Identities in Exceptional Mobility among Children of Mexican Immigrants." *Annals of the American Academy of Political and Social Science* 620:270–90.

Smith, Shirley J., Roger G. Kramer, and Audrey Singer. 1996. *Effects of the Immigration Reform and Control Act: Characteristics and Labor Market Behavior of the Legalized Population Five Years Following Legalization.* Washington, DC: US Department of Labor, Bureau of International Labor Affairs, Immigration Policy and Research. www.popline.org/node/312004.

Soysal, Yasemin. 1994. *Limits of Citizenship: Migrants and Postnational Membership in Europe.* Chicago: University of Chicago Press.

———. 2000. "Citizenship and Identity: Living in Diasporas in Post-war Europe?" *Ethnic and Racial Studies* 23(1): 1–15.

Standish, Katherine, V. Nandi, D.C. Ompad, S. Momper, and S. Galea. 2008. "Household Density among Undocumented Mexican Immigrants in New York City." *Journal of Immigrant Minority Health* 12 (3): 310–18.

Stanton-Salazar, Ricardo. 2001. *Manufacturing Hope and Despair: The School and Kin Support Networks of U.S.-Mexican Youth.* New York: Teachers College Press.

Stephen, Lynn. 2003. "Cultural Citizenship and Labor Rights for Oregon Farmworkers: The Case of *Pineros y Campesinos Unidos del Nordoeste* (PCUN)." *Human Organization* 62 (1): 27–38.

Stumpf, Julia. 2006. "The Crimmigration Crisis: Immigrants, Crime, and Sovereign Power." Bepress Legal Series, Working Paper 1635. http://law.bepress.com/expresso/eps/1635.

Suárez-Orozco, Carola, and Marcelo Suárez-Orozco. 1995. *Transformations: Migration, Family Life, and Achievement Motivation among Latino Adolescents.* Stanford, CA: Stanford University Press.

———. 2001. *Children of Immigration.* Cambridge, MA: Harvard University Press.

Suárez-Orozco, Carola, Marcelo M. Suárez-Orozco, and Irina Todorova. 2008. *Learning a New Land: Immigrant Students in American Society.* Cambridge, MA: Harvard University Press.

Svajlenka, Nicole Prchal, and Audrey Singer. 2014. "DACA Renewals Ramp Up." Report, Immigration Facts Series, July 8, Brookings Institution, Washington, DC. www.brookings.edu/research/opinions/2014/07/08-daca-renewals-ramp-up-svajlenka-singer.

Telles, Edward E., and Vilma Ortiz. 2008. *Generations of Exclusion: Mexican Americans, Assimilation, and Race.* New York: Russell Sage Foundation.

Theodore, Nikolas. 2000. *A Fair Day's Pay? Homeless Day Laborers in Chicago.* Report prepared for the Chicago Coalition for the Homeless, Chicago Interfaith Committee on Worker Issues, and Chicago Jobs with Justice. www.nelp.org/content/uploads/2015/03/Fair-Days-Pay-Chicago.pdf.

Theodore, Nikolas, Abel Valenzuela, and Edwin Meléndez. 2006. "La Esquina (the Corner): Day Laborers on the Margins of New York's Formal Economy." *Working USA* 9 (4): 407–23.

Thompson, Ginger, and Sarah Cohen. 2014. "More Deportations Follow Minor Crimes, Records Show." *New York Times,* April 6.

Thorpe, Helen. 2011. *Just Like Us: The True Story of Four Mexican Girls Coming of Age in America.* New York: Scribner.

Tobar, Hector. 2010. "Undocumented UCLA Law Grad Is in a Legal Bind." *Los Angeles Times,* November 26.

TRAC Immigration. 2014. "Secure Communities and ICE Deportation: A Failed Program?" TRAC Report, April 8. http://trac.syr.edu/immigration/reports/349/.

Trent, William, Margaret Terry Orr, Sheri Ranis, and Jennifer Holdaway. 2007. "Transitions to College: Lessons from the Disciplines." *Teachers College Record* 109 (10): 2207–21.

Tuan, YiFu. 1977. *Space and Place: The Perspective of Experience*. Minneapolis: University of Minnesota Press.

Turner, Victor. 1967. "Betwixt and Between: The Liminal Period in Rites de Passage." In *The Forest of Symbols*, 93–111. Ithaca, NY: Cornell University Press.

Tyson, Karolyn. 2011. *Integration Interrupted: Tracking, Black Students, and Acting White after Brown*. New York: Oxford University Press.

University of California Admissions Office. 2014. "AB 540 Nonresident Tuition Exemption." http://admission.universityofcalifornia.edu/paying-for-uc/tuition-and-cost/ab540/index.html.

University of California. Office of the President. 2013. "Annual Report on AB 540 Tuition Exemptions, 2011–12 Academic Year." June. www.ucop.edu/student-affairs/_files/ab540_annualrpt_2012.pdf.

Urrea, Luis A. 2004. *The Devil's Highway: A True Story*. New York: Little, Brown.

US Citizenship and Immigration Services. 2014. "Victims of Criminal Activity: U Nonimmigrant Status." Last updated January 9. www.uscis.gov/humanitarian /victims-human-trafficking-other-crimes/victims-criminal-activity-u-nonimmigrant-status/victims-criminal-activity-u-nonimmigrant-status.

———. 2015a. "Number of I-821ID, Consideration of Deferred Action for Childhood Arrivals by Fiscal Year, Quarter, Intake, Biometrics and Case Status: 2012–2014." February 12. www.uscis.gov/sites/default/files/USCIS /Resources/Reports%20and%20Studies/Immigration%20Forms%20Data /All%20Form%20Types/DACA/I821d_daca_fy2014qtr2.pdf.

———. 2015b. "Number of I-821D, Consideration of Deferred Action for Childhood Arrivals by Fiscal Year, Quarter, Intake, Biometrics and Case Status: 2012–2015." April. www.uscis.gov/tools/reports-studies/immigration-forms-data/data-set-form-i-821d-deferred-action-childhood-arrivals.

US Department of Homeland Security. 2013. "Yearbook of Immigration Statistics: 2013 Enforcement Actions." www.dhs.gov/yearbook-immigration-statistics-2013-enforcement-actions.

———. 2014. "Policies for the Apprehension, Detention and Removal of Undocumented Immigrants." November 20. www.dhs.gov/sites/default/files /publications/14_1120_memo_prosecutorial_discretion.pdf.

US Immigration and Customs Enforcement. n.d.-a. "Delegation of Immigration Authority Section 287(g) Immigration and Nationality Act." www.ice .gov/287g/.

———. n.d.-b. "Priority Enforcement Program: How Is PEP Different from Secure Communities?" www.ice.gov/pep#wcm-survey-target-id.

US Senate. n.d. "Glossary." www.senate.gov/reference/glossary.htm.

Valenzuela, Abel. 1999. *Day Laborers in Southern California: Preliminary Findings from the Day Labor Survey*. Los Angeles: Center for the Study of Urban Poverty, Institute for Social Science Research, University of California, Los Angeles. www.popcenter.org/problems/day_labor_sites/pdfs/valenzuela_1999 .pdf.

Valenzuela, Angela. 1999. *Subtractive Schooling: US-Mexican Youth and the Politics of Caring*. Albany: SUNY Press.

Van Gennep, Arnold. 1960. *The Rites of Passage*. London: Routledge.

Vargas, Jose Antonio. 2011. "My Life as an Undocumented Immigrant." *New York Times Magazine*, June 22.

Viruell-Fuentes, Edna A. 2007. "Beyond Acculturation: Immigration, Discrimination, and Health Research among Mexicans in the United States." *Social Science and Medicine* 65 (7): 1524–35.

Voss, Kim, and Irene Bloemraad, eds. 2011. *Rallying for Immigrant Rights: The Fight for Inclusion in 21st Century America*. Berkeley: University of California Press.

Wacquant, Loïc J.D. 2004. *Body and Soul: Notebooks of an Apprentice Boxer*. New York: Oxford University Press.

Waldinger, Roger D. 1996. *Still the Promised City? African-Americans and New Immigrants in Postindustrial New York*. Cambridge, MA: Harvard University Press.

Waldinger, Roger, and Mehdi Bozorgmehr, eds. 1996. *Ethnic Los Angeles*. New York: Russell Sage Foundation.

Walker, Kyle E., and Helga Leitner. 2011. "The Variegated Landscape of Local Immigration Policies in the United States." *Urban Geography* 32 (2): 156–78.

Walter, Nicholas, Philippe Bourgois, and H. Margarita Loinaz. 2004. "Masculinity and Undocumented Labor Migration: Injured Latino Day Laborers in San Francisco." *Social Science and Medicine* 59 (6): 1159–68.

Walter, Nicholas, Philippe Bourgois, H. Margarita Loinaz, and Dean Schillinger. 2002. "Social Context of Work Injury among Undocumented Day Laborers in San Francisco." *Journal of General Internal Medicine* 17 (3): 221–29.

Warren, Paul. 2007. *Alternative Education in California*. Sacramento, CA: Legislative Analyst's Office.

Waters, Mary C. 1999. *Black Identities: West Indian Immigrant Dreams and American Realities*. New York: Russell Sage Press.

WestEd. 2009. "ASAM School Performance: Alternative School Performance on ASAM Accountability Indicators 2002–03, 2007–08." Report to the California Department of Education Policy and Evaluation Division. February. www.cde.ca.gov/ta/ac/am/documents/asamschoolperf.pdf.

Willen, Sarah S. 2007. "Towards a Critical Phenomenology of 'Illegality': State Power, Criminalization, and Abjectivity among Undocumented Migrant Workers in Tel Aviv, Israel." *International Migration* 45:7–38.

———. 2012. "Migration, 'Illegality,' and Health: Mapping Embodied Vulnerability and Debating Health-Related Deservingness." *Social Science and Medicine* 74 (6): 805–11.

Willen, Sarah S., Jessica Mulligan, and Heide Castañeda. 2011. "Take a Stand Commentary: How Can Medical Anthropologists Contribute to Contemporary Conversations on 'Illegal' Im/migration and Health?" *Medical Anthropology Quarterly* 25 (3): 331–56.

Willis, Paul. 1977. *Learning to Labour: How Working Class Kids Get Working Class Jobs*. New York: Columbia University Press.

Wolfe, Thomas. 1940. *You Can't Go Home Again*. London: William Heineman.

Yoshikawa, Hirokazu, and Ariel Kalil. 2011. "The Effects of Parental Undocumented Status on the Developmental Contexts of Young Children in Immigrant Families." *Child Development Perspectives* 5 (4): 291–97.

Yuval-Davis, Nira. 2006. "Belonging and the Politics of Belonging." *Patterns of Prejudice* 40 (3): 197–214.

Zhou, Min, and Carl L. Bankston III. 1998. *Growing Up American: How Vietnamese Children Adapt to Life in the United States.* New York: Russell Sage Foundation.

Zlolniski, Christian. 2006. *Janitors, Street Vendors and Activists: The Lives of Mexican in Silicon Valley.* Berkeley: University of California Press.

Zúñiga, Victor. 2012 "Comment" following "'Awakening to a Nightmare': Abjectivity and Illegality in the Lives of Undocumented 1.5 Generation Latino Immigrants in the United States," by Roberto G. Gonzales and Leo R. Chavez. *Current Anthropology* 53 (3): 255–81.

Index

Page references followed by t *indicate a table.*

Abbott, Edith, xvi–xvii
abjectivity, 188
Abrego, Leisy J., 101, 188, 250n3
ACCESS (Agreements of Cooperation in Communities to Enhance Safety and Security), 255n49
Addams, Jane, xvi–xvii
Adichie, Chimamanda Ngozi, 243n101
Administrative Procedure Act (1946), 254n17
adolescence as a liminal phase, 12
adolescents' transition to illegality, 92–119; anger/frustration, 102–3; awareness of implications of undocumented status, 99–101, 104; broken rites of passage, 95–100; college-goers' asserting belonging/hiding stigma, 109–15; college-goers' trust of teachers/counselors, 109–12; early exiters' coping with outsiderness/illegality, 115–17; enforced secrecy's effects, 118; exclusions to adult life, 96–98; helplessness/uncertainty, 101–2; Latinos depicted as a threat, 106–9; and learning of undocumented status, 97–98, 99t; liminal lives, 95, 100–104; overview of, 33, 92–95; papers, lack of, 97–98; and peer networks, 112–15; self-conscious awareness of stigma, 104–9; and time,

212–18; unequal transitions, 118–19
adulthood. *See* adolescents' transition to illegality; master status, immigration status as
advanced placement (AP) classes, 77, 79, 117, 293
AEDPA (Antiterrorism and Effective Death Penalty Act; 1996), 21, 241nn62,64
agency, 135–36, 145
Agreements of Cooperation in Communities to Enhance Safety and Security (ACCESS), 255n49
Agricultural Job Opportunity Benefits and Security (AgJOBS) Act, 253n1
Alabama, 23
Alba, Richard, 6, 193
Aldo (case study), 128–29, 138, 142, 181
Alex (case study), xvii–xviii, xxv
Alexia (case study), 69, 82
Alonso (case study), 64
Alternative Schools Accountability Model (ASAM), 246n16
American dream, 7, 27–28, 73, 107, 122, 175, 214, 219
Americans in waiting, 4, 223, 238n4
Ana (case study), 63–66, 74
Andrea (case study), 75–76, 81–82, 168, 171–72, 201
Angelica (case study), 99

anti-immigrant discourse/sentiment, 22–24
Antiterrorism and Effective Death Penalty
    Act (AEDPA; 1996), 21, 241nn62,64
Antonio (case study), 102
AP classes, 77, 79, 117, 293
Art (case study), 98, 125, 130, 133
ASAM (Alternative Schools Accountability
    Model), 246n16
Assembly Bill 60 (California), 24, 247n1
Assembly Bill 130 (California), 24–25
Assembly Bill 131 (California), 24–25
Assembly Bill 263 (California), 24
Assembly Bill 540 (California), 24–25, 89,
    154, 161–62, 164, 250nn3,4,6
Assembly Bill 1024 (California), 24
Assembly Bill 1159 (California), 24
Assembly Bill 2189 (California), 25
assimilation, xix, 6–7, 136, 179, 207
autonomy, 90, 133–34

Balderas, Eric, 211
Belinda (case study), 125, 133, 142
belonging/membership. See contested
    membership over time; inclusion/
    belonging
Berman, Howard, 253n1
Betancourt, Maria and Ramon (case study),
    2–4, 146–47, 184, 201, 205, 252n5
Bhabha, Homi K., 179
Blanca (case study), 85–86, 131, 140–41,
    144
Bloemraad, Irene, 8
Boston Globe, 211
Bourgois, Philippe, 16, 32
Bracero Program (Mexican Farm Labor
    Program), 18–19, 240n46
Brennan, William, 11
bright boundaries, 193
Brown, Jerry, 24, 252n17
Brown v. Board of Education, 13
Bush, George W., 209–10, 228

California: high school enrollment levels in,
    247nn17,19; immigration stances of,
    23–25, 224–25, 242n85; K-12 vs.
    college/university enrollments in, 38;
    policy toward immigrants, xiii; schools'
    failings in, 37–38, 243n13,14, 244n15;
    undocumented immigrants, number of,
    36–37
California Basic Educational Skills Test
    (CBEST), 166
California Community Colleges system,
    38–39, 159, 167–68, 244n17

California Master Plan (Donahoe Higher
    Education Act; 1960), 38, 244n16
California State University system, 38,
    159–60, 167–68, 244n17, 250n8
Cannon, Chris, 253n1
Carla (case study), 185–86
Carlos (case study), 104, 156, 158
Carter, Donald, 244n22
CBEST (California Basic Educational Skills
    Test), 166
Celina (case study), 79, 81, 114–15
Cesar (case study), 150, 156–57, 171, 193,
    196, 251n31, 253n22
Cesar Chavez Continuation High School
    (Los Angeles), 37
Chacon, Jennifer, 27
Chavez, Leo, 64, 100, 188
Chicago, xv–xvi, 256n59
Choi, Inhe, xvi
Chuy (case study), 106
CIRCLE Project (UCLA Labor Center),
    256n60
citizenship: advocacy/extension of
    college-goers' claims, 167–68; and
    belonging, 5, 134–35; cultural, 165,
    168, 170, 187; definitions of, 5; via
    immigration, 4, 238n4; and legal
    residency vs. legal permission to work,
    231, 255n55
Classroom Instructional Improvement and
    Accountability Act (Proposition 98;
    California), 221, 254n26
Clinton, Hillary, 211
cloture, 210–11, 254n6
Coleman, Matthew, 224
collective effervescence, 246n7
college degree, future success determined
    by, 10
college-goers, 149–75; activism of, 168–70;
    administrative barriers for, 161–64,
    251n19; alienation/not belonging,
    feelings of, 160–61, 251n16; as asserting
    belonging/hiding stigma, 109–15; broad-
    ened horizons as a mixed blessing,
    170–74; citizenship claims, advocacy/
    extension of, 167–68; college's
    challenges, 154; and cultural citizenship,
    165, 168, 170; financial aid for, 234;
    financial challenges for, 152, 154–60,
    250n8; first in family to attend college,
    153; immigration status of (see under
    master status, immigration status as);
    in-state tuition for, 152–54, 250nn4,6,7
    (see also Assembly Bill 540); open

doors/closed windows for, 174–75; overview of, 34, 149–52; in the postsecondary labyrinth, 152–64; secondary school experiences of, 77–82; student services for, 155, 165–67; time constraints on, 156–57; transportation constraints on, 156, 250n9; trust of teachers/counselors, 109–12; university structures' influence on sense of belonging, 154–64. *See also* college-goers vs. early exiters

college-goers vs. early exiters, 35–57; assessing future possibilities, 56–57; California schools' failings, 37–38, 243n13,14, 244n15; college-goers as learning to dream, 53–56, 244n31, 245n33; and the deserving/undeserving distinction, 223; early exiters as living in the present, 47–53; early exiters' multiple pathways, 49–53; educational level attained, 44, 45t; family obligations, 50–51; girls vs. boys, 54–55, 245n33; and illegality, 49, 51; and integration vs. segregation, 37, 39, 243n10; K-12 vs. college/university enrollments, 38; orientation to the present vs. the future, 39–47, 244n22; overview of, 32, 34–39; positive expectations, 55–56; students out of options, 52–53; students pushed out of school, 51–52. *See also* college-goers; early exiters; primary/secondary school experiences

community organizations, 132, 143–44, 224, 250n30
community support of undocumented youth, 233–34, 256n59
Comprehensive Immigration Reform Act (S. 1348; 2007), 210
Comprehensive Immigration Reform Act (S. 2611; 2006), 210
contested membership over time, 1–32; California's immigration stances, 23–25, 242n85; crime and immigration, 21–22, 241n64; deserving/undeserving distinction, 4, 26–27, 31; exclusion/belonging for 1.5 generation, 4–8, 239n13; growing up in a hostile environment, 22–23, 241nn73,74, 242n79; illegality as a master status, 15; legal context's effects on immigration flow, 20–21, 240nn57,58, 241nn59,61,62; and liminality, 8–10, 12, 28, 31–33; Mexican migration,

contemporary, 18–19, 240nn46,49,50; overview, 1–4; political changes over time, overview, 17–18, 240n44; researching undocumented Mexican youth, 16–17, 239n41; research on undocumented adults over time, 28–32, 242nn95,96, 243n101; transition to adulthood undocumented, 10–13; transition to illegality, 8–15, 212–18. *See also* DACA; DREAM Act

continuation schools, 85–87, 246–47nn16,17
Cory (case study), 100–101, 104, 158, 202–3
Coutin, Susan, 244n22
Craig, Larry, 253n1
credit cards, 131, 249n18
credit crisis, 252n4
crime: definitions of criminality, 26–27; deportations of criminals, 21–22, 220, 223, 241n62; deportations of noncriminals, 185, 228, 231; hate crimes, 22, 107; illegality and criminality, 107–9; "illegal" Mexican immigrants viewed as criminals, 219–20; and immigration, 21–22, 241n64
criminal justice reform, 231
Customs and Border Protection (CBP), 227

DACA (Deferred Action for Childhood Arrivals), 226–27; age requirements for, 25, 240n44; benefits under, 25, 180, 226–27, 230, 242n88, 255nn38,47; and contested membership over time, 1–4, 25–26, 34, 242n88; deterrents to applying for, 180, 191, 203–5, 226; eligibility for, 26; enrollments by area, 226–27, 255n45; expansion of, 1, 218; goals of, 191; impact of, 202–3, 253n31; initiation of, 179, 191, 202; limitations of, 202–5, 226–27, 234, 255nn38,47; scope of, 25, 202; uptake rates for, 25–26, 226
Dani (case study), 67–68, 113
Daniel (case study), 125
DAPA (Deferred Action for Parents of Americans and Permanent Residents), 1, 218
David (case study), 103
Davis, Gray, 24
DEEP (DREAM Educational Empowerment Program), 256n58
Deferred Action for Childhood Arrivals. *See* DACA

Deferred Action for Parents of Americans
and Permanent Residents (DAPA), 1, 218
Define America, xi, xiii
de Genova, Nicolas, 40, 184, 188, 244n22
Department of Defense Authorization Bill
(S. 2919; 2008), 210
Department of Homeland Security (DHS),
1, 227–28, 255n47
deportations: of criminals, 21–22, 220, 223,
241n62, 252n16; illegality and
deportability, 184–88, 217, 252n16;
laws regarding, 227; of noncriminals,
185, 228, 231; number of, 22, 185, 231;
under Obama, 231; after prison time,
252n16; rights surrounding, 185
deserving/undeserving distinction, 4, 26–27,
31, 91, 218–23, 229
Development, Relief, and Education for
Alien Minors Act. See DREAM Act
Dewey, John, xvi–xvii
DHS (Department of Homeland Security),
1, 227–28, 255n47
Doe, Plyler v., xiii, 11, 13, 220
domestic violence, 140–41
Donahoe Higher Education Act (California
Master Plan; 1960), 38, 244n16
Dora (case study), 40–42, 44–47, 133, 182
Dream Act (California), 24–25
DREAM Act (Development, Relief, and
Education for Alien Minors Act), 207,
220; advocacy for/endorsement of, 3,
135, 167, 192, 244n31; eligibility for,
26; goals of, 238n2, 251n1; introduc-
tion/defeat of, 1–2, 178, 209–12, 238n2,
251n1, 254n3; potential impact of, 30;
purpose of, 209–10
DREAM Act (Illinois), 256n58
DREAM Educational Empowerment
Program (DEEP), 256n58
DREAMers, 53, 244n31
Dream resource centers, 233
Dream Summer National Internship
Program (UCLA), 256n59
driver's licenses, 242n85; driving without a
license, 189, 253n20; eligibility for, 97,
131, 252n17; importance of, 94; Social
Security number required for, 24, 247n1
dropouts, 136–37, 147
Durbin, Richard, 209–10, 238n2, 251n1,
254n3
Durkheim, Émile, 246n7

E4FC (Educators for Fair Consideration),
234

early exiters, 120–48; adjusting to limited
choices, 130–32, 249nn15,16,17,18;
agency of, 134–45; community
organizations used by, 132, 143–44,
250n30; diminished hopes of, 145–47;
early friendships' importance, 140–41;
family resources and networking,
132–34; finding work, 122, 125–26;
joining clubs/teams/artistic groups,
144–45; learning to be illegal, 122–34,
248n6, 249n9; mobility limitations for,
148; overview of, 34, 120–22; refusing
to live in a cage (withdrawing from
adult life), 137–38; resistance, respite of,
136–37; risk taking, 138–40; in routines
of illegality, 181–90, 252n16, 253n20;
searching for better jobs, 128–30;
secondary school experiences of, 82–90;
solidarity among undocumented
migrants, 141–42; work environments
of, 126–28, 249n12. See also college-
goers vs. early exiters
education, upward mobility via, 33, 123
Educators for Fair Consideration (E4FC),
234
Elizabeth (case study), 58–63, 67–68, 70
Eloy (case study), 132, 140
Enrique (case study), 156, 166
Eric (case study), 52–53, 108, 122
Esmeralda (case study), 77–78, 246n8
Esperanza (case study). See Rivas,
Esperanza
Estefania (case study), 105–6

fake documents, 102, 138, 139, 181
fandangos, 144, 250n30
FBI, 228
Felipe (case study), 48–49
Fernando (case study), 160
fieldwork, ethnographic, 16–17, 28–32
financial aid, 24–26, 234, 242n92
Flor (case study), 50–51, 53, 76, 88, 98,
124–25, 127–28, 134, 136
Flores-Gonzalez, Nilda, 84
Foner, Nancy, 30
Fourteenth Amendment, 11
Fox, Vicente, 210
Frisch, Max, 135

Gabriel (case study), 120–21, 125–26, 183
gay undocumented individuals, 110, 140
Georgia, 23
Geraldo (case study), 201
Gloria (case study), 74, 76–77

Goffman, Erving, 105
Grace (case study), 156
Graham, Donald, 234
Great Society, 249n15
green cards (alien registration cards), 130
Griselda (case study), 102, 104–5
Guadalupe (case study), 59–60, 62–63

H-2A Reform and Agricultural Worker
    Adjustment Act (H.R. 2736), 253n1
Hagel, Charles, 210
Hanen, Andrew, 218, 254n17
Hansberry, Lorraine: A Raisin in the Sun,
    237n1 (Preface)
Hanson, Victor David, 107
"Harlem" (Hughes), 237n1 (Preface)
Hart-Celler Act (1965), 18–19
Hatch, Orrin, 238n2, 251n1, 253n1, 254n3
hate crimes, 22, 107
health needs of undocumented youth,
    234–35, 256n60
Hector (case study), 129, 137
Hispanic Scholarship Fund General
    Scholarship, 234
Holmes, Seth, 127
Homeland Security (DHS), 1, 227–28,
    255n47
honors classes, 77, 112, 117, 293
housing instability, 64, 180, 245n12
housing prices, 252n4
H.R. 1918, 253n1
Hughes, Everett, 15
Hughes, Langston, xv, 209; "Harlem,"
    237n1 (Preface)
Huntington, Samuel P., 107

ICE (Immigration and Customs Enforce-
    ment): and DACA, 227; deportation
    quotas of, 185, 288; fear of, 188; and
    local law enforcement, 22, 185, 218,
    224, 228, 255n49; racial profiling by,
    22; raids by, 49
IIRAIRA (Illegal Immigration Reform and
    Immigrant Responsibility Act; 1996),
    20–21, 238n12, 241nn62,64
Illegal Immigration Reform and Immigrant
    Responsibility Act (IIRAIRA; 1996),
    20–21, 238n12, 241nn62,64
illegality: conceptions of, xix; and
    criminality, 107–9; and deportability,
    184–88, 217, 252n16; embodiment of,
    249n9; and enforced orientation to the
    present, 40, 244n22; learning to be
    illegal, 122–34, 222–23, 248n6, 249n9;

as produced and experienced, 125,
    216–17; school as a defense against, 49;
    as a stigma, xix, 15, 148, 175, 213, 231;
    transition to, 8–15, 212–18 (see also
    adolescents' transition to illegality)
"illegals," usage of, 107–8
immigrant rights marches (2006), 167,
    250n4
Immigration and Customs Enforcement. See
    ICE
Immigration and Nationality Act (INA;
    1965), 20, 240nn57,58, 241n64,
    252n16
immigration history/flow: Asian, 18,
    240n47; Canadian, 240n49; legal
    context's effects on, 20–21, 240nn57,58,
    241nn59,61,62; Mexican, 18–21,
    240nn46,49,50, 241n61
immigration laws: in California, 23–25,
    242n85; effects on subjective experi-
    ences of illegality, 216–17; enforcement
    of, 5, 184, 188 (see also deportations);
    Hart-Celler Act (1965), 18–19;
    IIRAIRA, 20–21, 238n12, 241nn62,64;
    INA, 20, 240nn57,58, 241n64; IRCA,
    19–20, 96, 190, 225, 230; legislative/
    administrative commitment to
    enforcement, 223, 227–29, 255n49; list
    of, 241n74; local, 223–24; number of,
    22–23; PRWORA, 238n12; restrictions
    on noncitizens' rights by, 6, 238n12;
    and rights of undocumented children, 6,
    238n11; "Show me your papers"
    (Arizona S.B. 1070), 23, 241n73;
    TRUST Act, 24
immigration policy: closed, militarized
    borders, 19–20; contemporary, and
    undocumented youth, 225–29,
    255nn47,49; and the "impossible
    subject," 4, 238n4; Plyler v. Doe, xiii,
    11, 13, 220; quotas, 19, 240nn49,50;
    recommendations regarding, 229–35,
    255n55, 256nn58,59,60; reform efforts,
    209–10, 253n1; uneven policies, 224
Immigration Reform and Control Act. See
    IRCA
INA (Immigration and Nationality Act;
    1965), 20, 240nn57,58, 241n64,
    252n16
inclusion/belonging, 58–72; assertions of
    home, 70–72; of college-goers (see under
    college-goers); and constraints of
    undocumented life, 62–65; and
    cramped/unstable housing, 64–65,

inclusion/belonging *(continued)*
245n19; cultural/social belonging,
61–62, 245n1; factors affecting, 217–18;
and feeling at home/safe, 61, 245n1;
knowing and being known, 68–70;
overview of, 32, 58–61; overworked/
absent parents, 65–66; and place,
66–72; and poverty, 61, 63–65
inferiority narratives, 32
Inslee, Jay, 242n92
intergenerational mobility, xix, 121, 151,
250n2
IRCA (Immigration Reform and Control
Act; 1986), 19–20, 96, 190, 225, 230
Irene (case study), 78, 80, 111–12, 194–95,
203

Janet (case study), 99, 122, 126
JD (case study), 78, 80–81, 246n8
Jenny (case study), 132
Joanna (case study), 145
Job Corps, 130, 249n15
Jonathan (case study), 131, 137, 141,
144–45, 176–79
Jorge (case study), 88
Jose (case study), 146–47, 184
Josue (case study), 51–53, 88, 126, 143,
181–82
Juan (case study), 83, 118, 130
Julliard School of Music, 209
Junior (case study), 86

K–12 schools. *See* school
Kanstroom, Daniel, 184–85
Karina (case study), 89
Kathy (case study), 116, 134
Kennedy, Ted, 210

Lathrop, Julia, xvi–xvii
lawful presence vs. lawful status, 255n47
LBGT undocumented individuals, 110, 140
Lee, Taeku, 8
Lee, Thereza, 209–10
legal immigrants' rights, 12
legal liminality, 9
legal non-existence, 244n22
legal violence, 188
life-course ethnography, 28
Lilia (case study), 68, 76
liminality, 230; of adolescence, 12; and
contested membership over time, 8–10,
12, 28, 31–33; definition of, 100–101;
legal, 9; in transition to illegality, 95,
100–104

Lina (case study), 118
lives in limbo, managing, 208–35;
contemporary immigration policy and
undocumented youth, 225–29,
255nn47,49; DACA's benefits/
limitations, 226–27, 234, 255nn38,47;
and the deserving/undeserving
distinction, 218–23, 229; and interven-
tions to support undocumented youth,
need for, 232–35, 256nn58,59,60;
legalization, arguments for, 209,
230–32, 255n55; and legislative/
administrative commitment to
enforcement, 223, 227–29, 255n49;
mediating influence of local contexts,
223–25; overview of, 34, 208–12; and
policy recommendations, 229–35,
255n55, 256nn58,59,60; returning to
communities after incarceration, 223,
254n30; and stigma management, 213;
time and the transition to illegality,
212–18
lockdown girls, 245n33
Lopez-Sanchez, Juan Francisco, 218
Lorena (case study), 98, 116
Los Angeles: community organizations in,
143–44; immigrant population's size,
35, 224, 243n1; immigration integration
policies of, 224; Mexican population of,
xv, 7, 36, 255n34; minorities in/ethnic
diversity of, 35, 243n1; public
transportation in, 35, 156; undocu-
mented immigrants, number of, 37, 224.
See also college-goers vs. early exiters
Loyola University, 234
Lozano, Rudy, xvi
Lugar, Richard, 210
Luis (case study), 80, 82, 173
Luisa (case study), 64–65
Luna, Joaquin, Jr., 199, 253n24
Lupe (case study), 131
Lupita (case study), 54–55, 101
Luz (case study), 136, 139, 189

MacLeod, Jay, 123
Mann, Horace, 73
Manuel (case study), 116, 143–44, 201
Marco (case study), 169–70
Margarita (case study), 124
Mario (case study), 146, 182
Marisol (case study), 54
Massey, Douglas S., 18–19
master status, immigration status as,
176–207; college-goers after college,

191–93; college-goers' coming to grips
with illegality, 197–99; college-goers'
dreams denied, 193–95, 253n22;
college-goers' family needs, 195–97;
DACA's limitations, 202–5; discardable
lives of college-goers/early exiters,
205–7; early exiters' routines of
illegality, 181–90, 252n16, 253n20;
experiential dimension of, 199–202,
253n27; illegality and deportability,
184–88, 252n16; illegality as a stigma,
xix, 15, 148, 175, 213, 231; and job
stability, 182–84; and living in the
moment, 188–90, 253n20; overview of,
34, 176–79; when doors stop opening to
college-goers, 190–99, 253n22
McCain, John, 210
Medi-Cal, 25, 242n88
membership/belonging. *See* contested
membership over time; inclusion/
belonging
Menjívar, Cecilia, 9, 188, 217
mental health professionals, 234–35,
256n60
mentors, 45–46, 111–12, 248n28
meritocracy, 13, 28, 47, 82, 152, 191, 220
Mexican Farm Labor Program (Bracero
Program), 18–19, 240n46
Mexican labor, 18–20, 240n46
Mexican migration: contemporary, 18–19,
240nn46,49,50; history/flow of, 18–21,
240nn46,49,50, 241n61; "illegal"
Mexican immigrants viewed as
criminals/undeserving, 219–20; Mexican
percentage of undocumented immigrants, 36–37; Mexican population of
Los Angeles, xv, 7, 36, 255n34;
Mexican population of United States,
36, 243n5
migrant laborers, 18, 20, 39, 240n50,
244n19
Miguel (case study), 101–2, 104–5, 125,
132–33
military service, 130, 249nn16,17
Mills, C. Wright, xx
minimum wage, 249n12
Misto (case study), 92–95, 100, 201
Motomura, Hiroshi, 238n4
music, 144, 250n30

nativism, 23–24, 220
Nee, Victor, 6
Negrón-Gonzales, Genevieve, 107–8
New York Times, 22, 231

Ngai, Mae, 238n4
Nieves, Esther, xvi
Nimo (case study), 43, 45, 56, 112–13, 169,
195–96
9/11 terrorist attacks (2001), 210
North Carolina, 242n79

Obama, Barack, 1–3, 22, 31, 203, 211,
218–19, 228, 231
Olivas, Michael, 23
Olivia (case study), 195
Omar (case study), 113
Oscar (case study), 80, 112, 166, 171, 196

Padilla Peralta, Dan-el, 210–11
Pancho (case study), 158–59, 251n11
partner abuse, 140–41
Pedro (case study), 41–42, 44–45, 66, 69,
76, 118, 126, 132, 136, 138, 183–84
Pell Grants, 234
Perez, William, 175
Personal Responsibility and Work
Opportunity Reconciliation Act
(PRWORA; 1996), 238n12
Pew Hispanic Center, 23, 64
Piore, Michael, 62
Pledge of Allegiance, 76
Plyler v. Doe, xiii, 11, 13, 220
Portes, Alejandro, 179, 224
Pren, Karen, 18–19
primary/secondary school experiences,
73–91; and autonomy, desire for, 90;
benefits of adult support, 76–77;
college-goers' secondary school
experiences, 77–82, 246n11; and the
deserving/undeserving distinction, 91,
222–23; early exiters' secondary school
experiences, 82–90; early school years,
75–77, 246n7; enhanced resources,
79–80; environmental effects on school
success, 74–75; extracurricular
activities, 81–82, 246n11; and family
needs, 89; integration into tracks,
90–91; integrative/Americanizing
influences, 75–76, 246n7; isolation's
implications, 83–84; labeling of
students, 84–88, 90, 222; overview of,
33, 73; peer networks, 80–81. *See also*
school
Priority Enforcement Program, 228
Priscilla (case study), 163
Proposition 98 (Classroom Instructional
Improvement and Accountability Act;
California), 221, 254n26

Proposition 187 (California), xiii, 24
Proposition 209 (California), 24, 38
Proposition 227 (California), 24
PRWORA (Personal Responsibility and
Work Opportunity Reconciliation Act;
1996), 238n12
Public Schools Accountability Act
(California, 1999), 246n16
Puente Project, 246n11
Purple Group (University of Washington),
256n60

race, and physical appearance, 104–6, 108
racial profiling, 22–23, 108
Rafael (case study), 108, 110–11
A Raisin in the Sun (Hansberry), 237n1
(Preface)
Ramon (case study). See Betancourt, Maria
and Ramon
Ramona (case study), 193
Real Hope Act (Washington State),
242n92
recession (2007–9), 252n4
revocability of the promise of the future,
244n22
Ricardo (case study), 110–11, 176–79
Rivas, Esperanza (case study), 3–4, 100,
112–14, 149–55, 197–99, 201, 203–4,
208, 248n29
Rodolfo (case study), 96–97
Rogelio (case study), 160
Rosalba (case study), 42–43, 45–47,
166–69, 190
Rosaldo, Renato, 165
Rosaura (case study), 97–98
Rosie (case study), 70–71
Rumbaut, Rubén G., 6, 91, 224

S. 1033 (Secure America and Orderly
Immigration Act; "McCain-Kennedy"),
210
S. 1291, 253n1
S. 1348 (Comprehensive Immigration
Reform Act; 2007), 210
S. 2611 (Comprehensive Immigration
Reform Act; 2006), 210
S. 2919 (Department of Defense Authoriza-
tion Bill; 2008), 210
Sal (case study), 79, 108, 113
Sandra (case study), 101–2
S.B. 666 (California), 24
S.B. 976 (California), 247n1
S.B. 1070 ("Show me your papers";
Arizona), 23, 241n73

Scarlet (case study), 81, 100, 157, 159–60,
192–93
scholarships, 234
school: culture of, 43; desegregation in, 13;
funding for, 221, 254n26; inequality in,
220–21; open access to, 9–11, 221–22;
resistance to, 136–37; social membership shaped by, 13–14, 222; support for
undocumented students in, 233–35;
tracking in, 13–14. See also primary/
secondary school experiences
Schwarzenegger, Arnold, 24
Second Chance Act (2008), 254n30
Secure America and Orderly Immigration
Act (S. 1033; "McCain-Kennedy"),
210
Secure Communities, 228, 231
segmented assimilation, 136, 207
Sergio (case study), 76, 88, 97, 117, 139,
186–87, 189
settlement houses, xvi
Sigona, Nando, 135
Silvia (case study), 132, 137, 140, 142
Simon (case study), 122
Singer, Audrey, 255n45
Smith, Robert Courtney, 28, 245n33
snowball sampling, 16–17, 239n41
Social Security no-match letters, 42, 49,
120, 244n24, 248n1
Social Security number, 97–98, 166–67
sociological imagination, xx
Sofia (case study), 160
Sonny (case study), 70–71, 127, 144,
187–88
South Carolina, 23
Southern Poverty Law Center, 107
sports, 144–45
Statement of Legal Residence, 161
stigma: and concealing disappointment,
113–14; hiding markers of, 105;
illegality as, xix, 15, 148, 175, 213, 231;
of labels, 84–88, 90, 222; management
of, 213; research on, 105
Suárez-Orozco, Carola, 90
subtractive schooling, 248n6
Suzie (case study), 83–84
Svajlenka, Nicole Prchal, 255n45

Taylor, Graham, xvi–xvii
Temporary Protected Status (TPS), 9
Tezca (case study), 150, 162–64, 166, 203
TheDream.US, 234
time. See contested membership over time
Tony (case study), 87, 90

TPS (Temporary Protected Status), 9
transitions in life, 8–9. *See also* liminality
transportation, 35, 156, 250n9. *See also* driver's licenses
Trump, Donald J., 218
TRUST Act (California), 24
Tuan, Yi-Fu, 68–69
tuition rates, 26, 242n91
Turner, Victor, 9
turning points, 96
Tyson, Karolyn, 13, 75

Undocuhealth (National Immigrant Youth Alliance), 256n60
undocumented immigrants: alcohol/drug use by, 201; in California, number of, 36–37; children vs. adults, 220–21, 225, 229; marriage between, 252n5; Mexican percentage of, 36–37; return to Mexico by, 186; rise in, 21, 225, 241n59; stress/ailments of, 200–202, 253n27, 256n60; viewed as criminals/undeserving, 219–20; workforce percentage of, 39, 244n19; youth framed as innocent, 175, 220, 223. *See also entries beginning with "immigration"*
undocumented immigrant status: and discretion to prioritize the removal, 237n1 (Ch 1); limits of, xvi–xx; priority status for minors, 240n44; youth defined by, xix–xxi
UndocuNation, 256n59
United States, Mexican population of, 36, 243n5
United We Dream (UWD), 256n58
University of California: A.B. 540 benefits within, 154; activism at, 167–68; vs. Cal State, 159–60; Dream Summer National Internship Program (UCLA), 256n59; feelings of isolation at, 150, 154–55; in-state tuition at, 153 (*see*

also Assembly Bill 540); Latino vs. Asian students at, 38, 154
University of Chicago School of Social Service Administration, xvi–xvii
U nonimmigrant visas, 180, 252n3
USA PATRIOT Act (2001), 241n62, 252n15
US Citizenship and Immigration Services (USCIS), 227
US–Mexican border, 19–20, 247n13
UWD (United We Dream), 256n58

Valenzuela, Angela, 248n6
van Gennep, Arnold, 8–9, 100
Vargas, Jose Antonio, 140
Vicente (case study), 163
Victims of Trafficking and Violence Protection Act (2000), 252n3
Victor (case study), 116
Voss, Kim, 8

Wage and Tax Statement (Form W-2), 248n1
Wall Street Journal, 210–11
Washington State, 242n92
welfare abusers, 219
welfare programs, 238n12
Wendy (case study), 162
"wetbacks," usage of, 106
Willemsen, Karen, xiii
Willen, Sarah, 125, 200, 249n9
Willis, Paul, 123, 136
Wilson, Pete, 23–24
Wolfe, Thomas: *You Can't Go Home Again*, 173

You Can't Go Home Again (Wolfe), 173
Yuval-Davis, Nira, 61, 245n1
Yuvi (case study), 104, 110

Zulima (case study), 78, 246n8